ENGLISH PLACE-NAME SOCIETY. VOLUME V

GENERAL EDITORS
A. MAWER *and* F. M. STENTON

THE PLACE-NAMES OF THE NORTH RIDING OF YORKSHIRE

ENGLISH PLACE-NAME SOCIETY

The English Place-Name Society was founded in 1924 to carry out the survey of English place-names and to issue annual volumes to members who subscribe to the work of the Society. The Society has issued the following volumes:

The volumes for the following counties are in an advanced state of preparation: *Berkshire, Cheshire, the City of London.*

All communications with regard to the Society and membership should be addressed to:

THE HON. SECRETARY, English Place-Name Society, University College, Gower Street, London, W.C.1.

ENGLISH PLACE-NAME SOCIETY. VOLUME V

THE PLACE-NAMES
OF THE
NORTH RIDING
OF YORKSHIRE

By

A. H. SMITH

CAMBRIDGE
AT THE UNIVERSITY PRESS
1969

Published by the Syndics of the Cambridge University Press
Bentley House, 200 Euston Road, London, N.W.1
American Branch: 32 East 57th Street, New York, N.Y. 10022

Standard Book Number: 521 07502 5

First published 1928
Reissued 1969

YN/9294/490,672

First printed in Great Britain
at the University Press, Cambridge
Reprinted in Great Britain
by William Lewis (Printers) Ltd, Cardiff

GENERAL EDITORS' PREFACE

HITHERTO the county-volumes of the English Place-name Survey have either been almost entirely the work of the Editors themselves, as was the case with volumes II and III, or else, as in volume IV, they wrote the volume on the basis of collections, identifications, and various topographical enquiries made by a collaborator. The present volume is the first in which the whole of the primary task of collection, identification, and interpretation has been undertaken by another scholar, working on the lines laid down for the Survey generally and under the general supervision of its Editors. Their part in the preparation of the volume and their interpretation of their editorial responsibility can best be explained by quoting briefly from the memorandum issued to all scholars preparing one of their volumes:

"The functions of the General Editors would seem to be (i) to see that the volumes in their general form follow the lines laid down by the promoters of the Survey, (ii) to place at their disposal such comparative material as they may have at their command, (iii) to see, so far as possible, that no interpretations, either general or particular, are offered which seem faulty in themselves or inconsistent with the general principles of place-name interpretation as the Editors conceive them."

Those functions have been exercised freely in the present volume. Without in any way detracting from the excellence of much of Dr Smith's work, it should be said that the volume as now published differs widely in detail, and at times in general ideas, from the manuscript submitted to them at various stages. At the same time, the editors desire to pay high tribute to the skill and energy of Dr Smith in collecting materials, more especially from unpublished sources, to the linguistic acumen which has led him to some brilliant solutions of problems, and to the unfailing readiness with which he has listened to their criticisms and accepted their suggestions. The task of the editors in volumes produced under the conditions which govern the Place-name Survey might not be an easy one. It is pleasant to record that on the first occasion on which they have carried out that task it has been entirely free from difficulty.

A. M.
F. M. S.

In die S. Johannis de Beverlaco,
1928

AUTHOR'S PREFACE

I WISH to express my deep gratitude to my old teacher and friend Professor E. V. Gordon. It is true that there are few direct references to his name in the following pages, but the obligation I owe him is in his untiring and illuminating assistance over a period of five or six years in reading through this work as it progressed, in pointing out valuable sources of material, in making corrections to my work, and giving me the benefit of his own researches.

Similarly my debt of gratitude to the Society's editors cannot be overestimated. For several years, both in his capacity as editor and as a personal friend, Professor Mawer has frequently devoted his time to reading my work, advising from his experience, and explaining far more cruces than are indicated by direct reference in the following pages. To Professor Stenton I am indebted for his notes on personal names, notes on the Anglo-Saxon charters, and for much advice in the preparation of the introduction.

Others I can but refer to in the alphabetical order of their names:

The Rev. Principal F. T. Cooper, M.A. and Captain J. Chance, M.A., for friendly help in the last stages of preparation for the press.

Professor G. H. Cowling, M.A., for help on the dialectal problems of the district.

Mr F. W. Dowson of Catford for help on topographical points.

Miss B. M. Fergusson, M.A., Secretary to the Director, for much help in checking forms and preparing the MS for press.

Mr J. P. Gilson, for valuable help on matters concerning MSS in the British Museum.

Mr T. S. Gowland, for lists of names from Tithe Awards which furnished several identifications of DB manors.

Mr W. R. Grist, B.Sc., for topographical information.

Rev. F. Harrison, M.A., Vicar-Choral of York Minster, for friendly assistance in connexion with the MSS preserved in the Zouch Chapel of the Minster.

Mr F. T. S. Houghton, M.A., for the forms of place-names in Worcestershire and Warwickshire.

The Librarian of the Library of the University of Leeds, and the Assistant Librarian, Mr G. Woledge, B.A.

The late Mr A. S. Lamprey, M.A., for forms of place-names in Kent.

Dr H. Lindkvist for reading through the proofs and for many valuable etymological notes on cruces which were presented to him.

Mr F. H. Marsden, M.A., for valuable information with regard to the dialectal pronunciations of place-names in the Riding, and for help in reading the proofs.

Professor L. V. D. Owen, M.A., for forms of place-names in Leicestershire.

Sir Alfred Pease, Bart., for many interesting dialect pronunciations of place-names in Cleveland.

Dr O. K. Schram for the forms of Norfolk place-names and for valuable etymological notes.

Mr A. H. Scott-Mackie, for his collections of Bulmer field-names.

Mr Walter Smith, editor of the *Yorkshire Weekly Post*, for his kind co-operation in giving publicity to the survey in Yorkshire in connexion with the Yorkshire Dialect Society's committee.

Professor A. Hamilton Thompson and the representatives of the late Dr Farrer for the loan of his transcripts of

Yorkshire documents, and to Professor Thompson for help in reading the proofs.

Professor J. R. R. Tolkien, M.A., for encouragement and valuable help in connexion with the philological problems which arose.

Miss H. P. Tomlinson, B.A., for assistance in the collection of forms, and indefatigable help in preparing the indexes and reading proofs.

Major R. B. Turton, of Kildale, for interesting notes from the Tithe Awards, especially in connexion with Cargo Fleet.

I also wish to thank the sub-committee on place-names of the Yorkshire Dialect Society, which came into existence on the initiative of Dr Hambley Rowe of Bradford, Miss Allison of Leeds, and Professor G. H. Cowling. I thank Col. J. Parker, who, as County organiser for Yorkshire, has also given valuable help in reading the proofs. I am also much indebted to the Ordnance Survey Office for their care and skill in preparing the map which accompanies the volume.

In addition to these acknowledgments I wish to record my personal gratitude to Professor Ekwall, who has solved many of the cruces which were presented to him in the course of preparation of the present volume.

A. H. SMITH

CONTENTS

INTRODUCTION

IN two respects the district now entered upon by the Survey differs widely from those which have already been dealt with. The North Riding of Yorkshire includes a vast region of high moorland which could not be occupied at an early date, and in which only scattered settlements could arise at a later time. In the second place, the Riding underwent in the ninth and tenth centuries a Scandinavian settlement of exceptional thoroughness, which has left innumerable traces in the local nomenclature of the present day.

The North Riding is an important agricultural region. Its production of oats and barley is considerable, in view of the limited area available for their growth. In sheep farming it comes third or fourth amongst English counties. This agricultural variety is due to the geographical structure of the region. The Vale of York (roughly Bulmer, Birdforth and Allertonshire wapentakes) is a broad plain connecting the Trent valley with the north. It rises nowhere (even at the Tees-Ouse watershed) to more than 200 ft. and its southern portion is covered with glacial deposits which make rich agricultural land. The southern part of the Vale was formerly covered by the Forest of Galtres. The Derwent valley (comprising the wapentakes of Ryedale, Pickering Lythe, and part of Whitby Strand) includes the small agricultural region known as Pickering Vale, which was apparently the bed of an old lake before the Derwent cut through into the Vale of York by the Kirkham Gorge. Pickering Vale is covered with alluvial deposits, and though formerly very marshy it has been turned by extensive drainage into the second productive area of the riding. The Vale of Pickering has a further importance in that it connects the Vale of York directly with the sea. The north-eastern part of the Riding is occupied by the Hambleton and Cleveland Hills which extend from the Kirkham Gorge in the form of a crescent to the north-east coast. The hills themselves are high and are covered with bleak moorland which offers pasture for many sheep. The lower parts of the valleys, many of which find direct outlet into the little bays of the precipitous coast, are covered with boulder clay which makes the valleys themselves fertile. In the extreme north, the discovery of iron ore, the presence of limestone, and salt-workings have facilitated the development of an industrial region round Middlesborough (the population of which in 1827 was 40). On the west of the Vale of York is the extensive Pennine region of which the portion included in the North Riding is nearly identical with Richmondshire. On the Westmoreland border there are lofty fells from which streams flow down to the main valleys of the Ure, the Swale, and the Tees. The scenery is typical of a mountain limestone district—steep hillsides often scarred, numerous potholes, and precipitous waterfalls. In the lower reaches of the rivers, where they approach the Vale of York, the land is arable and fairly well wooded, but in the upper reaches the arable land disappears and in its place there is pasture land which stretches far up the fell sides. As on the Cleveland Hills this permanent pasturage permits of sheep farming on a great scale, and most of the sheep of the Riding are to be found in these western dales.

As the term *riding* is of Scandinavian origin the division of Yorkshire into ridings must be later than the Danish settlement of 876. The ridings of Yorkshire are parallel to those of the ancient kingdom of Lindsey. There, as in Yorkshire, there was no attempt to secure equality of area or assessment in the ridings[1]. In Yorkshire, the riding boundaries converge on the city of York. The East and North Ridings are separated by the Derwent, and the West and North Ridings by the Ouse and the Ure-Nidd watershed[2]. The boundary between the North Riding and Westmoreland is the Pennine watershed, but the boundary was long uncertain and during the thirteenth and fourteenth centuries there were several attempts to define it. In 1338, for example, because of the "great disputes touching the confines thereof" a commission was made "to define by a

---

[1] Cf. F. M. Stenton, *Essays presented to R. Lane Poole*, 147.

[2] This was possibly the boundary between Deira and the old British kingdom which had its centre in Elmet. The existence of such a boundary would be confirmed if, as is probable, the names of two places near Ripon (YWR), Markington and Markenfield (*Mercingatun*, c. 1039 YCh 7, *Merchintone* 1086 DB; *Merchefeld* 1086 DB, *Merchingfeld* 1135-53 YCh 64), are geonymics derived from OE *mearc* 'march, boundary.'

perambulation the metes and bounds between those two counties"[1]. The northern boundary of the Riding is the river Tees, separating it from Durham, which according to Symeon of Durham was a barren waste and formerly considered to be the natural boundary between the ancient kingdoms of Bernicia and Deira[2].

The materials which are collected in this volume give little evidence of the survival of a British population in this region. This evidence is confined to some eight place-names, to half-a-dozen names which possibly contain OE *Wealh*, and to a dozen river-names. Of the eight place-names, Alne, Glaisdale, and Leeming are old river-names, Crayke refers to the precipice on which the village is built, Dinnand and Penhill are old hill-names, and Catterick alone is the name of a British settlement. British place-names are no less rare in the East and West Ridings. This rarity, however, does not necessarily prove a scanty British population, for there is good independent evidence of the survival of a British kingdom till well into the seventh century in the Leeds district, where there is similarly little evidence for it in place-names. On the contrary, it only serves to show how thorough were the later Anglian and Scandinavian settlements. Many British names which survived the Anglian settlement may afterwards have been displaced in the twofold settlement of Danes and Norwegians. This settlement affected even river-names, such as Wiske, Swale, Bain, and Greta, conservative though such names usually are. When compared with Durham and Northumberland we find in those counties a larger number of Celtic names than in the North Riding. But this disproportion is not necessarily due to the survival of a larger Celtic population north of the Tees but rather to the fact that the displacement of Celtic by Scandinavian names was far less extensive there than in Yorkshire. Conditions were different across the Pennines in Lancashire, where the British population survived in small well-defined islands of territory and in the hills. It would, therefore, be dangerous to draw conclusions as to the survival of the British population from the British names of the North Riding. Nevertheless, the persistence of the district name *Deira*[3] as the name of an Anglian

[1] Pat. 186.   [2] SD (Rolls ed.), i. 339.   [3] *v.* IPN 21.

kingdom and the distribution of such British names as survived the Anglian and Scandinavian settlements may indicate that the surviving Britons were not driven to the west but remained in their original homes in the more fertile parts. On the coast there is Wapley and in Eskdale there are Glaisdale and Dinnand; in Pickering Vale there is Wardle Rigg and in a fertile part of Ryedale the lost *Walton*. In the Vale of York there are Alne and Crayke in Bulmer wapentake and further north there are Leeming, Catterick, and the adjacent Walburn, and Walmire a little distance across the Swale. Only Penhill and Walden in Wensleydale are in any way isolated from the rest. It is an important fact that such British names as survived occur in fertile parts like the Vale of York, and it shows that the surviving Britons were not isolated by natural obstacles nor on the other hand did they survive in isolated groups as in Lancashire.

The evidence of place-names is, however, too scanty for us to determine whether the Britons lived apart from the Angles or in close contact with them. The view that the Britons lived side by side with the Angles[1] and perhaps mingled freely with them is supported by the use of British personal names amongst the Angles of the North Riding. Thus, *Cædmon*, the name of the Christian poet of St Hild's monastery at *Streonæshalch*, is from British **Catumannos*; *Ceadda* and *Ced(di)*, the names of the Abbot of Lastingham, later Bishop of Lichfield, and his brother the Bishop of the East Saxons, represent hypocoristic forms of late British **Caduc* (Old Welsh *Catuc*)[2]. In this respect the North Riding is similar to Durham and Northumberland, where the use of British personal names in Old English is shown by such names as *Arthan*, *Coluduc*, *Cundigeorn* and *Ūnust*[3].

The first specific reference to the Angles in Northumbria is the tradition that Ida began to reign at Bamburgh in 547. From

---

[1] There is, of course, no reason to suppose that the Britons of the North Riding lived with the Angles in anything but a state of subjection to them.

[2] Cf. RNY 5. The forms of these pers. names and p.n.'s show that they were borrowed in sixth and seventh century British forms: e.g. Brit 'soft-mutation' of *t* to *d* as in *Cædmon* and *Ceadda* by the side of Catterick, of *b* to *f* as in Leven (Brit **libna*), Dove (Brit **dubo-*); Brit 'affection' of *a* to *e* as in Crayke (OE *Crec*) which in other spellings also shows the later Brit change of *e* to *ai* (for further illustrations *v.* RNY 9 ff.).

[3] Förster, *Keltisches Wortgut* 62 ff.

this and other evidence it would seem that the Anglian settlement of Bernicia was at least a century later than that of the
south and east of England. The settlement of Deira had apparently begun before the middle of the sixth century, and archæological evidence, such as urn-burials found at Saltburn, points
to a date about 500[1]. Heathen burial-grounds which must be
earlier than the reception of Christianity after the baptism of
Edwin in 627 occur in the North Riding at Hob Hill near
Saltburn and Robin Hood's Bay not far from Fylingdales, both
on the coast, and finds of early sixth century brooches suggest that
they once existed at Bulmer, and at Thornbrough near Catterick.
In the rarity of heathen Anglian burial-places the North and
West Ridings stand in contrast to the East Riding, where such
sites are numerous. It is safe to argue from this that the Angles
did not advance to occupy the north and west of Yorkshire
until they were well established in the east.

The distribution of names in -ing and -ingaham suggests the
same conclusion. The existence of these names should not be
rigorously interpreted in Yorkshire as proving settlement before
the year 600. The first Anglian settlement in Airedale, represented by names like Bowling, Cowling and Manningham[2],
could not have taken place before the fall of the kingdom of
Elmet during the reign of Edwin. This suggests that names in
-ing and -ingaham were still living types in Yorkshire in the first
half of the seventh century.

The distribution of these names throws some light on the
extent of the original Anglian settlement of the North Riding.
In Bulmer wapentake in the Derwent valley there are East and
West Lilling not far from the supposed burial-ground at Bulmer;
in Ryedale there are Gilling, Hovingham and Lastingham, and
further east in the low-lying land of the Derwent valley is
Pickering. On the coast is Fylingdales, near the Robin Hood's
Bay burial-ground. Other names of this type are Kiplin, Gilling
in Richmondshire, and Barningham. These and the burial-
ground at Thornbrough are all on or near the great Roman
road, known as Leeming Lane or Watling Street, which passes

[1] VCHY, ii. 72.
[2] It is by no means certain that either Bowling or Cowling is a plural
name in -ingas. v. Ekwall, PN in -ing 92.

b 2

through the Riding. The burial-grounds at Saltburn and Robin Hood's Bay and the name Fylingdales are probably due to settlers entering the country immediately from the North Sea, but most of the settlements in the Derwent valley should be regarded as extensions of the early Anglian settlements in the northern parts of the East Riding. The group of early names along Watling Street bears out the archæological evidence that the Angles did not avoid Roman roads in Yorkshire and the north as they generally did in other counties to the south[1]. These two groups in the Derwent valley and in the Vale of York were probably connected with each other, for Gilling in Ryedale has its counterpart in Gilling in Richmondshire. The settlements, as already indicated, cannot have been as extensive in the North Riding as they were in the East, but geographical factors are partly responsible for their comparative rarity. The hilly country of Cleveland and the western dales, and the great forest of Galtres which covered the district north of York must have been unattractive to early settlers. To a certain extent, too, this rarity of ancient Anglian names may be explained by the thorough nature of the Scandinavian settlement. The element *worð*, for example, which probably became obsolete soon after the Anglian settlement[2], is common both in the south-east of the West Riding and in Durham (where Scandinavian influence was slight), but is found only once in the North Riding at Heworth in the extreme south, and once in the East Riding at Luddith[3]. The absence of the element in the North Riding, which lies between Durham and the West Riding, must be explained as due to the replacement of names containing *worð* by Scandinavian names rather than by the assumption that *worð* was never used in this district. There may be a similar danger in drawing inferences from the present distribution of names in -*ing* and -*ingaham*.

The varying fortunes of Northumbria in the seventh century have left no marks on local nomenclature. The fall of the British kingdom of Elmet and a partial colonisation from Mercia of that district, which possibly extended to the borders of the

---

[1] E. Thurlow Leeds, *Archæology of the AS Settlements*, 71.
[2] *v.* EPN s.v.
[3] A. Mawer, *Yorkshire History* (Leeds, 1924), 43.

North Riding (cf. xiv *supra* note), did not extend to the North Riding itself. The Anglian place-names of this Riding are all Northumbrian in form and include such distinctively Northumbrian types as *bōðltūn* (*v.* Bolton in Index). All we can say is that in the seventh century extensions must have been made from settlements already established. Gillamoor, for instance, appears to be an offshoot of the settlement of Gilling in Ryedale, and *Hoveton* must be connected with Hovingham. In the process of time farms would spring up in the neighbourhood of the original settlements and the land would be gradually cleared of forest and cultivated. It seems probable that places with Anglian names mentioned in Domesday Book and found in the neighbourhood of places with names in *-ing* or *-ingaham* belong to this period. Thus, in Bulmer there is mention in Domesday Book of some 45 manors with English names (besides 30 with Scandinavian) and of these 28 are names in *tun*, 2 in *wic* and 2 in *burh*. Fifteen are coupled with personal names, some of which, such as *Wippede* (in Wide Open Farm) and *Ēsa* (in Easingwold), are found only at a very early date. The use of hypocoristic personal names in place-names also points to early settlements, for it was only at an early date that names of this type were common among the landed aristocracy[1] whose members were likely to give their names to places. In Bulmer wapentake Benningbrough and (possibly) Harton contain hypocoristic names of this type and both these are on the banks of rivers not far from York, whilst Strensall, which is identical in form with Bede's *Streonæshalch*, contains a very ancient personal name.

Similar considerations apply to other districts of the Riding. In the Derwent valley Ryedale and Pickering Lythe include several place-names in *-ing* and in this district Domesday Book shows more Anglian than Scandinavian names. Other personal names which point to early settlement are *Nunna* (Nunnington), *Fadda* (Fadmoor), and *Hofa* (Hovingham and *Hoveton*) in Ryedale and possibly *Hab(b)a* (Habton) and *Ēaden* (Edstone) in Pickering Lythe. Few Anglian names have survived in Whitby Strand, for, though Fylingdales, and the ancient Hackness and *Streonæshalch* occur here, Scandinavian names outnumber

[1] Redin, 187 ff.

Anglian by two to one. A similar proportion is found in the wapentakes of Langbargh East and Langbargh West. Moreover, in Langbargh West the name Ingleby occurs three times and must indicate that distinctively Anglian survivals amid the Scandinavian population were sufficiently rare to find record in place-names. In the Vale of York (Birdforth and Allerton-shire wapentakes) Anglian and Scandinavian names are found in approximately equal numbers, and only a few of the former, such as Rainton, Fawdington, Yearsley, Coxwold, Kilvington, Otterington, Northallerton, Winton and Harlsey, contain personal names. Most of these are near the river Swale or its affluent the Wiske. The western dales were rough woodland and poorly accessible. Only occasional names like Witton, Wensley and Bolton (in Wensleydale) and Reeth, Fremington, Hudswell, and Downholme (in Swaledale) survive from the Anglian settlement in these parts, but within a few miles of Watling Street which runs along the foot of the dales there occur many Anglian names such as Kirklington, Tanfield and Burneston, Masham, Ellington, Bedale and Hunton, Fing-hall and Gilling, Moulton, Whashton, Barningham, and Mortham.

This distribution shows that Anglian names were most persistent in the fertile river valleys and along the central Roman road. Here, as indicated by names in -ing and -ingaham and heathen burial-grounds, the original settlements took place. From such centres the settlers expanded into the surrounding districts, chiefly by clearing forest land, as in Wensleydale or in the district round Hackness, where there are two well-defined groups of names containing OE leah 'forest clearing.'

Scandinavian raiders had touched the Northumbrian coast before the end of the eighth century, but it was not till 867 that Northumbria was invaded in force. In that year "the marauding army (*here*) crossed the Humber estuary from East Anglia to York in Northumbria"[1], and captured York. These invaders were undoubtedly of Danish origin. The great Scandinavian army which had landed in the previous year came from Denmark under the leadership of the sons of the famous Danish Viking, Ragnarr Loðbrók. This is important, for it points to the Danish

[1] ASC s.a. 867.

origin of the army which was to colonise Yorkshire in the next decade.

In 875 this army, which had wintered at Repton in Derbyshire, divided its forces. One part under Guthrum moved southwards to Cambridge, and the other under Healfdene returned to the north. After spending the winter by the Tyne Healfdene proceeded to attack the Picts and the kingdom of Strathclyde. There can be little doubt that the enterprise was intended, as Lindkvist suggests, to secure a peaceful colonisation of Yorkshire in the following year.

"In 876 Healfdene portioned out the land of the Northumbrians and they (the Danes) tilled it and made a livelihood by it."[1] This is the first recorded settlement of Scandinavians in England and, as already pointed out, it was effected by a Danish army. Its extent was limited on the north by the broken country which forms the modern county of Durham, for it is only in the extreme south of this county, in Upper Teesdale, that place-names point to a Scandinavian settlement. In Yorkshire, place-names[2] indicate that the Danish settlement was confined to the most fertile parts of the county, including the East Riding, the eastern parts of the West Riding, and the central and southern parts of the North Riding.

Early in the next century a new Scandinavian invasion began, this time of Norwegians from Ireland. There had been intimate association between the Irish and the Norwegian settlers. The Irish had adopted a number of Scandinavian words and names such as *Glunieran*[3], and the Norwegians had borrowed Irish names (*infra* xxvi ff.) and words such as Middle English *kapall* 'horse' and perhaps cros, and their sculpture frequently betrays the influence of Irish fashions. The Norwegian settlements in Northumbria had probably begun before 915. There is evidence of piratical descents on the North-West during the episcopate of Cuthheard, Bishop of Chester le Street (*c.* 899–915)[4], and this movement culminated in 915 in the capture of York by

[1] ASC s.a.
[2] Such as those containing *thorp, bōð, hulm, brink*, personal names such as *Ēsi, Ēskell, Frithi, Malti*, etc., and place-names such as Danby. *v.* IPN 60 ff.
[3] Adapted from ON *Járnkné*.
[4] Cf. E. V. Gordon, *Scandinavian influence on Yorkshire Dialects* (YDS) 7.

Ragnall mac Bicloch, who was the first of a series of Irish Viking kings of York which lasted for thirty-five years, during which intercourse must have been maintained between Ireland and Yorkshire. The evidence of place-names[1] goes far to show that the Norwegians entered Yorkshire from the North-West. Names of Irish-Norwegian type are especially well represented in Craven in the West Riding, the western dales of the North Riding and in Lower Teesdale, and in the Cleveland district, where the Scandinavian place-names strikingly resemble those of the Lake District through which most of these new settlers presumably came.

The effects of the Scandinavian settlement of Yorkshire were manifold. The county was divided into Scandinavian *ridings*, the ridings were divided into Scandinavian *wapentakes*, and the Vikings set up meeting-places for their own *things* on such sites as *Thingwall* and Fingay Hill (*infra* 128, 213). The characteristic Scandinavian type of place-name ending in *-by* probably belongs in the main to the earlier, Danish, settlement. There are over 150 names of this type in the North Riding and more than 100 of these contain a personal name as their first element. These new names must often have replaced earlier Anglian names. Later, the fusion of Angles and Scandinavians was such that an Anglo-Scandinavian dialect appears to have been spoken for a time[2]. Crosses at Skelton and Thornaby on Tees[3] bear Anglo-Scandinavian inscriptions, such a place-name as Loskay House (ON *lopt í skógi*) contains Scandinavian expressions, and hybrid place-names such as Osmotherley (*infra* 213) form perhaps the clearest evidence of amalgamation. The common use of Scandinavian or Irish personal names such as *Arkil*, *Asbeorn*, or *Grim*, and *Coleman*, *Ghile*, *Ghilander*, *Melmidoc*, or *Patric*[4], patronymics of a Scandinavian type such as *Orm Gamalsuna* on the Kirkdale

---

[1] Such as those which contain *brekka*, *slakki*, *foss*, *gil*, or *skáli*; types such as Normanby, Irby; place-names in which the order of the elements is reversed according to Irish methods of nomenclature; names containing *erg* and OIr personal names such as *Colman*, *Finegal*, *Maelmuire*, etc. *v*. IPN 32 ff., 60 ff., and more especially in relation to Yorkshire *v*. *Revue Celtique*, XLIV. 34 ff.

[2] Cf. Gordon, *op. cit.* 14 ff., *v*. Osmotherley *infra* 213.

[3] Cf. W. G. Collingwood, *Anglian and Anglo-Danish Sculpture in the North Riding* (YAJ, XIX), 386, 402.

[4] *v*. NP, ZEN, and *Revue Celtique*, XLIV. 40 ff.

inscription (*infra* 66) and *þorcetel Unbainasu(na)*, *Raganald Asbeornnas suna*, and *Hálwærð Sæfugalasuna* in the list of Alfric's *festermen*[1], and the use of women's names of Scandinavian origin in place-names such as Helperby, Hinderskelfe, or Whenby, indicate still further the closeness of the fusion. Finally, spellings show the frequent substitution of Scandinavian for English forms in Anglian names which survived the settlement. Such are Newton and Newsham, where ON *nýr* 'new' is occasionally substituted for the more common OE *nīwe*, Ousey Carr and Ovington, where OE initial *w-* is lost under the influence of ON *úlfr*, and the very interesting case of Rawcliff Bank (*infra* 146), where ON *rauðr* is substituted for OE *rēad*.

The evidence of place-names is borne out by that of archæology, with regard not only to the fusion of Angles and Scandinavians, but also to the distribution of Norwegian settlers in the North Riding. Besides the Norse crosses at Skelton and Thornaby on Tees, for example, there is also at Kildale a burial-ground which contains typical Viking burials[2]. Crosses of the Viking Age, carved according to Irish fashions of ornamentation, are found in Ryedale, Cleveland, the northern part of Allertonshire, the east of Hang East, and the eastern part of Gilling West in Teesdale[3]. Such types of carving were undoubtedly introduced by Norwegians who had been in contact with Ireland, and the distribution of these crosses agrees closely with the distribution of place-names of a Norwegian character.

A late connexion with Scandinavia seems to be indicated by the forms which some of the Norwegian place-names take. Shunner Howe arose from the late Old Norwegian form *Sjónar-* by a sound change somewhat analogous to that found in Shipton, whilst Old Norwegian stress-shifting appears in Yarna Beck and the lost place-names *Hyarlesholm*, *Yernekeldale*, *Jukeleholm*, and *Jatstaineswad*[4]. Goathland has been influenced by the ONorw change of *d* to *th*. Old Norse *u*-mutation of *a* to *o* is found in

---

[1] YCh 9.   [2] VCHY, ii. 96.
[3] Collingwood, *op. cit.* 265 ff.
[4] From ON *Jarl*, *Járnketill, *Jókell* and *Játsteinn, which is a Scandinavianised form of OE *Ēadstān* parallel to ON *Játvarðr* and *Játmundr*, found in Egils Saga as forms of OE *Ēadweard* and *Ēadmund*, the names of AS kings.

such words as *hǫld*, *hǫfuð*, of which the mutated forms sometimes appear in place-names such as *Holdlythe*, Middle Head,
and in the personal name *Svarthǫfði*[1]. Similarly, the words
brekka, *slakki*, *foss*, and the curious form *Son-* in South Otterington, which exhibit Scandinavian consonant assimilation, are
due to a Scandinavian sound-change which took place about
1000 A.D. The Domesday Book form *Locte-* for Old Norse *lopt*
(in Loft Marshes) seems to indicate that the bilabial nature of
Old Norse *p* was partly preserved in England and the history of
the name Snilesworth shows that Old Norse *-g-* between front
vowels had already been palatalised.

The general distribution of Danish and Norwegian settlements is clearly marked by the distribution of place-names.
The settlement of the Danes was far greater in the south of the
Riding than in the north. In Bulmer wapentake there are a
number of *thorps*, *Fornthorpe*, Ganthorpe, Mowthorpe, Tholthorpe, Towthorpe (from Danish *Tofi*), and Wiganthorpe,
whilst Rice Lane in its original form contains Danish *kunung*,
and Claxton contains a distinctively Danish personal name.
This group of Danish names extends from the south of Ryedale where we find Howthorpe, Coneysthorpe (from Danish
kunung), Easthorpe and Laysthorpe, and Fryton (from Danish
Frithi). In Pickering Lythe, further along the Derwent valley,
the line of Danish settlements seems to be continued. In the
western and central parts there are Kingthorpe and *Kettlethorpe*, Foulbridge and Sil Howe containing Danish personal
names, Beedale and the lost *Bothum*[2] (from *bōð*), and in the
extreme east in Cayton parish there is a group of *thorps* on
the coast, Gristhorpe, *Etersthorpe*, *Roberthorpe* and *Scawthorpe*.
There is thus a line of Danish settlements running across the
south of the Riding into Bulmer, whence it proceeds still further
west. In the south of Birdforth there are Ellenthorpe and
Langthorpe and the lost *Easby* (Old Danish *Ēsi*). In the neigh-

---

[1] This change shows a late connexion with Scandinavia as the older sound
usually appears in English as *a* in those words where it was mutated to *ǫ* in
late ONorw; cf. Howden (YER) which appears in the late tenth century as
to *Hæafuddæne* (YCh 4), but in DB as *Houedene*, where OE *hēafod* was replaced by ON *hǫfuð* in its mutated form.

[2] For lost places mentioned hereafter *v.* Field and other minor names
infra 324 ff., s.v. *bōð*, *brekka*, *klint*, *gil*, *skáli*, *slakki*, etc.

bourhood of Thirsk, itself possibly a Danish name, there are Ravensthorpe, Brink Hill, and *Crafclynt* (Old Danish *klint*) in Byland, besides a number of names containing specifically Danish personal names as Dowber Lane, Cold Kirby, *Fridebi*, the old name of Felixkirk, Kepwick, Silton. Such personal names also appear in the names of a number of lost places as *Esebrygg* (Danish *Ési*) in Wildon, *Eskeldic* (Danish *Éskel*) in Boltby, and *Fulkeholm* (Danish *Fulki*) in Thornton le Beans, and in Bullamoor, the latter in the adjacent part of Allertonshire. In Halikeld and the neighbouring parts of Hang East there are Allerthorpe, Carthorpe, Holme (Danish *hulm*), Exelby (Danish *Éskel*), Firby and Hornby, of which the last three contain Danish personal names. Danby on Ure in the east of Hang West and Danby Wiske in the south of Gilling East probably represent the western extremity of this Danish settlement. In Bulmer as we have no distinctively Norwegian names we may safely ascribe Scandinavian names such as Wigginton, Helperby, Dalby, Whenby and Skewsby to the Danes. The same may be said of the Scandinavian names in the south and central parts of Birdforth and to a certain extent in Halikeld, where there are few traces of Norwegian settlement. In Ryedale and Pickering Lythe, however, there are very definite examples of Norwegian influence and other Scandinavian place-names may be Danish or Norwegian in origin. In Whitby Strand it is known traditionally that the Danes Ingwar and Ubba destroyed the monastery of *Streonæshalch*[1], but the Danes do not seem to have settled there to any great extent. Silpho in the south of the wapentake and Sneaton and Wragby contain Danish personal names. Danby in Cleveland, the only other name pointing to Danish settlement, though in Langbargh East, belongs to the geographical district of Eskdale, and if the name Danby has any racial significance it suggests that the Danes were only present there in small numbers. In Whitby Strand, therefore, the very high proportion of Scandinavian names must be due to Norwegian influence. In the north of the Riding there are a few traces of Danish colonisation. Near the coast in Langbargh East there are a couple of *thorps*, Ugthorpe and *Roskelthorpe*. Further inland, there are Linthorpe (*thorp*), Easby, Maltby, and

[1] *Whitby Cartulary*, 1.

Lonsdale containing Danish personal names, and Dromonby (*infra* 168).

From this survey it will be seen that the Danish settlements in the North Riding were in three groups, the first and most extensive stretching from east to west across Pickering Lythe, the south of Ryedale, and Bulmer wapentake, and terminating in the wapentake of Hang East in a few sporadic settlements, the others being isolated settlements in Whitby Strand including Eskdale, and in Cleveland. The first is probably due to Healf-dene's apportionment of the land of Northumbria in 876 and is inseparable from the Danish settlement in the East Riding; the others are probably independent settlements made by Danes who invaded the respective districts directly from the sea.

The material available for determining the presence of Nor-wegian settlements is more complete than that for the Danes, because the tests of Norwegian influence are more numerous. In Bulmer wapentake there is no trace of Norwegian influence either in place-names or archæological material. In Ryedale there are many names of Norwegian and Irish-Norwegian origin, including Laskill Pasture which contains Old Norwegian *skáli*, Dowthwaite, Appleton le Moors, and *Colthmanelandes* which contain Irish personal names, and Normanby, all north of the river Rye. Airyholme, the lost *Ircroft* (Old Norse *Íri*) in Helmsley, and Oswaldkirk, which in early forms some-times has its elements reversed according to the Irish fashion, point to a small Norwegian settlement on the south of the river, in a district which had already been populated by Angles and Danes (*supra* xix, xxiv). Many of the Scandinavian names in the upper part of the valley are probably Norwegian, though there is nothing to prove it except the entire absence in these parts of names of specifically Danish origin. Irish influence has been observed on the crosses at Stonegrave, Amotherby, Hovingham, Lastingham, Kirkdale, Kirkby Moorside, and Helmsley.

In the adjacent parts of Pickering Lythe there are many Norwegian names, such as Scarf Hill and West Gill, *Mulfoss* (Norse *foss*) in Hartoft, *Westslak* (Norse *slakki*) in King-thorpe and *Hyndeslak* in Thornton Dale. *Ghilander* (cf. Gaelic *Gilleandrais*) is the name of a local tenant in 1066 and crosses at Sinnington, Ellerburn, and Levisham show Irish influence.

In the extreme east of the wapentake the name Irton points to a small Norwegian colony amid the Danish *thorps*, whilst Scarborough was founded by the Norseman Thorgils *Skarthi* (*infra* 105–6).

In Whitby Strand, where there was little Danish settlement (*supra* xxv), place-names show many Norwegian features, such as *Burstadgile* (Norse *gil*) in Suffield and *Waterslakgille* (Norse *slakki*, *gil*) in Thirley Cotes, *Breck*, Normanby and Airy Hill. Many of the common Scandinavian names like Whitby and Gnipe How, should, therefore, probably be ascribed to the Norwegians.

In Langbargh East and Langbargh West, where Danish influence was not extensive, there are indications of a thorough settlement by Norwegians, especially round Guisborough and the district to the west. Norwegian influence is evident in such names as *Scalebec* in Liverton, *Burnolfscales* in Guisborough, *Raufscales* in Kildale, *Scalestedes* in Tocketts, *Stainschale* in Upleatham, Scale Foot and Scaling (all containing *skáli*), *Endebrec* in Guisborough, *Bakestanbrec* in Tocketts and *Likkebreke* in Coatham (containing *brekka*); Coldman Hargos (*erg*) and Commondale contain the Irish personal name *Colmán*. *Patricius* (Old Irish *Patric*) and *Magbanet*[1] are the names of early tenants, and crosses at Easington and Skelton exhibit Irish forms of decoration. A little to the west occur Normanby, Airy Holme, Lackenby, and *Hillbraith*, whilst *Dunlangabrotes* in Great Broughton contains the OIr personal name *Dunlang*, and *Colman* is the name of an early tenant. The series is continued further west in the northern parts of Allertonshire and Birdforth, by Fowgill, Blow Gill, Irby and *Irton*. Sawcock is an Irish-Norwegian inversion compound (*v. supra* xxii, n. 1), and Birkby probably refers to a village of Britons or Brito-Scandinavians who had joined the Norwegians as they were passing through Cumberland. *Melmidoc, Gilemicel, Dughel*, and *Malgrin* are Irish names borne by local landholders in 1066. Irish forms of carving are found on crosses at Birkby, Northallerton, Brompton, and Osmotherley all in the north of Allertonshire, and at Crathorne and Kirk Leavington in the adjacent part of Langbargh West.

---

[1] Cf. *Revue Celtique*, XLIV. 45.

In Richmondshire Norwegian influence was very strong, and the large proportion of local Scandinavian names, not in themselves distinctive, must be due almost entirely to Norwegians, for, except in the wapentake of Halikeld and the east of Hang East, there are no definite traces of Danish influence. In Halikeld, the great Danish colonisation seems to have ended; we find Gatenby, the lost *Normanby*, mention in Domesday Book of a man called *Sudan* (Old Irish **Suthan*), and at Pickhill a cross bearing traces of Irish influence. These few pieces of evidence seem to show that Halikeld was the eastern limit of the very strong Norwegian colonisation of Hang wapentake. In Hang East, south of Catterick, there was a large settlement, as indicated by such names as *Scalerig* in Hudswell and *Scaleflath* in Colburn (containing *skáli*), *Leveracgille* near *Miregrim*, Thieves Gill, *Helegile* and *Wythegile* (containing *gil*), all near Hipswell. Patrick Brompton, Arrathorne, Oran, and *Miregrim* are examples of Irish influence, whilst *Ghille* (Old Irish *Gilla*) was the name of a local tenant in 1066. In Hang West there are far more Scandinavian than English names, and as many of these are certainly Norwegian in origin it is probable that most of the others are Norwegian also. Specifically Norwegian are Gammersgill, *Scalestedes* in Wensley, and Skell Gill (containing *skáli*), *Ulegile* in Wensley, *Wantegile* in Castle Bolton, *Thwertlanggille* in West Bolton, High and Low Gill, Howgill, *Ackegile* and *Stiwardgile* in Widdale, and Hell Gill (containing *gil*), *Hungrebrekes* in West Bolton (*brekka*), Fossdale (*foss*), and the river-name Bain (from Old Norwegian *beinn* 'short, quick'). Cragdale possibly contains Old Irish *creag*, which must have been introduced by Norwegians from Ireland, and Irish personal names are found in *Paterik-keld* in Harmby, Melmerby and Carperby, and as the names of early tenants such as *Glunier*, *Gilmychel*, *Ghilpatric*, *Colman*, and *Meriaduc*. At Finghall, Thornton Steward, Middleham and Wensley crosses have been found which show Irish influence. In Swaledale the traces of Scandinavian settlement are not so frequent as in Wensleydale, but in Swaledale the evidence of Anglian settlement is stronger. *Crin* is the Irish name of a local landowner in 1066, and *Skaleflat* (Norse *skáli*) is found in Feetham. The few traces of Scandinavian influence in south and upper Swaledale suggest

that the Scandinavian settlement of those parts was slight compared with that on the north side of the valley, but that the
few Scandinavians who did settle were Norwegians rather than
Danes.

In Gilling East the Norwegian settlement seems to be closely
connected with that of the north of Allertonshire and Cleveland.
Brekelandes (Norse *brekka*) in Jolby, Eryholme, Brettanby, and
the Irish name *Finegal* borne by a local tenant are all in the
north of the wapentake. In Gilling West there are many Norwegian names, including Priest Gill, Faggergill, *Waltergille* in
Arkengarthdale, William Gill, and Easegill in Swaledale, and
Scargill and Wemmergill in Teesdale (all containing *gil*), Scales,
Hang Bank (which in one of its forms contains *brekka*), Melsonby
and *Finegalgraft* (Old Irish *Finngail*) in Easby, both containing
Irish personal names. Kilmond in upper Teesdale is an interesting name of Gaelic origin and was perhaps introduced at this
time. Irish influence has been noticed on the crosses found at
Croft, Stanwick, and Wycliffe.

The general conclusion as to the distribution of the Scandinavian element in the North Riding is that the Danes settled
chiefly in the south of the Riding in the level fertile valleys of
the Derwent, Rye, Ouse, in the lower parts of the Ure valley
and in Birdforth in the central Vale of York. The Norwegians
settled chiefly in Ryedale, Whitby Strand, Cleveland and Teesdale and in Richmondshire. Whereas the Danes and Norwegians
indifferently occupied districts already settled by Angles, the
distribution of place-names suggests that the Norwegian settlers
tended to avoid the districts occupied by the Danes in the
previous century. Most of the Danes undoubtedly moved out
from the centre of their kingdom at York; others entered the
Riding independently. The Norwegians as a whole came over
the Pennines from Cumberland, occasionally bringing with them
Britons from that district, although the name Scarborough points
to incursions of Norwegians from the North Sea, which probably
explains the settlements in Pickering Lythe, Ryedale and Whitby
Strand.

The materials on which the following pages are based differ
from those used in other volumes in this series in that they
include hardly any Old English forms. The Domesday Survey

is generally accurate, and the inaccuracies which occur are usually explicable. Under these conditions the Domesday forms become unusually important. To some extent the rarity of Old English material is counterbalanced by a large mass of twelfth century material drawn chiefly from the published Cartularies of Rievaulx, Whitby, and Guisborough. From the Cartularies which are not published separately many twelfth century charters are printed in the late Dr Farrer's *Early Yorkshire Charters*. Material has also been drawn from several unpublished cartularies, such as those of Malton, Kirkham, St Leonard's York, Easby, and the *Magnum Registrum Album* of the Minster Church of York. The Assize Rolls provide valuable forms for the thirteenth century, whilst the series of Forest Rolls relating to Galtres and the Pleas of the Forest entered in the *Great Coucher Book of the Duchy of Lancaster* have been invaluable as sources of material for a slightly later time.

NOTES ON THE DIALECT OF THE NORTH RIDING
AS ILLUSTRATED BY ITS PLACE-NAMES

Professor G. H. Cowling's *The Dialect of Hackness* covers the problems of the dialect of the North Riding in a very adequate manner, and in every instance the place-names bear out the results achieved by that book. The actual sound-changes between the fourteenth and seventeenth centuries may be dated more precisely by the p.n. material.

Unlike the other counties already covered by the Survey, the North Riding belongs to the Northumbrian group, and in modern times to the Northern area.

OE, ON *a* **usually remains,** but Breckenbrough, Eppleby show a modern dialectal variant [ɛ].

OE, ON *al* (which remained unfractured in OE) **became** *au* in the middle of the sixteenth century **and later** [ɔː], as Scawton, Cawton, Cawthorne, Autherlands; Swaledale, Scalby, Salton, etc. preserve the older spelling. The spelling of Wardle Rigg is noteworthy.

OE *a* **before nasals is invariably preserved.**

OE, ON *ā* **was raised to** [eː], when it was diphthongised to [iə], as in Blea Wyke, Bluewath Beck, Breaday, etc. and initially this new diphthong became [jæ], as in the pronunciation of Ayton [jætn], Acomb [jækəm], Oak Dale [jægdil], etc. The actual line of division in the ME development of *ā* passed a little to the south of the Riding.

OE i-mutation of *a* before *l* + a consonant resulted in æ in parts of Mercia and there are evidences for the Mercian form in YWR. In YNR, however, it invariably became *e*, as in wella, Eldmire and Ellermire containing ONb *elfitu* (= southern OE *aelbitu*). The pers. name *Ella* (Ellington) occurs only in ONb area, but the forms *Ælla*, *Ælle*, are found in OE texts from the midlands and south.

OE, ON *au* usually becomes [ɔu] in the dialect, **but it has become** [a] in Marsett, Addlebrough and Laskill.

OE æ became *e* in parts of Mercia, but it **was always retained in YNR,** as in Masham, etc., usually as [a].

OE, ME *er* became *ar* by the middle of the fifteenth century and with loss of *r* it had become [aː] by the end of the sixteenth, whence such forms as *Maske* for Marske, Wath Cote, etc.

OE, ON *i* was lengthened in an open syllable and lowered to [eː], when it fell in with early modern English [eː] and became [iː], as in Cleveland, Feetham, Healam Beck, Kirkleatham, Reeth, Skeeby, Smeaton, and Upleatham.

OE, ON *i* and *y* followed by *r* often became er in ME and together with ur and sometimes er (as in Borrowby) it ultimately became [ɔr] or [ɔ(ː)], as in Worton, Storthwaite, Borrowby, Burneston, Cock Flat, and Irton (olim *Urton*), Irby, and Girlington, etc.

OE, ON *i* or *y* preceded by *r* often became [u], as in Ruddings, Ruswarp, Ruswick, Runswick.

OE, ON *ol* followed by a consonant had become [ou] or [ɔu] by the middle of the fifteenth century, as in Howthorpe, Colburn, etc.

OE, ON *ō* became ME [øu], [ɛu] (Cowling, *op. cit.* 49, 159) and in the early modern period it became [iu] (fifteenth and sixteenth centuries). This has remained in some parts of the Riding, whilst in others it has further developed to [iə], as in Beadlam and Beedale. Other examples of the earlier stage are Aiskew, Cotescue and other names containing skogr, Huby, etc.

OE, ON *ū* has remained in the dialect, as in Booze.

OE, ON *ul* followed by a consonant fell in with ME *ol* and became [ɔu], as in Ovington, Oulston, Bowforth, Owlands, Ousey Carr, Mowthorpe, and in the pronunciation of Holme (Halik), Bulmer, and Mulgrave.

ME *s* has in a few cases become [ʃ], as in Dishforth and Whashton and the pronunciation of Exelby.

OE *t* has become [ð] in Gatherley and Sutherland and in the pronunciation of Catterick. OE *d* in *ford* became [θ] during the fifteenth century.

ME *ks* often became z, s (with loss of *k*) as Exelby, Aiskew, Aysgarth, etc. From confusion of [z] from this source with z from other sources there have been curious unetymological back-formations in the spellings of Coxwold, Moxby, Throxenby, Roxby, etc.

OE *hw*, ON *hv* usually preserved their aspiration during

the ME period, when there are sporadic instances of over-aspiration as represented by *Qu-*, as in the spellings of Whitby, Whinholme, and Falsgrave. The North Riding was, therefore, rather to the south of the *Qu*-area. In the modern period, however, **aspiration was lost** (with the extraordinary exception of Falsgrave) and confusion of *Qu-* which represents over-aspiration with *Qu-* which is etymologically correct led to some of the latter being included in the change, as Whaw, Whenby, and Quernhow in some of its spellings.

Initial [j] has developed in Yafforth, Yearby, Yearsley, Yedmandale, and in some of the forms of Everley.

ABBREVIATIONS

Abbr	*Placitorum Abbreviatio*, 1811.
AD	*Catalogue of Ancient Deeds*. (In progress.)
Add	Additional MSS in the Brit. Museum.
Allert	Allerton wap.
AN	Anglo-Norman.
Angl	Anglian dialect of OE.
AntIt	*Itinerarium Antonini Augusti* (MHB).
Archd	*Registers of the Archdeaconry of Richmond*, an Abstract made by M. Hutton, Harl. 6978 (18th cent.).
ASC	Anglo-Saxon Chronicle.
AScand	Anglo-Scandinavian.
Ass	Yorkshire Assize Rolls (YAS 44).
Ass	Yorkshire Assize Rolls, unpublished (PRO).
Baildon	W. P. Baildon, *Monastic Notes* (YAS 17).
Banco	*De Banco Rolls* (PRO Lists and Indexes no. 32).
BCS	Birch, *Cartularium Saxonicum*, 3 vols., 1885–93.
Bede	Bede's *Historia eccles. gentis Anglorum*, 1896.
BedeOE	*The Old English Bede*, ed. Miller (EETS) 1890.
Beds	Bedfordshire.
Birdf	Birdforth wap.
Bk	Buckinghamshire.
BM	*Index to the Charters and Rolls in the British Museum*, 2 vols., 1900–12.
Bodl	Yorkshire Charters (unpublished) in the Bodleian Library.
Bridl	*Bridlington Cartulary*, ed. Lancaster. (Privately published.)
Brit	British.
Bulm	Bulmer wap.
Burton	Burton's *Monasticon Eboracense*, 1758.
BylD	*Byland Cartulary*, Dods. 63, 91, 94.
BylE	*Byland Cartulary*, Egerton 2823 (MS t. Hy 4).
C	Cambridgeshire.
Cai	*Admissions to Gonville and Caius College*, ed. Venn, 1887.
Ch	*Calendar of Charter Rolls*. (In progress.)
Ch	Cheshire.
ChR	*Rotuli Chartarum*, 1837.
Cl	*Calendar of Close Rolls*. (In progress.)
ClR	*Rotuli Litterarum Clausarum*, 2 vols., 1833–44.
Cockers	*Cartulary of Cockersand* (Chetham Soc.) 1898–1909, MS 18th cent.
Cover	Collections relating to Coverham, Sloane MS 4934 (MS late).
Crawf	*The Crawford Charters*, 1895.
Cu	Cumberland.
Cur	*Curia Regis Rolls*. (In progress.)
Cur	*Curia Regis Rolls*. (PRO, unpublished.)
D	Devonshire.
DB	*Domesday Book*.
Db	Derbyshire.
dial	dialect(al).
Dods	Dodsworth's MSS in the Bodleian Library (17th cent.).
Du	Durham.
Dugd	Dugdale's *Monasticon*, 6 vols. in 8, 1817–30.

Dunelm	*Registrum Palatinum Dunelmense* (Rolls Series), 4 vols. 1873–8.
e	early.
Easby	*Easby Cartulary*, Egerton MS 2827. (MS compiled c. 1281, with additions from late 13th and 14th cents.)
Ebor	*Registers of the Archbishops of York*: Surt 56, 109, 123, 128, 137
Ebor	*Registers of the Archbishops of York.* (Unpublished.)
EDD	*English Dialect Dictionary.*
EETS	Early English Text Society.
EPN	*Chief Elements in English Place-Names*, 1923.
ES	*Englische Studien.* (In progress.)
Ess	Essex.
f	feminine.
FA	*Feudal Aids*, 6 vols., 1899–1920.
Fabr	*Fabric Rolls of York Minster* (Surt 35).
Farrer MS	Transcripts of Y. documents by the late Dr W. Farrer.
Fees	*Book of Fees*, 2 vols., 1922–3.
FF	Yorkshire *Feet of Fines* (YAJ, xi, Surt 94, YAS 2, 5, 7, 8, 42, 52, 53, 58, 62).
Fine	*Calendar of Fine Rolls.* (In progress.)
For	Forest Proceedings, unpublished (PRO).
ForP	*Pleas of the Forest*, PRO Duchy of Lanc. Misc. Books, vol. 1 (MS late 14th cent.).
Förstemann	*Altdeutsches Namenbuch*, 2 vols. in 3, 1901–16.
Förster	M. Förster, *Keltisches Wortgut*, 1921.
Fount	*Memorials of Fountains Abbey* (Surt 42, 67).
FountA	*Fountains Cartulary, Add MS* 37770 (15th cent.).
FountT	*Fountains Cartulary*, Cotton MS Tiber. C. xii (15th cent.).
Fr	French.
Gael	Gaelic.
GillE	Gilling East wap.
GillW	Gilling West wap.
Godr	*De vita S. Godrici* (Surt 20).
Gosp	The York Gospel Book (Library of the Dean and Chapter, York).
GP	Rygh, *Gamle Personnavne i Norske Stedsnavne*, 1901.
Guis	*Guisborough Cartulary*, Surt 86, 89 (MS 15th cent.).
Ha	Hampshire.
Hailstone	Hailstone MSS in the Minster Library, York.
Halik	Halikeld wap.
HangE	Hang East wap.
HangW	Hang West wap.
HCY	*Historians of the Church of York* (Rolls Series), 3 vols., 1879–94.
He	Hereford.
Heal	*Cartularium de Parco Helagh*, Cotton MS Vespas. A. iv (MS c. 1498, fols. 175–189 *d* mid. 16th cent.).
HSC	*Historia de Sancto Cuthberto* in SD *infra*.
Hu	Huntingdonshire.
Icel	Icelandic
Ipm	*Calendar of Inquisitions post mortem.* (In progress.)
IpmR	*Inquisitiones post mortem*, Record Commission, 4 vols., 1806–28.
IPN	*Introduction to the Survey of English Place-Names*, 1923.

Sanct	*Sanctuarium Dunelm. et Beverlac* (Surt 5).
Saxton	Saxton's *Map of Yorkshire*, 1577.
Schönfeld	Schönfeld, *Wörterbuch der Altgermanischen Personen- und Völker-namen*, 1911.
SD	*Symeon of Durham* (Rolls Series), 2 vols., 1882–5.
Searle	Searle, *Onomasticon Anglo-Saxonicum*, 1897.
Speed	Speed's *Map of Yorkshire*, 1610.
St	Staffordshire.
Surt	Surtees Society Publications.
SurvDu	*Survey of Durham* (Surt 32).
Swed	Swedish.
Sx	Sussex.
Test	*Testamenta Eboracensia* (Surt 4, 30, 45, 53, 79, 106).
Thorpe	Thorpe, *Diplomatarium Anglicanum*, 1865.
Var	*Calendar of Various Chancery Rolls*, 1912.
VCH	*Victoria County History of the North Riding*, 2 vols. and index, 1914–25.
VCHY	*Victoria County History of Yorkshire*, 3 vols. and index, 1907–25.
VE	*Valor Ecclesiasticus*, 6 vols., 1810–34.
Vill	*Nomina Villarum*, 1316 (Surt 49).
Visit	*Heraldic Visitations of Yorks* (Surt 36, 41, 122, 127).
W	Wiltshire.
Wa	Warwickshire.
wap	wapentake.
WCR	*Wakefield Court Rolls* (YAS 29, 36, 57).
We	Westmoreland.
Whit	Whitby Strand wap.
Whitby	*Whitby Cartulary* (Surt 69, 72, MS 15th cent.).
Wo	Worcestershire.
WSax	West Saxon.
YAJ	*Yorkshire Archæological Journal.*
YAS	Yorkshire Archæological Soc., Record Series.
YCh	Farrer's *Early Yorkshire Charters*, 3 vols., 1914 ff.
YChant	*Yorkshire Chantry Surveys* (Surt 91, 92).
YD	*Yorkshire Deeds* (YAS 39, 50, 63, 64).
YDS	Transactions of the Yorkshire Dialect Society.
YER	East Riding of Yorkshire.
YI	*Yorkshire Inquisitions* (YAS 12, 23, 31, 37, 59).
YNR	North Riding of Yorkshire.
YWR	West Riding of Yorkshire.
ZEN	Björkman, *Zur Englische Namenkunde*, 1912.

Reference is made to the various county place-name books already published (*v.* summary bibliography in *Chief Elements in English Place-Names*) by using the abbreviation PN followed by the recognised abbreviation for the county, e.g. PN Gl for Baddeley's *Place-Names of Gloucestershire*.

Reference is made to the parish register of any particular parish by giving the name of the parish in full, e.g. 1663 Pickhill indicates a form found in the Pickhill Parish Registers, s.a. 1663.

PHONETIC SYMBOLS USED IN TRANSCRIPTION
OF PRONUNCIATIONS OF PLACE-NAMES

p	*p*ay	ʃ	*sh*one	tʃ	*ch*urch	ei	fl*ay*
b	*b*ay	ʒ	a*z*ure	dʒ	*j*udge	ɛ	Fr. jam*ai*s
t	*t*ea	θ	*th*in	ɑː	f*a*ther	ɛː	th*ere*
d	*d*ay	ð	*th*en	ɑu	c*ow*	i	p*i*t
k	*k*ey	j	*y*ou	a	Ger. m*a*nn	iː	f*ee*l
g	*g*o	χ	lo*ch*	ai	fl*y*	ou	l*ow*
ᴧ	*wh*en	h	*h*is	æ	c*a*b	u	g*oo*d
w	*w*in	m	*m*an	ɔ	p*o*t	uː	r*u*le
f	*f*oe	n	*n*o	ɔː	s*aw*	ᴧ	m*u*ch
v	*v*ote	ŋ	si*ng*	oi	*oi*l	ə	*e*ver
s	*s*ay	r	*r*un	e	r*e*d	əː	b*ir*d
z	*z*one	l	*l*and				

Examples:

Harwich (hæridʒ), Shrewsbury (ʃrouzbəri, ʃruːbəri),
Beaulieu (bjuːli).

(7) In the case of all forms for which reference has been made to unprinted authorities, that fact is indicated by printing the reference to the authority in italic instead of ordinary type, e.g. 1280 *Ass* denotes a form derived from a MS authority in contrast to 1259 Ass which denotes one taken from a printed text.

(8) Where two dates are given, e.g. 1285 (16th), the first is the date at which the document purports to have been composed, the second is that of the copy which has come down to us. For most of the cartularies only one date has been given, but the date of the cartulary itself will as a rule be found in the list of Abbreviations.

(9) Where a letter in an early place-name form is placed within brackets, the forms with and without that letter are found, e.g. *Hot(t)une* means that the forms *Hottune* and *Hotune* are alike found.

(10) All words are quoted in their West-Saxon form (cf. note 6 *supra*) or their OIcel form unless otherwise stated. ON personal names are quoted in the forms under which they will be found in LindN and LindBN.

(11) No explanation of a name is added when its meaning is obvious.

NOTES

(1) The names are arranged topographically according to wapentakes, and the parishes within the wapentakes are similarly arranged. Within the parishes the townships are arranged in alphabetical order, and the place-names within each township are similarly arranged. The only exceptions to this rule are that river- and road-names are taken at the beginning, whilst district-names are taken at the beginning of the wapentake in which they are found.

(2) Every township name is preceded by a figure (its number in the parish), and after every township name will be found the reference to the sheet and square of the 1-in. O.S. map (Popular Edition) on which it may be found. Thus, 2. Saltburn 16 C 5. With the exception of Kirkdale and Mashamshire, the parish name is also a township name and the parish name is therefore dealt with in its proper order within the parish, or as in the case of Kirkdale within the township in which it is situated.

(3) Where a place-name is only found on the 6-in. O.S. map this is indicated by putting 6″ after it in brackets, e.g. Halligill Cote (6″).

(4) Place-names now no longer current are marked as 'Lost.' This does not necessarily mean that the site to which the name was once applied is unknown. We are dealing primarily with names and the names are lost. These names are printed in italics when referred to elsewhere in the volume.

(5) The local pronunciation of the place-name is given, wherever it is of interest, in phonetic script within squared brackets, e.g. [jægdil].

(6) In explaining the various place-names summary reference is made to the detailed account of such elements as are found in the *Chief Elements in English Place-Names* by printing those elements in Clarendon type, e.g. Clifton, *v.* **clif**, **tun**. As the place-names are derived from Anglian forms without OE fracture this is indicated by putting the *e* representing fracture within brackets, e.g. **h(e)alh**, which means that the word will be found in EPN under the full form of the word, but that the place-name is actually derived from the form *halh*.

ADDENDA ET CORRIGENDA

[For numerous corrections of detail we are indebted to the
watchful kindness of Mr Geoffrey Marsland.]

VOL. I, PART I

p. 148. Dr Ritter (ES 62, 109) has an interesting note on the element
cistel, ce(a)stel, cæstel in OE charters. *stan cestil* in BCS 282 is given as the
name of *uno acerbo lapidum* and he suggests that this should be connected
with ON *kǫstr*, 'heap,' rather than with Lat *castellum*, such an etymology
agreeing closely with its actual usage in the one passage which is in any way
helpful as to its meaning.

VOL. I, PART II

p. viii, l. 6, for '1913' read '1916.'

s.v. bi(g). Dr Ritter (ES 62, 108–9) suggests with much probability that this
element in English place-names should be interpreted as a prefix rather than
as a preposition which has coalesced with the following word. He quotes
Germanic parallels for such a usage both in common nouns and in place-
names, where the prefix denotes 'surrounding.' Thus he would render
Bythorne as 'encircling thorn-hedge,' Bygrave as 'surrounding thicket.' This
is no doubt the best solution for a good many of the names in question but
is hardly applicable to them all. It will not fit Byford; Byfleet is 'by' a
stream but there is no 'surrounding stream' here. So also Bywell is difficult
to interpret in this way.

p. 37, s.v. hlinc. Delete 'Liscombe (Bk).'

p. 38, s.v. holegn. Delete 'Holdfast (Wo).'

s.v. hop. Delete 'It seems...Thames.'

p. 40, s.v. hwæte. Whaddon (W) is the Whaddon near Salisbury.

p. 44, s.v. læfer. Delete 'Livermere (Sf).'

p. 63, s.v. wad. Whaddon (W) is the Whaddon near Melksham.

p. 66, s.v. woh. Delete 'Wooburn (Bk).'

VOL. II

p. 26, WILLEN. Professor Zachrisson (ES 62, 97) calls attention to the
omission of the 12th cent. form *Wilinges* (France). This is an AN spelling
of the name.

p. 102, s.n. POLLICOTT. Mr P. H. Reaney calls attention to the form
Polingtote (sic) found c. 1150 (France). This confirms the *Poling-* derivation suggested in the text.

p. 151, HAMPDEN. Mr M. W. Hughes suggests with a good deal of likelihood that the first element may be OE hamm referring to the curved shape
of the valley at this point, hence 'valley suggesting the shape of the ham.'

p. 155, HALEACRE. Mr M. W. Hughes calls attention to another *Haleaker*
(c. 1200) in Chesham in the Missenden Cartulary, which makes the suggestions put forward for this name impossible.

HYDE. This is the 'Hida predictorum canonicorum que dicitur Hunfridi' of the Missenden Cartulary (12th cent.). This Humphrey was a brother of Walter de Broc and great-uncle of Elias de Wymbervile. (M.W.H.)

p. 159, DINTON. Mr M. W. Hughes quotes a form *Donentona* (c. 1180) from the Missenden Cartulary.

p. 170, RISBOROUGH. Professor Zachrisson (ES 62, 96) calls attention to some important additional OE forms, viz. *Hrisanbeorgen*, dat. pl. KCD 721, 1012 (13th), *at Risenburga* KCD 689, *Risberghe* KCD 690, 995 (12th), *Hrisbeorgan*, dat. pl. KCD 1321, 1336, 1033 (12th) and suggests that the first element in some of the forms may be an unrecorded OE *hrise*, 'land covered with brushwood' and in others the ordinary hris.

p. 198, GLORYHILL. It should have been made clear that this contains the same pers. name as Glory Fm (PN Bk 230). The etymology given is not that of the place-name but of the name of the family after which it was called. An earlier reference to *Gloryhill* is the holding of John de *Glorie* in Wooburn in 1242 (Fees 875).

VOL. III

p. 4, l. 4. The '*v.* Addenda' should be transferred to p. 2, l. 12 from bottom.

p. 55, a.n. BASMEAD. Mr P. H. Reaney calls attention to an interesting series of names in which final *d* has been lost, viz. Hullasey (Gl), DB *Hunlafsed* (from hid), Coxtie (Ess), *Cocstede* (1286 Ch), Sugstys Green (Ess), *Sucksted* in 1523, so that possibly the forms without final *d* may really be from earlier ones with a *d* which has by chance survived in the modern form.

p. 89. Delete 'In this case...difficulties' at the end of the first full paragraph.

p. 129, SEWELL. Professor Zachrisson points out that the pers. name *Seofa* is on record in the Latinised form *Seofus* in the *Hyde Liber Vitæ*, *v.* Searle 575.

p. 137, HERNE. Professor Mansion (*English Studies* 10, 14) points out that Dutch *haar*, 'height covered with wood,' does not actually exist. The definition is an attempt by Jellinghaus to interpret a place-name element of which the exact meaning is unknown.

p. 138, s.n. WADLOW. Mr P. H. Reaney calls attention to the forms and phonetic development of Weybridge (in the same volume, p. 232) which make it quite possible that the original first-element was weald.

p. 150, l. 11 from bottom, for '64' read '65.'

p. 227, l. 6. For 'Wardington' read 'Warrington.'

p. 272, l. 4 from bottom, for 'elation' read 'relation.'

p. 310, Index, s.n. Godmanchester. Delete ref. to p. 152.

p. 311, s.n. Yelling. For '276' read '275.'

VOL. IV

p. 1, THE COTSWOLDS. Additional early forms are *Coddeswold* (1294 Cl), *Coteswold* (1305 id.) ex inf. Major J. de C. Laffan.

p. 12, HONEYBROOK, etc. Mr C. A. Seyler suggests with a good deal of likelihood that the application of the term 'honey' to streams may have arisen from the fondness of bees for swarming in pollarded willows by the side of a stream.

p. 60, MAMBLE. The Rev. J. B. Johnston kindly calls attention to the omission of the DB form *Mamele* for this name.

NoB	*Namn och Bygd.* (In progress.)
Norw	Norwegian.
Nostell	*Nostell Cartulary*, Cotton MS Vespas. E. xix (principally 13th cent.).
NP	Björkman, *Nordische Personennamen*, 1910.
NR	North Riding Record Society Publications, 1st series.
NRS	North Riding Record Society Publications, 2nd series.
Nt	Nottinghamshire.
Nth	Northamptonshire.
O	Oxfordshire.
OblR	*Rotuli de Oblatis*, 1835.
ODan	Old Danish.
OE	Old English.
OEScand	Old East Scandinavian.
OFr	Old French.
OHG	Old High German.
OIcel	Old Icelandic.
ON	Old Norse.
ONb	Old Northumbrian.
ONorw	Old Norwegian.
O.S.	Ordnance Survey.
OSwed	Old Swedish.
OWScand	Old West Scandinavian.
P	*Pipe Rolls* (Pipe Roll Society (in progress), Great Roll of the Pipe for 26 Hy 3, ed. Cannon, 1918).
Pap	*Calendar of entries in Papal Registers.* (In progress.)
Pat	*Calendar of Patent Rolls.* (In progress.)
PatR	*Rotul. Litt. Patentium*, 1835.
Percy	*Percy Cartulary* (Surt 117).
pers. name	personal name.
Pick	Pickering Lythe wap.
p.n.	place-name.
Pont	*Pontefract Cartulary* (YAS 25).
PrN	Primitive Norse.
PRO	Public Record Office.
QW	*Placita de quo Warranto*, 1818.
Redin	Redin, *Uncompounded Personal Names in OE*, 1919.
RES	*Review of English Studies.*
RH	*Rotuli Hundredorum*, 2 vols., 1812–8.
Rich	*Extent of Knights' Fees in Richmond*, PRO, Exch. TR, Books 69.
RichReg	*Registrum Honoris Richmondiae*, Cotton MS Faustina B. vii (15th cent. transcript).
RichWills	*Wills of Richmond* (Surt 28).
Riev	*Rievaulx Cartulary* (Surt 83, MS 16th cent.).
Ripon	*Memorials of Ripon* (Surt 74, 78, 81, 115).
RNY	E. V. Gordon and A. H. Smith, *River-Names of Yorks* (YDS xxvi), 1925.
RotDom	*Rotuli de Dominabus et pueris et puellis* (Pipe Roll Soc. 35), 1913.
RSE	Received Standard English.
Ryed	Ryedale wap.
s.a.	sub anno.
Sa	Shropshire.
Saints	*Die Heiligen Englands*, ed. Liebermann, 1889.

Ir	Irish.
Jerv	*Charter of Jervaulx Abbey*, MS Harl. 1808 (late 14th cent.).
K	Kent.
KCD	Kemble, *Codex Diplomaticus Aevi Saxonici*, 6 vols., 1839–48.
KF	*Knights' Fees* 1303 (Surt 49).
KF	*Feoda Militum* 1316 (Library of the Dean and Chapter, York, MS Zouch L. 2. 2).
KI	*Kirkby's Inquest* 1285 (Surt 49).
Kirkham	*Kirkham Cartulary*, Bodl. Fairfax VII.
Kirkst	*Coucher Book of Kirkstall Abbey* (Thoresby Soc), 1904.
L	Lincolnshire.
La	Lancashire.
LangE	Langbargh East wap.
LangW	Langbargh West wap.
Lat	Latin.
LDD	*Lincoln Diocese Documents* (EETS), 1914.
Lei	Leicestershire.
LGerm	Low German.
Leon	*Registrum Cartarum Hospit. St Leonardi Ebor.* MS Cotton Nero D. III (MS 15th cent.).
Lib	*Calendar of Liberate Rolls.* (In progress.)
LindN	Lind, *Norsk-Isländska dopnamn och fingerade namn*,1905–15.
LindBN	Lind, *Norsk-Isländska Personbinamn*, 1920–1.
Lindkvist	Lindkvist, *Middle English Place-Names of Scand. Origin*, 1912.
LS	*Yorkshire Lay Subsidy* 1301 (YAS 21).
Lundgren-Brate	M. F. Lundgren and E. Brate, *Personnamn från medeltiden*, 1892 ff.
LVD	*Liber Vitae Dunelmensis*, facsimile ed. Surt 1921.
Malton	*Malton Cartulary*, Cotton MS Claudius D. XI (mid 13th cent. with 14th cent. interpolations).
Marrick	*Marrick Cartulary* (Collectanea Topogr. et Geneal. no. 820, v), London, 1838.
MaryH	*Cartulary of St Mary's York*, MS Harl. 236 (early 14th cent.).
Mary Y	*Cartulary of St Mary's York*, MS Dean and Chapter, York (15th cent.).
ME	Middle English.
Merc	Mercian.
MHB	*Monumenta Historica Britannica*, 1848.
MHG	Middle High German.
MIr	Middle Irish.
Misc	*Calendar of Inquisitions Miscellaneous*, 2 vols., 1916.
MLG	Middle Low German.
ModEng	Modern English.
Mx	Middlesex.
Naumann	Naumann, *Altnordische Namenstudien*, 1912.
Nb	Northumberland.
NCyWills	*Wills of the Northern Counties* (Surt 1, 26, 112).
NED	*New English Dictionary.*
NElv	Rygh, *Norske Elvenavne*, 1904.
Nf	Norfolk.
NG	Rygh, *Norske Gaardnavne*, 18 vols., 1897–1919.
Nielsen	Nielsen, *Olddanske Personnavne*, 1883.

p. 75, ll. 6–7 from bottom. Delete the reference to Harpsford (Sr). Mr Gerdström calls attention to a form *Harpedesford* which shows that this is a compound of **herepæð**. This is of special interest as Harpsford was by Virginia Water, where the Roman Road from Silchester to Staines crossed a small stream (VCH Sr i. 358, iii. 420, iv. 355). We may note further Harpford (So), *Herpoðford* in KCD 816 at an important ford across the Tone.

p. 78, SHRAWLEY. Mr F. T. S. Houghton calls attention to a very pleasant illustration of the use of OE *scræf* in p.n.'s. In Aston by Birmingham (Wa) there is a Salford Bridge, of which the early forms are *Scraford*, *Schrafford*, clearly 'ford with one or more examples of a *scræf* by it.' Close at hand is a *Scrave medwe* (1319) and, much more significant, *Dwarfeholys* (1490). It is clear therefore that these particular 'caves' or 'dens' were known in popular phrase as 'dwarf-holes.' The building of modern Birmingham alas makes it impossible to find just what they were like.

p. 100, l. 7. Delete 'Ess.'

p. 154, l. 8 from bottom. For '197' read '198.'

p. 156, REDMARLEY D'ABITOT. The *Abbetot* from which it is suggested that Urse derived his family name is the one for which we have a form *Apetot* in 1198 (Fabricius, *Danske Minder i Normandiet* 313). The Rev. J. B. Johnston calls attention to an *Abetot* in a Norman Charter of the 11th cent., which may or may not be the same place. If it is, the first element would be a pers. name *Abbe* rather than *Api* or the common word *æble*.

p. 216, l. 2 from bottom. For 'above' read 'below.'

p. 221, l. 9 from bottom. Mr Gerdström rightly points out that *pedanhrycg* is to be identified with Petridge in Horley (Sr) and not with Pettridge (K).

p. 254, l. 11. For the pers. name *Wraba*, Mr P. H. Reaney calls our attention to Rapton (Sf) which is *Wrabetun* in the 12th cent. (BM) and to William *Wrabbe* in 1256 Ass (So).

p. 264, l. 8. For '11' read '12.'

p. 286, l. 6 from bottom. For '13th' read '15th.'

p. 304, l. 13 from bottom. After tun add 'and þorp.'

VOL. V

p. 51, s.n. SCACKLETON. Mr F. H. Marsden calls attention to a word [ʃekəl] which he has heard used in YNR of a kind of circular depression in the limestone districts caused by subsidence of surface earth into small cavities underground. This word may possibly enter into some of the *Shackle-*names.

p. 123, s.n. SHAWM RIGG. Professor Ekwall points out that a 'straw' name is very unlikely at this particular spot and suggests that the *halm-* form offers no difficulty as ON *hjalmr* would, at an early date, have such a form as *healm* and that the substitution of ONb *halm* for this would be quite natural.

p. 131, s.n. CLITHERBECK. Professor Ekwall would prefer now to associate these names with Swed dial. *klädra*, *klera*, 'song-thrush,' going back to earlier **kliðra*.

p. 172, s.n. SEAMER. Add the lost DB manor of *Berguluesbi* or *Bergolbi* containing the ON pers. name *Bergúlfr* (LindN).

p. 181, s.n. LECKBY. Professor Ekwall suggests that a weak **Ljóti* or fem. *Ljóta* (LindN) would better explain the early forms.

p. 275, s.n. AINDERBY STEEPLE. The important form *Enderdeby* (1280 Ipm) should be added.

p. 305, s.n. RERE or REY CROSS. Professor Ekwall calls attention to the article by Mr W. G. Collingwood in the *Cu. and We. Arch. Soc. Trans.* (27, 1 ff.) in which he gives an early form *Redecros* (sic) (1314) and points to the parallel of Rear or Ray Crag on the old boundary of Coniston. Professor Ekwall suggests that the first element is OScand *hreyrr*, 'cairn,' still used in Swedish (in the form *rör*) of a boundary-mark, often in the combination *rå och rör*. In *Rey* Cross, as in *Rey* Crag, the final *r* was occasionally lost owing to dissimilation, but it is also possible that the name varied between *hreyr-kros* and *rá-kros*. Both would mean the same thing. Rere Cross is on the Yorkshire-Westmoreland boundary.

NORTH RIDING OF YORKSHIRE[1]

on Eoferwicscire 1055–64 Thorpe 391, 1066–9 ib. 438
Eboracensisira 1061–5 YCh 11; *-sc(h)ira* 1089–95 *RegAlb* i. 62,
  12 ib. i. 36 *d*
Euroicsira 1066–90 (1433) PatR
Euruic-, Eurewicscire 1086 DB, etc.
le Counte d'Everwyk c. 1416, 1456 Fount
the Counte of Yorke 1456, 1538 Fount
Yorkshire 1577 Saxton, 1610 Speed
Nort Treding 1086 DB
Nortrithing' 1198 Fees, 1233 Cl
Nortriding 1235, 1237 Cl
Northrithing' 1240 Lib, 1279–81 QW
Nordriding' 1235–6 Fees
(Weststriding et) Nortstriding 1287 Ebor
Northridding(e) 1285 KI, 1296 YI

The etymology of the name is OE, ON *norð*, 'north,' and
ON *þriðjungr* 'third part,' late OE *þriðing*. On the form of the
second element *v.* IPN 109 ff. For the origin of the Riding
name *v.* Introduction xiv, xxii.

NORTH RIDING ROAD-NAMES

LEEMING LANE

This is the name of the great Roman road which crosses the
North Riding from Borough Bridge to Catterick and the north.
In the 16th cent. it was called Watling Street (cf. Healam House
220 *infra* and Watling Street *infra*). *v.* Leeming 227 *infra*.

WATLING STREET

ad magnam stratam 12 *Easby* 57
Watlinge Stre(e)te 1613 NR, 17 Felon Sew of Rokeby

This is the name sometimes applied to that part of the Great
North Road in Gilling West wapentake; its southern part is

---

[1] The names of York and other places within the city will be dealt with
in the West Riding volume.

known as Leeming Lane 1 *supra*, whilst that part which runs through Allerton Bywater (YWR) is referred to in the 13th cent. as *Watlinge Strete*. For the etymology of this name *v.* PN BedsHu 5–7.

NORTH RIDING RIVER-NAMES

The forms of the river-names, so far as they are found in early documents, are as follows. For their interpretation reference may be made to the *River-Names of Yorkshire* (YDS 1925), by E. V. Gordon and A. H. Smith, and to the forthcoming volume upon the *River-Names of England* by Professor Ekwall.

BAIN, R., an affluent of the Ure

> *Bayn(e)* 1153 Dugd v. 573 *et passim*
> *Baine, Bein* 1218 FF

Cf. the river Bain (L), *Beinam* 12, 13 BM. *v.* RNY 17, and Bainbridge 262 *infra*.

BALDER, R., an affluent of the Tees

> *Balder* 13 YD
> *Bauder flu'* 1577 Saxton, 1626 Drayton (*Polyolbion*)

A back-formation from the name Baldersdale (*v.* 306 *infra*).

BURN, R., an affluent of the Ure

> *Brunne* 12 Fount, 1330 Ch
> *v.* RNY 17 and brunnr, burna.

COD BECK, an affluent of the Swale

> *Cotesbec* 13 Riev
> *Codbek flu* 1577 Saxton

COSTA BECK, an affluent of the Derwent

> *aquam de Costa* c. 1180–1212 YCh 394, 1189 Riev *et passim*
> *Costham* (Latinised) 1189 Riev, 1252 Ch
> *Costey* 1536 YChant
> *Costtow flu'* 1577 Saxton

COVER, R., an affluent of the Ure

> *Couer* 1279 *Ass*, 1577 Saxton *Cover* 1336 Pat.
> *The Cour* 1565 FF

Also found in Coverdale:

Coverdale 1202 FF, 1270 YI *et passim*
Coferdale 1543 FF

The name is found in Coverham 254 *infra*. It should be compared with OE *Coveresgiet* BCS 912 (in Brockenborough W), OE *on cofer fros* BCS 1056 (Cornw), and OE *on cofring treow* BCS 1051 (in Clere, Ha).

CRAMBECK, an affluent of the Derwent

Crambech 13 *Malton* 71 d
v. bekkr. Cf. Crambe 38 *infra*.

DERWENT, R., an affluent of the Ouse

Deruuentio, Doruuentio 8 Bede
Deorwentan (acc. and dat.) 959 YCh 4
Derewent(a-m) a. 1133, 1154–89, 1199 Whitby *et passim* to 1339 Percy
Derwent 1177 HCY, 1225 FF *et passim*
Derwynte 1322 NRS
Darwent 1448 Test
The Darwen 1573 FF, 1619 NRS

From Romano-British *Deruentio, -a*, the name of a Roman station on the Derwent in the East Riding. The name is paralleled by the other Derwents (*e.g.* Db, *ea Deorwentan* 10 Saints) and probably by the Darenth (K), OE *Diorente* 822 BM, *Darente* 1345 BM. The etymology is discussed in RNY 21.

DOVE, R., an affluent of the Rye

Duue 1100–3 YCh, 1227 Riev, 13 *Malton* 115
Duua, Duva, Duve 1207 FF, 1255 Ch, 1308 Ch
Dovve 1306 NRS
Dow 1577 Saxton, 1626 Drayton (*Polyolbion*)
Dovebeck 1614 NR

Cf. Dove, R. (Db), *an dufan* 951 BCS 890 and *v.* RNY 22.

ESK, R.

Esch 1109–14 YCh 865, a. 1133, 1154–89, 1199 Whitby
Esc 1129, c. 1199 Guis
Esk(e) 1204 ChR, 1279–81 QW, 15 Whitby *et passim*

Cf. Esk Dale and Esklets 119, 134 *infra*, and *v.* RNY 13.

Foss, R., an affluent of the Ouse

   Foss(e) 13 *Kirkham* 9, 1227 Ch, 1228 Lib *et passim*

   The name of this river is found in Fossgate (York), *Fossegate* 13 *Leon* 126 *d*, and a parallel name is that of the river Foss, an affluent of the river Wharfe near Tadcaster, *aque de Fosse* 1230, 1250 Percy. The river flows through the city of York through a cut channel, cf. Lat. *fossa*, 'ditch.'

Greta, R., an affluent of the Tees

   Great' flu' 1577 Saxton   *Greta* 1606 NR

   Cf. the name of the river Greet (Nt), OE *Greotan* (acc., dat.) 958 *RegAlb* i. 58, and *le Grayegrete*, the name of a lost place in Bowes, 13 *RichReg* 127 *d*. *v*. RNY 12.

Keas Beck, an affluent of the Derwent

   Kesbek 1335 *ForP* 211 *d*

   v. Keasbeck (Whit) 114 *infra*.

Kyle, R., an affluent of the Ouse

   Ki-, Kyle 1289, 1293–5 *For* (*passim*), 1316 For

   Kyle was also the name of a bailiwick in 1317 etc. (*For*).

Leven, R., an affluent of the Tees

   Leuen(e) 1218–31 *Heal* 113, H3 BM, 1293 YI, 1301 LS
   Leaven 1615, 1621 NR

   v. RNY, p. 12, and Castle Leavington and Kirk Leavington 173 *infra*.

Lune, R. [liun], an affluent of the Tees

   vallem de Loon 1201 ChR   *Lune* 1561 FF, 1577 Saxton

   This name is found in Lancashire (*v*. Ekwall, *PN La*) and its etymology is further discussed in RNY 11. Cf. Alne 21 *infra*.

Murk Esk, R., an affluent of the Esk

   Mirchesc 1230 Whitby   *Mirkhesk* 1231 *Ass*
   Mirke Eske 1252 YI, 15 Whitby, 1619 NRS

   v. RNY 14.

Ouse, R. [uːz][1]

> *andlang usan* 959 YCh 4, 963 *RegAlb* i. 56 *d*
> *Use* 1066 ASC *et passim* to 1308 Ch
> *Huse* 1286 Ebor
> *Ouse* 1314 Fount
> *Ouze* c. 1314 Fount, 1626 Drayton (*Polyolbion*)
> *Úsa* 13 *Fagrskinna* and other Scand sagas

This river-name is often found elsewhere in England.

Riccal, R., an affluent of the Rye

> *Ricalf* 1086 DB (then a manor), 1293 QW
> *Richale* 1227 FF
> *Ricolf(e)* 1283 YI, 1293 QW
> *Riclofe, Riclose* 1285 KI
> *Ricolf* 1301 LS
> *Rycal* 1316 Vill, etc.
> *Rycolf* 1418 YI

The river-name is also found as

> *Rycaluegy* (? = -*greynes*), *Ricolvegreines* 1251, 1333 Riev

The DB form, the KI forms and one or two others refer to a lost vill which may have stood near to Riccal Moor and Riccal House on the north bank of the river Riccal in the south-east of Harome township. It should be noted that for 6 or 7 miles from its mouth the Riccal is never more than a mile distant from the Rye. On the etymology of the name *v.* RNY 23. *Ricolvegreines* contains an additional element, ON *greinn* 'a branch' (here applied to the river); the following references apply to the Riccal valley: *Graynes* 13 *Kirkham* 2, *þe graynes* 14 ib. 50.

Rye, R., an affluent of the Derwent

> *Rye* 1181 BylE 103 *d*, 1282 *Malton* 102, 1577 Saxton

Found also as the first element of Rievaulx, Ryton 73, 76 *infra*, and the river Riccal *supra*. This name should be compared with the river Ryburn (YWR); *v.* RNY 20, 21.

---

[1] For Dr Grundy's identification of this river with the *wusan* of BCS 875 *v.* Overton 15 *infra* note.

SKITTERICK (lost), an affluent of the Derwent (in Pick.)

 Sciteric 1201 ChR, 1204 Riev *Skyterik* 1328 Banco

 Both these references are to a stream, and should be compared with *Schiterike* 1313 WCR, the name of a lost place (or stream) in Wakefield (YWR), and possibly with Skitter (L), earlier *Schitere, Scitra,* c. 1150–5 BM. Cf. Shatterford, PN Wo 32.

SEPH, R., an affluent of the Rye

 Sef 1170–85 YCh 1845, 1201 FF
 Cepht 13 *Kirkham* 51 *d* *Cepth* 1260 Riev
 On the etymology of this name *v.* RNY 23.

SEVEN, R., an affluent of the Rye

 Si-, Syvene 1155–8 *Mary Y* 179, 1204 ChR *et passim* to
  1306 NRS
 Sivena 1180 YCh 352, 1308 Ch, 1339 PatR
 Sivona 13 Whitby
 Si-, Syven 1290 Baildon, 1326, 1577 NRS
 Seven 1577 Saxton
 Cf. Sinnington 76 *infra* and RNY 22.

SWALE, R., an affluent of the Ouse

 Sualua, Swalwa 8 Bede
 Swalwan, Swalewan, Swealwan, Swealewan 10 BedeOE
 Swale 1157 *RichReg* 82 *d*, 13 ib. 127 *d et passim*
 Suale c. 1205 *FountA* 25
 Swalle 1219 *Easby* 11, 1442 NR
 Swaill 1654 Grinton
 cf. also Swaledale 269 *infra.*

 The name is paralleled by Swalecliff (K), OE *æt Swalewanclife* BCS 874, near the Swale (K), OE *sualuæ* (gen.) BCS 353, *Suuealuue fluminis* BCS 341, and by Swallow (L), *Sualue* 1203–6 BM, *Swalough* 1395 BM. *v.* RNY 15.

TAME, R., an affluent of the Tees

 Tame 1129 Guis

 This name is identical with the river-names Tame (St, Wa) and Thames, with Welsh *Taff* and the old Indian river-name *Tamassa. v.* RNY 13 and cf. Tanton 170 *infra.*

TACKRIVELING (lost), an affluent of the Derwent

Tacriveling 1157–8 YCh 402, 1176–9 YCh 406, 1201 ChR

Cf. *Rivelingdale* 1231 Guis, the name of a lost place in Guisborough. *v.* RNY 25, s.n. Rivelin, R. (YWR).

TEES, R.

Teisa, Teysa c. 1130 SD, 1166 P (p)

Tesa c. 1130 SD, 1162 P, 1204 ChR

Taisa, Taysa c. 1130 SD, 1192–9 Guis, 14 Whitby

Teysiam 1139–57 Guis, c. 1230 *Bodl* a. i. 57, 1239–57 Guis

Theise, -am c. 1160 Riev, 1170–80 YCh, 1204 ChR; *Theyse* 13 *BylE* 38 d

Teyse 1177 HCY, 1229 FF, 1237 Cl, 1252 *Ass*, 1268 Abbr

Tayse 13 *Easby* 40

Tésa 13 *Knýtlinga Saga*

Tese 13 *Easby* 243, 1279–81 QW, 1300 *RichReg* 97

Tees 1348 FF, 1404 YI, 1577 Saxton

These 1396 Pap

The name also appears in Teesdale 279 n. *infra*. The etymology of this name is discussed in RNY 11.

THORDISA (lost), a stream flowing to the sea in Whit.

Thordeisa 12 Whitby

Thordisa 1108–14, R 1, 1204 Whitby, 1279–81 QW

Tordisa c. 1166 Whitby, 1204 ChR, 1308 Whitby

Tordesay 1282 Whitby

Tordsaybek E 2 Whitby

TILLA BECK (lost), an affluent of the Derwent

Tillabek 1222–4 Whitby, -bec(k) 13 Percy, 1619 NRS

Tyllaybeke 13 Whitby

URE, R., an affluent of the Ouse

Earp (? for *earp*) late 10 Saints

Jor(e) 1142–96 Dugd v. 596 *et passim* to 1314 Fount

Yor 1175–1203 YCh, 1280 *Ass*, 1300 YI

Yhor 1202 FF

Gior 1199–1210 Abbr

Your(e) 1295 Ch, 1314 Fount, 1577 Saxton

ʒuram 1465 YD
Yeure 1530 Visit

Cf. RNY 17, and Jervaulx 250 *infra*.

WISKE, R., an affluent of the Swale

Wisca 1088 *LVD* 50 *d*
Wi-, Wysk, Wisc 1157 *RichReg* 82, 1210 Abbr *et passim* to
  1483 Test
Wyx 1281 Ebor
Wi-, Wyske late 13 BM, 1371 FF

The river in its upper course is also referred to as *foulbroke*
in 1508 Guis. On the etymology *v.* RNY 16.

I. BULMER WAPENTAKE

Bolesford Wapentac 1086 DB
Wap' de Bvlem' svr' 1166 P   *Bulemer* 1219 Fees, 1231 *Ass*,
  1252 YI, 1285 KI, 1286 Ebor
Bullemere 1226–8 Fees
Bulmer 1231 *Ass*, Fees *et passim*
Bulmers(c)hire 1238 Guis *et passim* to 14 *Kirkham* 24 *d*

The name of the wapentake at the time of the DB survey is
derived from that of Bulford, a lost place (*v.* 13 *infra*). The site
of the meeting-place was probably not far from the Forest of
Galtres, for the forest mill (*Buleford*) is named as standing on
the SE boundary of the forest and its position may be exactly
determined from a list of bounds of the forest in 1316 (Dunelm):
"and by the same river Foss...and so to *le Brendmilne de
Ferlinton* and then along the aforesaid river to the mill of
Bulford and so to Strensall." Bulford, therefore, seems to have
been a ford across the river Foss somewhere in Strensall parish,
practically in the centre of the wapentake.

After the 12th cent. the wapentake is named from Bulmer
39 *infra*. For the suffix *v.* scir.

GALTRES [gɔːtriz]

Galtres is the name of the old royal forest which covered
a great part of this wapentake. Its existence is still perpetuated

in the additional *le Forest*, etc. in some of the place-names within its area.

> Galtrys, -ris 1155–89 *Kirkham* 5, 1171, 1179 P, 1222 ClR
> *et passim* to 1451 Test
> Galtres 1177 HCY, 1226–9 *RegAlb* ii. 39 d *et passim* to
> 1577 NRS
> Galteriz 1222 Pat, 1223 ClR; -ris 1227 Cl
> Gautric 1227, 1229, 1233 Cl
> Gaut(e)ris 1227, 1230 Cl, Ch, 1236 Cl, 1250 Pat, 1296 YI
> Gautres 1270 YI, 1290, 1310 Ch, 1577 Saxton
> Gawtrees 1416 YD   Gawtryce 1510 Sanct

This interesting name is a compound of ON *goltr* (PrN *galtuR*), 'boar,' and hris, 'brushwood.' Turberville tells how boars when being hunted make for the thickest brushwood they can find. "Bores lie most commonly in the strongest holdes of Thornes and thicke Bushes" (*The Noble Art of Venerie or Hunting*, Oxford ed., p. 151).

Holtby

1. HOLTBY 27 F 9 [ɔutbi]

> Boltebi (sic) 1086 DB
> Holteby 12 *RegAlb* i. 67 d *et passim* to 1316 Vill

The persistence of medial -*e*- in the spellings shows that the first element had an originally inflected form (gen. sg.). 'Holti's farm' from the ON personal name *Holti* and by.

Osbaldwick

1. HEWORTH 27 F 8

> Heuuorde, -uuarde 1086 DB   Heword 1177 HCY
> Hewrd(e) c. 1148–59 YCh 1060, 1294, 1335 Ch, 1295 *For*
> Hewrth(e) 1244 *Ass*   Heworth(e) 1285 KI *et passim*

v. heah, worð. Heworth is on low-lying ground and the meaning must, therefore, be 'chief enclosure' rather than 'high, lofty enclosure.' Cf. the common use of *High* in *High* Street. There are other instances of OE *hēah* used in this sense, as in Broad Hinton (Berks). Heworth is the only name in the North Riding containing the element worþ. *v.* Introd. xviii.

2. MURTON 27 F 8

Mortun, -ton 1086 DB *et passim* to 1295 *For*
Murton 1391 Test

'Farm on the mor,' *v.* tun.

TANG HALL

Tange 1219 *Ass*, 1279 YI   *The Tanghawle* 1519 Fabr

v. tang. The second element is from ME *hall*, 'hall, residence.' Tang Hall stands on the south bank of a stream now called Tang Hall Beck, and the name probably refers to the spit of land formed by the confluence of Tang Hall Beck and Osbaldwick Beck.

3. OSBALDWICK 27 F 8 [ɔzbəwik]

Osboldeuuic 1086 DB
Osebaldewyke 1198–1216 *RegAlb* ii. 54 *d*
Osbaldewyk(e) 1199 *RegAlb* i. 38, 1316 Vill, 1330 *For*
Ossebaldewyke 1280 Ebor
Osbaldwyk(e) 1280, 1289 Ebor, 1354 Pap, 1416 Fabr
Osberwick 1577 Saxton

'Osbald's dwelling place,' *v.* wic. The first element is the OE (Angl) personal name *Ósbald*.

Gate Helmsley

1. GATE HELMSLEY 27 E 10 [geːt emzlə]

Hamelsec 1086 DB
Hemelsi 1145–53 *Leon* 35
Hemelesay H 2 *Leon* 3 *d*; *-eia* 1199 *RegAlb* i. 38
Hemelsay, -ey 1177 HCY, 1198–1216 *RegAlb* ii. 54, 1285 KI,
   1287 Ebor, 1300 YI   *Hemilsay* 1295 *For*
Hamelesia c. 1200 *For*
Helmyslay 1418 YI
Gatehemelsay 1438 Baildon   *Gaythamulsay* 15 VCH ii. 139
Gethemsley 1574 FF   *Gate-hemesley* 1577 Saxton

'Hemele's eg.' The OE personal name *Hemele* is also found in Hemsworth (YWR) (*Hamelsuurde* 1086 DB, *Hemeleswrthe* 1288 Ebor) and Hemlington 170 *infra*. The prefixed element

Gate- refers to the Roman road from York to Malton on which Gate Helmsley stands. ON *gata* is used instead of the more common OE *stræt*. OE *eg* is used in its broader sense here.

The modern form of the name is due in part to metathesis of *Hemelsay* to *Helmyslay* and in part to the analogy of Helmsley (Ryed) 71 *infra*.

2. UPPER HELMSLEY 27 E 10

Hamelsec(h) 1086 DB

Other forms follow those of Gate Helmsley. First distinguished as *Over* in 1301 LS. *Over*, as usual, is later replaced by *Upper*.

Upper Helmsley stands on higher ground than Gate Helmsley. *v.* ufera.

3. WARTHILL 27 E 9 [waːtil]

Wardhilla, Wardille 1086 DB
Warthill(e), -hil, -hyll 1194–8 *Dods* vii. 168 *et passim* to 1416 Fabr
Warthehill 1295 *For*
Warthull 1330 Ch
Warthell 1536 YChant
Wathell 1574 FF

'Beacon hill,' *v.* weard or varða, and hyll. The 1295 form is slightly in favour of Scand varða as against OE weard.

Stockton on the Forest

1. STOCKTON ON THE FOREST 27 E 9

Stocthun, Stochetun 1086 DB
Stocatuna 1145–53 *Leon* 35
Stoke-, Stoceton' 1170–88 *Leon* 288 *et passim* to 1316 Vill
Stoc(k)ton 1218 Pat, 1316 *KF*, (*on the more*) 1577 Saxton

'Stockaded enclosure,' *v.* stocc, tun. The early forms clearly indicate that the original form of the first element was the OE gen. plur. *stocca*.

CARLTON

> *Careltone, -tun* 1086 DB   *C-, Karleton'* 1167 P *et passim*
> *v.* karlatun.

SANDBURN HOUSE

> *Sābura* 1086 DB   *Sandeburn* 1269 Ch, etc.
> Self-explanatory.

Huntington

1. EARSWICK 27 E 8 [iːəzwik]

> *Edresuuic, Edrezuic* 1086 DB
> *Ethericewyk* e. 13 *RegAlb* ii. 47 *d*
> (*H*)*everswyk'* 1292, 1295 *For*, 1301 LS
> *Herswyk* 1295 *For*
> *Etheirwike* 1316 *KF*
> *Etherswik* 1322 Abbr
> *Ereswick* 1577 Saxton
> *Erswick* 1665 Visit

This is a compound of **wic** and the common OE personal name *Æþelric*, early reduced to *Æþeric*.

The later forms of the name in *Ever-* are due to the common interchange of *th* and *v* as in *fever* for *feather*. Cf. also the change of initial *th* to *f* in such names as Throxenby, Fingay Hill 110, 213 *infra*.

2. HUNTINGTON 27 E 8

> *Huntindune* 1086 DB
> *Huntingtuna* 1145–53 *Leon* 35, 1308 Ch
> *Hunting-, Huntyngdon* 1159 YCh 1059; 1266, 1286, 1295, 1317 *For*
> *Huntendune* c. 1160 Whitby
> *Hunting-, Huntyngton*(*a*) H 2 *MaryH* 6 *d et passim*
> *Huntinton*(*a*) c. 1180 Whitby, 1231 FF, 1237 Cl, 1294 Ch
> *Huntingedon'* 1187 P
> *Huntin-, Huntyndon* 1241 Cl, 1536 YChant

OE *Huntingdūn*, with the same pers. name *Hunta* as in Huntingdon (PNBedsHu 261). *v.* ingtun, dun.

3. TOWTHORPE 27 D 8 [tɔuθrəp]

> *Touetorp* 1086 DB
> *Touthorp(e)* c. 1157–70 YCh 1084 *et freq* to 1310 Ch
> *Thouthorp(h)* 1180–c. 1200 YCh 65, 1280 Ebor, 1295 *For*
> *Towethorp* 1372 FF *Towthorpp* 1419 YI; *-throppe* 1316
> (Eliz) *KF*

'Tofi's farm,' *v.* þorp. The name *Tofi* though found once in
Iceland and also in late Norwegian is by Lind and Björkman
(NP 142) considered to be originally Danish. Cf. ODan *Towi*
(Nielsen). It is found also in Towthorpe (YER), *Touetorp*
1086 DB. Cf. the name *Toui* (LVD) and the common use of
Toue in the medieval Danelaw.

Strensall

1. STRENSALL 27 C 8

> *Strenshale* 1086 DB
> *Strensale* 1127–8 YCh 785 *et freq* to 1319 *For*
> *Strenehal'* 1167 P
> *Streneshal(e)* 1222 Pat, 1251 Ass (p), 1252 *Ass*, 1281 Ebor
> *Strenesale* 1286, 1292 *For*, 1299 Ebor, 1302 *Ebor* 196 *d*
> *Strensall* 1316 Vill, 1451 Test

'Streon's nook of land,' *v.* h(e)alh. The name *Strēon(a)* is
found in Bede's *Streonæshalch* (*v.* Whitby 126 *infra*), and in two
lost places in Wo, (1) *in Streoneshalh* (KCD 1358) near Bengeworth and (2) *on streon halh, be streonen halæ* (BCS 1139)
near Wick Episcopi. It appears as a name-element in OE
Strēonbercht (LVD) and as a by-name in *Godric Strēona*. Cf.
Stevenson's note in *The Academy* (July 11, 1885, 29).

BULFORD (lost)

> *Bul(e)ford(a)* 1145–53 *Leon* 35, 1154–89 ib. 3 *d*, 12 *MaryH*
> 6 *d*, 1231 *Ass*, etc.
> *Bulforthtoftes* 1286 *For*

'Bull ford,' *v.* bula, ford and Bowforth 64 *infra*. On the
identification of Bulford with the site of the wapentake meeting
place *v.* 8 *supra*.

Wigginton

1. HAXBY 27 D 7

> *Haxebi, -by* 1086 DB, 1177 HCY, 1223 ClR, *et passim* to
> 1319 *For, Axebi* 1167 P
> *Haxby* 1317, 1330 *For et passim*

v. by. The personal name which forms the first element is
recorded in Lincs in the early 13th cent. in the form *Haac*,
and goes back to ON *Hákr*, used as a by-name. On the form
Haxe-, which represents the ON gen. sg. in *-s*, *v.* IPN 62

2. WIGGINTON 27 D 7

> *Wichistun, Wichintun* 1086 DB
> *Wi-, Wyginton'* 1231 *Ass*, 1295 YI, 1301 LS, 1317, 1330 *For*,
> 1337 Ch
> *Wi-, Wygington'* 1291 YI (p), 1293, 1330 *For*
> *Wiggenton* 1579 FF

The forms are difficult but are perhaps most easily explained
if we take the name to be derived from the ON personal name
Víkingr (LindN) and tun. The voicing of intervocalic *k* is
evidenced in many other English place-names. Cf. Wiganthorpe
35 *infra* and Wigston Magna (Lei), DB *Wichingestone*.

CORBURN LANE (6″)

> *Coteborne, -burun* 1086 DB; *-burn'* 1295 *For*
> *Corteburc* 1155–c. 1170 YCh 422
> *Cortburne* 1343 PatR, 1409 YI
> *Coriburne* 1363 PatR

v. burna. The first element is obscure, but may contain the
same element as Courteenhall (Nth), *Cortenhale* 1086 DB,
Curtenhale 1328 Banco, and a lost place in Surrey, OE *curten
stapele* (BCS 34). The common element is probably a personal
name *Curta* or *Corta*, possibly identical with PrGerm *Crotus*
(given by Werle, *Die ältesten germanischen Personennamen*)
with metathesis. If this is correct the name must have existed
in PrOE to have given the OE derivative names *Cyrtel* (found
in Kirklington 220 *infra*) and *Cortela*, as in Costock (Nt),
Cortelingstocke 1302 FA.

Overton

1. CLIFTON 27 F 7

    Cliftune 1086 DB, etc.

    Self-explanatory.

2. OVERTON[1] 27 E 5 [ɔuətən]

    Ovre-, Overtun 1086 DB, *Ouerton* 1086 DB *et passim*
    Orton 1327 Ch

    'Farm on the bank (overlooking the river Ouse),' *v.* ofer, tun.

    MORTON (lost)

    Mortune 1086 DB; *-tona* 1292 *For*

    'Farm on the mor,' *v.* tun.

3. RAWCLIFFE 27 E 6

    Roud(e)clife 1086 DB
    Rout(h)ecliua, Routhecliue 1170 P (p), 1208 FF, e. 13 *RegAlb*
        ii. 47 *d*, 1294 Ch; *-klif* 1295 *For*; *-clyff* 1301 LS, 1323 Pat
    Rauþeclif 1295 *For*
    Roucliff, -clyf(f) 1309 Dugd iii. 565, 1318 Pap, 1330 *For*,
        1342 Test, 1364 FF
    Roclyff 1540 Dugd iii. 570

    'Red cliff,' *v.* rauðr, klif. The name refers to the high reddish
    bank of the Ouse at this point.

4. SHIPTON 27 D 5 [ʃiptən]

    Hipton 1086 DB
    Hepeton' 1167 P
    Hieptuna 1154–89 *MaryH* 6 *d*, 1308 Ch, *Hyepton (Yheptona)*
        1176 P
    Yhupton 12 *RegAlb* ii. 16 *d*   *Hupton'* 1231 *Ass*, 1244 Fees
    Supton' 1244 *Ass*

---

[1] Dr Grundy (*Arch. Journal*, 76, 247) identifies *æt Ofærtune, to ofertune*
(BCS 875) with this place on the ground that both places are on a river Ouse
(*Wusa* in the charter) and the charter is witnessed by the Archbishop of
York. This evidence is hardly sufficient to counterbalance the difficulties
on the other side, namely, how a charter dealing with land in Yorkshire
got into a Winchester cartulary, and how King Eadred could have made a
grant of land in Yorkshire at all in the troublous years to which this charter
belongs.

S(c)hupton 13 *MaryH* 122 *d et passim* to 1541 Dugd iii. 570
Scuppeton 1295 YI
Schippeton 1295 YI
Shipton 1328 Banco, 1522 FF, 1577 Saxton
Schiptun 1405 HCY

The etymology of this name is OE heope 'briar, bramble,'
and tun; cf. Heptonstall (Moorman, *PN YWR* s.n.).

The phonology of this name is peculiar and the problem is
treated more fully in RES i. 437 ff. There it is shown from other
place-names such as Shap (We), Shawm Rigg 122 *infra*, etc.
that OE *hēo-* and *hēa-* in certain cases became ME *shē-* or *shō-*.
In addition there is a Y dialect-word *shoop*, 'dog-rose,' which is
derived from OE *hēope.* So far the evidence seems to indicate
that the change took place only in Scandinavian England but
how far it was due to Scandinavian influence it is impossible to
say. It certainly cannot be explained by the later Norw sound-
change of ON *hj-* to *sh-*, for that did not take place till long
after Scandinavian connexions with England had ceased. The
phonetic development of the name is that OE *hēo-* became *hyē-*
(or with stress on the second element of the diphthong *hyō-*),
and that *hy-*, being acoustically near to *sh-*, became *sh* in the 13th
cent. The variant forms *Shup-* and *Ship-* are due to shifting of
the stress from one element to the other of the original OE
diphthong *ēo, héo* giving *Shi-* and *heó-* giving *Shu-*. Shipton
(YER), *Epton* 1086 DB, *Shupton* 1316 Vill, is probably of the
same origin.

5. SKELTON 27 E 6

Sc(h)eltun 1086 DB
Escheltona 1090–5 (1433) Pat
Skelton 1181–4 YCh 423, 1244 *Ass et passim*
Schelton 1248 Ebor, 1289, 1295 *For*; -*tunam* 1308 Ch

Skelton is a common name in Yorkshire; there are two more
in the North Riding, and others in the East and West Ridings.
The spellings in each case are identical and the places are on
or near streams, but there is some doubt as to the etymology
of the first element. There are two possibilities.

The first is that the name is of the same origin as several English Sheltons, which contain OE *scelf*, 'shelf, shelving terrain of land' (*v.* scylf). There is, however, only a slight rise of land at Skelton and it is doubtful if this could be called a *scelf* when compared with the ledges of land which are certainly referred to in this word, as at Raskelf. Skelton in LangE (145 *infra*) is in the valley-bottom, whilst Skelton in GillW (293 *infra*) may well contain OE *scelf*. If this is the correct etymology, there is no difficulty over the phonology, for -*f* was lost at an early date in Raskelf 26 *infra*. Initial *Sk-* (for *Sh-*) is due to Scandinavian influence. It has been observed however that there is difficulty in the topography of this Skelton, and, as in the case of Skelton (LangE) and Skelton near Leeds (YWR, *Sceltune* 1086 DB, *Scheltunam* 1154–66 YCh 1770), standing on the bank of the Aire, there is more likelihood of the alternative explanation being the right one.

In addition to the parallel names already cited we must take into consideration the name of the river Skell near Ripon (YWR), *Schelbec* 1170–5 *RegAlb* i. 72, *Scheldene* 1179 ib. i. 71 d, *Scheldale* c. 1200 Fount, and Skelfleet, the name of a stream near Broomfleet (YER), *Skelflete* in the 17th cent.. From this it appears that Skell was a river-name and in some cases such as the present Skelton, Skelton (LangE), and Skelton near Leeds, this river-name may form the first element. This Skelton stands a little distance from a stream which rises at Skelton Spring, Skelton (LangE) is by Skelton Beck, and Skelton near Leeds is on the Aire. On the river Skell near Ripon is another Skelton (olim *Schelton*). Probably the river-name Skell is identical with the Norw river-name *Skjellaen*, from ON *skellr*, 'clatter, splash,' being related to the ON verb *skalla*, 'to clatter' (cf. NElv 219); the Norw stream-name *Skjelle*, evidenced in ONorw as *i Skælli* (NG i. 85) is of the same origin.

The probability is that Skelton in this case means 'farm near the river Skell' and the river-name has not survived independently. *v.* tun.

WIDE OPEN FARM

Wibedstune 1086 DB
Wipestune 1086 DB, 1429 IpmR
Wipetuna 1308 Ch

The modern name is not a derivative of the early forms, unless by popular corruption. The early forms themselves are not conclusive, but probably point to 'Wipped's farm,' v. tun. The pers. name is identical with the first element of *Wippedes-fleote* (ASC), named from *Wipped(e)* who was slain there. Wide Open Farm may be the same place as the OE *pibustun*[1] *socn* of BCS 1279.

Sutton on the Forest

1. HUBY 27 B 6 [iubi]

Hobi 1086 DB, 1167, 1172, 1178, 1179 P
Hoby 1135–54 *Kirkham* 5 *d*, 1180–1 YCh 420 *et passim* to 1399 Pat
Houby 1326 NRS
Huby, -bie 1398 Pat, 1571 FF, 1577 NRS
Hewby 1538 Dugd iv. 567, 1614 NR

Lindkvist is mistaken in his etymology of Huby; there probably was no *hór* (= ON *hár*) in Anglo-Scandinavian. Hoby (Lei) appears as *Houcbig* 1066 Thorpe, *Houbia* 1086 DB, *Hou(e)by* 1326, 1349 Cl, 1407 Pat, and the first form gives the clue to the etymology. Both names mean 'farm on the spur of land,' v. hoh, by, and are to be compared with the numerous Huttons (*passim*). Huby is also the name of a little village near Harrogate (YWR), which stands on a ridge of land similar to that at the present Huby.

KELSIT GRANGE

Chelestuit, Chelesterd (sic) 1086 DB
Kelst(h)wait 1300 Leon 6 *d*, 1338 Ch
Kel(e)thwait 1317, 1330 *For*

'Kel's enclosure' v. þveit. A pers. name *Kel(le)* is best explained as a short-form of such an ON name as *Grímkell* or *Úlfkell* from earlier names in *-ketill*. Cf. *Kelle* found in Lincs in 1219. Cf. also Björkman, *ZEN* 52.

---

[1] Birch reads *pibustan*, but Miss F. E. Harmer has kindly collated the MS and says that the vowel may be a *u* and the reading in the Harleian copy is a *u*.

LAUND HOUSE

le Londe 1404 YI

v. land, 'land, cultivated land,' later influenced by launde.

2. SUTTON ON THE FOREST 27 B 7

Su(d)tune, Suton 1086 DB
Suttune 1145–53 *Leon* 35, 1252 Ch
Sutton(e) 1166 YCh 777, 1167 P *et passim* (*sub* (*in*) *Galtris*) 1242 Ebor, (*in the Forest*) 1577 Saxton

In the 13th and 14th cents. it is sometimes distinguished as:

Onegatesinton' (sic) 1229 Cl
Ouergate Sutton' 1231 *Ass*
Ougate Sutton' 1301 LS, *Sutton Ouvgate* 1316 For

'South farm' *v.* suþ, tun. If the form *Onegatesinton'* is correct, its origin is probably an OE *sūþingatūn*, 'farm of the dwellers south (of Stillington)'; cf. Westonby 130 *infra*.

On the common addition *v.* Galtres 8 *supra*. The prefixed name *Ougate* appears independently as *houergate* 1246 *RegAlb* iii. 2, and there is no doubt that it contains ME *over*, 'upper,' and gata, 'road.' The spellings with *Ou-* arise from the omission of the diacritic used in 13th cent. handwriting to denote *er*.

GREENTHWAITE [griːnfit]

Grenthwayt, -thwait 1226–9 *RegAlb* ii. 39 *d*, etc.

v. grene, þveit.

Newton on Ouse

1. BENINGBROUGH 27 D 5

Benniburg 1086 DB
Bennigburg 1160–70 *Bodl* a. i. 105 (p)
Beninburc(g) 1167 P, 1293 For
Bening-, Benyngburg(h) 1180 YCh 550 *et passim* to 1317 For
Beningeburg 1223 FF
Benigburgh' 1301 LS

'Benna's fortified place' *v.* ing, burh. For this personal name *v.* Bengeworth, PN Wo 95.

2. LINTON UPON OUSE 27 D 4

Lingtona 1086 DB
Lin-, Lynton' 1176 P *et passim*, (*super Usam*) 1336 Ch

v. tun. The origin of the first element is not clear; but it is probably OE *lin*, 'flax,' and so 'enclosure where flax is grown.' It can hardly be OE *hlynn* (= Lat *torrens*, as pointed out in PNS II. xxxii), for the river Ouse cannot be termed *torrens*.

3. NEWTON UPON OUSE 27 D 4

Neuton 1086 DB
Neweton(e) 1086 DB, 1231 *Ass*, 1330 *For*
Niwenton' 1167 P
Niweton' super Vsam 1176 P, etc.

'New farm' *v.* niwe, tun. The form *Niwenton* presupposes an OE (*æt þæm*) *niwan tūne*, an inflexional form one would not expect in the North.

NIDDERMYN (lost)

Nidderminne 1294 Ch

'Confluence of the river Nidd (and the Ouse),' *v.* mynni. On the etymology of Nidd *v.* RNY 18. The river Nidd joins the Ouse in this parish. The actual form of the river-name here contains the ON genitive in *-ar*, also found in Nidderdale (cf. RNY 18).

Alne

1. ALDWARK 27 C 3 [ɔːdwaːk]

A(l)deuuerc 1086 DB
Aldwerc 1176 P
Aldewerk(e) 1175–1203 YCh 797 *et passim* to 1410 YI
Audewerk 1224, 1230 FF
Aldewark 1316 (Eliz) Vill, 1399 Test
Oldewarke 1536 YChant

'The ancient fortification,' *v.* (e)ald, weorc. Similar names are Aldwark (Db) and a lost *Aldwark* in York, found in 'regiam stratam de *Aldewerk*' in 1331 (*Leon* 75). There are now no traces of fortifications of any kind at Aldwark.

RICE LANE

Probably preserves the second element of the lost *Cuningesris*
1175–1203 YCh 793.

'The king's brushwood' *v.* konungr, hris. The form *Cuning-*
is from ODan *kunung*.

2. ALNE 27 B 4 [ɔːn], [ɑˑn]

Alne, Alna 1086 DB, c. 1130 SD *et passim*
Aulna 1167 P
Aune 1237 Ebor
Alen 1316 Vill
Awne 1402, 1454 Test, 1577 Saxton, 1581 FF

Alne stands on the river Kyle to which the name must have
referred originally. It is derived from some British name
similar to Ptolemy's *Alauna* (= Allen, Scotland) or *Alaunos*
(= Alne, Nb), which sometimes appears as OE *lōn (*v.* RNY 11).

3. FLAWITH 27 B 3 [flawiθ]

Flathwayth c. 1180–94 YCh 796
Flathewath(e) 1207 *Easby* 256 *d*, 1251 Ass, 1252 *Ass*, 1259
  Ass, 1282 YI, 1301 LS
Flaþewath 1289 *For*
Flathewat' 1295 *For*
Flatwath 1316 Vill
Flawythe, Flawith 1316 (Eliz) *KF*, 1582 FF

The second element is ON vað, 'ford.' Professor Ekwall
suggests that the first element is the same word as Norw *flade*,
Sw dial. *flada*, 'flat-meadow.' The whole name would then
mean 'ford by the flat meadow-land.' Dr Lindkvist notes
evidence for Norw *flað- with the same meaning as *flat-*, in
Flaðkar (Rygh, *NG* xiv, 323).

4. THOLTHORPE 27 B 3 [θɔuθrəp]

þurulfestune 972 (11th) BCS 1279
Turulfestorp 1086 DB
Turoluestorp 1086 DB
Turold' Torp 1176 P (p)
Toraldethorpe 1282 YI, 1292, 1293 *For*
Thoraldethorp 1285 KI, 1316 Vill, 1328 Banco

Thoralthorp' 1295 *For*
Thoraldesthorp 1337 Ch
Thoraldthropp' 1316 (Eliz) *KF*
Thorlothorpp' 1301 LS
Tholthorp 1505 Test; *-thropp* 1614 NR

'Thurulf's village' *v.* þorp. The name *Thurulf* is from ON þórólfr, ODan *Thorulw.* A similar change of *-ulf* to *-ald* is noticed in Inglethwaite 25 *infra*, Barnoldswick (YWR), *Bernulfeswic* 1086 DB and in Gonalston (PN Nt 56), and is due to the weakening of the stress on *-ulf*. The OE form þurulfestune is of interest as it shows that the OE tun might be replaced by Scandinavian þorp.

5. TOLLERTON 27 B 4 [toulətən]

Toletun 972 (11th) BCS 1279
Tolentun, Tolletun 1086 DB
Tolereton' 1167 P
Tolreton 1230 Ebor
Tollerton' 1256 *RegAlb* iii. 55 *d*, 1291 Ch *et passim*
Tollirton 1289 *For*
Tolnorton 1292, 1293 *For*   *Tolnertona* 1293 *For*

v. tun. The first element can hardly be identical with Toller (Do), *Tollor* in KCD 1322. In this case it is probably from OE *tollere*, 'tax-gatherer,' perhaps used as a man's second name. The *Tolner-* forms are from the OE by-form *tolnere*. Both *Toller* and *Tolner* are still used as surnames (*v.* Harrison, *Surnames of the United Kingdom*, s.n.).

6. YOULTON 27 C 4 [jɔultən]

Ioletun, Loletune 1086 DB
Yolton' 1295 *For*, 1301 LS, 1330 *For*, 1369 FF, 1508 Test
Yiolton' 1301 LS
Yowl-, Youlton 1574 FF, 1666 Visit

The first element is the pers. name *Yol*, found in Lincs and Yorks in the 12th cent. and in Yawthorpe (L), LindsSurv *Joltorp*, Liber Niger *Goletorp*. This must be a short form of such an ON pers. name as *Jólgeirr* (LindN). *Geola*, the name of an 11th cent. moneyer at York, must be an Anglicised form of it.

Myton on Swale

1. MYTON ON SWALE 27 B 2 [mitən]

æt nyðtune (sic) 972 (11th) BCS 1278
mytun 972 BCS 1279   *Mitune* 1086 DB
My-, *Miton(e)* c. 1100–6 YCh 791, 1130–5 YCh 792 *et passim*
Mitton 1247 Pap, 1344 *Ebor* 9, 1406 Test
Mytoun 1375 Barbour's *Bruce* xvii. 1. 536

'Farm at the confluence' *v*. myðe, tun. Myton is half a mile from the meeting of the river Swale and the Ure, and the site of the White Battle in 1319, mentioned by Barbour, is said to have been at the confluence, on the land between the two rivers.

Brafferton

1. BRAFFERTON 27 A 2

Brad-, *Bratfortune*, *Bratfortone* 1086 DB
Bradfortonam c. 1180–94 *Mary Y* 138
Braferton 1226 Ebor, 1285 KI, 1290 Ebor, 1316 Vill, 1451 Test
Brafferton 1292 *For*, Pap *et passim*
Brauerton' 1295 *For*
Braffirton' 1301 LS, YI

'Farm near the broad ford' *v*. brad, ford, tun. Brafferton is near the river Swale. The name is also found in Durham (PN NbDu s.n.).

PILMOOR

Pilemor 1254 YI

'Pila's mor.' The name *Pīl(a)* is not adduced in independent use, but it is found in a number of place-names: Pilsworth (PN La 54), Pilsgate (Nth), *Pilesgete* BCS 1128, and Pilsbury (Db), *Pilesberie* 1086 DB. A weak form *Pīla* enters into Pilham (L).

2. HELPERBY 27 A 2

Helperby 972 (11th) BCS 1278, 1177 HCY *et passim*
æt heolperbi 972 (11th) BCS 1279

(H)ilprebi 1086 DB
Helprebi, -by 1086 DB, 1109–19 *RegAlb* i. 68 *d*, 1166 P (p),
1202 FF (p)
Helparby 1576 FF

'Hjalp's farm' *v.* by. The ON woman's name *Hjálp*, gen.
Hjálpar (LindN) is also found in Helperthorpe (YER), *Elpetorp*
1086 DB, *Helprethorp* 1109–19 *RegAlb* i. 69. Cf. Norw *Jerberg*
(Hiolperbergh) and ONorw *Hialparsteinn* (NG i. 98). The inflexional *-er* and the presence of a woman's name in a *by*-
compound are noteworthy.

3. THORNTON BRIDGE 22 J 2

Torenton(e) 1086 DB
Thorneton(a) 13 *BylA* 32 *et passim*, *(brigge)* 1576 FF
Thorenton on Swale 1275 YI

Thornton is a common name in Y. It means 'enclosure made
of thorn bushes' and is parallel to such compounds as *Stockton*,
Stanton (Stainton), 'enclosure made of stocks (stone).' *v.* þorn,
tun.

Easingwold

1. EASINGWOLD 27 A 5 [iːəzinud]

Eisicewalt, Eisincewald 1086 DB
Esing-, Esyngwald 1167, 1177 P, 1187 *Leon* 5 *d et passim* to
1451 Test
Esingewald(e) 1169 P, 1218 FF, 1230 Cl, 1247 YI
Hesiwald' 1179 P
Hesingewald' 1187 P
Esingaud 1208 FF
Esingwaud 1219, 1231 *Ass*, 1221 ClR, 1232, 1236 Cl, 1236
Lib, 1269 Ebor
Esingewaud 1220, 1222 ClR, 1247 Cl, 1250 Pat
Hesingwaud', -woud' 1236 Cl
Easingwould 1666 Visit

'The high land of Esa and his followers' *v.* w(e)ald. The
pers. name *Ēsa* is adduced by Redin and is of common appearance in place-names (cf. Easington 140 *infra*). *v.* ing.

ALWALDTOFTS (lost)

Alwald(e)toftes 1292 Pat, 1295 YI, 1330 *For*
Alwald(e)cotes 1295 Fine, 1318 *For*

v. topt. The first element is a personal name derived from
OE *Ælfwald* or *Æþelwald* or from ON *Olvaldi* (LindN), ODan
Alwaldi (Nielsen). There was an alternative form with OE cot
'cottage.'

HAWKHILLS

Houkeshill 1226–9 *RegAlb* ii. 39 *d*

'Hawk's hill' *v.* hyll. The ME personal name *Houk*, common
in the Danelaw, is derived from the ON name *Haukr* (LindN),
OSwed *Høk* (Lundgren-Brate). Originally the name here may
have been OE *Heafoc* (*v.* Hauxwell 269 *infra*).

INGLETHWAITE (lost)

Inguluestuet 1086 DB
Ingolthweyt, -thwait(e), -t(h)wayt 1236 Cl, 1318 *For et passim*
    to 1411 Pat
Ingoluet(h)wayt 1292, 1293 *For*
Ingoldethwayte 1295 Fine
Ingold-, Ingaldtweyt 1295 *For*, YI
Ingolftwayt 1295 YI

'Ingulf's clearing' from ON *Ingólfr* and þveit. On the
Ingolde- forms *v.* Tholthorpe 22 *supra*.

LEXMERE (lost)

Lexemer' 1187 *Leon* 5 *d*, 1248 Cl

'Salmon pool' from OE *leax*, 'salmon,' and mere. Normally
OE *leax* appears in ME as *lax*, in the same way as OE *feax*
appears as ME *fax*, but there is an example of *lex* cited by
Stratmann-Bradley (*ME Dict.* s.v. *lax* from a 12th cent. version
of Ælfric's Grammar, etc.). For the *e*-vowel cf. also DB
Lexintune, Hy 3 Ipm *Lexinton*, now Laxton (Nt).

THE LUND

le Lound 1280 ClR

v. lundr.

WHITECARR (6″)

Whiteker 1286 *For*, c. 1300 *BylE* 36

v. hwit, kjarr.

2. RASKELF 22 J 3 [ræskil]

Raschel 1086 DB
Raskel(l) 1169–93 YCh 790, 1289 *For*, 1316 *KF*, 1409 YI,
    1613 NRS i, *Raskill* 1577 Saxton, *Raskall* 1613 NR
Raskelf 1243 Fees, 1282 YI *et passim*
Raschelf 1265 Ebor
Raskelue 1292 *For*

The first element is probably ra, 'roe.' The second is more difficult. Final *-f* is organic but was lost early in certain forms. The original form would be *skelf* which appears again in Hinderskelfe 40 *infra* and in Ulleskelfe (YWR), *Oleschel* 1086 DB. It is either from ON *skjálf*, 'shelf, seat' (used here in the sense of OE *scelf*, 'shelving terrain of land') or a Scandinavianised form of that word. Raskelf is on a jutting ridge of land overlooking the river Kyle. *v.* ra, scylf.

BOSCAR [bɔskə]

Balschaw(e) 1142 Dugd v. 352, 13 *BylE* 8
Bal(e)schagh 1247 Ch, c. 1300 *BylE* 35 *d*
Balska 1301 LS
Baskaa 1541 Dugd v. 355

This must be the same name as the lost Balshaw (PN La 7), earlier *Balghschae* (1296) which Ekwall connects with ME *balgh*, 'rounded,' used in *Sir Gawayne* in the phrase *a balȝ berȝ* (l. 2172), 'a rounded hill.' The second element is OE sceaga, 'wood.' In the later forms this has been Scandinavianised.

3. THORMANBY 22 H 4 [θɔnəmbi]

Turmoz-, Tormozbi 1086 DB
T͞modesbi 1167 P
Thormodeby 1193–1208 YCh 786, 1230 Cl (p)
Tormodeby 1234, 1281 Ebor
Thormoteby 1275, 1287 Ebor, 1293 *For*, 1301 LS, 1303 KF
Thormotheby 1295 *For*

Thormotby 1295 *For*, 1316 *KF*, Vill
Thormanby 1481, 1491 Test, 1577 Saxton
Thornamby 1541 Dugd v. 355

'Thormoth's farm' *v.* by. The personal name is from ON *þórmóðr*, found also in Thurmaston (Lei), Thrumpton (Nt), Thornaby 172 *infra* and in Tremauville and Turmauville in Normandy.

Stillington

1. STILLINGTON 27 A 6

Stiuelinctun 1086 DB
Stiuelinton' 1176 P
Stiuil(l)ington 1242 P, 1301 LS
Sti-, Styvelington(e) 1280, 1286 Ebor *et passim* to 1351 Pap
Stillyngton 1371 Baildon, 1442 Test

'Styfel(a)'s farm' *v.* ingtun. The first element is a personal name *Styfel(a)*, not actually on record, but a derivative of the OE personal name *Stuf* (ASC). It enters also into Stillingfleet (YER), *Steflingefled* 1086 DB, *Stivelingflet* 1208 Ass, 1252 Ch.

Crayke

1. CRAYKE 22 J 6 [krɛək]

Crec 685 (17th) BCS 66 (? spurious; cf. YCh 918)
(on) Creic c. 980 (10th) BCS 1255, c. 1000 *LVD* 43 d, 1086 DB, 1088 *LVD* 50 d, *et passim* to 1229 Ch
Creca, Cric c. 1130 SD
Craic, Crayk 1176 P, 1346 Test, 1435 NCyWills
Cre(c)k 1227, 1236, 1237 Cl
Creik, Creyk 1227 Pat, 1244 Cl, 1295 Pat, 1309 Pap, 1349 Test, 1364 FF
Crake 1440 Test, 1470 Pat, 1577 Saxton
Creake 1530 Visit

The name is of Celtic origin, from Brit **krakịo*, which became OW *craig*, 'a rock.' The word appears to have been borrowed in two forms, one with Celtic 'affection' giving **kraik-*, the other without, giving *krek* by OE mutation. There is a very steep cliff at Crayke, on which is built Crayke castle.

Brandsby

1. BRANDSBY 22 J 7

Branzbi 1086 DB
Brendesbi 1167 P
Brandeby 1224–30 Fees
Branceby 1231 FF
Brandesby 1221–5 *RegAlb* ii. 56 *d et passim* to 1458 Test
Brandsby 1316 *KF*, 1665 Visit
Bransby 1316 *KF*

'Brand's farm' *v.* by. This personal name, common in the Danelaw, represents ON *Brandr*. The form *Brance-* represents the ON gen. sing. in -*s* (cf. Haxby 14 *supra*), as in Bransby (L), *Braunceby* 1243 Cl, and some forms of Bransdale 65 *infra*. Other forms are due to the substitution of the OE gen. -*es*, voiced in ME to [*z*].

FOULRICE

Fulryse 1301 LS   *Fowlerice* 1538 Dugd iv. 567

'Foul brushwood,' probably referring to 'a miry place overgrown with brushwood,' *v.* ful, hris.

STEARSBY

Estires-, Stirsbi 1086 DB
Stiresbi c. 1110–25 YCh 1094, 1308 Ch
Steresbi, -by 1167 P, 1251 Ass, *et passim* to 1399 YI
Sterisby 1285 KI, 1316 *KF*

'Styr's farm' *v.* by. The ON personal name *Stýrr*, ODan *Styr* is found in DB as *Stir*, and enters into Starston (Nf), DB *Sterestuna*, Streetthorpe (Y), c. 1170 Wollaton MS *Stirestorp*, Sturston (Db), DB *Sterstune*.

Marton le Forest

1. MARTON IN THE FOREST 27 A 7

Martun 1086 DB
Marton(a) 1160–75 YCh 656 *et passim*; (*in Galtres*) 1278 Baildon
Mareton' 1167, 1172, 1178, 1179 P

The name Marton is of frequent appearance in Y. On phonological (and in many cases topographical) grounds the

first element cannot be identified with OE *mere*, 'pool,' which
in DB and 12th and 13th cent. sources would scarcely appear
as *Mar-* and in many cases there is no evidence for the presence
of a pool. There is, however, a Yorks dialect word *mar* (EDD)
used of 'marshy land, sodden or reedy ground,' a sense which
would suit the topography of the Yorkshire Martons. Zachrisson
(*PN in Ing* 113, 114) derives this word from Scandinavian and
compares Swed *mar* (from OSwed *mar*, 'sea') which has the
meaning of 'marsh' in some dialects, and Dan *mar*, 'fen, marshland.' If so, the first element of Marton is from an ON *marr*,
'fen, marsh,' and the name means 'farm in the marshy land.'
v. tun.

Moxby [mɔuzbi]

    Molzbi, Molscebi 1086 DB
    Molesby, -bi 1158 YCh 419, 1161, 1165, 1167 P, 1318 Ch
    Molebi 1172, 1178, 1179 P
    Molseby 1234 Ebor, 1242 P, 1248 HCY, 1268, 1281, 1284,
        1287 Ebor, 1301 LS, 1345 Pap
    Molsby 1538 Dugd iv. 567

    v. by. The first element is probably a personal name. The
DB forms imply some such form as *Mold*, gen. sing. *Molds*.
An ON weak personal name *Moldi*, gen. *Molda*, existed in
Scandinavian (LindN), and a strong form *Moldr*, gen. *Molds*,
is not an unlikely supposition; cf. Mouldsworth (Ch) from an
OE *Mold* and *v.* Mildenham PN Wo 112. The place-name
would, therefore, mean 'Mold's farm.'
    The modern form of the name offers some difficulty. The
development of ME *Mols-* in the local dialect would be *Mouz-*,
and this too is the form we should get if the ME form had
been *Mox-*; association of the two has probably led to confusion
in the modern English spelling. In fact, *x* appears to have
been inserted for NEDial *z* in other cases, such as Roxby
(Pick), Throxenby, and Coxwold 90, 110, 191 *infra*.

Dalby

1. DALBY 22 J 8 [dɔːbi]

    Dalbi, -by 1086 DB, 1154–89 *MaryH* 6 d
    Dalebi, -by 13 *Malton* 99, 1283, 1287 Ebor, 1308 Ch

'Valley farm' *v.* dæl (ON *dalr*), by. Cf. OSwed *Dalby* (Hellquist, *ON på -by*, 6).

FORNTHORPE (lost)

> *Fornetorp* 1086 DB, 13 *Malton* 95 *d*   *Fornthorp* 1301 LS

'Forni's village' *v.* þorp. The ON personal name *Forni* (LindN, Nielsen, etc.) enters into the Norw place-name *Fornebu* (NG ii. 134) and is adduced in independent use in English as *Forne* (c. 1200 *For*).

SKEWSBY [skiuzbi]

> *Scoxebi* 1086 DB
> *Stoggesbi* (sic) 1167 P
> *Scog(h)esby* 13 *RegAlb* ii. 47 *d*, 1328 Banco
> *Scousby* 1226 FF
> *Schouse-, Shouesby* 1295 YI
> *Sc-, Skouesby* 1299, 1310 YD, 1354 FF
> *Scoseby* 1301 LS
> *Scewysbye* 1316 (Eliz) *KF*
> *Skuesby* 1408 YI, 1611 NR   *Skewsby* 1666 Visit

Skewsby is identical in form with the Swedish place-names *Skogsby* and *Skogby* (Hellquist, *Svenska ON på -by*, 13), and all three may mean 'farm in the wood' *v.* skogr, by. The gen. form of the first element is a type frequently met with in Scandinavian place-names, e.g. Swed *Brunnsby* by the side of *Brunnby*, *Högsby* by *Högby*, etc. (*op. cit. passim*). The normal gen. sing. of ON *skógr*, was *skógar*, but a gen. in -*s* is often found in OSwed and in OIcel poetry.

It is at least equally possible that the first element is the ON by-name *Skógr*, gen. *Skógs* (LindBN).

Whenby

1. WHENBY 27 A 8 [weŋbi]

> *Quennebi* 1086 DB
> *Quenebi, -by* 1202 FF *et passim* to 1333 Ch
> *Quenby* 1338 Baildon, 1394 Test
> *Qwheneby* 1408 YI
> *Whenby(e)* 1316 (Eliz) *KF*, 1454 Test, 1530 Visit

v. **by.** The first element is ON *kona*, 'a woman,' gen. plur. *kvenna.* Cf. Swed *Kvinneby*, OSwed *Quinnæby* from the same OSwed *kona* (Hellquist, *Svenska ON på -by*, 72). Hence, 'women's farm.'

The modern form with loss of initial *k-* arises from (1) the falling together of ON (OE) *cw-* and the over-aspirated OE *hw-* (ME *qwh-*), and (2) subsequent loss of aspiration, a regular feature in the dialect. Cf. Wheldrake (YER), earlier *Queldryk* 1285 KI, *Wheldryke* 1519 Test, and Quernhow and Whaw 224, 296 *infra*.

Sheriff Hutton

1. FARLINGTON 27 A 7

> *Ferlin-, Farlintun* 1086 DB
> *Ferlinton(a)* 1167 P, 1170–85 YCh 1055, 1310 Ch
> *Ferlington* 1249 *Heal* 127 (p), 1285 KI, 1286, 1295 *For*, 1295 YI, 1301 LS, 1316 *KF*
> *Farling-, Farlyngton* 1316 *KF*, 1400 YI
> *Farrelyngton* 1536 YChant

This name is of the same origin as Farlington (Ha), *Ferlinton* 1231 Cl, and Farleton (We), *Fareltun* 1086 DB, and in each case the first element is a personal name *Færela*, which is not adduced in independent use in OE. It is a diminutive in *-ela* (cf. IPN 171) of the OE personal-name theme *Fær*, found in OE *Wilfær* (evidenced in Bede's OE *Uilffaresdun*, YNR, 'Wilfær's hill') and in a patronymic form in a 12th cent. *Feringus* (Sumner, *Gavelkind* 1726 ed. p. 175) and in Fringford (O), *Feringeford* 1086 DB[1]. 'Færela's farm' *v.* ingtun.

2. SHERIFF HUTTON 27 B 9

> *Hotun(e), -ton(e)* 1086 DB, 1154–60 YCh 1052
> *Shi-, Shyref-, Schirefhoton* 1199–1213 YCh 1054, 1244 *Ass*, et passim
> *Hoton(e) Vicecomitis, Vescunt* 1281 *For et passim*, (*Neville'*) 1281 Ebor
> *Hotonscireve* 1282 YI

---

[1] Possibly it is a surname in *Ricardus Ferling* (13 Kirkst 166 n.).

S(c)erif-, Sheryf-Hoton (Huton) 1316 *KF, et passim* to
1572 FF
Sherofhooton 1505 Test
Sherefhoton 1548 YChant
'Farm on the spur of land' *v.* hoh, tun.

MedLat *vicecomes* and AN *vescunt* are both equivalent to OE
scir-gerefa, 'sheriff,' and the land was held originally by Bertram
de Bulmer, the *Sheriff* of York, who died in 1166. Through the
marriage of his daughter Emma to Geoffrey de *Neville*, the land
passed into the hands of the Nevilles, who in the 13th cent.
became Sheriffs of York.

CORNBROUGH
  Corlebroc 1086 DB
  Cornburc, -burgh 1154–8 *Kirkham* 94, 1166 P (p), 1213 Abbr,
    1316 *KF*, 1317, 1330 *For*, 1333 Riev (p)
  Corneburc(h), -burg(h) 1167 P, 1204 Ass, 1219, 1231 *Ass*,
    1285 KI, 1289, 1295 *For*, 1301 Abbr, LS, 1316 Vill, 1333
    Ch, 1372 FF, 1391 Test
  Cornisbour' 1295 *For*
  Corneborowe 1537 Dugd vi. 199

Names with initial *Corn-* are always difficult. Some may
contain OE *corn*, 'crane, heron' (cf. Cornwood, PN Wo 54)
but it is difficult to believe that such a compound could be
formed with burh. Cornbrough is not on a stream, so DB
-broc is probably an error for *-borc* from a Scandinavianised
form in borg.

CRANBERRYMOSS (lost)
  mora de Cranberimos 1155–89 YCh 421
  Tranberimose 1235 Cl

v. cran, mos. The first element is probably Engl *cranberry*,
'peat bog where cranberries abound.' The form *Tran-* arises
from interchange of OE cran and ON trani.

3. WEST LILLING 27 B 8, EAST LILLING
  Lilinge, -inga 1086 DB
  Lilling(a) 1167 P, 1202 FF (p), 1295 *For*; *West Lillinge* 1282
    YI, *Estlillyng* 1317 *For* etc.

'The settlement of Lilla and his dependants,' the name being originally a family name based on the OE personal name *Lilla*; *v. ing*. There is here no evidence for an OE form *Lillingas*, 'the Lillings,' but in Yorkshire the nom. plur. ending *-as* in *ing*-names of this type fell into disuse at an early date. That this took place is clear from such names as Gilling (Ryed) and Pickering 53, 85 *infra*. These names are much better evidenced in early spellings than Lilling and in them we have definite traces of the survival of the OE plur. ending *-as* as ME *-es*. The absence of this ending may be due to a certain extent to the original OE form of the name being in the dat. plur. *-um* as in Bede's *Ingetlingum*.

4. STITTENHAM 27 A 9 [stitnəm]

> *Stidnun* 1086 DB
> *Stitlum* 1185 P (p), 1208 Riev, 1295 *For*
> *Stiklum* c. 1260 *Malton* 39
> *Sti-, Stytel(l)um* 1275 YI, 1284 Ebor (p), 1289 Ebor
> *Stitelom* 1301 LS
> *Stitnum* 1250 Riev, 1310 Ch, 1333 Riev
> *Stytenom* 1316 Vill
> *Stytnam* 1316 *KF*, 1443 Test, 1615 NR

The difficulty of interpreting this name is largely brought about by two facts, (1) that *c* and *t* are in the court hand of the 12th and 13th cents. scarcely distinguishable, and (2) that *c* and *t* often interchange phonetically in ME, so that it is almost impossible to say whether we have here to deal with an original *Stitlum* or *Sticlum*. Most of the *Stitlum*-spellings may therefore represent *Sticlum*; the form *Stiklum*, however, is orthographically unambiguous, and it points to an original *Sticlum*. There is no evidence for a word like *stitel* or *stitle* which we should have to assume if the original form were *Stitlum*, but OE *sticol* (adj.) is frequently used in place-names in the sense 'steep,' and the meaning of Stittenham may, therefore, be 'at the steep (places)' from the dat. plur. *sticlum*. As a matter of fact this meaning may well be applied to Stittenham, for the village stands on the top of a very steep hill, surrounded on three sides by valleys; the hill rises in places more than 150 feet in a third of a mile.

Professor Ekwall suggests that we may have to do with a noun-derivative *sticele*, formed from *sticol*, meaning 'steep place' or the like. The topography is so striking that a name which refers to it is antecedently probable.

On the interchange of *c* and *t* before a following *l*, cf. Kirklington 220 *infra*. The later change of *l* to *n* is evidenced also in Hinderskelfe and Hinderwell 40, 138 *infra*. The DB form with -*n*- should be explained according to Zachrisson (*IPN* 106 ff.) as due to AN interchange of *l* and *n*, and no conclusions should be drawn from this name, as by Goodall (*NoB* v. 102) as to the use of the ON suffixed definite article in English place-names.

Terrington

1. GANTHORPE 22 J 10 [gɔnθrəp]

   Gameltorp   1086 DB
   Galmestorp   1169 P
   Galmethorp   1202 FF,   1290 YI,   1301 LS,   1344 FF; -*torp* 1244 *Ass*
   Gametorp'   1200 Cur
   Gaumisthorp   1202 FF
   Yalmethrope   1316 *KF*
   Ganthorp(e)   1577 Saxton, 1665 Visit

'Galm's village' *v.* þorp. The ON personal name *Gálmr* (LindN) is found also in Ganton (YER), *Galmeton* 1086 DB, 1207 FF. In both names the phonetic change is that -*alm*- became -*awm*- and *m* became *n* through the influence of the following *t*. The DB form is due to confusion with the common Anglo-Scand *Gamel*.

2. TERRINGTON 22 J 9

   Teurintone, Teurin(c)tun(e)   1086 DB
   Thiverinton   1202 FF
   Tivering-, Tyverington   1226 FF, 1261, 1275 YI, 1287 Ebor, 1288 YI, 1301 LS, 1302 Ch, 1316 Vill, 1367 FF
   Tyuerinton   1233 Ebor, 1244 *Ass*
   Teverington   1275 Fine
   Tyrrington   1316 (Eliz) *KF*, 1536 YChant
   Teryngton   1495, 1496 Test, 1545 NCyWills, RichWills

The first element of this name is doubtful, but it is a personal name, and certain other place-names should be taken into account: Teversham (C), *Teuresha'* 1086 DB, Teversall (Nt), *Teureshalt* 1086 DB, 1204 FF, *Tiueresheult, Tyversalt* 1297 Ebor, and Tyersall (YWR), *Tyversolde* 1280 Ebor, *Teversholte* 1535 VE. There is in each case variation between forms with *Tev-* and *Tiv-*. *Tev-* forms are always earlier than *Tiv-* except in Tyersall where none of the forms are really early. The name then probably goes back to an earlier *Tefringtun,* and *e* became *i* before the following labio-dental *f*.

There is an OE (Anglian) pers. name *Teoful* (*v.* Bede, ed. Plummer ii. 391) which suggests a name-theme *Tĕof*. There may well have been an *r*-derivative of this theme (cf. Pickering 85 *infra*), and a name *Teofer* would explain all the above names which, it may be noted, are confined to Anglian territory.

MOWTHORPE [mɔuθrəp]

Muletorp 1086 DB, 1167 P, 1244 *Ass*
Mulethorp 1227, 1238 Cl
Multhorp(e) 13 *Kirkham* 13, 1219 Fees, 1275, 1288 YI, 1316 Vill
Molthorp(e) 13 *Kirkham* 13, 1284, 1288 YI
Molthropp 1316 (Eliz) *KF*
Mowthropp(e) 1571 FF, 1615 NR

'Muli's village' *v.* þorp. Björkman (*NP*) notes that *Múli* is adduced in OEScand sources only, but LindBN cites *Múli* from OWScand sources and notes in addition the ONorw place-name *Mulaþorp*. In LVD mention is made of *þorkitell Mule*, and another example of its use in English is the place-name Mowthorpe (YER), *Muletorp* 1086 DB. Cf. also Muneville (Normandy), earlier *Muleville*.

WIGANTHORPE [wigənθrəp]

Wichingastorp 1086 DB
Wyggenthorpe 1275 YI
Wyginthorpe 1284, 1288 YI   *Wygenthorp* 1316 Vill
Wykenthorp 1304 Ch
Wiging-, Wygyngthorp(e) 1497 Test, 1530 Visit
Wiginthroppe 1316 (Eliz) *KF*

'Viking's village' *v.* þorp and Wigginton 14 *supra*.

Bossall

1. BOSSALL 27 C 11 [bɔsəl]

> *Boscele, Bosciale* 1086 DB
> *Boz(h)al(e)* 1225 Ebor, 1226 *RegAlb* ii. 56, 1238, 1289 Ebor
> *Boszale* 1257 Ch
> *Bosehale* 1265–78 Riev (p)
> *Boscale, Boscehale* 1269, 1289 Ebor
> *Bossal(e)* 1295 *For*, 1301 LS, 1346 Test, 1416 YI
> *Bossall* 1316 *KF*, 1397 Pap   *Boshal* 1336 Ch
> *Bosschall* 1404 Pap

ME *sc, z* were AN devices for representing the sound *ts*; early forms like *Bozhale*, therefore, indicate an OE form *Bōtesh(e)ale*, meaning 'Bot's nook of land' from the OE personal *Bōt* and h(e)alh. The early loss of medial *e* is probably due to Scand infl. where the gen. is simply *s*; cf. Cossall (Nt) which not infrequently appears as *Cozale* though DB has *Coteshale*, and Foston 39 *infra*.

BARNBY

> *Barnebi, -by* 1086 DB *et passim* to 1416 YI
> *Barnby(e)* 14 *Kirkham* 23, 1316 *KF*

This name, together with Barnby (135 *infra*), other Barnbys in YWR and two in Nt, offers difficulties. There is an ON pers. name *Bjarni* but this should appear in ME as *Berne*. Nielsen gives a reconstructed Danish *Barni* but it is doubtful if we should use such to explain so common a p.n. and for the moment judgment must be reserved as to the precise name involved.

BUTTERCRAMBE

> *Butecram(e)* 1086 DB, 1234 Cl
> *Botercram(e)* c. 1150–60 YCh 828, 1282 YI, 1301 LS, 1416 YI
> *But(t)ercram* 1208 FF, 1228 Ebor, 1276 YI, 1282 Fine
> *Butrecram* 1308 Ch
> *Buttercramp* 1316 Vill; *Botter-* 1365 FF
> *Buttercramm* 1344 *Ebor* 9, 1396 Pap
> *Butercrambe* 1350 Test

The meaning of the name is 'rich piece of land in the bend of the river (Derwent)' *v.* butere, and cf. Crambe 38 *infra*.

2. CLAXTON 27 D 10

Claxtorp 1086 DB
Claxton(a) 1282 YI *et passim*
Clauston 1295 *For*

The first element is probably the OEScand name *Klak*, recorded in Swedish runes as *KlakR* and as the ODan personal
name *Klak* (Nielsen), gen. *Klaks*. The one example of the
name recorded by Lind in West Scandinavia is a *Klakkr*, reconstructed from *Reider Klagsson*, but this man is said to
have come from Bohuslän, which then bordered on and is
now part of Sweden. This would suggest that the name *Klak*
(commonly found in the Danelaw) is a definite test of East
Scandinavian settlement. The form *Clacc* is found in *clacces
wadlond* (BCS 216) in the bounds of an Oxfordshire charter
dated 774. These bounds are certainly not original and probably
belong to the 11th cent. by which date an Anglo-Scand personal name might well be found in Oxfordshire.

3. FLAXTON 27 C 9

Flaxtune, -ton(a) 1086 DB, 1129-35 YCh 1056 *et passim*
Flastun, -tona 1086 DB
Flacstune 1147-63 Riev
Flasse-, Flaxeton' 1295 *For*

The first element may be the Scandinavian pers. name *Flak*.
It is found as a by-name in ON (LindBN), and as the word
now means 'fool' in Norw it is the kind of name which would
thus have been used in earlier times. *v.* tun. One might also suggest 'flax farm' from OE *fleax* and tun but the form *Flacstune* is
against this.

4. HARTON 27 C 10

Heretun(e) 1086 DB
Harton(a) 1293 *For, et passim*
Haretona 1308 Ch

v. tun. The first element is not clear. One possibility is
that the first element is OE *here* 'marauding band of more
than 35 men.' In this case Harton would indicate an enclosure
which had been or might be frequented by such a band.

In view of the rarity of compounds with *here* we should consider the second possibility that the first element is a personal name of some form like *Her(r)a*, a possible hypocoristic form of a personal name such as OE *Hereric, Herred*, etc.

5. SAND HUTTON 27 D 10

Hot(t)un(e) 1086 DB
Hoton(e) 1086 DB, 1228 Ebor, 1399 YI
Sandhoton' 1231 *Ass, et passim* to 1498 Test
Sandhuton' 1577 Saxton

'Farm on the sandy spur of land' *v.* hoh, tun.

Crambe

1. BARTON LE WILLOWS 27 C 11

Bartun 1086 DB
Barton' c. 1280 *Kirkham* 15 *et passim, (in Bulmer(e)schir)* 14 *Kirkham* 24 d, *(in the Willos)* 1574 FF

v. beretun. The regularity of *Bar-* forms for this and other Bartons in the North Riding in DB and other early sources points to an OE side-form *Bæretūn* (cf. OE *bærlic* 'barley'); indeed there is no case which can safely be ascribed to the more common form OE *beretūn*. The affix *le Willows* is from the OFr definite article *le* and ME *willugh*, 'willow tree,' and indicates the proximity of Barton to willow trees, cf. Zachrisson in *Anglia*, xxxiv. 336.

2. CRAMBE 27 B 11

Crambom, Cranbon(e) 1086 DB
Crambum 1086 DB, c. 1145–80 YCh 691 *et passim* to 1391 Test
Cranbu' 1168 P
Crambom 1301 LS, 1336 Ch
Crambumb' 1303 Ebor
Crambhom 1316 Vill
Cramb(e) 1577 Saxton, 1578 FF

This name seems to contain ME *crome, cromb*, 'hook, crook' (found *post* 1400), from OE **cramb, cromb* (*v.* NED s.v. *crome*); cf. OE *crumb, cromb*, 'crooked, bent.' The ultimate origin of this seems to be a Germanic word cognate with Brit *krumbos*, later evidenced as W *crwm, crom*, Ir *crom*, OGael *cromb*, 'bent, crooked.'

The original form of the name Crambe is OE (*æt þæm*) *crambum*, 'at the crooks,' and the crooks must refer, as in the case of Buttercrambe 36 *supra*, to the serpentine bends of the river Derwent in the midst of which both places are situated. See also Croome, PN Wo 118, for a similar type of name.

3. WHITWELL ON THE HILL 27 B 11

Witeu(u)elle 1086 DB
Whyttewell 1154–9 *Kirkham* 94
Qwyttwell 1187–91 *Kirkham* 93
Other forms are without interest.

'White, clear spring' *v.* hwit, w(i)ella.

Foston

1. FOSTON 27 B 10

Fostun(a) 1086 DB, 1167 P
Foston(e) 12 *MaryY* 168, 1145–61 YCh 1050 *et passim*
Fotestun 1231 *Ass*
Fotston 1233 Pat

v. tun. This name is identical with Foston (Lei), Hy2 Ch *Foteston*, which contains a personal name *Fōt*, not adduced in independent use in OE. For loss of *t* cf. Bossall *supra*.

2. THORNTON LE CLAY 27 B 9

Torentun(e) 1086 DB
Thorneton c. 1100–15 YCh 1001, 1301 LS

v. Thornton Bridge 24 *supra*. The affix is from OE clæg and the French def. art. *le*; cf. Barton le Willows 38 *supra* and Norton le Clay 182 *infra*.

Bulmer

1. BULMER 27 A 10 [bɔumə]

Bolemere, Boleber 1086 DB
Bvlem', Bulemer' 1159, 1160, 1165 P, *et freq* to 1285 KI
Bulmer(e) 1190 Guis *et passim*
Bolmere 1335 For

Boulmere 1350 Test (p)
Bowmer(e) 1577 Saxton, 1610 Speed
'Bull pool' *v.* bula, mere. Cf. Boulmer (Nb), Bulmer (Ess).

2. HINDERSKELFE (6″) [indəskəl]

Hildreschelf, Ilderschelf 1086 DB
Hi-, Hyldreskelf 1159–81 *Kirkham* 94, 1167 P
Hi-, Hylderskelf 1207 FF, 1253 Ch, 1259 Ass, 1301 LS,
    1336 Ch, 1418 YI
Hyldyrschelf c. 1280 *Kirkham* 15
Hi-, Hynderskelfe 1316 KF, 1483 Test
Hilderskilf 1344 FF
He-, Hyldresskelf 1436 NCyWills
Hilderskill 1577 Saxton, 1610 Speed

This is probably a purely Scandinavian name, the first element being *Hildar*, the gen. of ON *Hildr*, a woman's name, and the second being ON *skjálf*, 'shelf, seat.' The latter element no doubt refers to the small plateau in the west of the township. For the change of *l* to *n* cf. Stittenham 34 *supra* and Hinderwell 138 *infra*.

CASTLE HOWARD

The modern mansion was built by the Howard family (VCH ii. 107). The name is gradually displacing the name Hinderskelfe, which is now only the name of the township.

3. WELBURN 27 A 11

Wellebrun(e) 1086 DB, 1251 Ch
Welbrun 1243 Fees
Welleburn(e) 1167 P, 1279 YI, 1310 Ch
Welburn(e) 1301 LS *et passim*

v. w(i)ella, burna, and cf. Welburn (Ryed) 66 *infra*. The forms with *-brun* are due to the influence of the cognate ON brunnr. Cf. Welbourne (L).

Huttons Ambo

1. HIGH HUTTON 27 A 12

Hotun 1086 DB
Bardolf Hoton 1186–1202 *Malton* 68, *Hoton* (*Bardolfi*)
    1202 FF, *Hotton Bardouf* 1226 FF

The three Huttons (Huttons Ambo refers to High and Low Hutton) in this parish may all derive their names from a single hoh. High Hutton and Hutton Hill stand on small ridges of land, but Low Hutton is on the bank of the river Derwent. A ridge of land traverses the parish from north to south and juts into a bend of the Derwent in the shape of a tongue. This spur of land may have given rise to all three Hutton names. *v.* hoh, tun. The Bardolfs held land in this district in the 12th and 13th cents.

Low Hutton

>   *Hotun* 1086 DB, 1250 Fees
>   *Houton* 1304 Ch
>   *Huton* 1316 *KF*, 1581 FF

The distinguishing name *Colswain* occurs frequently in combination with *Hoton*, in the earlier instances it follows, but in later cases it precedes *Hoton*:

>   *Colsuain, -sweyn, -swayn* 1227 Ch *et passim*; *Colswan* 1279 YI;
>   *Colsuen* 1282–6 *Malton* 68 *d*; *Colesweyn* 1285 KI

The name is later

>   *Hoton upon Derwent* 1316 Vill

v. High Hutton *supra*. *Colswain* from OWScand **Kolsveinn*, ODan *Kolswen* (NP) is the name of the first tenant of this manor of whom there is any record (VCH ii. 150). The name is ill-recorded in Scandinavia but is common in England (L, W, Wa, etc.).

Hutton Hill

>   *Hoton* 1086 DB
>   *Minchon Hoton* e. 13 *Kirkham* 27, *Minechunhoton* 1286
>   *Malton* 68 *d*
>   *Hoton Mynchon* 1294 *Malton* 74 *d*; *Minchun* 1303 Abbr
>   *Huton on the Hill* 1581 FF

v. High Hutton *supra* and myncen, 'nun.' There is no recorded tenure of land here by nuns.

Musley Bank

>   *Musecliue, -clyve* 13 *Malton* 78, 14 *Kirkham* 25
>   *Musecleue* 13 *Kirkham* 59 *d*

'Musi's bank' *v.* clif. There is a steep declivity here. Cf. ON *Músi* in LindN. The name *Muse* is recorded in Lincs in 1207.

STONE CLIFF WOOD (6")

Staynecliue 13 *Kirkham* 26 *d*

Self-explanatory. *v.* steinn, clif.

II. RYEDALE WAPENTAKE

All the parishes of the modern wapentake except Lastingham which was in *Dic* (now Pickering Lythe wapentake), were in 1086 in the wapentake known as

Maneshou wapentac 1086 DB

'Man's mound' *v.* haugr. The meeting place was a hill or tumulus which cannot now be identified. The first element is a personal name such as OE *Mann*, ON *Mani*, ODan *Man*. The same name enters into Mansergh (We), Ekwall, *Scands. and Celts* 77.

In the 12th cent. the name of the wapentake was changed to Ryedale:

(*wapentagium de*) *Ri-*, *Rydal(e)* c. 1160–75 YCh 195, *et passim* to 1298 YI

Ry-, *Ridall(e)* 1283 Ebor, 1508 Test, 1619 NR

The wapentake lies in the valley of the river Rye. *v.* Rye 5 *supra* and dæl.

HOLDLYTHE (lost), a district, probably embracing the south of the wapentake judging by the name *Apeltone in Holdelithe* (*v.* Appleton 46 *infra*)

Holdelith, *Holdelythe* c. 1160–85 *Leon* 10 *d*, 1287 YI

The first element is probably ON *hǫldr*, the name of a class, corresponding generally to the English *þegn*, (from PrN **haluðr*, cognate with OE *hæleþ* and Germ *held*, 'warrior'). This is a form which exhibits Scand *u*-mutation, and examples of this change are rare in English loans from ON. The form *hold* occurs in independent use in OE (ASC and Laws), and Scand *u*-mutation of *a* to *ǫ* is also found in examples of ON *hǫfuð*. An interesting case in this light is Howden (YER), which appears in OE as *æt Heafuddæne* (BCS 1052), but later forms such as DB *Houedene* show that OE *hēafod* was in the 11th cent. replaced by ON *hǫfuð*, the *u*-mutated form. The second element of Holdlythe is hliŏ, 'a slope.' Hence 'slope of the *holds*.'

Malton

1. OLD MALTON 22 J 13 [ɔːd mɔːtən]

   Maaltun c. 1130 SD
   Maltune 1086 DB, 1160–80 Riev
   Malton(e) (*Veteris*) 1173 YCh 1888, 1219 *Ass et passim*,
     (*Ald*) 1399 YI
   Mealton 1191 P
   Miauton' 1200 Cur
   Mialton 1204 Ass
   Meautun, -ton 1218 ClR, FF, 1221 ClR, 1227 Ch, 1231 *Ass*,
     1253 Ch
   Mealtune c. 1270 Gerv
   Meuton 1218 FF, 1244 Fees, 1260 Baildon
   Mauton 1250 Fees, c. 1260–7 *Malton* 34 *d*
   Melton 1294 Ch

This name should be taken together with the *Madaltune* found in a charter of 1148 (YCh 179). It would seem to be beyond question that in that name we have a compound of OE *mæðel*, 'speech,' used especially of formal speech in council. The same compound here would explain all the forms, their great variety being due to loss of inter-vocalic *th*. The name would mean 'discussion-village' and would refer to the holding of some moot here (cf. Matlask in IPN 65). *Madaltune* refers beyond question to Melton-on-the-Hill *al.* High Melton (YWR), which appears in DB as *Medeltone*, *Middeltun*, *Mideltone*, as *Methylton* in 1252 and as *Meuton* in 1269 (Ch). This has commonly been interpreted (PN YWR 130, PN SWY 212) as 'middle farm,' from ON *meðal*, but the 1148 form makes this less likely and we should probably explain the DB forms as due to confusion between *Methel* from OE *mæðel* and ON *meðel*, OE *midel*. In that case Melton has the same meaning as Malton.

ACOMB [jækəm]

> *Acum* 1222 FF

'(At the) oaks' *v.* ac.

GREENGATE (6″), a street

> *Grengate* 1323 YD

'Green way' *v.* grene, gata.

HOWE

> *How(e)* 1322 *Malton* 53 *d, et passim*

HOWE BRIDGE (Fm)

> *ponte de Hou* 12 *Malton* 7, 37 *d,* c. 1260–7 ib. 48; *ponte de How* 15 Whitby
> *ponte de Holm* 1157–89 *Malton* 28 *d*
> *ponte de Houm* 1169 *Malton* 7 *d*

The repetition of the *Hou*-forms in this cartulary, the appearance of *How* in the Whitby Cartulary, the modern form of the name, and the forms of Howe *supra* seem to show that *Hou* is the original form of the name.

Howe and Howe Bridge are within half a mile of each other and contain the same element. Howe Bridge crosses the river Rye at the northern extremity of a piece of land round which the river flows, whilst Howe is further south on a spit of land similarly encircled by the river. The meaning of the names, therefore, is clearly 'spur of land.' *v.* hoh.

Howe is from the OE dat. sing. *hōhe,* and Howe Bridge from the OE dat. plur. *hōhum* (as well as *Hou, How* from the dat. sing. *hōhe*). This will explain the discrepant *Hou* and *Houm* in the forms of Howe Bridge. In addition to this *Houm* also became *Holm* on the analogy of the common ON *holmr.* In the same way Holme on the Wolds (YER), which appears variously as *Hougon* DB, *Holm* 1279–81 QW, and *Howm* 1303 KF, has an intrusive *l.* That name may be derived from the dat. pl. of ON *haugr* rather than OE hoh, but the topography of Howe and Howe Bridge makes derivation from hoh more likely for those names. Variation between the dat. sing. and the dat. plur. is noticed in Wykeham, Newsham and Downholme 45, 270 *infra,* and in Blubber houses (YWR), earlier

Bluberhusum 1172 YCh 511, *Bluberhous* 1195–c. 1210 YCh 512, and Woodhouse near Leeds (YWR), *Wdehuse* c. 1160–74 YCh 1562 and *Wdahusum* 1165–75 YCh 1567.

NEW MALTON, commonly called *Malton*
> *Maltune* 1086 DB

Further forms as for Old Malton 43 *supra*. First called *Nova* in 1301 (LS).

WYKEHAM [wɑikəm]
> *Wich, Wic(h)um* 1086 DB
> *Vycum, Wicum* 1268 *Malton* 48, 1301 LS
> *Wycom* 1322 *Malton* 53 *d*, 1387 *Bodl* a. i. 68
> *Wycomb* 1399 YI

'(At) the dwellings' *v.* wic. All forms except the first are from the OE dat. plur. *wīcum*.

Appleton le Street

1. AMOTHERBY 22 H 12 [æməbi], [eməbi]
> *Aimundrebi, Edmundrebia* 1086 DB
> *Eimundrebi, -by* e. 13 *Malton* 86 *d*, 1240 ib. 90
> *Aymunderby* e. 13 *Malton* 76 *d*, 1226 FF, 1242 P *et passim*
>   to 1415 Fabr
> *Aymundresby* 1308 Pat
> *Aymonderby* 1368 FF
> *Amonderby* 1614 NR

'Eymund's farm' *v.* by. The ON personal name *Øymundr*, gen. *Øymundar* (LindN), ODan *Ømund* (Nielsen) is found in Norfolk records of the 12th cent. as *Eimund*.

NEWSHAM
> *Newehusum, Neuhuse, Niehusum* 1086 DB
> *Neusum* 13 *Malton* 95 *d et passim*
> *Newesum* 1300 Baildon
> *Neusom* 1301 LS, 1368 FF

'(At the) new houses' from OE (*æt þǣm*) *nīwum hūsum*. *v.* niwe, hus. Ekwall (*IPN* 68) suggests that the DB form *Niehusum* may contain ON *nýr*, 'new.'

2. APPLETON LE STREET 22 H 11

> *Apletun, Apeltun* 1086 DB
> *Apel(l)ton(e)* 13 *Malton* 47 *et passim*; (*in Holdelithe*) 1349
>   NRS; (*in Rydale*) 1369 FF

v. æppel, tun. The termination *le Street* is of late appearance,
as in the case of Barton le Street 47 *infra*. It refers to a supposed
Roman road (6″ OS sheet 123 NE 4), on which Appleton and
Barton stand. *v.* stræt. On the element *le v.* Barton le Willows
38 *supra*. For *Holdelithe v.* 42 *supra*.

EASTHORPE [jiəstrəp]

> *Estorp* 1086 DB, 1227, 1241 Ebor
> *Esttorp* 1182 P
> *Easthorpe* 1231 FF
> *Estthorp* 1280 *Ass*, 1377 Test
> *Esthorpe* 1288 YI

This seems to be the original form of the name but there
is also another series of a different type. There can be no
doubt of the identification, for the types are found indifferently
in parallel documents (e.g. 1275 and 1288 YI). Examples of
this type are as follows:

> *Jarpesthorp* 1201 ChR   *Iarpestorp* 13 *Malton* 71, 71 *d*, 73 *d*
> *Yarpestorp', Yarpestrop* 1243 Fees, 1259 Ass
> *Yarpesthorp* 1275 YI, 1279 *Malton* 74, 1301 LS, 1304 Ch,
>   1369 FF
> *Yaresthorp* 1285 (16th cent.) KI
> *Yaistropp* 1621 NR.

The *Estorp* forms are the earlier and denote 'east village,'
v. east, þorp. It is not phonetically possible to derive the
obviously later *Yarpesthorp* forms from this. This must be
'Yarp's village.' Cf. the lost *Iarpestune* in the Norfolk DB.
The personal name *Yarp* is from the ON personal name *Iarpr*
(LindN), from *jarpr*, 'brown of hair'; cf. OE *Earp* (Redin 65,
s.n. *Eoppa*).

3. BROUGHTON 22 J 12 [brɔutən]

> *Broctun(e), Brostone* 1086 DB
> *Broctuna, -ton* 1145–53 *Leon* 35 *et passim* to 1285 KI

Brochton 1258 Ch
Broutton 1301 LS
Broghton 1328 Banco, 1369 FF
'Farm by a stream' *v.* broc, tun.

4. HILDENLEY 22 J 11

(*H*)*ildingeslei* 1086 DB
Hildingle 13 *Malton* 87, 1336 Ch   *Hildinglaye* 1344 Test
'Hilding's clearing' *v.* leah. The name *Hilding* is based on the common OE name-theme *Hild.* A similar formation *Hildingr* is recorded in ON but in view of the English second element an English pers. name is the more likely.

5. SWINTON 22 J 12

Suintun(*e*) 1086 DB
Swin-, Swynton' 1219 *Ass, et passim*
'Pig farm' *v.* swin, tun.

BRAYGATE STREET (6")

Braiþagate 13 *Kirkham* 59 *d*   *Breyegate* 13 *Malton* 87
'Broad way' *v.* breiðr, gata. Cf. the common ONorw *Breiðgata.*

Barton le Street

1. BARTON LE STREET 22 H 11

Bartun(*e*), *-ton*(*e*) 1086 DB; (*in Rydale*) 1280 Ebor; (*in le Strete*) 1614 NR

v. bere-tun; and cf. Barton le Willows and Appleton le Street *supra.*

2. BUTTERWICK 22 G 11

Butruic 1086 DB
Buttrewyc, But(*t*)*erwic, -wyk*(*e*) 1145–8 Whitby, 1227 FF *et passim*
Buttirwyk 1279 YI
Butrawic 1308 Ch
Botrewyk 1399 YI
'Dairy farm with rich pastures' *v.* butere, wic. Butterwick is by the river Rye and the land is very fertile. Cf. Butterwick (YER, *Buterwic* c. 1260 *Malton* 95 *d*).

3. CONEYSTHORPE 22 J 10 [kunistrəp]

Coningistorp, Coungestorp 1086 DB
Cunighestorp 1125 YD
Cuningestorp 1167 P, 1204 Ass
Cunnigestorp 1200 Cur
Coninges-, Conyngesthorp 1251 Ass, 1252 *Ass*, 1316 Vill, 1327 Baildon, 1436 NCyWills
Cunigthorp 1254 Pat
Conis-, Conysthorp 1285 (16th cent.) KI, 1577 Saxton
Conistropp 1615 NR

'The king's village' *v.* þorp. The first element is ODan *kunung* (= ONorw *konungr*). The Danish form is also found in Coneythorpe near Knaresborough (YWR), *Cunningesthorp* 1293 QW, *Conyngesthorp* 1316 Vill, and in several other Yorkshire place-names, e.g. Conisborough (YWR), *Cunugesburh* KCD 1298, *Cuningesburg* DB, Coney Street (York), *Cunyngesstrete* 1150–61 YCh 232, and Cold Coniston (YWR), *Cuningestone* DB. *v.* Introduction xxiv.

Slingsby

1. SLINGSBY 22 H 10

Selunges-, Eslingesbi 1086 DB
Slengesbi, -by 1161–84 Whitby, 1164–72 YCh 882 *et passim* to 1403 YI
Eslenggesbi 13 *Malton* 83 *d*
Slengeby 1203 Whitby, 1226 FF, 1251 Ass, 1282 YI
Lengesbi, -by e. 13 *Malton* 96 *d*, 97
Lengeby 1224–30 Fees, 1251 Ass, 1280 Ebor
Slingebi 1155–65 Whitby, 1167 P
Sli-, Slyngesby 1202 FF *et passim* to 1578 FF
Selingesby 1347 Pap
Slingysby 1402 Whitby

The persistence of *Slenges-* forms (approximately in the proportion of 2 : 1 to the *Slinges-* forms) shows that we have to deal with an original *Sleng*. Zachrisson (*Some English Place-Name Etymologies*, 142) suggests OWScand *Slyngr* (LindBN) rather than the hypothetical ON *Sløngr* or *Slengr* (ZEN), suggested as the first element of Slingley (PN NbDu s.n.). ON

Slyngr will not, however, explain the *Slenges-* forms of the place-name, whereas if the first element be taken as *Sleng* we can explain the *Slinges-* forms as due to the ME sound-change of *eng* to *ing* (cf. Ingleby 167 *infra*) which took place in the 13th cent., if not earlier. Further, it will be seen that whilst no *Slenges-* forms are found after the 13th cent. the majority of *Slinges-* forms are of the 13th and following cents. The DB form *Eslinges-* cannot be taken seriously as in that source there is frequent interchange of *e* and *i*. Slingsby, therefore, means 'Sleng's farm.' *v.* **by**. The name *Sleng* appears in the surname of Robert *Slenge* (1298 WCR).

For loss of *s-* and spellings with *Esl-, Sel- v.* IPN 103.

THE FIRTH WOOD (6″)

le Frythe 1301 YI

'The wood' *v.* fyrhþ.

THURTLE WOOD

Thurkelwode 1301 YI

'Thurkel's wood' *v.* **wudu**. *Thurkel* is a common ME name from ODan *Thurkil*, etc. For interchange of *t* and *k* before *l* cf. Kirklington 220 *infra*.

Hovingham

1. AIRYHOLME 22 J 9

Erghum 1138 Dugd v. 350 *Ergum* 1218 FF, 1236 Cl (p)

'(At) the shielings' *v.* **erg**. The word is derived ultimately from OIr *airgh* 'a place for summer pastures in the mountains,' and as Airyholme stands on the top of a hill overlooking Wath Beck in the hilly district south of Hovingham, it seems probable that the meaning of the name is 'summer pastures.' The phonology of this word is of interest; the MIr form was *airge* but this does not indicate a diphthong; medial -*i*- is here used to indicate the palatal quality of OIr *a*, whilst *gh* represents a spirant consonant aspirated from original stopped *g* between vowels. The pronunciation, therefore, of OIr *airgh* would be [ǽrg]. This would normally develop into [erj(əm)] in Yorkshire.

HOWTHORPE [ɔuθrəp]

> Holtorp 1086 DB, 1167 P, 13 YD, 1244 *Ass*
> Holetorp' 1166, 1167 P (p)
> Holthorp(e) 13 *RegAlb* ii. 47 d, *et passim* to 1399 YI

'Village in the hollow' *v.* hol, þorp. Howthorpe is in a slight depression on rather high ground.

2. COULTON 22 H 8 [kɔutən]

> Cole-, Coltun(e) 1086 DB
> Colton 1086 DB, 1208, 1223 FF *et passim* to 1399 YI
> Coltun 1167 P, 13 *Malton* 101, c. 1285 ib. 99
> Cowlton 1578 FF

The rarity of medial -*e*- in early forms is against a derivation from the OE pers. name *Cola*; the first element is more probably OE *col* 'charcoal.' 'Farm where charcoal was burnt' *v.* tun.

STOCKING

> Le Stockinges 1333 Riev

v. stocking.

3. FRYTON 22 H 10 [fritən]

> Frideton, Fritun 1086 DB
> Friton(a), Fry- 1086 DB, 12 *BylE* 43 d, 1224–30 Fees, 1244
>   *Malton* 65, 1251 Cl, 1300 Ch, 1301 LS, YI
> Firton 1577 Saxton

'Frithi's farm' *v.* tun. The first element is ODan *Frithi* (Nielsen) as in *Fridebi*, the old name for Felixkirk 199 *infra*, and Freeby (Lei), DB *Fredebi*.

4. SOUTH HOLME 22 G 10

> Holm(e) 1086 DB, *Southolme* 1301 YI

v. holmr. The name refers to the low-lying land between Hole Beck, the river Rye and Wath Beck. "South" in relation to North Holme 59 *infra*.

5. HOVINGHAM 22 H 9 [ɔvinəm, ɔuiŋəm]

Hoving-, Houing-, Hovyngham 1086 DB, 1142–50 YCh 638,
  et passim
Hovingeham 1157 YCh 354, 1228 Cl, 1308 Ch

Ekwall (*PN in -ing* 148) suggests that the first element is
derived in some way or other from OE *hof* 'temple.' It would
seem probable that there is some connexion between this name
and the lost *Hoveton* 66 *infra*, which can only have been some six
miles to the north. If that is so, the further probability is that
we have to do with a pers. name in both cases, and if so it is
difficult to keep these names entirely apart from Hoveringham
(Nt), *Houringam* (p), c. 1160 Db Charters no. 1397 and *Houer-
ingeham* 1167 P. This latter name can only be explained on the
basis of a name-theme *Hof*, to which *Hofer* would stand in the
same relation as the *Picer* of Pickering 85 *infra* to the recorded
Pic. For the use of *hof* 'temple' as a name-theme we may
compare the common use of *Ealh-* in OE, of which the earliest
sense was also 'temple.'

6. EAST NESS 22 G 10, including WEST NESS

Ne(i)sse 1086 DB, (*West-*) 1243 Fees, (*Est*) 1416 YI

v. næs. Both these names refer to the east end of a ridge of
land enclosed between the river Rye and Hole Beck. Cf. Norw
Nes used with this sense of 'headland' (NG i. 90, etc.).

WATERHOLMES

Waterholm(e) 1243 Fees *et passim*
From OE *wæter* 'water' and holmr.

7. SCACKLETON 22 J 8

Scachelden(e), Eschalchedene 1086 DB
Skakilden 1138 Dugd v. 350, 1243 *BylE* 81 *d*, 1408 YI
Scakeldana 1142–50 YCh 638
Skakelden(a) 1154–89 *MaryH* 6 *d*, 1231 *Ass*
Scakelden' 13 *BylE* 70 *d*, 1244 *Ass*, 1247 Ch, 1328 Banco
Schacheldene 1308 Ch

v. denu 'valley.' The first element may be a Scandinavianised
form of OE *sc(e)acol* though in what sense is not clear. The

same element occurs in two OE field names in Berks, *on scaeceling aecere* (BCS 971) and *on scaecyling aecer* (BCS 1002), in Shacklecross (Db), *Shakelcros* 1235 Ch, Shackleford (Sr), *Shakelford* 1355 Pat, Shackleton (YWR), *v.* Goodall s.n., and a lost place in Shackleton (YWR) called *Schakelhull* 1219 *Ass.* Shacklecross possibly indicates that OE *sceacol* (the only recorded meaning of which is 'shackle, fetter') could also mean 'pole to which shackles were attached,' like ON *skǫkull* and Swed *skakel.* If this is correct, Shackleford would be 'a ford indicated by a pole,' Shackleton would be 'a farm by a pole' (cf. such names as Stapleton, Rounton 217, 283 *infra*) and the lost *Schakelhull* 'a hill with a pole on top.' Similarly Scackleton would be 'a valley in which a pole, used as a landmark, was a prominent feature'; initial *sk-* in this case would be due to the substitution of ON *sk-* for OE *sc-.* *v.* Addenda xlv.

8. WATH 22 H 9 [wæθ]

Wad 1086 DB

Wath 1224–30 Fees

'The ford' *v.* vaδ. Wath stands at the point where the supposed Roman road (*v.* Appleton le Street 46 *supra*) crosses the stream now known as Wath Beck. There is also a lost place near here called

Hawade 1086 DB

Probably it was in this township (possibly in Wath Wood higher up the stream) and means 'high ford' from ON *hár* 'high' and vaδ.

Gilling

1. CAWTON 22 H 8 [kɔːtən]

Caluetun, -tone 1086 DB

C-, *Kalueton(a)* 1160–75 *Dods* vii. 116 *d*, 1167 P *et passim* to 1416 YI

Calton 1316 (Eliz) Vill, 1393 Test

Caulton 1418 YI

Caw(e)ton 1538 Riev, 1579 FF, 1665 Visit

'Calves' farm' from OE calf and tun. Cf. such names as Swinton, Shipton, Cowton. A similar combination is Calverton, Callerton (PN Nt, NbDu s.n.), from the OE gen. plur. *calfra.*

This is the normal form of the gen. plur. of *calf*. Cawton, however, seems to be from an OE gen. plur. *calfa*, which is found in Challock (K), OE *cealfa locum* BCS 378, and in the name of a lost place near Alton (Ha) called in OE *cealfa mære* (BCS 390).

2. GILLING 22 H 7

Ghellinge, Gellinge 1086 DB
Gy-, Gilling' 1135–47 *MaryY* 215, 1167 P *et passim*
Gillinges 1239 *RegAlb* iii. 34
Gillingaridale 1308 Ch (= "in Ryedale")

Cf. Gillamoor and Gilling (GillW) 64, 288 *infra*. It is of the common OE -*ingas* type of place-name and indicates the settlement of some man and his dependants. The ultimate origin of the first element, which is of course a personal name, is open to doubt. Professor Zachrisson (*Some Yorkshire Place-Names*, 39 ff) thinks that Givendale (YWR, OE *Gyþinga deal, Gyðlinga-dale*, c. 1020 YCh 7), Givendale and Gillamoor 94, 64 *infra* and the two Gillings in the North Riding all contain the same personal name, an OE patronymic *Gȳþling* formed from *Gūða* with *i*-mutation of *u* to *y* due to the patronymic suffix -*ling* (*op. cit.* p. 41). Early forms with *ge*- he explains as being the regular AN rendering of OE *y*, *i*. All this is quite true for Givendale (YWR), but the early forms leave it uncertain how far it may be accepted for the North Riding Gillings.

A second possibility is that the personal name found in Gilling and Gillamoor is either an OE pers. name *Getla* derived from WGerm **Gautila* (a diminutive of the name-theme found in ON *Gautar*, the *Gēatas* of *Beowulf*) as suggested by Ekwall (*PN in -ing* 94) or an OE cognate of the recorded Germanic name *Gattila* (Schönfeld) which is the base of OSwed *Getlinge* (Hellquist, *Svenska ON på Inge*, 34).

This name is certainly the basis of Bede's *Ingetlingum* (Bede iii. 14), the *Ingætlingum* of the *Historia Abbatum* and the Tanner MS of the OE Bede and probably also of Gilling 288 *infra* and of Yetlington (Nb). In that case OE initial palatal *g* (= [*j*]) has been replaced by Scand velar *g*. For *e* > *i*, cf. Zachrisson, *PN in *Vis, *Vask* 54.

3. GRIMSTON 22 H 7

Gri-, Grymeston(a) 1086 DB, 1166 P (p) *et passim*

'Grim's farm' from the common ON personal name *Grímr* and tun. Grimston is a common name, found in YWR and four times in YER, once in Lei and once in Nt.

Stonegrave

1. NEWTON 22 G 8

Newentune, Neutun, Neweton 1086 DB
Neuton(e) 1086 DB, 1268 Ch *et passim*
Niwenton' 1167 P

'The new farm' *v.* niwe, tun. For the *-en-* forms, cf. Newton upon Ouse 20 *supra*.

LAYSTHORPE [lɛəsθrəp]

Lechestorp 1086 DB
Leisthorp 1170–83 *Dods* vii. 148 *d*
Lai-, Laystorp 1219 *Ass*, 1293 QW
Laysethorp 13 *BylE* 55
Lai-, Laysthorp(e) 1266 Baildon, 1285 KI, 1316 Vill
Lasthorp 1301 LS

'Leik's village' from the ON personal name *Leikr* (LindN); cf. the ODan weak form *Leki* (Nielsen). DB often represents ON *ei* by *e*; cf. Laceby (L), DB *Leuesbi*, from ON *Leifr* (LindN). *v.* þorp.

2. NUNNINGTON 22 G 9

Nonnin-, Nonninc-, Noning-, Nunnige-tun(e) 1086 DB
Nunintun, -ton' 1167 P, 1257, 1308 Ch
Nunnington 1169 Riev, 1295 YI

'Nunna's farm' from the OE personal name *Nunna* and ingtun.

3. STONEGRAVE 22 G 9

Staine-, Stein(e)-, Stanegrif 1086 DB
Steingrave c. 1150 RegDun
Staingrive 1190 *Bodl* a. i. 48
Stay-, Staingreue 1200–10 *Bodl* a. i. 50, *et freq* to 1301 YI
Stei-, Steyngreve 1242 P, *et freq* to 1306 Pap

Staynegrive 1251 Ass (p), 1301 LS
Stei-, *Steyngrive* 1267, 1269 Ebor, 1277 Pat, 1279–81 QW
Stangreve 1418 YI, 1483 Test
Stan(e)grave 1508 Test, 1613 NR

v. steinn, gryfja. *Griff* is still used in the YNR dialect for a small steep-sided valley. The application to the topography of Stonegrave is not very clear. In the modern form of the name the earlier *steinn* has been replaced by Standard English *stone* as in Stony Keld etc. 305 *infra*.

Interesting problems are, however, raised by the mention in BCS 184, in the same letter in which Coxwold 191 *infra* occurs, of a monastery at *Staningagrave*. Is this an earlier form of Stonegrave and was the name later Scandinavianised? The form in Reginald of Durham suggests that the form of the second element may once have been OE grafa or græfe or græf and the latter would readily account for the numerous -*greve* forms later. The interpretation in that case would be 'copse or thicket or quarry of the people of a man called *Stan*' with later substitution of ON *steinn* for OE *stan* and of Anglo-Scandinavian *grif*, *grive* for OE *graf* or *græfe*.

Oswaldkirk

1. OSWALDKIRK 22 G 8

Oswaldescherca 1086 DB
Villa tota de S̄cō Oswaldo 1167 P
Oswaldkirke c. 1170 Riev, etc.
Chirch-, *Ki(e)rkos(e)wald* 1201 ChR, 1214 Abbr, 1239 *RegAlb* iii. 34
Oswoldchurch 1613 NR

'The church dedicated to Saint Oswald' *v.* kirkja and cf. Felixkirk and Romaldkirk 199, 309 *infra*. On the form *Kirkoswald* *v.* Introduction xxvi. The St Oswald referred to in this place-name is probably the well-known Archbishop of York, who was regarded as a saint in OE times (cf. Saints: "þonne resteð sanctus Oswaldus arcebiscop on Wigeraceastre") and whose name is found in the dedication of Worcester Cathedral. This identification of St Oswald in the place-name is supported by the fact that part of the land of Oswaldkirk was held by the Archbishops of York.

WEST NEWTON GRANGE

Neutun(e), *Newetune* 1086 DB   *Westneuton'* 1228 Pat

Self-explanatory.

Ampleforth

1. AMPLEFORTH 22 G 6

Ampreforde, Ambreforde 1086 DB

Ampilford c. 1142 Dugd v. 352, 1290 Ebor, 1323 *BylE* 4,
1414 YI, 1444 NCyWills

Ampleford 1167, 1187 P, 1202 FF, 1327 Banco

Ampelford 1221–5 *RegAlb* ii. 56 *d*, 1247 Ch, 1284 YI, 1285
KI, 1301 LS, 1316 Vill, 1347 Pap

Amplesford 1243 Fees   *Ampilforth* 1472 Fabr

v. ford. Probably the first element of Ampleforth is OE
ampre 'dock, sorrel' and the forms with -*l*- are due to AN interchange of *l* and *r* (*v.* IPN 107). Hence, 'ford where sorrel grows.'
Cf. Clatford (W) from clate and Larford and Ribbesford (PN
Wo 34, 68).

DRAKEDALE (6″)

Drakedalehevid 1376 Dugd v. 348

The first element is OE *draca* 'dragon,' found in Drakelow
(Db), DB *Drachelauue* and Drakenedge (Wa). *v.* dæl, heafod.

HOLBECK, HOLE BECK, a stream

Holebec(k) 1154–63, c. 1170 Riev   *Holbek* 1418 YI

'Stream in the hollow' *v.* hol, bekkr. Cf. also the name of
a lost road in Gilling near this stream called *Holegate* c. 1170
Riev.

Scawton

1. SCAWTON 22 E 5 [skɔːtən]

Scaltun 1086 DB, 1154–60 YCh 1830, c. 1155 Riev, 1181
BylE 103 *d*

Sc-, Skalton(a) 1189 Riev *et passim* to 1414 YI

Scaulton 1328 Banco   *Scawton* 1575 FF

'Farm in the hollow' from ON *skál* 'hollow' (cf. Rygh,
NG Indledning s.v.) and tun. Scawton lies in a short but steep-
sided valley.

ANTOFTS

Aldwinetoftes, Aldenetoftes 1193–1203 Riev

'Aldwine's fields' from OE *Aldwine* and topt.

BROCK HILL (6")

Brochesholes c. 1150 Riev

v. brocc-hol.

BUNGDALE [bɔndil]

Brunesdale c. 1150, c. 1170 Riev

'Brun's valley' *v.* dæl. The first element is the OE personal name *Brūn* which also enters into a lost place in this valley called *Brunescale* 1181 BylE 103 *d* (from skali). The modern form offers some difficulty but its phonetic development was probably *Brundale* > *Burndale* > [bɔndil]; the last stage represents the regular development of NE *ur* in the dialect (*v.* Introd. xxxii).

STOCKING HOUSE

Stocking 1249 Baildon

v. stocking.

Salton

1. BRAWBY 22 G 11 [brɔːbi]

Bragebi, Brageby 1086 DB *Brahebi* 1165 YCh 778

Brauby 1301 LS (p) *Braby* 1577 Saxton

'Bragi's farm' from the ON personal name *Bragi* and by.

2. SALTON 22 F 10 [sɔːtən]

Saletun, -ton 1086 DB, 1167–80 YCh 415 (p)

Salton 1285 KI, 1396 Pap, 1536 YChant

Saulton 1286 Ch *Sauton* 1577 Saxton

'Enclosure of or by the willows' *v.* s(e)alh, tun. The early forms suggest OE *s(e)ala-tun* from the gen. plur. *s(e)ala*.

Normanby

1. NORMANBY 22 F 11

Normanebi, -by 1086 DB, c. 1200 *For*, 1204 (1433) Pat 1308 Ch

Northmannabi c. 1130 SD

Normnebi 1167 P
Normanby 1147–61 YCh 414, 1154–89 *MaryH* 6 d
North(e)manby 1285 KI, 1301 LS
Normannebi 1308 Ch

'Village of the Norwegians' from OE *Norþman* (gen. plur. *Norþmanna*) and by. *v.* Introduction xxvi.

ROOK BARUGH [riukbaːf, riukbarə]

Rochesberc, -berg(e) c. 1140, c. 1180, 1333 Riev
Rocheberch 1160 Riev *Rokeberg* 1301 LS
Rogeberg 1201 ChR

'Rook's hill' from the ON personal name *Hrókr* or OE *Hrōc* and berg. The spelling *Roge-* is probably to be explained in the same way as Wigginton 14 *supra*.

Great Edstone

1. GREAT EDSTONE 22 E 10

Micheledestun 1086 DB
Edestun 1140, 1333 Riev
Edeston' 1167 P, 13 *Malton* 115, 1201 YCh 598, 1285 KI *et passim*
Edneston' 1231 *Ass*
Ed(d)iston' 1202 FF, 1285 KI
Heddestone 1276 YI

Cf. also the spellings of Little Edstone 76 *infra*.

Professor Stenton (IPN 171, note 5) discusses a type of OE personal name derived from a single theme and extended by the addition of an *-n* suffix. Taking the P form *Edenston'* (Little E) and the later forms *Ed(d)is-* it is clear that we have here an OE personal name *Ēaden*, an *n*-derivative of the name-stem *Ēad-*. Hence 'Eaden's farm.' *v.* tun.

COWLDYKE [kɔuldɑik]

Coldic 1154–63, 1333 Riev

The first element seems to be ON *kola*, a common Scand stream-name meaning 'coal-black river' (from ON *kol* and *á*) (Rygh, *NElv* 30). It is probably a stream-name in this case, for

Cowldyke stands very near to the river Dove (which actually means 'black') and to a stream (possibly identical with the river Dove) called *Colebecke* (13 *Malton* 115). *v*. dic, bekkr.

WANDALES

Sanwandeiles 1333 Riev

Lindkvist (*PN Scand Origin* 35, n. 2) notes the survival in NE of *wandale* 'a share of the large open arable land of a township' (cf. EDD s.v.) and the existence of ODan *wang* in the special sense of 'cultivated field in which all the villagers hold a share.' From this evidence Lindkvist suggests that the first element of *wandale* is ON *vangr*. There are objections to this: (1) none of the spellings of *wandale* (either in the YNR or frequent examples elsewhere) ever exhibits a form *wangdale*, and the loss of -*g*- in that position is unlikely as it is usually preserved in such names as Langdale, etc.; (2) there is a form *wanddayles* (*v*. Wandale, LangE 157 *infra*) which points to an original first element *wand*. ON *vǫndr* 'a twig' etc. is used in the compound *vand-balkr* to denote 'a wall of wands'; the meaning of *wandale*, therefore, is probably 'a share of the common field fenced off with wands or stakes.' The final element of *wandale* is either OE dal 'share' or ON deill. The distinguishing element in this name is sand.

2. NORTH HOLME 22 F 10

Holm(e), *Hom* 1086 DB, 1154–63 Riev
Northolm(e) 13 *Malton* 115

v. holmr and South Holme 50 *supra*.

Lastingham

1. APPLETON LE MOORS 22 D 11

Apeltun 1086 DB *Duueld' Apelton'* 1301 LS

v. æppel, tun and cf. Appleton le Street 46 *supra*. The element *Duueld'* is difficult but it is possibly from the OIr personal name *Dubhgall* (cf. *Revue Celtique*, XLIV. 46), found as the first element of Duggleby (YER) and independently as *Duuegald* (12 YCh 217), a man of York. The name was borrowed through a Scandinavian source (*v*. Introd. xxvi); LindN adduces Scand forms *Dugal*, *Duggal*, from the same OIr name. The affix *le Moors* indicates the proximity of Appleton to the moors (cf. Barton le Willows 38 *supra*).

2. HUTTON LE HOLE 22 C 10

Hotun 1086 DB
(*Hege*)*hoton* 1204 Ass, (*subtus le Hegh*) 13 Dugd iii. 560, (*Underheg*) 1285 KI
Hewton under Heighe 1579 FF

'Farm on the projecting ridge of land' *v.* hoh, tun. The added element *heg(e)* denotes land enclosed for hunting; *v.* (ge)hæg. The modern affix is simply *hole* or *hollow* (cf. Barton le Willows 38 *supra* for the element *le*).

DOUTHWAITE HALL

Duvanesthwat c. 1154–63 Riev   *Duthethwayt* 1276 YI
Dowthwayte, *-thwait* 1540 Dugd iii. 570, 1613 NR

'Duvan's clearing' *v.* þveit. The first element is from the OIr personal name *Dubhan*, *v. Revue Celtique*, XLIV. 47 and Introduction xxvi.

3. LASTINGHAM 22 C 11

læstinga-, *lestinga eu*, *laestinga-*, *laestenga eu* (*ig*), *læstingæ*, *læstinga æi*, *lęstinga ei* 8 Bede
Læstinga ea 10 BedeOE
Lestingaheu, *Lestingaea* c. 1130 SD
Lestingay 12 Dugd i. 343

All other post-Conquest spellings are of the ingaham type:
Lesting(e)ham 1086 DB
Lesting-, *Lestyngham* 1086–9 MaryH 1, *et freq* to 1665 Visit
Laystyngham 1285 KI
Lasting-, *Lastyngham* 1393 Test, 1396 Pap, 1508 Test

Ekwall (*PN in -ing* 148) supposes that there was an OE personal name equivalent to the ON by-name *Leistr* (LindBN); this would be a name *Lāst*, which in the *-ing* forms might be mutated to OE *Læsting-*. Lastingham, therefore, means 'the settlement of the *Læstingas* (or of *Lāst* and his dependants).' *v.* ing, ham.

The explanation of the two forms *eu* and *ig* in the suffix of Bede's forms seems to be this: the PrGerm nominative was **auhwi* and the oblique cases were formed with **auhwj-*. Apparently *eu* comes from the PrGerm nominative **auhwi* and *ig* from the PrGerm oblique **auhwj-*. OE *ei, æi* are for *eg*, another Anglian form from the PrGerm oblique **auhwj-*. There can be no doubt that these are different forms for the same word, for *eu* is regularly translated by Bede as *insula* 'island' in such names as *Heroteu*. The site of the abbey at Lastingham is on the west bank of the river on a piece of land round which Hole Beck flows. *v.* eg.

The form *ea* in the OEBede is probably due to confusion, since OE *ēa* 'a river' (from PrGerm **ahwa*, cf. Latin *aqua*) can hardly have had such a form as *eu*.

ANSERDALE LANE, a road

> *Hansterdaile* 1336 Ch

Dr Lindkvist suggests that the first element may be ON *ǫmstr* (*amstr*), 'heap (of corn or dung).' The whole name would probably mean deill or dole of land marked by a dung-heap. The *h* is clearly inorganic and *ms* has become *ns* by dissimilation.

4. SPAUNTON 22 C 11 [spɔːntən]

> *Spantun(e)* 1086 DB
>
> *Spaunton(a)* 1086–9 *MaryH* 1 *et passim*
>
> *Spantona* 1154–6 *MaryH* 6 *d*, 12 *Cur* 46, m. 3 *d*, 1225 Baildon, 1285 KI, 1308 Ch
>
> *Spawnton* 1665 Visit

'Farm with shingle tiling' (or 'farm where shingle for tiling was obtained') from ON **spann** and **tun**. *v.* Lindkvist 196. For *-aun- v.* IPN 105.

THE LUND

> *Lund(e)* 1154–63, c. 1170 Riev
>
> *v.* lundr.

Kirkby Moorside

1. FADMOOR 22 D 9

Fademor(a) 1086 DB, 1221 FF, 1231 *Ass*
Faddemor c. 1150 Riev, 1185–1201 *Dods* vii. 179, 1201 ChR, 1219 *Ass*
Fadmore 1285 KI, 1301 LS, 1399 YI, 1462 Test
Fadymor 1301 LS

v. mor. The first element is probably a personal name but its source is uncertain and it is almost impossible to do more than speculate amongst possibilities. As the neighbouring Gillamoor is of very early origin it is probable that this name belongs to the same period. There is an ON by-name *Faddi* (LindBN) which Lind suggests is a short form of ON *faðir*, but it may be of common Germanic origin: cf. OGerm *Fato*, *Fadiko* (Förstemann, *NP* 492), *Fadi* (Fick, *Wörterbuch der Indogerman. Sprachen*, iii. 168), all cognate with Gothic *-faþs* 'man, warrior.' *Fadenus* is adduced from a Latin source as being similar to OHG *Fadi* (Werle, *Die ältesten german. Personennamen*, 36); it is probably *Fadi* extended by an *-n* suffix. An OE example of this common Germanic name is, therefore, not improbable, especially if we take Fadmoor to be an early name. Its form would be *Fad(d)a*, and further evidence of this pers. name is found in the OE pers. n. *Fadol* and in the p.n.'s Vaddicott (D), *Faddecote* 1212 and Faddiley (Ch), *Faddelee* 1259.

LOSKAY HOUSE

Loftischo 1282 YI   *Loftisco* 1332 Pat (p)

'Loft in the wood' from ON *lopt í skógi*; *v.* lopt, skogr. Cf. Loscoe (YWR), *Loft Scoh* 13 Kirkst 150. Cf. Loftus 140 *infra*.

SLEIGHTHOLME DALE [sleitumdil]

Sletholme 1301 LS (p)
Slehtholme 1386 Riev (p)
Sl(e)ightholm(e)dale 1538 Riev, 1621 NR

'Flat ground near water' *v.* sletta, holmr, and cf. Barnby Sleights and Sleightholme 135, 305 *infra*.

The first element is from early ON *sleht-* (which later became *slétta*), and the normal development of this in the dialect would be [sliːt] (*v.* Sleightholme 305 *infra*). The modern pronunciation [slɛit] is irregular, and, as Cowling (§§ 149, 172, 226) suggests for some other word, it is a borrowing from RSE.

SLEIGHTS HOUSE [slɛits uːs]

> *Slectes* 1154–63 Riev

ut supra and cf. the Latin form *in parvis slectis* in a West Lincs charter of c. 1160. The context suggests that it refers to marshland (*AD*, AS 280).

2. FARNDALE 22 ABC 9

> *Farnedale* c. 1154–63 Riev, 1276, 1416 YI
> *Farendale, -dal(a)* late 12 *Cur* 46, m. 3 *d*, 1201 ChR, 1229 Cl, 1255 Ch, 1286 *For*, 1301 LS
> *Farndal(e)* 1279–81 QW, 1301 LS, 1371 Baildon, 1577 Saxton

'Fern valley' *v.* fearn, dæl.

HARLAND

> *Harlonde* 1282 YI

Harland is on the top of a hill and in the neighbourhood are a large number of tumuli. With this in view it is possible that the first element is an OE *har* meaning apparently 'a rock, tumulus, heap of stones' (cf. PN BedsHu 137). Harome 70 *infra* seems to contain the same element.

MIDDLE HEAD

> *Middelhoved* 13 Riev

v. middel, hǫfuð.

SWINACLE 22 B 8

> *Swenekelis* 1282 YI

This name is probably identical with the Norw place-name *Svinekle*, which Rygh suggests is from ON *svín* and ONorw *ekla* 'want' (NG i. 47). Hence, 'place where pigs are lacking.'

3. GILLAMOOR 22 C 9 [giləmuə]

Gedlingesmore 1086 DB
Gillingamor late 12 *Cur* 46, m. 3 *d*
Gillingemor' 1231 *Ass*
Gilling-, *Gillyngmore* 1195–1200 Guis, 1285 KI, 1301 LS, YI, 1399 YI
Gillemore 1282 YI *Gillimore* 1577 Saxton

'The open expanse of land belonging to the *Getlingas*.' If this is the folk-name which lies behind Gilling 53 *supra* there may actually be a reference to the same folk. *v.* mor.

4. KIRKBY MOORSIDE 22 D 10

Chirchebi 1086 DB
Ki-, *Kyrkebi*, *-by (Moresheved)* c. 1170 Riev, *et passim* to 1391 Test
Kirkebymoreshede 1399 YI *Kirkeby Moresyd* 1489 Test

'Farm by the church' *v.* kirkja, by. The termination Moorside means 'head of the moor' *v.* mor, heafod.

BOWFORTH [bɔufəþ]

Buleford(e) 1154–63 Riev, 1167, 1175 P, 1278–84 *Malton*, 109 (p), 1333 Riev
Bulford(e) 1301 LS, YI, 1302 Baildon, 1328 Banco
Bouforth 1538 Riev

'Bull ford' *v.* bula, ford and Bulford (Bulm) 13 *supra*.

HAGG FARM

Hagh 1414, 1421 YI *unius copicii sive le Hagge* 1538 Riev
v. hǫgg.

KELDHOLME

Keld(e)holm 1170–86 *Dods* vii. 157, 1201 ChR *et passim*

'Water-meadow near the spring' *v.* kelda, holmr.

RAVENSWYKE

Revenwich 1201 ChR

'Raven's nook in the hills' from the ON personal name *Hrafn* and vik. The name refers to the steep-sided valley of the river Dove.

Kirkdale

1. BRANSDALE 22 ABC 8

Brannesdale c. 1150 Riev   *Brauncedale* 1276 YI, 1301 LS
Brandesdal' 1279–81 QW   *Bransdale* 1577 Saxton

'Brand's valley' from ON *Brandr* (*v.* Brandsby 28 *supra*)
and dæl.

2. MUSCOATES 22 F 10

Musecote(s) 1154–63 Riev, 1198–1214 *RegAlb* ii. 62, 1227 FF,
   1282 YI, 1333 Riev
Muskote c. 1260 *Malton* 39; *-cotes* 1385 Baildon, 1416 YI
Mouscotes 1293 QW
Mosekotes 1301 LS; *-cotes* 1301 YI
Muscoites 1417 YI

'Musi's cottages' *v.* cot. The ON name *Músi* (LindBN,
Nielsen) is from ON *mús* 'mouse' and enters into Muscote
(Nth).

3. NAWTON 22 E 9 [nɔːtən]

Naghelton, Nageltone, Nagletune, Nageltune 1086 DB
Nagelt', -ton 1160–5 YCh 164, c. 1160 Riev, 1190–1200 *Bodl*
   a. i. 30
Nathelton c. 1160 Riev
Nau-, Nawelton 1170 Riev, 1202 FF, 1285 KI, 1298 Abbr
Nalton(a) 1301 LS, 1316 Vill, 1333 Riev
Nawton 1665 Visit

'Nagli's farm,' from the ON personal name *Nagli* (LindN)
and tun. On the form *Nathel-* cf. Fearby 232 *infra*.

NAWTONDALE (6″)

Nageltundale c. 1170 Riev

4. SKIPLAM 22 D 9

Skipenum c. 1150 Riev
Sc(h)-, Skipnum c. 1160, c. 1180 Riev, 1259 Ass, 1268 Ch,
   1293 QW, 1333 Riev
Skiplom(e) 1526, 1538 Riev   *Skiplam* 1577 Saxton

'(At) the cowshed' *v.* scipen with substitution of Scand *sk-*
for Engl. *sh-*. The modern form with *-lam* probably arose
under the influence of the neighbouring Beadlam 67 *infra*.

5. WELBURN 22 E 9
Wellebrune 1086 DB
With the same run of forms and meaning as Welburn (Bulm)
40 *supra*.

HOVETON (lost)
Houetune 1086 DB   *Houeton* 12 Riev, 1252 Ch
v. tun. Identical with Hoveton (Nf), DB *Hovetuna*. For
the first element *v.* Hovingham 51 *supra*.

KIRKDALE
Kirkedale 1202 FF
Kirkdale 1518 Test   *Kyrkdayle* 1572 FF
'Church valley' *v.* kirkja, dæl. A church existed here before
the conquest for "Orm Gamalsuna bought the church of St.
Gregory when it was badly in disrepair and ruinous, and
he had it rebuilt from the ground for Christ and St. Gregory
in the days of king Edward and the earl Tosti." (Inscription
translated from OE on the famous dial-stone at Kirkdale Church
1055–65.) The same church is recorded in DB, where the place
is called *Chirchebi*; *v.* kirkja, by. Like the name of the place,
the name of the man who built the church is of Scandinavian
origin; *Orm* is from OWScand *Ormr* and *Gamal* from OWScand
Gamall, whilst the patronymic *Gamalsuna* is of a Scandinavian
type.

SUNLEY HILL
Sunnolvehou 1192–9 Riev   *Suneley* 1572 FF
'Sunnolf's mound' *v.* haugr. The first element is the ON
pers. name *Sunnólfr* found independently as ME *Sunnulf*
(*LVD* 14).

WALTON (lost)
Waletun, -ton 1086 DB
'Village of the Britons (or serfs)' from OE *W(e)alh*, gen. plur.
W(e)ala 'Briton, foreigner, Welshman' and tun. (*v.* IPN 18.)

6. WOMBLETON 22 E 9

Winbel-, Wilbetun 1086 DB
Wimbaltuna 1145–53 *Leon* 35
Wimbeltun c. 1159, 1154–63 Riev, 1190–1200 *Bodl* a. i. 30,
   c. 1250 *Malton* 108 *d*
Wi-, Wymbelton(a) 1231 *Ass*, 1233 Cl *et passim* to 1385
   Baildon
Wimbil-, Wymbylton 13 *Malton* 242, 1285 KI, 1417 YI
Wimilton c. 1260 *Malton* 39
Wimbleton 1301 LS   *Wymbulton* 1399 YI

From the OE personal name *Wynnbeald* or *Winebeald* and
tun. The modern form is due to the development of *i* to [u]
in the neighbourhood of *r* and *w* as in such names as Ruddings,
Runswick, Ruswarp and Ruswick 85, 121, 139, 191 *infra*.

Helmsley

1. BEADLAM 22 E 8 [biədləm]

Bodlun 1086 DB
Bodlum 1086 DB, 1201 ChR, 1202 FF, 1285 KI; -*lom* 1336 Ch
Bothlum c. 1170, 1333 Riev
Bothelum 1259 Ass
Bolum 1259 Ass, 1260 Riev, 1285 KI
Bodelum 1301 LS, 1316 Vill; -*lom* 1328 Banco
Budelom 1414, 1421 YI
Bewdlom 1578 FF; -*lam* 1613, 1614 NR
Beaudlam 1616 NR

'(At) the buildings' *v.* boðl; the name is from the OE dat.
plur. *boðlum*. The modern form of the name has arisen from
the dialectal change of OE *ō* to [iu] and later to [iə] in this
part of the North Riding. The modern form with -*d*- has
come from an AN form *Bodlum* (*v.* IPN 110).

2. BILSDALE 22 ABC 6

Bi-, Byldesdale (-a) 1153–9, 1180–5 Riev *et passim* to 1316 Vill
Bilsdale 1577 Saxton

'Bild's valley' *v.* dæl. The first element is the ON pers.
name *Bíldr* as in Bildeston (Sf), Bilsthorpe (Nt) and Bilstone
(Lei).

BROAD FIELDS

Bradfelde 1301 LS

v. brad, feld.

COCK FLAT

Kyrkflat 13 *Kirkham* 50 *d*

'Church field' *v.* kirkja, flat. Probably 'land held by the church of Kirkham.' The modern form *Cock* is phonetically derived from ME *kyrk*. The normal development of *kirk* in the dialect is [kɔ·k]; this is near enough acoustically to be confused with *cock*.

COLD MOOR

Kaldmore 14 *Kirkham* 51 *d*

Self-explanatory.

CROSSLETS

Kirkesletes 1260 Riev   *Kirkeslectes* 1333 Riev

v. kirkja, sletta.

ELLERMIRE

Elvemire 1260 Riev   *Eluitemercote* 1301 LS

'Swan pool' from OE *elfitu* and myrr. Cf. Eldmire 184 *infra* and Elvet, PN NbDu s.n.

FANGDALE

Fangedala c. 1160 Riev, 1170–85 YCh 1845

'Fangi's valley' *v.* dæl. The first element is a personal name *Fangi* of Scandinavian origin. A personal name *Fangulf* (from ODan *Fangulf*) is evidenced in medieval Nf records and in York records of the 12th cent. (e.g. *Waltero filio Fannulfi* 1164–75 YCh 282, *filio Faganulph'* 1170–6 YCh 225), and enters into Fangfoss (YER), *Frangefos* (sic) 1086 DB, *Fangelfosse* 1200 Cur (p), *Fangefosse* 1208 FF, 1260 YI. A short form *Fangi* would be normal and this enters into Fangdale.

FANGDALE BECK

Flandgedalebec (sic) 1201 Riev

GARFIT

Garthwayt 13 *Kirkham* 51   *Garthpheit* 13 *Kirkham* 52
Garthwat 1335 *Kirkham* 53
'Clearing with a garth on it' *v.* garðr, þveit.

HOWL BECK (6″)

Holbek 14 *Kirkham* 51 *d*
v. hol, bekkr and Holbeck 56 *supra.*

RAISDALE [reəzdil]

Riedesdal' 1204 FF
Reydhesdalle 1246 Riev
Raythesdale 1268 Ch, 1273 Riev, 1293 QW
Reythesdal' 1259 Ass (p)
Rai-, Raysedale 1301 LS, 1377 Baildon
Raysdale 1538 Riev
'Reith's valley' *v.* dæl. The first element, Lindkvist suggests, is an ON personal name *Hreiðr*, probably a short form of ON *Hreiðulfr* (LindN). There are, however, Norw place-names *Røsæk* (ONorw *i Røydesæik*) and ONorw *i Røydiseim* (Rygh, *NG* i. 121), and from these cases its original form seems rather to have been *Røyðr* or *Røyðir*, an *i*-mutated form of the well-evidenced ON pers. name *Rauðr* (LindN).

SMIDDALES (6″)

Smidhesdala c. 1180 Riev
'The smith's valley' from OE *smið* and dæl.

STAINDALE

Steindal(e) 1247, 1260 Riev
'Rocky valley' *v.* steinn, dæl.

STONEHOUSE COTE

Staynhouse 14 *Kirkham* 51 *d*
'Stone house' *v.* steinn, hus.

TRIPSDALE

Thriplesdala c. 1180 Riev
v. dæl. Professor Ekwall suggests that the first element may be connected with OE *þripel* 'instrument of torture,' which has

yielded dial. *thripple* 'movable framework fitted on a cart.' In that case we have a genitival compound and the meaning of the whole name would be 'valley marked by a *þripel*,' whatever the exact sense of the word in this context may be. The Anglian form would be *þrēpel*, but we may assume early shortening and raising of the vowel to *i*.

URRA

> *Horhowe* 1301 LS   *Orrow(e)* 1377 Baildon, 1382 *Kirkham* 55
>
> *v.* haugr. The first element is OE horh 'filth' as in Horcum (Pick) 91 *infra*.

WILLIAM BECK

> *Willelmesbec(h)* 1160, c. 1180 Riev
> *Williambek* 1192 *Kirkham* 70 d, 14 ib. 50 d, 100 d
> *Wylȝambek* c. 1250 *Kirkham* 101
> 'William's stream' *v.* bekkr.

3. HAROME   22 F 8

> *Harun, Harem, Harum* 1086 DB
> *Harum* c. 1170 Riev, 1192 *Kirkham* 70 d, *et passim* to 1471 Test
> *Harom(e)* 1301 LS, 1572 FF
> *Haram* 1336 Ch, 1614 NR
> *Harom* 1572 FF

Harome is probably derived from OE dat. pl. *harum* 'amongst the stones' from OE *har, *v.* Harland 63 *supra*.

4. SPROXTON   22 F 7 [sprɔustən]

> *Sprostune* 1086 DB
> *Sproxtun(a)* 1165–75 YCh 410, 1192 *Kirkham* 70 d, 1202 FF
> *Sprocston'* 1186 P (p)
> *Sproxton(a)* 1226 FF, 1228 Pat, 1252 *Ass*, 1285 KI, 1298 YI, 1301 LS, 1308 Ch, 1417 YI

v. tun. For the first element the following names should be compared: Sproxton (Lei) and *Sproxmire* (13 *Easby* 142 d), the name of a lost place in Crakehall (HangE) *infra*. Professor Ekwall suggests that it is the same as the OSwed pers. name

Sprok found in *Sproxstatha* (1376) recorded by Lundgren-Brate. This pers. name is probably to be associated with OFris, LGerm *sprock* 'brittle.'

5. HELMSLEY 22 E 7 [emzlə]

Elmeslac, Almeslai 1086 DB

Helmeslac(h) 1155 Riev, 1165–75 YCh 410, 1170–85 YCh 1845, 1189 Riev, 1252 Ch

Helmesleia, -ley, -legh, -lay c. 1170 Whitby *et passim*

Helmele 1251 Ass

Hemesley 1548 YChant, 1597 NR   *Hemsley* 1602 NR, 1665 Visit

The following spellings also occur:

Hamylac 1133–9 Riev

Hamelac 1229 Pat, 1230 Riev; *-lak(e)* 1231 Ebor *et freq.* to 1414 YI; *-lek* 1251 Ass

Haumelak 1232 Riev; *-lake* 1283 YI; *-lac* 1336 Ch

Heaumele 1231 *Ass*; *-lake* 1258 Baildon

The meaning of the name is clearly 'Helm's forest-clearing' *v.* leah. The OE pers. name *Helm* is only adduced in independent use in *Widsith* and in a Lincs Ass Roll of 1202, but it enters into Helmdon (Nth), Hemswell (L) and Helmingham (Nf, Sf).

The secondary forms are all due to French influence; as late as Camden's time we are told that there were two pronunciations of the name *Helmesley* and *Hamelack* and the barony of Roos of *Hamlake* only became extinct in 1632. OE *Helm-* became *heaume-* or *haume-* by AN influence. At the same time *a* + nasal was often written *au* (*v.* IPN 105, 4). The form *Hame-*, therefore, is due to confusion of *aum* representing AN vocalisation of *l* before *m*, and *aum* arising by nasalisation from earlier *am*, which was also still written *am* in many cases. *Hamelac* is therefore an inverted spelling for *Haumelac*. The pronunciation of the final element as *lak* is shown by the orthography and is further confirmed by Gaimar's rime *Helmeslac–Espac*. It may perhaps be best explained as an AN pronunciation of late Nthb *lǣh*, shortened in the unstressed syllable (cf. IPN 113, 3). An AN pronunciation of the name of a famous barony is very natural. Cf. also the DB form for Pockley 72 *infra* in the immediate neighbourhood.

CARLTON

> K-, *Carlton* e. 13 *Kirkham* 2, 13 ib., 1414 YI
> *Carletona* 1301 LS
>
> v. karlatun.

PLOCKWOODS [plɔkudz]

> *Plocw(o)de* 1232, 1251 Riev
>
> v. wudu. The first element is not clear, but Professor Ekwall notes *plock* 'block of wood, log,' *plockwood*, the same (EDD).

ROPPA [rɔpə]

> *Rauthepathe* 1160 Riev   *Raudepade* c. 1180 Riev
>
> 'Red path' v. rauðr, pæð. The soil is here of a reddish hue.

6. LASKILL PASTURE 22 C 6

> *Lauesc(h)ales* 1170 Riev, 1200 FF, 1201 Riev
> *Laygskales* 1301 LS
>
> 'Low pastures' v. lagr, skali. Laskill is in the bottom of the deep valley of the river Rye. On the change of ME *laue* to *la* cf. Addlebrough 262 *infra. v.* Introduction xxvi.

HAGG END

> *Haghe* 1285 YI
>
> v. hɔgg.

7. POCKLEY 22 E 8

> *Pochelaf, -lac* 1086 DB
> *Pokelai, -lay* 1184–98 Riev, 1279–81 QW; *-le* 1232 Riev,
>   13 *Kirkham* 1; *-ley(e)* 1282 Baildon, 1301 LS
> *Pockeley(a)* 1252 Ch, 1259 Ass
> *Poklee, Pockele* 1285 KI
>
> 'Poca's forest-clearing' v. leah. The name *Poc(c)a* is not adduced in OE, but it may be assumed from Pockthorpe (YER), *Pochetorp* DB, (Nf, 4 examples) and Pocklington (YER), *Poclinton* DB, which contains **Pocela*, a derivative in *-ela* of *Poca*. It is probably connected with OE *pocc* 'small-pox.' For the DB form v. Helmsley 71 *supra*.

8. RIEVAULX 22 E 6 [rivis, rivəz]

Rievalle, Ry-, Rieualle 1157 YCh 401, *et freq.* to 1202 FF
Riesuals 1161 P
Ri-, Ryvall(e) 1204 Ass, 1226 FF *et freq.* to 1299 YI
Rivallis 1228 Pat
Ri-, Ryevallis 1252 Ch, 1285 KI
Ryvaus 1301 LS, 1324, 1326 NRS, 1491 Test
Rywaus 1301 LS, c. 1310 *Bodl* a. i. 58
Riweus, Ryfuowis 1375 Barbour's *Bruce*
Ryvaux 1390, 1486, 1497 Test

'The Rye valley' from the river-name Rye (*v.* 5 *supra*) and OFr *val-s*. Cf. Jervaulx 250 *infra*. The name is of AN origin and was applied to the monastery here in the first place.

ABBOT HAG

Hagg c. 1180 Riev

v. hǫgg. The land here belonged to the abbot of Rievaulx.

CRINGLE CARR (6″)

Krynglecarre 1538 Riev

'Circular marsh' *v.* kringla, kjarr, cf. *Cryngelflath* 13 *Easby* 214, *Krinkelker* 1212 FF.

GRIFF FARM

Grif 1086 DB *et passim* to 1301 LS
Griff(e) 1229 Pat, 1333 Riev

'Narrow valley' *v.* gryfja.

NEWLASS

Newlathes 1301 LS

'The new barns' *v.* niwe, hlaða. Cf. Wass 195 *infra*.

STILTONS FM

Tilstun(e) 1086 DB
Thilleston', Thyllestonam c. 1180 Riev, 1252 Ch
Tyleston 1229 Pat
Tilston' 1230 Cl
Tylleston' 1293 QW

The origin of the first element is open to speculation, but
the best suggestion seems to be the OE personal name *Tili*
or *Tilli*. Interchange of initial *t-* and *th-* is noticed in other
names such as Thirlby, Thirsk and Theakston 188, 195, 228
infra. Initial *s* may possibly be due, as Dr Lindkvist suggests,
to prefixed *east* or *west*.

III. PICKERING LYTHE WAPENTAKE

Dic wapentac 1086 DB
Pikiringelit 1135–55 YCh 377
Pikeringelid, -lith 1158 YCh 403, 1252 Ch
Pykeringlidh, Pykerynglyth c. 1169–85 YCh 196 *et freq* to
    1485 Test
wap' (wapentacco) de Picheringe 1166 P *et passim* to 1301 LS
Pikringlith 1172–9 YCh 379
Pikaringalith 1176–9 YCh 406, 1201 ChR

v. Pickering 85 *infra* and hlið. The original name of the wapentake, *Dic*, probably refers to one of the numerous dykes in the
district which would be the wapentake meeting-place, *v.* dic.
Dykes were frequently the sites of the meeting-places of the
hundreds, as in Wrangdike Hundred (R), Flendish Hundred
(C), DB *Flamingdic*, and Abdich Hundred (So).

The later name of the wapentake is taken from some slope
near Pickering, but this cannot now be identified.

Kirby Misperton

1. GREAT BARUGH, LITTLE BARUGH 22 G 11 [ba:f]
    Berg(a) 1086 DB, 1170 P, 1285 KI
    Berch 1086 DB, (*magna, parua*) c. 1200 *For*
    Bergh(e) 1219 Ass, *et passim* to 1409 YI
    (*Great*) *Bargh(e)* 1526 NRS
    'The hill' *v.* beorg.

2. GREAT HABTON, LITTLE HABTON 22 H 12
    Habetun, Ab(b)etune 1086 DB
    (*parva*) *Habeton* c. 1163–85 YCh 781, c. 1200 *For*, 1201 ChR,
    1219 FF

Habbeton 13 *Malton* 97, 1231 *Ass,* 1285 KI, 1301 LS, 1333
   Riev
Habbenton 1231 FF
Great, parua Habton 1365 FF
Great Hapton 1368 FF

'Hab(b)a's farm' *v.* tun. The first element is a hypocoristic
pers. name *Hab(b)a* from some OE pers. name such as *Hēah-
beorht* or *Heardbeorht.* Cf. Hapton (Nf), *Habetuna* DB. A pers.
name *Habe* is recorded (L) in *Danelaw Charters* 573, possibly
derived from ON *Hábjǫrn,* which would also suitably explain
the first element of Habton.

3. KIRBY MISPERTON (KIRBY OVERCARR) 22 G 12

In DB survey Kirby and Misperton are separate manors. In
all later records they are joined together under the common
name of Kirby Misperton.

Chirchebi 1086 DB
Ki-, Kyrkeby, -bi 1094–9 YCh 601 *et passim* to 1408 *For*
Kirkabi 1308 Ch, *Kirkby* 1414 Test, *Kirby* 1665 Visit
Mispeton 1086 DB
Mi-, Mysperton(a) 1137–61 YCh 602 *et passim*

In the 16th and 17th cents. it is also called

Kirkebye Overkare 1549 YChant   *Kyrkby Overcarr* 1573 FF

'Farm by the church' *v.* kirkja, by.

The first element in Misperton is not clear but Dr O. K.
Schram suggests that there may have been an OE word *mispel*
or *mispeler* denoting the medlar-tree. LL *mespila* is found in
LG and HG as *mespel* (OHG *mespila*) and there is a side-form
mispel from MHG *mispel(e).* Both forms are found in the LG
dialects, and Frisian *mispel(beam)* is well-evidenced.

LL *mespilarius* var. *mispilarius* appears in Dutch and Flemish
as *mespelare* and is found in the Belgian p.n. *Mespelaere* in
the form *Mespilarios* in 899. (Vincent, *Les noms de lieux de la
Belgique,* § 181.)

Hoops (*Waldbäume* 606) suggests that there may have been
an OE form of LG *mespila.* The word actually occurs in late
ME as *mespile,* by the side of *mespiler* (NED s.v.) but these
are probably late borrowings from Latin itself.

OE *mespiler-tun* might readily become *misp(l)erton* and if
that is the history the name means 'farm with the medlar-tree.'
Such might well grow in the low-lying ground, or *carr*, from
which the place takes its alternative appellation. *v.* kjarr.

4. RYTON 22 H 13

Ritun, Ritone 1086 DB   *Ri-, Ryton* 1282 *Malton* 102 *et passim*
Rihtona c. 1145 Riev
Rictona 1189 Riev
Rigeton c. 1200 *For*

'Farm by the river Rye' *v.* Rye, R. 5 *supra* and tun.

LUND FOREST

Lund(e) 1176–9 YCh 406 *et passim*
Lond' 1184 P
Loundhouse 1577 Saxton

v. lundr. There is now no wood at Lund, but in 1335 Richard
de Breaus had enclosed his wood at Lund (*ForP* 251 *d*).

Sinnington

1. LITTLE EDSTONE (6″) 90 NE 7

Parva Edestun 1086 DB   *Edenston'* 1167 P

For meaning and further forms *v.* Great Edstone 58 *supra*.

2. MARTON 22 E 11

Martun, Martone 1086 DB
Marton' 1167 P, c. 1200 *For* (*on Syuen*) 1290 Baildon *et
   passim*

v. Marton le Forest 28 *supra*. Marton is on the Seven R.

3. SINNINGTON 22 E 11

Siuenintun, Sevenictun 1086 DB
Siuerinctune 1086 DB
Siuilinton' 1167 P, c. 1200 *For*
Sivilington 1183–93 YCh 595, 1201 ChR
Si-, Syvelington, -thun 1185–1205 YCh 597 *et passim* to
   1327 Banco
Synnyngton 1580 FF   *Sinington* 1665 Visit

This p.n. is probably derived from the name of the river on which it stands, *v*. Seven, R. 6 *supra*. One would have expected ME *Siueningetune*, with inflexional *e*, at least in a few forms, going back to OE *Syfeningatūn*, 'farm of the dwellers on the Seven' (*v*. ing). The forms as they are actually on record point to OE *Syfeningtun*, 'farm having to do with or belonging to the R. Seven.' For this general sense, v. ingtun, and for a similar use of *ing* cf. Tavistock (D), *Tauistoce* (KCD 629), *Tefingstoce* (997 ASC), which is on the Tavy.

4. THORNTON RISEBOROUGH (6″) 90 SE 12

> *Tornitun, Tornentun* 1086 DB
> *Torinton'* 1167 P
> *Torneton sub Riseberg* c. 1200 *For*
> *Torenton* (*voc. Riseberge*) 1310 Ch
> *Thornton under Isbergh* 1406 YI

v. þorn, tun and Riseborough *infra*. It is interesting to compare the form *under Isbergh* with the later forms of Roseberry and Newton under Roseberry 163–4 *infra*.

RISEBOROUGH HILL

> *Ri-, Ryseberg(h)', -berch* c. 1200 *For*, (*in Aselakeby*) 1260 Ch
> *et passim* to 1318 Ch
> *Reysebergh* 1293 QW

Lindkvist (134) on the evidence of the QW spelling derives the first element from ON *hrøysi* 'cairn.' It should, however, be noted that in the other cases of ON *hrøysi* cited by Lindkvist there is not a single instance of ON *hrøysi* appearing as ME *rise*. More probably the name should be connected with Risborough (PNBk 170) and a lost place called *Riseberga* 1158 YCh 419 from OE hris 'brushwood' and beorg.

Middleton

1. AISLABY 22 E 12 [ɛəzləbi]

> *Aslache(s)bi* 1086 DB
> *Aselacbi* c. 1160 Riev
> *Aslakebi, -by* 1167 P *et passim* to 1303 KF

Aselakeby c. 1200 *For*, 1244 Fees, c. 1250–63 *Malton* 3, 1260 Ch
Aslakesby 1253 Pap
Aslacby 1285 KI, 1299 Baildon, 1316 Vill, 1519 FF
Asle-, *Asleyby* 1536 YChant *Aslabye* 1572 FF

'Aslak's farm' *v.* by. The ON pers. name *Aslákr* is found in the similar Norw place-name *Aslaksby* (Rygh, *NG* i. 30, *GP* 17), in Aislaby (Du) and Aslackby (L), *Aselachebi* 1086 DB, locally called [eizəlbi].

2. CAWTHORN 22 D 12

Caltorn(e), *-torna* 1086 DB, c. 1200 *For*
Calthorn(e) 1175 P (p), c. 1190 Guis *et passim* to 1572 FF
Kaldthorn 1202 FF
Cawlthorne 1561 FF *Cawthorne* 1571 FF

'Cold thorn' *v.* cald, þorn. OE *cald* is coupled with a tree-name in Chold Ash (D). Cawthorne (YWR), for which Moorman suggests OE *calu*, is probably identical with this name. OE *calu* 'bare' would however give ME *Caluethorn* from the dat. *calwe*.

3. CROPTON 22 D 12

Croptun(e) 1086 DB, 1167 P
Cropton(a) c. 1200 *For et passim*
Cropetun c. 1260 *Malton* 3
Croppeton 1260 Ch

Cropton is near the summit of a hill, and probably the meaning of the name is 'hill-top farm.' The earliest spellings of the name do not suggest any connexion with Cropthorne (Wo), which contains the OE pers. name **Croppa*, found also· in OE *Croppanhulle* BCS 112 now Crapnell (Ha). We should rather compare it with Crofton in Orpington (K), OE *Croptunes gemæro* KCD iii. 465, which stands on a well-marked hill, and Cropwell (Nt), *Crophille* 1086 DB. *v.* tun.

BECKHOUSE

(le) Bekhus early 13 *Malton* 98, 1260 ib. 3
Self-explanatory.

LEAF HOWE

Lefehowe 1335 *ForP* 224

The name of a tumulus, *v.* **haugr.** The first element is probably a pers. name, such as ODan *Lefi* (Nielsen).

SUTHERLAND and SUTHERLAND BECK

Suterlund 1334 *ForP* 304
Soter-, Souterlund, Suterlundbek 1335 *ForP* 218 *d*, 219 *d*

'Sutari's wood' *v.* **lundr.** The first element is the ON by-name *Sútari* from Latin *sutor* 'shoe-maker'; the word was borrowed in ME from ON (*v.* Stratmann-Bradley s.v. *sūtare*). The change of intervocalic *t* to *th* is seen in other place-names, e.g. Catterick 242 *infra*, and Souther Scales (YWR), *Suterscales* 1214 Abbr, which contains the same element.

4. HARTOFT 22 B 11

Haretoft 1316 Vill, 1335 *ForP* 246, 1349 IpmR
Hartoft 1335 *ForP* 244, 1408 *For*

v. **topt.** For the first element *v.* Harome 70 *supra*. 'Messuage by the stony or rocky place.'

GRUNDSTONE WATH (6″)

Grunstan Wath 1334 *ForP* 304
vadum de Grindstone wath 1619 NRS

'Ford made of ground-stones' *v.* **vað.** The first element is OE *grund-stān*, glossing Latin *cementa*, i.e. *petre* which is well evidenced and survives in NEDial *ground-stone* 'foundation stone.'

HANCOW HO

Anchou 1210 Dugd iv. 317

Possibly 'Haneca's spur of land' *v.* **hoh.** The OE pers. name *Haneca* is not found in independent use in OE, but it is the first element of Hankerton (W), *Hanekyntone* BCS 589, Hannakin (Ekwall, *PNLa* 218), and OE *Hanecanham* BCS 821–2, now Hankham (Sx). One may also note the Anglo-Scand pers. n. *Hanke, Hanc*.

5. MIDDLETON 22 E 13

   Mid(d)eltun(e) 1086 DB

   v. middel, tun. Middleton is the centre of other Anglian farmsteads in the district, such as Edstone, Nunnington, Salton, Sinnington and Wrelton.

6. ROSEDALE 22 A 11 [roːzdil]

   Russedal(e) 1130–c. 1158 (1201) ChR, 1155–70 *Mary Y* 179
   Rossedal(e) 1186–95 YCh 694 *et passim* to 1541 Dugd iii. 570
   Rossdale 1328 Ch
   Rosedale, -dall 1376, 1390 Test, 1408 YI, 1420 Test
   Rosedaile 1561 FF
   Rosdale 1416 YI, 1577 Saxton

   'Russi's valley' from the ON by-name *Russi* (LindBN); most of the dale-names in this part of the Riding have a pers. name as their first element. The long vowel in *Rose-* is quite a late phenomenon and is due to folk-etymology, as in Roseden (PN NbDu s.n.). *v.* dæl.

ALDER CARR (6″)

   Ellerker 1537 Dugd iv. 319
   Self-explanatory.

AYMOT (lost)

   Amoth 1210 Dugd iv. 317

   'River-meet' *v.* a, mot. Cf. Beckermonds (YWR), *Beckermotes* 1241 Percy, and the ONorw *Bekkiarmote* (Lindkvist 6, note 2). The streams referred to are the river Seven and Northdale Beck.

HAMLEY, HAMLEY BECK

   Hamclife 1201 ChR   *Hamcliuebek* 1335 *ForP* 211 d

   Possibly 'scarred cliff' *v.* hamel, clif, bekkr. For the change from *clif* to *-ley* cf. Crunkly 133 *infra*, Cronkley, Aycliffe (PN NbDu s.n.), Hockliffe (PN BedsHu 126).

LOOSE HOWE (tumulus) [luːsou]

   Lushov, -hou c. 1200 Guis, 1223 FF, Guis
   Lowsohowes 15 *Whitby*   *Lowsehowes* 1619 NRS

Cf. OE *lusebyrge* (Herts) BCS 745, *Lusabeorg* BCS 699, and *lusdun* BCS 1020, which all contain OE *lūs* 'louse.' *v.* haugr. 'Louse mound.' One should also note the ON name *Lúsi* (LindBN) from ON *lús.* Perhaps here a pers. name would give the better sense.

MIDDLEHEAD (6″)

Middelheued 1334 *ForP* 304
'Middle hill' *v.* middel, heafod.

WEST GILL (6″)

Westgill 1335 *ForP* 205 *d*
v. west, gil.

WILLIAM HOWES (6″)

Willelmi howes 15 Whitby
v. haugr. Cf. William Beck 70 *supra.*

7. WRELTON 22 E 12

Wereltun 1086 DB
Wrelton 1282 YI, 1285 KI *et passim*
Wherlton 1316 FA
Wrelleton' 1301 LS, 1303 KF, 1416 YI
Wrielton 1526 FF

This is a difficult name but, as Professor Ekwall suggests, the first element may be OE *wearg-hyll*, 'felon-hill,' found in Wreighill (PN NbDu s.n.), pronounced [ri·hil]. The whole name would mean 'farm by or on the gallows-hill.'

Pickering

1. GOATHLAND 16 J 9 [goːədlənd]

Godeland(ia) 1108–14 Whitby, 1109–14 YCh 396, 1201, 1205 ChR, 1240 Lib
Golanda c. 1170–88 YCh 393
Gotheland(e) c. 1180 *Add* 4715 *f* 98 *et freq* to 1408 *For*
Gothe-, Goþelaund' 1297 YI, 1301 LS
Goodland 1497 NRS
Gotland 1576 FF
Goteland 1577 NRS, 1612 NR
Goutland 1613 NR

'Goda's land' *v.* land. The OE pers. name *Gōda* here appears to have undergone a Scandinavian sound-change from *d* to *ð* (*v.* IPN 65). For the form *Golanda v.* IPN 110.

ALLAN TOPS (6")

Aleinetoften 1204 ChR; *-toftes* 1286 *ForP* 194
Al(l)antoftes 1408 *For*, 1619 NRS

'Allen's enclosures' *v.* topt. The name *Allen*, earlier *Alain*, was brought into England by the Normans; its origin is OFr *Alain*. It enters also into Alain Seat (near Barnoldswick, YWR), *Alainesete* 13 Kirkst. Allan Tops is the name of a hill on the top of which are a number of ancient enclosures. The alteration of *toft* to *top* is due to the fact that these enclosures are on the top of the hill.

BLAWATH BECK (6")

Blawath 1334 *ForP* 304   *Blawoth* 1619 NRS
'Dark or black ford' *v.* blar, vað, bekkr.

BRAITHWAITE

Braghtwaht 1335 *ForP* 223 *d*
'Broad enclosure' *v.* breiðr, þveit.

BROCKA BECK

Brocholebec(h) 1109–14 YCh 865
'Badger hole stream' *v.* brocc-hol, bekkr.

ELLER BECK

Helrebec 1201 ChR
Ellerbe(c)k 1335 *ForP* 204 *d*, 205, 217 *d*, 1619 NRS

'Alder stream' *v.* elri, bekkr. The initial *h-* of the first spelling is inorganic.

HAWTHORN HILL

Howghton Hill 1619 NRS

v. hyll. Hawthorn is a corruption of the common *Hutton* or *Hoton* 'farm on the hoh or hill.'

HUNT HOUSE

Huntereshuses 1252 YI

v. hus. The first element is ME *huntere*, 'hunter.'

RUDMOOR

Rotemur 1334 *ForP* 304   *Rotymyr* 1335 *ForP* 223

From ON *rotinn* 'rotten, putrid,' and myrr, later replaced by mor. ON *mýrr* would normally become [mɔr] in the dialect.

SIL HOWE

Si-, Sylehou 1108–14, a. 1133, 1154–89, 1199 Whitby, 1204 ChR, 1314 NRS

Silhou 1308 Whitby   *Sill howes* 1619 NRS

OE *syle* 'miry place' would hardly suit topographically. We should rather connect the first element with ODan *Sile* (Nielsen) and OSwed *Sil* (Lundgren-Brate). 'Sile's mound' v. haugr.

SIMON HOWE (6")

Simondeshou 1335 *ForP* 206

'Sigemund's mound' v. haugr.

WAITS HOUSE (6")

dom' le Weyte 1296 YI   *Whaytes* 1322 NRS

The name probably means 'watch house' from NFr **wait* 'watch'; cf. NE *wait* used in the sense of 'watch' and Waytail Gate 142 *infra.* v. hus. The form *dom'* = Lat. *domus.*

2. KINGTHORPE 22 E 14

Chinetorp 1086 DB

Ki-, Kynthorp(e) 1139 *RegAlb* ii. 11 *d*, 1198 Fees *et passim* to 1577 Saxton

Ki-, Kyntorp 1176 P (p), c. 1200 *For*, early 13 *Malton* 96 *d*, 1226–8 Fees

Kynestorp 1205 ChR

Kynethorpe 1322 NRS

'Cyna's village' from the OE pers. name *Cyna* (Redin 47), or 'royal village' from OE *cyne* 'royal.' The change from *Kin-* to *King-* is due to folk-etymology and parallels are found in Kingthorpe (L) DB *Chinetorp* and Kingsbury (Wa) DB *Chinesburie*, 1322 BM *Kinesbury.* v. þorp.

6-2

3. MARISHES 22 G 14

Marishes parish includes a great part of the very low-lying land in the south of the wapentake and takes its name from the extensive marshes which it embraced till the land was drained. *v.* mersc. These probably included *Aschilesmares, Aschelesmere* 1086 DB (from ON *Áskell*), *Chiluesmares, Chiluesmarsc* 1086 DB, *Kilverdesmersh* 1152–6 Riev, *Culverthesmersch* 1160 Riev (cf. Killerby 103 *infra*), *Maxudesmares, Maxudesmersc* 1086 DB (first elements possibly being, as suggested by Dr Lindkvist, the ON pers. n. *Mákr* (LindN) and wudu), *Odulfesmare, Ouduluesmersc* (from ON *Auðulfr*) and *Theokemarais* 1189 Riev, 1252 Ch, *-mar* 1201 ChR, in which the first element is perhaps an unrecorded ON by-name *þjokka* (gen. *þjokku*) 'thick'; *v.* LindBN s.n. *þjokkubeinn* 'thick leg.' The suffix in some of these forms has been influenced by OFr *marais*.

BELLYFAX GRANGE

Bellyfaxe (pasturis) 1538 Riev

This name is of peculiar interest as apparently it contains the same final element as Halifax (YWR). This, as Mr Goodall (*PN SWY* s.n.) suggests, is OE *feax* 'hair,' used of '(a place covered with) shrubs and rough grass,' a meaning paralleled by Norw dialect *faks* 'coarse-grass' and South German *fachs* 'poor mountain grass.' This is probably the meaning also in OE *to feaxum* (BCS 880). The material is insufficient to allow of any explanation of the first element.

KEKMARISH (lost)

Kekemar(r)ays 1206, 1241 Riev, 1301 LS
Kekmar(r)eys 1335 ForP 216, 260, 1369 Riev
Kekmaresse 1538 Riev

'Kekkja's marsh' *v.* mersc. The first element is probably the ON by-name *Kekkja* (LindBN).

4. NEWTON 22 C 13

Neuton, Newetone, Newetun(e) 1086 DB, 1242 P
'New farm' *v.* niwe, tun.

HOWLGATE (6")
Holgate 1335 *ForP* 235
'Road through the hollow' *v.* hol, gata.

NEWTON BECK and NEWTONDALE
Neutonebekke 1240 Riev, *Neuton(e)dale* 1322 NRS

RUDDINGS (6")
le Ridding 1262 *Malton* 4 *d*
'The clearing' *v.* hryding. Cf. Ruswarp 125 *infra.*

SCARF HILL
Scarthougill 1335 *ForP* 205 *d*
'Ravine near the mound in the mountain pass' *v.* skarð,
haugr, gil. For the *f* cf. Earswick 12 *supra.*

5. PICKERING 22 E 13
Pichering(a) 1086 DB, 1165 P (p), 1173–88 Riev
Pic(h)rinch 1109–14 YCh 397
Pikeringes 1109–14 *RegAlb* ii. 12, 1120–5 ib. ii. 10 *d*, 1138
    ib. ii. 11 *d*, 1234 Cl; *Pykerynges* 13 *Leon* 10 *d*
Picaringes 1119–35 *RegAlb* ii. 5 *d*
Pikering(a-m, -e) 1157 YCh 401, 1157–89 ib. 408, 1160 Riev
    et passim
Pekeryng 1579 FF
'The settlement of Picer and his dependants' from OE
Piceringas. The base of the place-name is an OE pers. name
Picer, not adduced in independent use in OE. It is found also
as the first element of Pixham (PN Wo 225). *v.* ing. In the
name Pickering there is some evidence for the survival in ME
of the OE plur. *-ingas.*

BIRDGATE (6") [bɔrgət]
Burghgate 1408 *For*
'Road to the stronghold' (i.e. Pickering Castle). *v.* burh, gata.

BLANSBY
Blandebi, -by 1086 DB *et passim* to 1335 *ForP* 219
Blaundeby, -bi 1251 NRS, 1297 YI
Blandesby 1408 *For* Blansby 1577 Saxton

'Blanda's farm' v. by. The ON by-name *Blanda* (gen. *Blǫndu*) is adduced by Lind(BN) and means 'one who mixes his drinks.' For *Blaundebi* cf. Spaunton 61 *supra*. For Blansby cf. Baldersby 182 *infra*.

BROATES

Brootes, Brottes 1538 Riev

The name occurs elsewhere in the North Riding, in Broats in Dalton 183 *infra* and as a field-name, and it is the same as the Norw p.n. *Braaten* (Rygh, *NG Indledning* 45 and *NG passim* and particularly i. 17, ii. 116) which is derived from ON *broti* 'a heap of trees felled in a wood' and so 'a clearing in a wood.' Cf. *Fenbrotes, Lang(e)brotes, Morbrotes, Smalbrotes, Dunlanga-brotes* as 13th cent. field-names.

EDYMARSH (lost)

Eduiemersh, -mersc c. 1160, 1189 Riev
Ediue-, Edyuemersc(h) 1238 *Malton* 38
Edeuemerske 1333 Riev   *Edymarsh* 1619 NRS

'Edive's marsh' from the OE woman's name *Ēadgifu* and mersc.

FARWATH

Ferwath 1334 *ForP* 304   *farr-, farewath(e)* 1619 NRS

Possibly 'distant ford' from OE *feor* 'far' and vaδ. Professor Ekwall would take the first element to be ON *færr*, 'easily passable.'

FRIAR'S DITCH

Freredik 1334 *ForP* 304   *Freeredike* 1619 NRS

ME *frere* 'friar' and dic.

GREENGATE

Grenegate 1335 *ForP* 212

'Green road' v. grene, gata.

GUNDALE

Gundale 1335 *ForP* 206 d, 1619 NRS   *Gonddale* 1503 NRS

'Gunni's valley' v. dæl. ON *Gunni* is found also in Gunby (YER), *Gunnebi* DB.

KILLING NAB SCAR (6″)

Killyngnebbesker 1335 *ForP* 213 *d*

On the first element *v.* Lindkvist 201, note 5. The probability is that *Killing* is a pers. name derived from ON *Kyle* (LindBN). *Nab* is ME *nebbe, nab* 'projecting point of a hill' (ultimately from OE *nebb* 'beak'). The final element is ON *sker* 'rock.'

LITTLE DALE

Liteldale c. 1180–1212 YCh 394

Self-explanatory.

MIDSYKE DRAIN

Midsic(h), -syk c. 1160, 1189 Riev

'Middle stream' from OE *midd* and sic.

PICKERING BECK

aqua de Pykeringe c. 1180–1212 YCh 394, etc.

v. bekkr.

PICKERING VALE

valle de Pykerynge 1248 Whitby

Vale is from OFr *val* 'valley' (cf. Rievaulx *supra*).

POTTERHILL (6″)

Potterhill 1408 *For*

OE *potere* 'potter' and hyll.

RAWCLIFF

Rouclif, -clyff 1334 *ForP* 304, 1408 *For*
Rocliffe 1619 NRS

This is probably the same as Rawcliffe (Bulm) 15 *supra*.

SAINTOFT

Centoftdikes 1335 *ForP* 213 *d*, (-*heued*) ib. 235
Sentoftheued 1335 *ForP* 254

Probably 'clearing caused by burning' *v.* topt. The first element is identical with that of Sundridge (K), OE *sænget hryg* BCS 506, Syntley (PN Wo 36) and St Chloe (Gl), being a noun-derivative of OE *sengan* 'to burn.'

WARDLE RIGG [wɔːdəlrig]

   Waldalerigg 1252 YI

Possibly 'ridge above the valley of the Welshmen' v. w(e)ala, dæl, hrycg.

WATERPOOL (6")

   Wadelespole 1335 *ForP* 211 d

'Wædel's pool' v. pol. This contains an OE pers. name *Wædel* recorded in the form *Wadell* as the holder (TRE) of *Wadelscota*, now Waddlestone (D) in Lew Trenchard. It is found also in Woodluston (Sa), *Wadelestun* DB, and in a weak form in Wattlehurst (Sr), earlier *Wadelehurst*. The modern spelling is due to folk-etymology.

YATTS (6")

   Yates 1335 *ForP* 237 d   *Yattes* 1497 NRS
   v. geat.

Thornton Dale

1. THORNTON DALE 22 E 14

   Torentun(e), Torentona 1086 DB
   Thornetun, -ton 1157–8 YCh 402, (*in vallem de Pykerynge*)
      1248 Whitby *et passim*

With the same run of forms and meaning as Thornton Bridge 24 *supra*. The suffix *Dale* refers to the valley in which the village stands.

DALBY and DALBY BECK

   Dalbi, -by 1086 DB, 1408 *For*, (*rivulum de*) 1619 NRS
   Daleby 1251 NRS, 1279 YI
   Dawby 1500 NRS
   'Valley farm' v. dæl, by and Dalby (Bulm) 29 *supra*.

ELLERBURN

   Elreburne 1086 DB, 1225 Ebor
   Elrebrune 1086 DB
   Elraburna 1145–53 *Leon* 35
   Alrebrune 1155–67 YCh 380, Hy 2 *Leon* 4 d
   Ellebrone c. 1200 *For*; *-burn(e)* 1227 Pat, 1231 Ebor
   Ellerburn(e) 1252 Ebor, 1275 YI *et passim*

'Alder stream' *v.* elri, burna. There is indecision in the early forms between OE *alor* and ON *elrir* and between OE *burna* and ON *brunnr*. All these forms have their parallels in Y. In the light of the early forms quoted this place cannot be identical with OE *æt Helaþyrnum* (ASC 778 E). Cf. *Brandl Festschrift* i. 48 on this identification.

Elliker (6")

Helaghker 1335 *ForP* 208
'Marsh near the high forest-clearing' *v.* kjarr and cf. Healey 232 *infra*.

Farmanby

Farmanesbi 1086 DB
Farmanebi, -by 1155–65 Whitby, 1210 Dugd iv. 318
Farmanby Hy 2 *Leon* 4 *d*, 1155–67 YCh 380 *et passim*
Feremannebi 1170 P
Farmanneby 1225 Ebor, 1242 P, 1280 *Ass*
Faremanby 1231 Ebor
'Farman's farm' *v.* by. The ON pers. name *Farmann*, ODan *Farman* appears in OE as *Færeman*, the name of the priest who glossed the Rushforth Gospel of St John, and in ME as *Fareman* (12 *Easby* 13).

Flax Dale

Flaxdale 1334 *ForP* 252 *d*   *Flaxedale* 1619 NRS
'Flak's valley' or 'valley where flax is grown' *v.* fleax, dæl. On the first element *v.* Flaxton 37 *supra*.

Heck Dale

Ekkedale 1335 *ForP* 252 *d*
v. dæl. The first element is probably ME *hekk. v.* hæcc.

Kettlethorpe (lost)

Chetelestorp 1086 DB, c. 1250 *Malton* 118
'Ketill's village' *v.* þorp. A common Scand pers. name.

Lidyyate Way (6")

Lydeyate 1335 *ForP* 222 *d*   *Lidgate* 1619 NRS
v. hlid-geat.

NEWSTEAD

> *Neustede* 1335 *ForP* 260
> *Newstede in lez Marres* 1534 Riev

'New place' *v.* niwe, stede. Newstead is in Pickering Marishes. *Marres* is from Fr *marais* 'marsh.'

ROXBY [rɔuzbi]

> *Rozebi, Rosebi* 1086 DB
> *Roucesby* 1250 Fees (p), 1301 LS, 1335 *ForP* 207, 253 *d*, 1408 *For*
> *Roxbie* 1577 Saxton

'Rauth's farm' from the ON pers. name *Rauðr* (LindN) and **by.** Cf. Roxby (LangE) 139 *infra.* The spelling *Rox-* is due partly to influence of genuine Roxbys (from ON *Hrókr*) and partly to an inverted spelling arising from the change of ME *x* to *z*, which has confused the spelling of *z* from other sources in the dialect, cf. Moxby 29 *supra* and Coxwold 191 *infra.*

SELLEY BRIDGE

> *Selibrigg* 1301 LS   *Selybrygge* 1349 NRS

'Bridge by the willows' *v.* brycg. The first element is ON *selja* 'willow.' A field in this district was called *Seliflat* in 1201 ChR.

THORNTON BECK

> *Thorntonebech* 1167–79 Riev, etc.

2. WILTON 23 F 1

> *Wiltun(e)* 1086 DB, 1247 Dugd iv. 276, 1247 Ch
> *Wi-, Wylton(am)* 1167 P, 1180 YCh 610 *et passim*
> *Willeton* 1301 LS

There is another Wilton in LangW 159 *infra*, which is found in DB as *Wiltuna* and *Widtuna*. Bishop's Wilton in YER also has a form *Widtone* in DB. These forms suggest that the true form of the name at the time of DB was *Wildetuna*, in which presumably the first element is the common adj. *wild*, referring to the original state of the site. Cf. Wildon (193 *infra*) and the use of Wildbrook (twice in Sussex) to describe marshy uncultivated land, a name going back to medieval times.

Lockton

1. LOCKTON 22 C 14

Lochetun 1086 DB
Loketon 1167 P *et passim* to 1303 KF
Lokeintun 1170–88 YCh 398
Lokin-, Lokynton(e) 1198, 1250 Fees, 1322 NRS
Loquinton 1226–8 Fees
Locatun c. 1250 *Malton* 118
Lok-, Locton(e) 1285 KI *et passim* to 1577 FF

'Loca's farm' *v.* ingtun. The name *Loca* is a weak form of
the OE pers. name *Loc* adduced by Ekwall (*PN in -ing* 70).
Derivation from a pers. name explains the forms *Lokinton* (from
an OE by-form *Locingtun*, by the side of *Locantun*). Cf. also
Lockington (YER), *Lochetun* DB, *Lokyngton* 1285 KI, 1316 Vill.

CROSSDALE

Crossedale 1335 ForP 216, 253
Self-explanatory. *v.* cros, dæl.

HORCUM, HOLE OF HORCUM [ɔːkəm]

Hotcumbe c. 1250 NRS
Holcumbe 1322 NRS
Horcumbe, Horcombe 1326, 1619 NRS
Horkome 1500 NRS

The first two spellings are probably erratic; the first is not
supported by the later forms and the second would have become modern [ɔukəm]. The first element is probably identical
with that of Urra 70 *supra. v.* horh, cumb. Horcum is at the
head of a very deep valley.

SALTERGATE

Saltergate 1335 ForP 211, 214, 1619 NRS
v. gata. The road referred to is that over the moors from
Pickering to Whitby. The first element is OE *saltere* 'a salter'
which occurs in other place-names. Cf. the full account of
these names in PNWo 4 ff. Note also Saltergate near Harrogate
(YWR) and Salterhebble near Halifax (cf. RNY s.n. Hebble).

Mr W. B. Crump suggests to me that many of the *Salter*-names in YWR and La probably indicate roads along which salt was carried from the Cheshire mines. In the North Riding the name is possibly connected with the salt (or alum) mined in the Cleveland district (cf. Saltburn, etc. 143 *infra*).

STAINDALE

Staindal 1185–95 YCh 392

'Rocky valley' *v.* steinn, dæl.

THACK SIKE (6″)

Taksyk 1335 *ForP* 204 *d*   *Thaksyk* 1335 *ForP* 205

v. sic. The first element is ON *þakk* 'thatch' (cf. Thackthwaite Beck 266 *infra*). 'Stream by which thatching material grew.'

Levisham

1. LEVISHAM 22 C 14 [liusəm, levisəm]

Leuecen, Lewecen 1086 DB

Leuezham 13 *Malton* 116 *d*, c. 1230 ib. 117, 1226–1257 Ch, c. 1250 NRS

Leuezam, Leuesam 1231 *Malton* 29 *d*

Leu-, Levesham 1242 P *et passim* to 1619 NRS

Leuescem 1250 *Malton* 118

Leueshaim c. 1250 *Malton* 118

Levest-, Leveszham 1252 YI

Levisham 1289 Ebor, 1297 YI

Levesam 1301 LS

Leveysham, Lewsam 1577 FF

Leas(h)am 1577 Saxton, 1610 Speed

The DB spellings and others with *z*, *sc*, *st*, and *sz* show that the name is of the same origin as Ledsham (Ch), *Leuetesham* DB, 'Lēofgēat's homestead' *v.* ham. The spelling *Leueshaim* has been influenced by ON heimr.

HAWDALE (6″)

Haghdale 1335 *ForP* 223 *d*

'Enclosure-valley' *v.* haga, dæl.

NESS HEAD (6")

Undernesheued 1335 *ForP* 223 *d*

'Under the promontory head' *v.* næs, heafod.

RHUMBARD SNOUT (6")

Rumboldlyngeweit 1335 *ForP* 255

The þveit must have been near the snout. The first element is a pers. name *Rumbeald* and the second is lyng.

YORFALLS

Yorcfal 1335 *ForP* 255

Yorfalls was an enclosure in the Forest of Pickering. The second element is ON fall, 'place where trees have been felled.' The first is possibly adopted from the city of York or, as Dr Lindkvist suggests, may be the ON pers. name *Jórekr*.

Allerston

1. ALLERSTON 23 F 2 [ɔləstən]

Alurestan, -stain, Aluristan 1086 DB

Alvestain, -stein 1154–74 YCh 387, 1160 Riev, 1167 P, 1227 FF, 1233 Cl

Al(l)verstain, -stayn, -steyn, -stein 1086 DB, c. 1190–1214 YCh 389, *et freq* to 1335 *ForP* 252

Alverstan(e) 1219 Ass, *et freq* to 1335 *ForP* 214 *d*

Auverstan 1259 Ass   *Alvestane* 1322 NRS

Some of the early spellings have *tun* in the second element:

Aluestune 1086 DB   *Alveston, -tun* 1160 Riev, 1218 FF

Later forms include:

Allerstane 1285 KI, 1408 *For*

Alistan 1316 Vill   *Allestan* 1329 Ch

Allerston, Allarston 1518 FF, 1577 NRS, 1665 Visit

Ollerston 1577 Saxton

The original form of the name seems to have been OE *Ælfheresstān* 'Ælfhere's stone' *v.* stan. Forms like *Alve-* (with loss of *-r-*) may represent a pet form *Ælf* or a substitution of ON *Alfr* (LindN).

The second element fluctuates between OE stan and ON steinn. OE tun in the second element appears to be of early origin. The best explanation of this is to suppose that at an early date a farmstead was built in the neighbourhood of the *stan* and Ælfhere's name was applied to it also. *v.* tun.

ALLERSTON BECK

Alvestain(e)bec 1189 Riev   *Aluerstanbek* 1335 *ForP* 260, etc.

BLAKEY MOOR, BLAKEY TOPPING

Blakehou 1223 FF   *Blakhouloundes* 1335 *ForP* 210 d
Blakay more 1577 Saxton
'Black mound' *v.* blæc, haugr, lundr.

CRAKETHORN (6")

Crakethorn 1218 FF
'Crow thorn' *v.* kraki, þorn and cf. *Crakethirn* 13 Percy in Rainton.

CROSS CLIFF

Crosseclif, -clyff 1335 *ForP* 205, 217 d
v. cros, clif. The reference may be to some cross used as a boundary mark.

DERWENT HEAD (6")

Derewentspring(es) 1201 ChR, 1335 *ForP* 213
'The source(s) of the river Derwent' *v.* spring.

GIVENDALE [giːndil]

Gindala 1160 YCh 386, c. 1160 Riev
Geveldale 1227 FF, 1301 LS (p)
Geuendale 1231 FF
Gyvendale 1323 NRS
Gyndale 1500, 1619 NRS
Geyndell al. Gyuendale 1536 FF

This name possibly derives from a lost river *Gifle* found in Ivel (PN BedsHu 8), with Northern velar *g*. Cf. Zachrisson in NoB xiv. 52 f. on Givendale (YER). If so, we must explain the numerous *n*-forms as due to common AN confusion of *n* and *l* (cf. IPN 108).

LOFT MARISHES

Loctemares, -mersc 1086 DB
Loftmarays 1241 *RegAlb* ii. 13   *Loftmarreys* 1335 *ForP* 260
Loftemarrays 1301 LS

'Marsh near the loft' *v.* lopt, mersc. The DB *Locte-* probably indicates that the bilabial quality of ON *p* (= *f*) was preserved to a certain extent in the Anglo-Scand dialect of Y.

MAY MOSS

Mawemose 1335 *ForP* 205 *d*

v. mos 'a peat bog.' The first element is perhaps the ON by-name *Magi* (LindBN), which appears in ME as *Mawe* c. 1100 (Danelaw Ch 37) and *Maue* c. 1245 (Selby Cart. i. 374).

MOOR HOWE (6")

Morhou 1154-74 YCh 387

v. mor, haugr

WATER FLASH

Flaskes 1335 *ForP* 204 *d*
'Water pools' *v.* flasshe.

YARNA BECK (6")

Yarnolfbek 1324 NRS, 1335 *ForP* 216 *d*
Yorney beck 1619 NRS
'Yarnolf's stream' from ON *Járnólfr* (LindN) and bekkr.

Ebberston

1. EBBERSTON 23 F 2

Edbriztun(e) 1086 DB
E-, Ædbri(c)hteston 1163, 1167 P (p), 1167, 1187 P
Edbriston 1185-95 YCh 390, 1219 *Malton* 130 *d*, 1301 LS
Edbreston 1254 *RegAlb* ii. 17, 1259 Ass
Ebreston(a) 1114-9 YCh 371, *et freq* to 1359 FF
Ebriston(e) 1202 FF, 1322 NRS
Eberston 1316 Vill, 1408 *For*

'Eadbriht's farm' from OE *Éadbriht* and tun.

BICKLEY

Biggelea 1185 P
Bickele 1326 NRS
Bikle 1335 *ForP* 252   *Byklay* 1408 *For*   *Byckley* 1566 FF

'Bica's forest clearing' *v.* leah. The first element is the OE
Bica (Redin 85). For -*gg*- cf. Wigginton 14 *supra*.

DEEP DALE

Depedale 1335 *ForP* 215 *d*
Self-explanatory.

LITTLE MARISH (6″)

Littlemersk 1247 Dugd iv. 276
v. lytel, mersc.

STOCKLAND

Sto(c)k(e)lund 1335 *ForP* 219 *d*, 257 *d*
'Wood from which trees have been cut (leaving only the
stocks)' *v.* stocc, lundr

WELLDALE BECK, HO

Queldale 1322 NRS   *Weledale* 1335 *ForP* 291

v. hweol, dæl. The sense in which OE *hweol* is here used is
not clear. In Wheeldale 131 *infra* it certainly refers to the
circular course which the valley takes. There are in this neighbourhood a number of dikes and the meaning of *hweol* may be
'circular dike' (cf. Ekwall, *PN La* 132, s.n. Wheelton).

Brompton

1. BROMPTON   23 F 4 [brumptən, brɔmptən]

Bruntun(e) 1086 DB, c. 1170 Riev
Brunton 1086 DB, *et freq* to 1665 Visit
Birunton' 1167 P
Brumton' 1219 *Ass*, 1245 *Malton* 41 *d*, 1301 YI
Brumpton(e) 1253 Ch, *et freq* to 1399 YI
Brompton(e) 1285 KI *et passim*

The name Brompton occurs elsewhere in the Riding and in YER as Potter Brompton, *Bruneton* DB, *(Potter)-brumton* 1285 KI, 1306 Bridl. Most of the early spellings have *Brun-* and to explain this we must suppose either that the ME nasal sign ' or ¯ should be interpreted as *m* and not *n* (as is usually done) or that *n* later became *m*, a change which is unlikely before *t*. The reverse process is more probably correct and if we take the first element as being originally *Brum-* we can explain the *n* forms as due to the influence of the following *t*. A similar change of *m* to *n* at an early date is found in Bromley (K), OE *Bromleag* BCS 506, *Brunlei* in DB, and Bromley (St), OE *Bromleage*, c. 1096 FW, but *Brunlege* DB.

The origin and meaning of the first element are open to speculation, but the most likely explanation is the OE word brom 'broom,' which enters with certainty into many English place-names, such as the two Bromleys already noticed, Brumdon (Do), *Bromdun* KCD 1322, Broomhope, Broomley (PN NbDu s.n.), etc. The word seems to have become *brum* at an early date, as shown by the spellings of Broomley (Nb, *Brumleg* 1255) and the two Bromleys. If this is correct Brompton means 'enclosed piece of land overgrown with gorse' *v.* brom, tun and cf. Brampton 180 *infra*.

ROW HOWES

Ruchou c. 1242 *Malton* 141
'The rough mound' *v.* ruh, haugr.

SAWDON [sɔːdən]

Salden(e) early 13 *Malton* 138 *d, et passim* to 1562 FF
Sawden 1569 FF
Sawdon 1570, 1578 FF   *Saudon* 1577 Saxton
'Willow valley' *v.* s(e)alh, denu.

2. SNAINTON 23 F 3 [snɛəntən]

Snechintun(e), *-ton(e)* 1086 DB, *Snechint'* 1166 P (p)
Sneing-, *Sneyngton* 13 Percy, 1237 *Malton* 41
Snain-, *Snaynton* 13 *Malton* 137, 1204 Ass *et passim*
Sneynton 1304 BM, 1335 ForP 252
Snenton 1577 Saxton
No satisfactory solution of this name can be offered.

DARNCOMBE

Dernecombe 1335 *ForP* 252

'Hidden valley' *v.* d(i)erne, cumb. This is quite apt.

FOULBRIDGE [foubrig]

Fuchebruge 1178 P   *Fuchkebrige* 1179 P
Fulkebrig(g)e 1182, 1184 P
Fukbrigg 1285 KI, 1325 Ipm   *Foukebrigge* 1301 Ebor
Foulbridg 1577 Saxton

v. brycg. The local pronunciation of the name presupposes an original *-ul-* in the first element (*v.* Introduction xxxii), which is probably the pers. name *Fulk*. This is OEScand *Fulke* (Lundgren-Brate), cognate with OWScand *Folki* (LindN). If the original form were ON *Folki* it has been influenced by the Norman name *Fulk* (1124 ASC), which was a loan from OHG *Fulco*. The name enters also into Folkton (YER), *Fulcheton* DB, and *Fulkeholm* 1208 ChR, in Thornton le Beans.

WYDALE [widil]

Wyddale c. 1242 *Malton* 141

'Wood-valley' *v.* viðr, dalr, and cf. Widdale 267 *infra*.

3. TROUTS DALE 23 D 3 [truːtsdil]

Truzstal 1086 DB
Trucedal(e) 1314 Percy, 1335 *ForP* 206 *d*, 1619 NRS
Trowt(t)esdale, Troutesdale 1497 NRS, 1562 FF, 1619 NRS, 1665 Visit

'Trut's valley' *v.* dæl. It is reasonable to suppose that *Trut* is from the ON by-name *Trútr*, gen. *Trúts* (LindBN). The early spellings with *z*, *c* represent the ON gen. form *-s* (*v.* Haxby 14 *supra*).

BACKLEYS (6″)

Baklaus 1335 *ForP* 252

The forms are too few for any satisfactory explanation.

WILLIAM'S CROSS (6″)

crucem Willelmi 1335 *ForP* 207 *d*

v. cros and William Howes 81 *supra*.

Wykeham

1. WYKEHAM   23 E 4 [wɑikəm]

Wicam 1086 DB
Wic-, Wi-, Wykham 1086 DB, c. 1125–35 YCh 762 *et passim*
    to 1408 *For*
Wicheham c. 1180 Whitby   *Wi-, Wyckham* 1201 Dugd v.
    670, 1286 Ebor, 1301 LS, 1665 Visit
Wykkam 1244 Fees, *Wickeham* 1295 YD
Wykeham 1285 KI, 1375 FF
Wyc-, Wykam 1328 Banco, 1423 Test

v. wicham. The significance of the first element here is not clear.

BARLEY (6″)

Berlagh 1335 *ForP* 209 *d*, 210, 210 *d*

'Forest clearing used for growing barley' *v.* bere, leah.

BEEDALE [biədil]

Boddale c. 1153 Dugd v. 670   *Bodale* 1259 Ass
Budells 1619 NRS

The phonetic history of the name is parallel to that of Beadlam 67 *supra*, and the original vowel must have been ō. The first element is perhaps ODan boð. Hence, 'booth-valley.'

HIPPERLEY

Hepperle', Hiperle 1335 *ForP* 210, 210 *d*

The first element of this name is undoubtedly identical with the p.n. Hipperholme (YWR), *Hy-, Hiperum* DB, 1266 YI, 1286 WCR. There is a dialect word *hipper* 'osiers used in basket making' adduced from La, but its origin is obscure. *v.* leah.

LANGDALE

Lang(e)dale 1335 *ForP* 207

'Long valley' *v.* lang, dæl.

THE PARK

>*Ludeparc* c. 1190–9 YCh 381

'Luda's park' *v.* p(e)arroc. Cf. the pers. name *Luda* (Redin 67).

RUSTON

>*Rostun(e)* 1086 DB, 1208 Ass (p)
>*Ruston* 1167 P, 1393, 1450 Test
>*Roston(a)* c. 1190–9 YCh 381, 1226–8 Fees *et passim* to 1408 *For*
>*Royston* 1287 Ipm

Professor Ekwall suggests that this name contains OE *hrōst*, 'roof-beam,' but the sense of the compound is obscure. *v.* tun.

HIGH (LOW) WOOF HOWE (tumuli)

>*Woulfhow* 13 Whitby   *Wolfhow* 1446 Whitby
>*Wulhow, North-, Southewulfehow* 1619 NRS

'Wolf-mound' *v.* wulf, haugr.

Hutton Buscel

1. WEST AYTON 23 E 5 [jætən]

>*Atun(e)* 1086 DB
>*Aton(e, -a)* 1200–10 Whitby *et passim* to 1385 YD
>*Vestheton* 1393 Test
>*Ayton* 1555 BM, 1562 FF

'River-farm' *v.* a, tun, and cf. Norw *Aaby* (Rygh, *NG* ii. 158). West Ayton, like East Ayton 101 *infra*, is on the river Derwent: *Aton' ex parte occident. aque* (1408 *For*).

PRESTON ING (6")

>*Preste-enge* 1323 Whitby

v. preost, eng. The land here was in the possession of Whitby Abbey. The modern form arises from association with the neighbouring Preston Hill 101 *infra*.

YEDMANDALE [jedməndil]

>*Yedmundale* 1335 *ForP* 209 *d*

v. dæl. The first element is the OE pers. name *Ēadmund*. On the *y*- form *v.* Yearsley 193 *infra*.

2. HUTTON BUSHELL (BUSCEL) 23 E 5

Hotun(e) 1086 DB, and with the same run of forms as for
Sheriff Hutton 31 *supra*. The suffix appears as
Bussalle 1280 Ebor, *Bussel(l)* 1282 Ebor, *Buscel(l)* 1284 YI,
Bus(s)hell 1493 Test

v. hoh, tun. It was held in the 12th and 13th cents. by the
family of Bushell (*v.* YCh 371, Whitby *passim*).

PRESTON HILL (6")

Presteton, Prestetune 1086 DB   *Preston* 1259 Ass *et passim*
'Priests' farm' *v.* preost, tun.

WEST CROFT (6")

Westcroft 1135–55 YCh 373
Self-explanatory.

Seamer

1. EAST AYTON 23 E 5

Atun(e) 1086 DB
Forms as for West Ayton 100 *supra*.

HILL GRIPS (6")

Ildegrip 1086 DB
Hildegrip(e) 1086 DB, 1303 Percy
Hildegrippe c. 1260–70 *Bodl* 123.

The DB names have usually been identified with Hilla Green
in Hackness but the other references here given and the
fact that in DB *Hildegrip* is mentioned between *Iretune* (Irton
infra) and *Atune* (East Ayton) seem to show that the place
referred to was in East Ayton. Hill Grips is, therefore, more
likely.

The first element is OE *Hild* (f). The second element is
probably connected with ME *grip* 'furrow, ditch,' cf. OE *grype*
and MDu *grippe*.

2. IRTON 23 E 6 [ɔrtən]

Iretun(e) 1086 DB, 1170 P
I-,Yrton(a) c. 1223 Whitby *et passim*
Hi-, Hyrton(a) c. 1223 Whitby, 1244 Percy, 1301 LS
Urton 1572 FF

'The Irishman's or Irishmen's farm' *v*. tun. The first element is the ON *Íri*, gen. sg. or pl. *Ira*, used of a Scandinavian who had been in Ireland. *v*. Introduction xxvii.

3. SEAMER 23 E 6

> *Semær* 1086 DB
> *Semer(e)* 1086 DB *et passim* to 1534 *Bodl* i. 84
> *Samare, -mara* 1090–6 YCh 855, 13 Percy, c. 1200 Whitby, 1224 Pat
> *Semar(e, -a)* 1155–65 Whitby, c. 1160 *BylE* 22 *d et passim* to 1529 NCyWills

Cf. Seamer (LangW) 172 *infra*, and Semer (Sf), Semere (Nf), always with *mere*. The first element is OE *sæ* 'sea, lake.' The second is OE mere 'pool.' The significance of the name is not clear; in fact there is some doubt as to the meaning of the individual elements and apparently there is some confusion between OE *mere* 'pool' and ON *marr*. But it seems possible that, as Gothic *saiw-s* meant 'marsh' (besides 'sea') and the cognate OHG *gi-sig* meant 'ponds, marshes,' the OE word *sæ* could also mean 'marsh' in addition to 'sea, lake.' What makes it likely that the element is OE *mere* is the fact that a piece of land SW of the village is called *The Mere* and judging from the number of drains running in various directions across it it has every appearance of having formerly been a pool. If we start with ON *marr* as the original form it is hardly possible to explain the *-mere* forms which appear in the 13th cent. Whereas if we start with *mere*, the earlier *-mær, -mar* forms can be explained as due to an ONb by-form *mær* (*v*. EPN s.v. mere). 'Marshy pool,' probably indicating 'a partially drained pool.'

CRUMBCARR (6″)

> *Crumbker* 1337 Percy
> 'Crooked marsh' *v*. crumb, kjarr.

RAINCLIFFE

> *Ramescliua* 1170–80 YCh 412
> *Ravenesclif(fe)* 13 Percy, 1252 Pat; *-clive* 1252 NRS
> *Raveneclyff* c. 1250 Whitby
> *Ravenclif* 1335 *ForP* 209 *d*, 1337 Percy
> *Rancleiff* 1405 Pat   *Reyn-, Raynclyf(f)* 1461, 1475 Pat

'Raven's cliff' v. clif. The ON pers. name *Hrafn* had various forms for the gen., *Hrafns, Hramnes, Hrams* (LindN), and it is from the latter that the first spelling *Rames-* is derived.

Cayton[1]

1. CAYTON 23 E 7

Caitun(e), Caimton(a) 1086 DB
Chaituna a. 1087 Whitby
C-, Kaiton(a), C-, Kayton 12 Dods vii. 146 *et passim*

'Cæga's farm' v. tun. For the OE pers. name *Cǣga* v. IPN 180 and PN BedsHu 15, 147. Cf. also Cayton (YWR), *Caitun* etc. 12 YCh (*passim*).

DEEPDALE

Depedale (-am) 1086 DB *et passim* to 1572 FF
Dipedall' 1242 P *Deepdale* 1555 BM

'Deep valley' v. deop, dæl.

KILLERBY

Chilvertebi, Chiluertesbi 1086 DB
Kilverdebi, -by 1155–65 Whitby, 1231 *Ass*
Kiluerdby 13 BylE 20 d
Kilvardeby 1247 Ch
Kelwardeby 13 Percy
Ki-, Kylward(e)by 1285 KI *et freq* to 1487 FF
Kilwerbye 1572 FF

The first element is without doubt identical with the pers. name *Chiluert* which is found in DB. It enters into Kilverstone (Nf), and a lost *Kuluertestuna, Culuerdestuna* (DB) in Colneis Hundred (Sf), one of the forms of Marishes 84 *supra*, Killerby 245 *infra*, Killerwick (PN La 205), and a lost *Killerby* in Lei (IPN 86). Björkman (*NP* 81, *ZEN* 54, *Loanwords* 25) supposes that it is a hybrid pers. name of which the themes are ON *Ketill* (frequently reduced in Scand dithematic names to *Kil-*) and the common OE theme *-weard*. The persistence of *-verd* forms, however, may occasion some doubt as to the correctness of Björkman's suggestion, and one may suggest that

[1] A detached part of Whitby Strand Wapentake.

the name is from an OE compound name *Cēolfriþ, Cēolferð*, composed of the very common themes *Cēol-* and *-friþ*, or an ON name *Ketilferð composed of the themes *Ketill-* and *-ferð*. Later forms however show confusion with OE *-weard. v.* by.

OSGODBY

Asgozbi 1086 DB
Angotby c. 1160 *BylE* 22 *d*
Angoteby 1206 FF, 1247 Ch, 1268 Ebor
Osgotby c. 1160 *BylE* 22 *d*, 1285 KI, 1301 LS, 1408 *For*
Osgodebi c. 1170, 1252, 1333 Riev
Osgodby 1301 LS (p) *et passim*
Osgarby 1577 NRS

'Asgaut's farm' *v.* by. The first element is the ON pers. name *Ásgautr*, on the various forms of which *v.* NP 14 ff. Forms with *An-* are due to AN substitution of a continental form, and those with *Os-* to the substitution of the OE pers. name-theme *Ōs-* which was cognate with ON *Ás-*.

2. GRISTHORPE 23 F 8 [grisθrəp]

Grisetorp 1086 DB
Gris-, Grysthorp(p) 1175–89 YCh 370 *et freq*
Gri-, Grysethorp 1181 *BylE* 103 *d et freq*

'Gris's village' *v.* þorp. The first element is the ON pers. name *Griss*, from ON *griss* 'a pig,' found also in Gristhwaite and Girsby 186, 280 *infra*.

ETERSTHORPE (lost)

Eterstorp 1086 DB

The first element is a pers. n., possibly ON *Eitri* (LindN), found also as the first element of *Etresghilebec* (13 Riev) in Middleton in Teesdale (Du). *v.* þorp.

NEWBIGGIN

Niwebigginge 1187, 1190 P etc.

'New building' *v.* niwe, bigging.

ROBERTHORPE (lost)

Rodebestorp, Roudeluestorp 1086 DB   *Rodberthorp* 1328 Banco
The evidence is too conflicting for any certainty to be possible.

SCAWTHORPE (lost)

Scagestorp, Scagetorp 1086 DB

'Skagi's village' *v.* þorp. Cf. ON *Skagi* (LindBN), ODan *Skaghi* (Nielsen).

3. LEBBERSTON 23 F 8

Ledbestun, Ledbeztun 1086 DB
Ledbrithun 1181 BylE 103 *d*
Ledbreston(a) 1190–1227, 1251 Riev
Ledbrizton 1206 FF
Ledbriston 1208 FF, 1251 Ch
Ledberstona 1257 Riev
Lebreston 1285 KI, 1301 LS, 1303 KF, 1408 *For*
Lyberston 1550 FF

'Leodbriht's farm' from OE *Lēodbeorht* adduced only in ONb and tun.

Scarborough

1. SCARBOROUGH 23 D 6, 7

Escardeburg 1155–63 YCh 364, 1256 Pat
Scardeburc(h), -burg 1159–1190 P (*passim*) *et passim* to 1505
Scarðeborc c. 1200 *For*
Scartheburg(h) 1208 *Ass et freq*
Scareburgh 1414 Test   *Skarbrugh* 1538 Riev
Scarbrowgh 1573 FF

The name also appears in Scandinavian Sagas as

Skarðaborg Kormakssaga, Flateyjarbok; *Skarðabork* Ork-
   neyingasaga

'Skarthi's stronghold' *v.* burh (ON *borg*). The history of this name is fully dealt with in a paper by Professor E. V. Gordon in *Acta Philologica Scandinavica*, i. 320 ff. The following is a summary of Professor Gordon's account of the foundation of the borough.

Kormakssaga tells us that "the brothers Thorgils and Kor-mak went harrying in Ireland, Wales, England and Scotland, and were accounted the most excellent of men. They were the first men to set up the stronghold which is called Scarborough"

(*Kormaks Saga*, Reykjavik, p. 64). It seems probable that the place takes its name from Thorgils, for we know from two poems which his brother Kormak addresses to him under his by-name (*op. cit.* 44, 45) that he was nick-named *Skarði* 'the hare lip.' This account of the foundation of Scarborough must have been widely known, for Robert Mannyng of Brunne (*The Story of Inglande*, ed. Furnivall, Rolls Series, ii. ll. 14816 ff.) gives the summary of a story told by Mayster Edmund (not extant):

> When Engle had þe londe al þorow,
> He gaf to Scardyng Scardeburghe—
> Toward þᵒ northe, by þe see side,
> An hauene hit is, schipes in to ryde.

The date of Thorgils' harrying of England can be approximately determined. According to the saga, the brothers had joined the service of king Harald Gráfeld of Norway (king 960–965) and had accompanied his expedition to *Bjarmaland* (= Permia in North Russia) which took place in 966, and as the expedition to England took place immediately after this and as Kormak died in 967, the foundation of Scarborough as a centre of Scandinavian influence dates from 966–7[1].

BURTON DALE (6″)

Burtondal(e) 1210 Dugd iv. 319, 1298 YI, 1329 Percy

v. burhtun, dæl.

DUMPLE STREET, a street (6″)

the Dompyll 1500 Test

This name should be compared with Dumplington (PN La 38) which Professor Ekwall derives from an unrecorded OE *dympla* 'a small dent in the earth,' cf. OHG *dumphilo*. The word is probably the origin of the English word *dimple*, the earliest recorded sense of which is 'a small hollow in a plump

---

[1] Among Scarborough street-names, in addition to Dumple St *supra*, we may note Cartergate (id. 1252 Riev) and Sandgate (id. 1333 Riev, *Portum Sabulonis* (ib), 'Carter's road' (*v.* gata) and 'road to the sands.' Newbrough St takes its name from the *Novo Burgo* (1333 Riev), referring probably to Scarborough Castle.

part of the human body' (NED from 1400). The later meaning
'a dip in the surface of the earth,' judging from the cognate
words, is in reality probably earlier. The actual word *dumple*
found in this place-name is hardly a direct descendant of OE
dympla, but must be from an unmutated OE *dumpel* from a
Germanic base **dump-*; cf. ON *dump* 'pit, pool,' Germ dialect
dumpf, *dümpel* 'a deep place in flowing or stagnant water'
(Grimm), and the modern dialect (YNR) *dump* 'a deep hole in
the bed of a river or pond' (Atkinson, *Cleveland Glossary*),
dumble (Nt) 'stream with steep sides.'

FALSGRAVE [fɔːzgrif]

> *Wal(l)esgrif, Walesgrip* 1086 DB
> *Walesgraua, -grave* 1169, 1190 P *et freq* to 1619 NRS
> *Hwallisgrave* 1170 Riev
> *Hwallesgraue* 1181 *BylE* 103 *d*, 1334 *ForP* 318
> *Walegrive* 1175–89 YCh 370
> *Wallesgrave* 1201 ChR, 1228 Lib, 1275, 1298 YI, 1312 Ch
> *Walegrave* 1231 Fees *Whalegrave* 1237 Cl
> *Quallegrave* 1242 P
> *Whallesgrave* 1259 Ass, 1304 Abbr, 1312 *ForP* 377 *d*, 1487 FF
> *Walsgrave* 1575 FF, 1577 Saxton
> *Faulesgrave* 1568 FF

v. gryfja 'pit,' cf. Griff Farm and Stonegrave 54, 73 *supra*.
The first element is the ON pers. name *Hvalr*, gen. *Hvals*
(LindN). The change of *hw-* to *f-* is peculiar, but is probably
due to over-aspiration, in the same way as in some Scottish and
Northern Irish dialects *what* has become 'fat.'

SANDPITS (6″)

> *Sandepittes* 1298 YI

v. sand, pytt. There is a large number of sand-holes in the
parish.

Scalby

1. BURNISTON 23 B 6 [bɔnistən]

> *Brinctun, Brinniston, -tun* 1086 DB
> *Brinigstun* 1091–5 YCh 863, 1109–14 YCh 865
> *Brinigstona* 1185–95 YCh 369

Briniston(a) 1108–14, 1145–8, 1155–65 Whitby, 1314, 1322
   NRS
Brunieston 1150–60 Whitby
Bernestona 1161–84 Whitby
Bri-, Bryningeston(a) 1224–38 Whitby, 1279–81 QW, early
   14 Whitby, 1408 *For*
Brinneston 1259 Ass (p)
Bryneston' 1301 LS
Brenestona 1314 NRS   *Brenyston* 1395 Whitby
Byrnyngeston' 1408 *For*
Burnysshton 1550 FF
Burston 1577 Saxton

'Bryning's farm' *v.* tun. The name *Brȳning* (an *ing*-forma-
tion from OE *Brūn*) is found independently in OE (*v.* Redin
165) and as *Brȳningr* in ON (LindBN); cf. Burneston (Halik)
226 *infra*. The modern form of the place-name is due to metathesis of *Brin-* to *Birn-*, which later became [bən] in the dialect.

2. CLOUGHTON 22 B 6 [klɔutən]

Cloctune, -ton(a) 1086 DB, 1195–1225 *Dods* vii. 244, 1230
   Whitby, 1235 Ch
Clochton 1231 *Ass*   *Cloghton* 1368 FF, 1408 *For*
Clouchetone 1322 NRS   *Cloughton* 1577 NRS
Clawghton 1619 NRS

'Valley farm' *v.* cloh, tun.

ELLIS CROFT (6")

Elsicroft, Elsy- a. 1133, early 14 Whitby, 1204 ChR
Elliscrofte 1619 NRS

'Elsi's croft' *v.* croft. *Elsi* (cf. DB *Alsi*) is from OE *Ælf-*
or *Æþel-sige*.

3. SCALBY 23 C 6 [skɔːbi]

Sc-, Skallebi, -by 1086 DB *et passim* to 1400
Sc-, Skalebi, -by 1086 DB, 1169 P *et freq* to 1280 Ch
Escaleby 1251 Cl
Scalby 1322 NRS, 1376 FF, 1408 *For*, 1508 Test, 1665 Visit
Sc-, Skawby(e) 1570, 1575 FF, 1577 NRS

'Skalli's farm' *v.* **by.** The first element, as in Scawby (L), is the ON pers. name *Skalli*, gen. *Skalla* (LindN); cf. the Swed place-name *Skålby*, OSwed *Skallaby* (Hellquist, *Svenska ON på -by*, 37).

COLDY HILL (6")

    Caldhou 1244 Percy

    'Cold mound' *v.* **cald, haugr.**

COOMS (6")

    Cumbis 1252 Pat   *Cumbes* 1252 NRS

    'The valleys' *v.* **cumb.**

CROSS SIKE (6")

    Crossik 1244 Percy

    'Stream near the cross' *v.* **cros, sic.**

HATTERBOARD HILL (6")

    Hatterberga 1167 P

    Haterberg(e, -h) 1218 FF *et freq* to 1304 NRS

    Hatherbergh 1327 Banco

    Atterbergh 1550 FF

    Haterbargh 1577 NRS

    v. **berg.** The first element is the ON by-name *Hattr* (*Hǫttr*), gen. *Hattar* (LindBN).

NEWBY

    Neuby 1244 Percy *et passim*

    'New farm' *v.* **niwe, by.**

NORTHSTEAD

    Nort(h)stede 1550 FF, 1619 NRS

    'North place' *v.* **norþ, stede.**

SCALBY HAY

    haia (*haya*) *de Scallebi* 1190 P, 1201 ChR

    v. Scalby 108 *supra* and **gehæg.** Here it denotes a hunting enclosure in the forest of Scalby. Cf. Hayburn 111 *infra*.

SWINESALE [swɪnsɔː]

> *Swinestischal* 1109–14 YCh 865
> *Swi-, Swyn(e)stischage, -schache* a. 1133, 1154–89, 1189
>   Whitby *et freq* to 1308 Whitby
> *Swinsey* 1619 NRS

'Wood near the pig-sty' *v.* swin, stigu, sceaga. The final element offers some difficulty. The *-schall* forms in ME should probably be regarded as orthographic variants of the *-schaghe* forms, due to the development of a diphthong *-au-* from OE *-ag-*, which was similar in sound to the diphthong *-au-* from OFr *-al-*; the latter was often written *al* by French scribes after the Conquest, even though its phonetic character had changed. Apparently Norman scribes represented the ME *au* (from OE *ag*) in the same way as OFr *au*. OFr *al* had certainly become *au* soon after the Conquest (Schwann-Behrens, *Altfranz. Gram.* § 174) and the new diphthong was frequently written *al* (*op. cit.* §§ 174, 233). The probability that ME *au* (from OE *ag*) was sometimes represented by *al* in AN orthography is borne out by the evidence of other place-names. Oakenshaw (YWR), *Akanescale* 1255 YI, *Okeneschagh* 1355 YD (from acen and sceaga); cf. also the DB form of Aiskew (HangE) 236 *infra*, and Vinehall (Sx), earlier *Fynhawe*.

THROXENBY [θrɔsənbi]

> *Trstanebi* 1167 P
> *Thurstanby* 1276 Percy *et freq* to 1475 Pat
> *Thorstanby* 1301 LS, 1379 IpmR, 1417 YI
> *Throssenbye* 1537 FF   *Frostenby* 1577 Saxton

'Thorstan's farm' *v.* by. The ultimate origin of *Thorstan* is ON *þórsteinn* (LindN, Nielsen, etc.), with the OE name-theme *-stan* substituted. For the modern pronunciation and the last two spellings cf. Thrussington (Lei) from the same pers. name. The *x* in the modern spelling is probably explained in the same way as in Moxby and Roxby 29, 90 *supra* and Coxwold 191 *infra*. For *F-* in the last form cf. Fingay Hill 213 *infra*.

4. STAINTONDALE 23 A 5

> *Steintun* 1086 DB   *Staynton Dale* 1562 FF
> *v.* steinn, tun, dæl.

BLEA WYKE

Blauuich 1108–14 Whitby
Blawic, -k, -wyc 1109–14 YCh 865 *et passim* to 1314 NRS
Blawick 1619 NRS

'Exposed, cheerless sea-creek' *v.* blar, vik. Blowick near
Southport (PN La 126) is an exact parallel.

HAYBURN

Hai-, Hayburn(ia) 1135–54 YCh 362 *et passim*

The name referred originally to Hayburn Beck, *v.* burna. As
Hayburn was within the bounds of the forest of Scalby (a royal
hunting ground, cf. Cl and P *passim*) the first element is probably ME *hay* 'part of a forest fenced off for hunting'; hence
'brook by the hunting enclosure' (cf. Scalby Hay 109 *supra*).
v. (ge)hæg.

RAVENSCAR

Rauenesere 1312 *ForP* 378

'Hrafn's scar' from ON *Hrafn* and ON *sker* 'rock, skerry.'

IV. WHITBY STRAND WAPENTAKE

Wytebistrand 1200–22 Guis, 1294 Ebor
Libertate de Whiteby 1231 *Ass*

'Whitby shore' *v.* Whitby 126 *infra* and strand. Whitby Strand
was a liberty and at the time of the DB survey all its parishes
were in the wapentake of Langbargh except Hackness which
was in Pickering Lythe. As late as the end of the 13th cent.
the lord of Aislaby manor (in Whitby parish) did suit at the
wapentake court of Langbargh (cf. Whitby 718). Whitby Strand
(the older name of the district) was first called a wapentake in
1316 (Pat).

Hackness

1. BROXA 23 C 4 [brɔksə]

Brokesay(e), -eye 1090–6 YCh 855 *et passim* to 1335 *ForP*
Brochesei 1155–65 Whitby
Broxhay 1335 *ForP*
Brokessay 1395 Whitby

'Broc's hunting enclosure' v. (ge)hæg. The position does not admit of a second element eg. For the possibility of such a pers. name, v. MLR xiv. 235.

LANGDALE SIDE

Langadale c. 1200 Whitby

v. lang, dæl.

2. HACKNESS 23 C 4

Hacanos 8 Bede   *Heaconos* 10 BedeOE
Hagenesse 1086 DB   *Haganes* 1176 P
Hakenesse c. 1081–5 *LVD* 48 d et freq to 1354 Whitby
Hachanessa 1091–2 YCh 863, 1133 Whitby
Hakanes 1108–14 Whitby
Hakenes(s) 1114–40, 1145–8, 1149–53, c. 1180 Whitby, 1227 FF, 1234 Cl
Hachanes 1155–65 Whitby
Hakanessham 1314 NRS
Hakenasse 1385 Whitby   *Haknas* 1472 Test

The forms of this name, apart from those in Bede, offer no great difficulty. They may be interpreted as the 'næss or headland of one *Hac(c)a*.' The form in Bede suggests that there was an earlier form of the second element, and Professor Ekwall suggests that there may have been an OE *nōs*, cognate with Scand *nōs* (cf. Torp, *Nynorsk Etym. Ordbog*, s.v. *nôs*) bearing the same sense as næss. Hackness lies at the foot of a very prominent ridge projecting between the Derwent and Lowdales Beck.

FLOCK LEYS (6″)

Flok Leiz 1540 Whitby

'Sheepflock clearings' from OE *flocc* or ON *flokkr* and leah.

HARD DALE (6″)

Haradale 12 Whitby *Haredale* c. 1265–78 ib. *Hardale* 1286 ib.

These spellings have been taken to refer to the modern Harwood Dale 113 *infra* but the site of the place, so far as can be ascertained from the bounds in the Whitby Cartulary, is here rather than at Harwood Dale, and the latter name can scarcely be a direct descendant of the above spellings. The first element is perhaps OE *hara* 'hare.' *v.* dæl.

HILLA THWAITE

Thwayte, Thwaite 1372 IpmR

v. þveit.

HOLL GATE (6")

Holgate 1268 Whitby

v. hol, gata and cf. Howlgate 85 *supra*.

LANGDALE END, etc.

Langedalebek c. 1265–72 Whitby

LOW DALES, HIGH DALES

Dales 1155–65, c. 1265–78, 1395 Whitby

Self-explanatory.

3. HARWOOD DALE 23 B 4 [ǽrəddil]

Harewode 1301 LS, 1385 Baildon (p)
Harwod 1301 LS, 1395 Whitby
Harwoddale 1577 Saxton

v. Hard Dale 112 *supra*. The first element is doubtful. It may be OE *hara* 'hare,' hence 'hare wood.' It is possible however that we may have OE *har* 'rock,' (*v.* Harome 70 *supra*), which would certainly conform with the topography of Harwood Dale. Finally it might be OE (*æt þǣm*) *hāra(n) wuda* '(at the) grey wood.' Equally ambiguous is Harewood (YWR), ONb *æt Harawuda*, where Færeman Glossed the gospel of St John.

BLOODY BECK

Bludebec 1268 Whitby
Blode-, Blodybek 13 *Add* 4615 *f* 96 *d*

v. bekkr. The first element is from OE *blōd* 'blood' or OE adj. *blōdig* 'bloody.' The significance of this element in the place-name is not clear.

COP KELD BROOK (6")

Coppekeld(e)broc(h) 1108–14 Whitby *et freq*
Copcheldebroc 1109–14 YCh 865
Copkeldebroc, -brok 1199 Whitby, 1204 ChR, 1279–81 QW
Cocheldbrok 1308 Whitby
'Stream which flows from a spring on the top of a hill'
v. copp, kelda, broc.

DRY HEADS (6")

Drye Hede 1540 Whitby
Self-explanatory.

GATELA ROAD (6")

Gaytelaye, Gaitelei 1145–8, 1155–65 Whitby
Gatelaw 1619 NRS
'Goats' clearing' *v.* geit, leah.

KEASBECK

Kesebec, -bek 1155–65 Whitby, 1231 *Ass*, 1395 Whitby
Kesbek 1175–98 Whitby
The first element is ON *kjóss* 'a small creek, valley, recess,'
which enters into a number of Norw place-names (cf. Rygh, *NG
Indledning* 60); *v.* bekkr.

KIRKLESS

Kirkelach 1108–14 Whitby, 1204 ChR, 1308 Whitby
Kirkelac, -lak 1109–14 YCh 865 *et freq* to 1314 NRS
'Church clearing' *v.* kirkja, leah. On the form *-lac(h)*
v. Helmsley 71 *supra*.

MURK HEAD

Myrke Hede 1540 Whitby
'Dark hill' *v.* myrkr, heafod.

THIRLEY COTES [θɔrlə]

Tornelai, -lay, Torneslag 1086 DB, 1204 ChR
Thornelay(e) 1109–14 YCh 865 *et passim* to 1314 NRS
Thornelac 1199 Whitby
Thirley 1619 NRS
'Thorntree clearing' *v.* þorn, leah.

4. SILPHO 23 C 4 [silfə]

Sifthou (sic) 1145–8 Whitby
Silfhou, -how 1155–65, 1230, c. 1265–78, e. 14 Whitby
Silfho 1231 *Ass*
Silfow(e) 1301 LS, 1395 Whitby *Silfey* 1577 Saxton

v. haugr. The first element is probably the ODan pers. name *Sylve* (Nielsen). Cf. Silton 201 *infra*.

BREADAY HEIGHTS [bríəde]

Bradeie, Braday c. 1200, 1286 Whitby
Braderheved c. 1265–78 Whitby

'Broad eg' *v.* brad. The modern form is regularly developed from OE *ā*. The 'broad *eg*' was no doubt the level tract of land between Whisperdale Beck and Breaday Gill, bounded on the north by the end of the ridge now called Breaday Heights, formerly *heued* (*v.* heafod).

WHISPERDALES

Whitspotdale, Wytspotdale 12, c. 1200, 1286 Whitby

'White spot valley' *v.* dæl. For *spot* cf. Ekwall, *PN La* 59 (s.n. Spotland).

5. SUFFIELD 23 C 5

Sudfelt, Sudfeld 1086 DB *Suffeld* 1108–14 Whitby
Suthfeld 1155–65 ib.

v. suð, feld. Cf. Northfield *infra*.

EVERLEY [jiələ, evələ]

Eurelai, Eurelag 1086 DB
Euerlaye 1090–6 YCh 855
Everle 1177–89 FF *et passim* to 1328 Banco; *-lac* 1314 NRS
Yereley 1577 Saxton

'Wild boar clearing' *v.* eofor, leah. On the modern form cf. Yearsley 193 *infra* and for *lac v.* Helmsley 71 *supra*.

NORTHFIELD FM

Norfel, Nordfeld 1086 DB *Norfild* 1108–14 Whitby
Northfeld 1155–65 Whitby

v. norð, feld, and Suffield *supra*.

Thieves Dikes

Theovesdiches 1108–14, a. 1133, 1154–89 Whitby, *Theofves-dikes* 1204 ChR, 1314 NRS, *Theofesdikes* 1308 Whitby, 1314 NRS, *Thevisdykes* 15 Whitby

v. dic. The earthworks to which the name refers are still extant. The element OE *þēof* 'thief' enters into several OE names, e.g. *to þeofa dene* near Hallow (Wo), BCS 356. Cf. Thieves Gill 246 *infra*.

Fylingdales

1. FYLINGDALES 16 H 12

Figelinge, Nortfigelinge 1086 DB
Philinch 1114–40 Whitby
Figelingam a. 1133 Whitby; *-inge* c. 1175 YCh 366
Fieling(am) 1133, 1155–65, 1222–7, 1308 Whitby
(*Tribus*) *Figelinges* 1181 P
(*North*)*filinge, -fylyng(e)* c. 1280 Whitby *et freq*, (*in valle de*) ib.
Ffilingdales 1395 Whitby

'The settlement of the people of Fygela' *v.* ing. The district included by the settlement was probably the series of small valleys which meet the sea in Robin Hood's Bay. The pers. name *Fygela* is not adduced in independent use in OE, but it may be assumed (as by Ekwall, *PN in -ing* 93) from the place-names Figheldean (W), Fillingham (L), *Figelingeham* DB, and Filgrave (PN Bk 15). *v.* dæl.

Bilaer Howe

Bilrod 1145–8 Whitby   *Bilroche* 1155–65 Whitby

The second element is possibly OE rod, 'clearing.' If so, the *-roche* is an error for *-rothe*, a Scandinavianising of rod under the influence of ON *rióðr*. Dr Lindkvist suggests ON *Bili* or *Bil* (fem.) as the first element.

Bownhill

Bownehalle 1236 Whitby   *Bownelle* 1540 Whitby

'Buna's hall' from the OE pers. name *Būna* and h(e)all.

FYLING THORPE

This should be identified with the *aliam Fielingam* (1133 Whitby), *Sutfieling* (1140–65 ib.), i.e. South Fyling, of early sources. Other spellings agree with those of Fylingdales *supra*. In the 13th cent. the name is sometimes *Prestethorpe* (1280 Whitby). Here þorp is used in the sense of 'outlier.' The land was held by the monks of Whitby. *v.* preost, þorp.

GREEN DYKE (6")

Grenedic(h) 12 Whitby (*passim*)   *Greene dikes* 1619 NRS

'Green (grassy) dyke' *v.* grene, dic. The dyke is still extant.

HELWATH BECK

Helewath 1231 *Ass   Helwath* 1369 Whitby

'Ford made with flat stones' from ON *hella* 'flat stone' (cf. Rygh, *NG Indledning* s.v.) and vað. Cf. a lost *Hellawath* in Glaisdale (1119, 1129 Guis).

LILLA CROSS, LILLA HOWE, tumulus

Lillacros(se) 1108–14 Whitby *et passim* to 1314 NRS
Lilehaucros 1154–89 Whitby
Lillehowes 15 Whitby   *crucem de Lilhow* 1619 NRS

'Cross on Lilla's mound' from the OE *Lilla* and haugr and cros. Such a hybrid formation offers difficulties but seems here to be beyond question.

NORMANBY

Normanneby c. 1110 YCh 857   *Northmanbi* 1224 Whitby

This name has the same run of forms and meaning as Normanby (Ryed) 57 *supra*.

RAMSDALE

Ramesdale 1210 Dugd iv. 319, 1240 FF
Rammesdale 1240 FF

The early forms suggest that we have here OE *hramse*, *ramese* 'garlic, ramson,' as in Ramsey (Hu), *v.* PN Wo xli. Alternatively we may have OE ramm, hence either 'garlic valley' or 'ram's valley.'

ROBIN HOOD'S BAY

> *Robin Hoode Baye* 1532 Whitby

The name is not found before the 16th cent. and probably arose from the popular ballads.

ROW

> *Fyling Rawe* 16 Whitby

v. raw 'a row of houses, hamlet.'

STOUPE BROW [stɔup bru:]

> *Staupe* 1133 Whitby
> *Stoup(e)* 1155–65 Whitby, 1301 LS
> *Stowpe Browe* 1540 Whitby

From ON *staup* 'a steep declivity, precipice' (cf. Lindkvist 165) and OE *brū* 'brow.'

WRAGBY [rɔ:bi]

> *Wrauby* 1344 Test   *Wragby* 1476 Test, 1540 Whitby

'Wragi's farm' from the ODan pers. name *Wraghi* (Nielsen), found as the first element of ODan *Wraghæthorp* and of Wrawby (L), *Waragebi* DB, and Wragby (YWR), *Wraggeby* 1308 WCR. *v.* by. The *g* in this name is purely a spelling survival.

Sneaton

1. SNEATON 16 G 11

> *Snetune, Sneton* 1086 DB *et passim* to 1665 Visit
> *Snetton'* 1163, 1167, 1181 P
> *Ouersneyton'* 1231 *Ass*

'Snjo's farm' from the ODan *Snjó* (Nielsen); cf. OIcel *Snær* and the ON name-theme *Snæ-* (LindN). *v.* tun. Called *Ouer-* because it is on higher ground than Sneaton Thorpe 119 *infra*.

CATWICK

> *Kattewich* 1214–22 Whitby   *Catwyk* 1576 FF

Possibly 'Kati's vik.' ON *Káti* is adduced by LindBN, but the *tt* is difficult. Further forms are needed. ON *vík* seems to be used here of a nook or corner in the hills (*v.* EPN 62). Catwick stands on the side of a narrow valley.

SCOGRAINHOWES (lost)

Scograineshoues 12 Whitby (*passim*), 1177–81 YCh 871
Scogreineshoues 1109–14 YCh 865, 1308 Whitby
Scogranehouuis 1199 Whitby
Scogreneshoghes 1314 NRS
Skoggat howes 1619 NRS

Lindkvist (78) suggests that the first element is an unrecorded ON pers. name *Skóga-Hreinn* "from *skógr* 'a wood' prefixed to the man's name *Hreinn* and referring to the abode or usual whereabouts of the person in question." Such a type of pers. name is not without parallel; other cases are *Tungu-Karl, Tungu-Oddr*, etc. (LindBN). It should also be noted that frequently in this district ON *haugr* is coupled with a pers. name. *v.* haugr.

SNEATON THORPE

Sneton et Thorpe 1349 Whitby

This was formerly a hamlet attached to the larger village of Sneaton. *v.* þorp.

Whitby

1. AISLABY 16 G 10 [ɛəzəlbi]

Asulue(s)bi 1086 DB
Assulueby 1215 ClR   *Asolvebi* 1222–7 Whitby
Aselby c. 1300 Whitby *et freq* to 1339 Pat
Assulby 1487 Ipm
Ayslabye 1556 NCyWills

'Asulf's farm' *v.* by. ON *Ásulfr* (LindN) occurs independently in English as *Asulf, Asolf* on OE coins (NP) and in the Yorkshire DB as *Asulf, Asul*.

BRIGGSWATH

Briggwath 1230–50 Guis

'Bridge ford,' i.e. near a bridge, *v.* brycg, vað.

2. ESK DALE (SIDE) 16 G 9, 10

Eschedale, -dala 1086 DB
Aeschedale c. 1150 Godr
Eskedal(a) 1175–85 YCh 673 *et passim*   *Eskdale* 1336 Ch

v. Esk, R. 3 *supra* and dæl, sid.

FLAT HOWE

> *Flathou* 1252 YI; *-how* 1619 NRS

'Flat mound' *v.* flǫt, haugr. There is a tumulus here.

GROSMONT

> *Grosmunt'* 1226–8 Fees
> *Grosmont* 1540 Dugd iv. 75, 1665 Visit
> *Grandimont(e)* 1228 Ebor, 1287 Guis
> *Grauntmount* 1301 LS
> *Gromunde* 1301 LS   *Gromo(u)nd* 1469 Baildon, 1615 NR
> *Growmand* 1557 Saxton

Grosmont was a priory founded by John Fossard in 1200. He gave to the Prior and Brothers of the order of Grandmont near Limoges a mansion and land in the Forest of Egton (Dugd vi. 1025). Grosmont takes its name from that of the mother priory of Limoges. The meaning is 'big hill.' Cf. Grosmont (Mon), *Grosmont* 1232 Pat, so named for a similar reason.

IBURNDALE

> *Iburne, Yburn(e)* 1258–65, 1270, 1308, 1311 Whitby
> *Iborne* 1382 Whitby
> *Iburndall* 1349 Whitby   *Ibornedale* 1573 FF

v. burna, dæl. The first element should be compared with OE *on yburnan* BCS 1290 (Mx), Iden (Sx), DB *Idene*, and Ifield (Sx). DB *Ifelt*. Professor Ekwall suggests that the first element is OE iw with loss of *w* before the following labial, at least in Iburn and Ifield.

LYTHE BECK   (6″)

> *Lithebec(h)* 1109–1114 YCh 865 *et passim* to 1314 NRS
> *Lythebeck(e)* 1335 ForP 212 *d*

v. hlið 'slope' and bekkr.

SLEIGHTS [sliːts]

> *Slechetes* c. 1223 Whitby
> *Sleghtes* c. 1223, c. 1300 Whitby, 1347 Baildon, 1429 Test

v. sletta and cf. Sleightholme Dale and Sleights 62–3 *supra.*

UGGLEBARNBY [ugəlbaːnbi]

> *Ugleberdesbi* 1086 DB
> *Ugelbardeby, Ugle-* 1100–c. 1115 YCh 857, 1177–89, 1222–7
>   Whitby
> *Uggelbardebi, -by* 1145–8 Whitby, 1301 Abbr
> *Ucchelbardebi* 1155–65 Whitby
> *Vgulbardebi* 1181 P
> *Uglebardby* 1270 Whitby
> *W-, Ugelbardby* 1310 Whitby, 1335 *ForP*
> *Oggelberdesby* 1314 NRS
> *Ugglebarnby* 1613 NR

'Farm of a man nicknamed "Owl-beard"' from ON *Uglu-barði* (cf. Lindkvist lxii, and NP, ZEN s.n.) and *v.* by. The change of *-bardby* to *-barnby* is due to association of the name with Barnby across the river Esk.

3. HAWSKER 16 G 12 [ɔskə]

> *Houkesgart(h)*   c. 1100–c. 1125,   c. 1110 Whitby,   1181 P,
>   1226 FF
> *Haukesgard* c. 1115–35 YCh 859, a. 1133, c. 1230–40 Whitby
> *Houkesgard* 1145–8 YCh 872, 1222–7 Whitby
> *Hoches-, Hokesgard* 1163, 1167 P
> *Haukesgarð, Haukesgarth(e)* 1176 P (p), 1284 YI (p), 1298 YI,
>   1308, 1351 Whitby
> *Hakisgarth* 1330 Whitby
> *Housegarth* 1577 Saxton
> *Harrsker, Horskarse, Haskerth* 1611, 1613 NR

'Hawk's enclosure' *v.* garð. The first element is the ON pers. name *Haukr*. Cf. Lindkvist 143.

COCK MILL

> *Kocche-milne* 1155–65 Whitby   *Cokmylne* 1395 Whitby

Possibly 'cock mill' from OE cocc; though one may have rather to deal with OE *cocc* used as a pers. name. *Cocc(a)* is found in Cockbury (Gl), OE *Coccanburh* (BCS 246) and Cogshall (Ch), DB *Cocheshull*. Cf. Sawcock 217 *infra*.

GNIPE HOWE

Ghinipe 1086 DB   *Gnip(e)* c. 1110, 1145–8, 1155–65 Whitby

From ON **gnipa** 'a steep rock or peak,' probably referring to the high peak overlooking the sea-cliffs on which Gnipe Howe stands. *v.* **haugr**. There is a tumulus here.

HAWSKER BOTTOMS [ɔskə bɔdəmz]

Bothem c. 1230–40 Whitby   *Bothome* 1396 ib.

v. **botm**.

LARPOOL HALL

Lairpel, Layrpel 1145–8 YCh 872, 1301 LS
Leirpel 1155–65 Whitby
Lairpelle 1307 Whitby   *Lairepell* 1395 ib.   *Layerpelle* 1396 ib.
Larepoole c. 1540 Whitby   *Lirpoole* 1622 NR

The first element is **leirr**. The second is more difficult. Lindkvist (71, n. 2) suggests that it is OE **pyll**. The history and forms of Marple (Ch), *Merpille* in 1285 (Ass) and so generally, do not make this very likely. Professor Ekwall suggests that the second element is the Norse word from which comes Norw *pøyla*, 'pool.' This would suit the phonology and fit a Norse first element better.

LING HILL (6″)

Lingehou c. 1230–40 Whitby

v. **lyng** and **haugr**.

RIGG

le Rigge c. 1175–98 Whitby

v. **hrycg**.

SALTWICK

Saltewicke 1540 Whitby

From OE **s(e)alt** (*v.* Saltburn 143 *infra*) and ON **vik** 'creek.'

SHAWM RIGG (6″)

Halmerigg 1214–22 Whitby   *Scalmeryg* 1305–22 ib.   *Shalme-rigge* 1355–72 ib.

Ekwall (IPN 92) makes the interesting suggestion that this name exhibits a development in sound of the Scand dialect in England; he suggests that the first element is ON *Hjalm-* and that *Sh-* was substituted for this. Though this form would explain the later development to *Shalme-*, the earliest form could hardly arise from it. It is more probably OE *healm* 'straw, stubble'; the form *Halme-* is from the regular unfractured Anglian form *halm*; the *Shalme-* form must have arisen from confusion with ON *hjalmr*, 'helmet,' suggested by Professor Ekwall. On the change of *Healm* or *hjalm* to *Shalme-* *v.* Shipton 16 *supra* and Addenda xlv.

SPITAL BRIDGE (6″)

    Ad pontem Hospitalis c. 1175–98 Whitby
    Spittalle-brigge 1540 Whitby

    v. **brycg.** The first element is ME *spital*, an aphetised form of OFr *hospital*. There is still a farm called *Hospital* in the district.

STAINSACRE

    Stainsaker 1090–6 YCh 855
    Stainsecre, -echer, Staynseker c. 1110 Whitby, 1145–8 YCh
        872, e. 14, 1395 Whitby
    Steinsecher Steinseker 1155–65 Whitby, 1181 P
    Stanesacher 1177 P (p)
    Stanseker 1611 NR

    'Stein's field' from the ON pers. name *Steinn* and **akr.** ON *ekra* (a by-form of *akr*) occurs in some of the spellings.

WHITBY LAITHES

    Whitebi-lathes 1351 Whitby

    v. **hlaða** 'a barn' and Whitby 126 *infra*.

4. HELREDALE (6″) 32 SE 11

This is now the name of a township formed out of Hawsker. The name had fallen into disuse but has now been revived. The small valley originally called *Helredale* is now called Spital Vale (cf. Whitby Cartulary ii. 428).

Hellerdale 1145–8 Whitby *Helredale* 1155–65 ib., 12 *Leon* 66 *d*
Ellerdale 1351 Whitby

v. dæl. The first element is possibly ON *hella*, gen. *hellur*, 'flat stone, tableland of rocks,' common in Norw place-names, cf. Helwath Beck 117 *supra*.

5. NEWHOLM 16 F 10

Neu(e)ham 1086 DB   *Neweham* c. 1100–1125 Whitby

'New homestead' *v.* niwe, ham. Cf. Newham 163 *infra*.

DUNSLEY

Dunesla 1086 DB
Dunesle 1086 DB, 1219 *Ass*, 1227 Whitby, late 12th *Malton*
    137 *d*, -*lea*(*m*) 1139–48 Whitby, 1181 P
Duneslac 1100–c. 1115 YCh 857, 1133 Whitby
Doneslac 1136 YCh 868, 1314 NRS
Dunslaie 1145–8 YCh 872

Further forms are without interest.

'Dun's forest clearing' from the OE pers. name *Dun* and leah. For -*lac v.* Helmsley 71 *supra*.

GRAYSTONE

Graistan 1190–1206 YCh 725

'Grey rock' *v.* græg, stan.

RAITHWAITE

Raithwait 1351 Whitby   *Rathwayte* c. 1540 Whitby

v. þveit. The form *Rai-* is at first sight against Lindkvist's suggestion of derivation from ON *rá* 'landmark' (p. 119, n. 4, 5) but too much stress should not perhaps be laid on a form which first appears in 1351. It is worth noting also that in a Danelaw charter of c. 1190 (ed. Stenton no. 529) land lying compactly is contrasted with land described as lying *rái a rái*. It would seem that this can only mean 'strip by strip' and if so it is difficult to think that we have any other word than ON *rá* 'boundary-mark.' The spelling is exceedingly difficult but it is possibly an inversion due to the fact that OE *ā* alternates with ON *ai, ei*, so that ON *á* might possibly have been spelt *ai* on occasion, in an area where OE long *a* was preserved.

SWARTHOE CROSS (tumulus) (6")

Swarthouethcros 1108–14 Whitby *Swarthovthescros* 1204
ChR *Swarthouchescros* (? = *-houthes-*) 1314 NRS

'Swarthead's cross' *v*. cros. The first element is the common
ON pers. name *Svarthǫfði, -a* (LindN), found also in the name
of a lost place in Tolsby, *Swarhovedwath* 12 Whitby.

6. RUSWARP 16 F 11 [ruzəp]

Risewarp(e), Ryse- 1145–8 YCh 872 *et passim* to 1351 Whitby
Riswarp 1316 Vill *Ruswarpe* 1665 Visit

Ruswarp is on the north bank of the river Esk, and this fact
must be taken into consideration in deciding the etymology of
the second element. A dialect word *warp* 'the sediment de-
posited by a river, an accumulation of mud checking the flow
of a river' is found in the North Riding (EDD), and a compound
warp-land 'land formed by the silt of a river' is adduced from
the East Riding (EDD); this is the meaning required by the
geographical situation of Ruswarp. These two words and the
second element of the place-name are identical in form with
ON *varp* (neut.), *varpa* (fem.), found in the Norw place-name
Varpet (Rygh, *NG* i. 218, etc.), and the root idea of the whole
series is 'something cast up' from *varpa* 'to throw, cast.' The
meaning of Ruswarp is therefore 'silt-land overgrown with
brushwood' *v*. hris.

The change of *Rise-* to *Rus-* is probably due to the influence
of *w* especially in the neighbourhood of *r*; cf. Ruddings 85
supra and Ruswick and Runswick 241, 139 *infra*.

RUSWARP CARR

(*bosco qui vocat'*) *Le Ker* 1282 Whitby *Ruswarp Carr*
1623 NR

'Ruswarp marsh' *v*. kjarr.

STAKESBY

Staxebi 1086 DB
Stachesbi, -by 1090–6 YCh 855, 1133, 1155–65 Whitby,
1314 NRS
Stakesbi, -by 1100–c. 1115 YCh 857 *et passim*
Stakisby 1395 Whitby

'Staki's farm' *v.* by. The first element is probably the ON by-name *Stáki* (LindBN) with genitival -*s* substituted for -*a* (the weak form), rather than the by-name *Stakkr*, gen. *Staks* (LindBN) which would have become *Stax*-.

UPGANG

le Upgange 1540 Whitby

'Road or path leading up (from the sea shore)' from OE *up* and OE *gang* (cf. *gang* in EDD).

7. WHITBY 16 F 11 [widbi]

Witebi, -by, Wytebi, -by 1086 DB *et passim* to 1298 YI
Wyttebeia, -beya 1138 Dugd iii. 545 *passim*

Aspirated forms appear in the 12th cent. and are practically the only forms found after the 13th:

Whitby 1138 Whitby *et passim*
Whi-, Whyteby c. 1150–60 YCh 828 *et passim* to 1361 FF

Over-aspirated forms are of sporadic appearance:

Quiteby 1218 FF (p), 1267 Ebor   *Qwyteby* 1423 Baildon

The name appears also in the Heimskringla as *Hvítabýr*.

'Hviti's farmstead' from the ON by-name *Hvíti* (gen. *Hvíta*) and by.

Whitby was by early tradition identified with the *Streanæshalch* of Bede (cf. Simeon of Durham, *Hist. Dunelm. Eccles.*, Rolls Series, i. 111). Variant forms of the name in Bede are *Streaneshalh, Streonæshalch, Streaneshalh, Streneshælc*. The OE Bede has *Streoneshalh, Strineshalg*, whilst the ASC (s.a. 680) has *Streonesheal*. For this name *v.* Strensall 13 *supra*. Bede translates the name as *sinus fari*, which offers difficulty. The best explanation seems to be to look upon Bede's *fari* as a mistake for *fare* or *farae*, from Medieval Latin *fara* 'strain, descent,' which is, of course, the meaning of OE *streon*, here used as a pers. name, while healh is rendered by *sinus*.

AIRY HILL

Ergum 1090–6 YCh 855 *et passim* to 1314 NRS
Hergum 1155–65 Whitby

v. erg and cf. Airyholme 49 *supra*.

BALDBY FIELDS (lost)

Baldebi, Baldeby 1086 DB, 1133, 1155-65 Whitby, 1280 *Ass*

'Baldi's farm' from the ON pers. name *Baldi* (LindN) and by. For the site *v.* Whitby Cartulary 118, n. 9.

BRECK (lost)

Breche 1086 DB

Brecca(m) 1086 DB, 1100-c. 1115 YCh 857, 1133 Whitby

'The slope' *v.* brekka and Introduction xxvii.

CHURCH STREET (6")

Kirkgate 1318 Whitby

v. kirkja, gata.

THE FITTS (6")

Fyths 1395 Whitby

'Luxuriant grasslands on the bank of a river' from ON *fit*, which enters into a number of Icel place-names (cf. *Landnamabók*) and into such Norw place-names as *Fiane, Fidjane* (Rygh, *NG Indledning* 49). Cf. Feetham 271 *infra*.

FLOWERGATE, a street (6")

Florun 1086 DB

Flore 1086 DB, 1145-8 Whitby (*passim*), 1280 *Ass*

Floram 1133 Whitby, 1314 NRS

Floregate 1313 Whitby

'(At) the cow stalls' from ON *flórum* (dat. plur.) or *flóri* (dat. sg.) of ON *flórr*. *v.* gata. Cf. Skiplam 65 *supra*, which is a name of the same significance.

PRESTBY (lost)

Prestebi, -by 1086 DB *et passim* to 1345 Whitby

'Priests' farm' *v.* preost, by. Cf. Norw *Præstby* (Rygh, *NG* i. 66). SD and the Memorial of the Foundation of Whitby Abbey (Whitby Cartulary, p. 1) both say that *Prestebi* was the old name of Whitby. But the above references and spellings show that the name was in use in the 12th cent., contemporaneously with Whitby, and certainly not to refer to the same area as *Witebi*.

SOWERBY (lost)

> *Sourebi, -by* 1086 DB *et passim* to 1354 Whitby
> *Saurebi, -by* 1145–8 YCh 872, 1148–75 Whitby, c. 1170–9
>   YCh 861

The name Sowerby is common in the north of England and
that is identical with Norw *Sørby* (ONorw *i Saurby,* Rygh, *NG*
ii. 88, etc.) 'swampy farmstead.' An interesting explanation of
the Icel name is found in the *Landnamabók*: Steinolfr built a
farm and called it *Saurbœ, því at þar var myrlent mjǫk,* i.e.
'because it was very swampy there.' *v.* saurr, by.

THINGWALL (lost)

> *Tingwal* 1145–8 YCh 872   *Thingwala* 1155–65 Whitby

v. þingvǫllr. The name is undoubtedly that of the moatstead
of a very strong Scand colony in Eskdale. There is no clue to
the site. Cf. Fingay Hill 213 *infra.*

V. LANGBARGH EAST WAPENTAKE

> *Langeberg(e) Wapentac* 1086 DB *et passim* to 1339 Guis
> *Wap' de Lankeberga* 1166 P
> *Langebrigg'* 1226–8 Fees
> *Langebergh(e)* 1231 *Ass et passim* to 1335 Guis
> *Langeberewe* 1273 YI
> *Langbarffe* 1599 NR   *Langbarghe* 1612 NR

Langbargh Wapentake (now in two divisions East and West)
takes its name from a hill called Langbaurgh in Great Ayton
165 *infra,* practically in the centre of the whole wapentake, of
which it was the meeting-place. Part of the wapentake was
taken for the formation of the wapentake of Whitby Strand
and now the remainder goes by the general name of Cleveland.

CLEVELAND [kliːvlənd]

> *Clive-, Clyveland(a)* 1104–14 YCh 932, c. 1130 SD *et passim*
>   to 1452 Test
> *Clieveland* 1304 Dugd v. 508

Clifland bi Tese side 14 Horne Child (l. 54)
Cleueland c. 1270 *Heal* 103 *et passim Cleiveland* 1621 NR
In the Orkneyinga Saga (c. 40) it is called *Klifland*.
'Steep, precipitous district' *v.* clif,. land. One glance at the map will show the appropriateness of the name.
To explain the modern form we must assume that the original form of the name had a gen. plur. *clifa-land* 'district of cliffs,' for the short vowel *-i-* has undergone a lengthening which usually took place only in open syllables. Cf. Upleatham 153 *infra*.

Egton

1. EGTON 16 G 8
    Egetune, -ton 1086 DB, 1284 YI, 1291 Pap
    Eggeton' c. 1170–95 YCh 1041, 1181 P *et passim* to 1410 YI
    Egton 1285 KI
    'Ecga's farm' from the OE *Ecga* and tun. Cf. Egton (La).

ARNECLIFF
    Erneclive 1223 FF
    'Eagles' cliff' *v.* earn, clif.

BLUEWATH BECK
    Blawyth a. 1133 Whitby *Blawath* 13 Guis (3 X), 1252 YI
    'Dark, (possibly) cheerless, exposed ford' *v.* blar, vað and cf. Blawath 82 *supra*. The modern form arose from the dialect change of ON *á* to [iə] and then from the development of a glide-vowel [u] before the following *w*.

BRIDGE HOLME [brigɔum] (6″)
    Brigholme 1301 LS (p)
    v. brycg, holmr.

LEASE RIGG
    Lecerigge 1301 LS
    From OE læs 'pasture' and hrycg.

NEWBEGIN
    Neubiggin 1310 Ch
    'New building' *v.* niwe, bigging.

SHORT WAIT

> *Shortwaite* 1619 NR

'Short enclosure' *v.* sceort, þveit.

SHUNNER HOWE [ʃunərɔu]

> *Senerhou* 13 Guis (2), 1223 FF
> *Shonerhom* (sic) 1252 YI   *Shonerhowes* 15 Whitby
> *Shenerhoues* 1619 NRS

'Sjon's mound' *v.* haugr. The first element is ON *Sjónr*, gen. *Sjónar* (LindN), which enters into the parallel Norw placename *Sjonhaug* (ONorw *i Siónarhaugi*, Rygh *NG* i. 10): Ekwall (NoB ix. 162) would derive the name from ON *sjón* and explain it as 'look-out hill' and compares it with Shunner Fell (not evidenced in early documents) in Wensleydale.

The modern form of the name *Shunner* is borrowed directly from the late ON form *Sjónar*, for initial *sh-* can in this case be derived only from the acoustically neighbouring sound [sj], a tendency in sound development which is reflected in such modern English words as *sure*, *sugar* (18th cent. [siuə, siugə]). The earlier forms *Sener-* are what we should normally have in English for ON *Sjónar* (PrN *sēonaR*). The phonetic history of this name and possibly of Shunner Fell indicate a late connexion with the Scandinavians (*v.* IPN 92).

WESTONBY HOUSE

> *Westingebi* 1254 Pat
> *Westingby* 1279 YI, 1301 LS
> *Westynby* 1413 YI

'Farm of the western men' *v.* west, by. The hamlet lies in the west of the township. The use of *ing* in compounds of this type to indicate relative position is discussed by Zachrisson (*English Place-Names containing PrGerm *vis, *vask*, 8 ff.), where a number of parallels are cited.

WHEELDALE and WHEELDALE RIGG

> *Wheeldale, Welledale* 1252 YI
> *Wheledale* 1335 *ForP* 218 *d*, 15 Whitby
> *Weledalerygge* 1335 *ForP* 213 *d*

The first element is from OE *hwēol* 'a wheel' and the valley derives its name from the fact that its course forms a large arc of a circle; *v.* hweol, dæl, hrycg, and cf. Wheelden (PN Bk 212) and Welldale (Pick) 96 *supra*.

Danby

1. DANBY 16 J 5

Danebi, Daneby 1086 DB *et passim* to 1328 Banco
Danby 1285 KI *et passim* *Danby-Forest* 1665 Visit

'Village of the Danes' *v.* by. For the significance of this name, *v.* Introd. xxv.

BOTTON CROSS, BOTTON HALL and BOTTON GROVE (6″)

cruce de Bothine, le cuvert de Bothine, bosci de Bothine 1234, c. 1200, 1223 Guis

This may be ON botn used of the bottom of a valley but Professor Ekwall suggests that *Bothine* is an inexact rendering of *Bothme* from OE *boðm* for the more usual botm. Cf. Dial. *botham*. The change from *m* to *n* would then be due to assimilation or to the influence of the common Scand word just mentioned. Cf. further Botton (PN La 182).

CASTLETON

Castro de Daneby 1242 Guis *Castleton* 1577 Saxton

'Castle farm,' named from Danby Castle.

CLITHERBECK

Clitherbec 1273 YI

Clitherbeck should be compared with Clitheroe (La), early *Cliderhow, Clitherow,* (PN La 78) from *clider, clither,* probably identical with dial. *clitter* 'a pile of loose stones or granite debris' (EDD, from D), and possibly connected with OE *clidren(n)* 'clatter, noise.' Clitherbeck is a fast-flowing stream with a rocky bed. *v.* bekkr and Addenda xlv.

DANBY LAWNS

Laundis in foresta de Daneby 1242 Guis

v. launde and cf. Lawn of Postgate 133 *infra*. Lawns is within the bounds of the old Forest of Danby.

9-2

DINNAND (6")

> *le Dynant* 1273 YI

This is the name of a boundary stone on the hills in the north of Danby parish. Possibly we have here to deal with a Celtic name, for the name is not of a Germanic type. If this surmise is correct the name is no doubt from Brit *din* 'hill, fort' (cf. Welsh *din* 'hill,' Cornish *din* 'a fort') extended by a suffix *-ant*, which also enters into the name of the old Northumbrian kingdom of *Bernicia* (Brit **Briganticia*) and the tribal name *Brigantes*.

FRYUP [frɑiup]

> *Frehope* 12 Guis, 1301 LS   *Frihop(p)* 1223, 1234 Guis

v. hop, here used of a small valley branching off from Eskdale. The first element offers some difficulty, but the modern pronunciation and spelling indicates ME *-ī-*. It is possibly an OE pers. name *Frīga*, a hypocoristic form of some OE pers. name such as *Frīgȳð*.

HOLLINS

> *Hollenges* 1230–50 Guis
> *v.* holegn.

SOWERBY BOGS (6")

> *Souresby* 1242 Guis
> Cf. Sowerby (Whit) 128 *supra.*

TROUGH HOUSE

> *Troch* c. 1200, 1223, 1234 Guis   *Trochsich* 13 Guis
> *v.* trog, sic. Trough is a small valley branching off Fryup.

2. GLAISDALE 16 H 7 with GLAISDALE BECK

> *Glasedale* 12 Whitby, c. 1200, 1223 FF, Guis, 1224 Pat, 1665 Visit
> *Glasedalebech* 12 Guis
> *Glasdale* 1223 FF, 1227 Guis, 1369 FF

The modern form *Glais-* indicates that the ME vowel in the first element was long; the name may, therefore, be compared with Glazebrook (Ekwall, *PN La* 94) which is perhaps from the British word found in Welsh *glas* 'blue, green' etc. *v.* dæl.

BAINLEY BANK

Bainwith(e)lith c. 1200, 1223 Guis

'Holly bank' from ON *bein-viðr* 'the common holly' and hlið. Cf. Lindkvist 24, note 1.

BUSCO

Birkescoht, -scog(h) 1200, 1223 Guis, 1223 FF

'Birch wood' *v.* birki, skogr.

CRUNKLY GILL

Crūbeclif, Crūbeclive, -cliva 1086 DB

'Ravine by the crooked cliff' *v.* crumb, clif, gil and cf. Cronkley, PN NbDu s.n. and Hamley 80 *supra*.

GREY STONE HOUSE (6″)

Graystanes 12 Guis   *Graistan* 13 BylE 19

'Grey stone' *v.* græg, stan.

LAWN OF POSTGATE

la launde de Postgate c. 1200 Guis

v. Danby Lawns 131 *supra* and Postgate 134 *infra*.

LEALHOLM [liːləm]

Lelun, Laclum (sic) 1086 DB
Lelum(e) 1273 YI, 1301 LS   *Lellum* 1299 YI
Lelhom(e) 1273, 1410 YI   *Lelom* 1301 LS (p), 1349 Test
Leleholme 1579 FF

This name is probably derived from the dat. pl. of OE *lǣl(a)* '(amongst the) twigs' (*v.* Ritter 58, 207). Cf. Rysome (YER) from OE *hrīsum* (*v.* hris) and Snaizeholme 267 *infra*.

MOSS BECK (6″)

Mosebec(k) c. 1200, 1223 Guis, 1223 FF, 1234 Guis

'Stream through the swamp' *v.* mos, bekkr.

POSTGATE

> *Postgate* 12 Guis, 1223 FF, Guis   *Postegate* c. 1200 Guis
>
> 'Road marked by posts' from OFr *poste* and gata.

STONEGATE, BECK, WOOD

> *Stai-, Stayngateside* 12, 1223 Guis, 1223 FF
> *Staingatelith* 1233 Guis
>
> 'Hill-side along which the stone(-paved) road runs' *v.* steinn,

gata, sid. Cf. Stonegate (York), *Stainegate* 1118–35 *RegAlb* ii.
5 *d*, etc. *Staingatelith* contains hliδ.

Westerdale

1. WESTERDALE   16 G 4

> *Westerdale, -dala* 1154–81 Riev *et passim*
> *Westerdaill* 1285 (16) KI, 1582 FF
>
> 'More westerly valley' *v.* west, dæl. Westerdale is one of

the western valleys of Eskdale.

BAYSDALE and BAYSDALE BECK

> *Basdale* 1189–1204 YCh 564, 1301 LS
> *Basedale* c. 1230 Guis *et passim* to 1400 Test
> *Basedalebec* 1236 Dugd v. 508
> *Bosedal* 1236 Ch
> *Bassedale* c. 1291 Tax, 1390 Test
> *Baisedale* 1483 Test   *Baisdell* 1561 NCyWills, 1578 FF
>
> 'Cow-shed valley' from ON **báss*, OSwed *bás* (equivalent to

OE **bōs*, which has become YWR dial. *boois*, YNR dial. [biəs]);
cf. Björkman, *Loanwords* 99. The Ch form *Bosedal* contains
OE *bōs*. The modern forms of the place-name are due to the
regular Northern ME raising of OE, ON *ā*.

ESKLETS

> *Eskeletes* 1154–81 Riev
>
> The first element is the name of the river Esk which rises

in the vicinity. The second element is difficult to determine
but it is probably OE (ge)læte, the reference being to the
junctions of the three streams here which form the river Esk.

HUNTER'S STY (6")

Huntersty 1301 LS (p)

'Hunter's path' from ME *hunter* and stig.

RALPH CROSSES

crucem Radulphi c. 1200 Guis

v. cros.

WAITES HOUSE

Hogthaith c. 1180 Riev *Oggedwaith* 1160 ib. *Oggethuaith,*
Hogarthweit 12 ib. *Oghetwait* 13, 1333 ib. *Oggethwaite*
13 ib.

v. þveit. The first element is uncertain but one may derive
the name from the OE pers. name *Ogga* (Redin 103). The
form *Hogarthweit* is of secondary authority. On the loss of
the first element cf. Keld, Thwaite (HangW) 260, 272 *infra*.

WHYETT BECK (6")

Whitethwayt 1539 Dugd v. 510

v. þveit. The first element is OE hwit or a pers. name, ON
Hvíti (cf. Whitby 126 *supra*).

WOODALE BECK (6")

Wulvedalebec 1154–81 Riev

'Stream through the wolves' valley' *v.* wulf, dæl, bekkr.

Lythe

1. BARNBY 16 E 9

Barnebi 1086 DB

With the same range of forms and interpretation as Barnby
36 *supra*.

SLEIGHTHOLME (lost), identical with BARNBY SLEIGHTS (6")

Sletholm(e) 12 Guis, c. 1175–98 Whitby, 1279 YI

v. Sleightholme 62, 120 *supra*.

2. BORROWBY 16 D 7 [bɔrəbi]

Bergebi, Bergesbi 1086 DB
Berg(h)by 1279 YI, 1327 Banco
Berygby 1301 LS
Barube 1483 Sanct
Boruby, Borabye 1415 YI, 1513 FF

'Hill farm' from berg, by. Borrowby is on a hill. Cf. Borrowby (Allert) 205 *infra* and Norw *Berby* (ONorw *i Bærghabø*, NG i. 97), and Swed *Bergby* (OSwed *Bærghby*, Hellquist, *Svenska ON på -by*, 5).

GRIMSBY (lost)

Grimesbi 1086 DB

'Grim's farm' from the common ON pers. name *Grímr* and by.

3. ELLERBY 16 E 8

Elwordebi, Alwardebi 1086 DB
Elverdeby c. 13 Whitby, 1279 YI, 1316 Vill
Elferby 1252 *Ass*
Eluuerdeby 1254 Pat
Elred(d)eby 1301 LS, 1316 Vill   *Elred-, Elleredby* 1303 KF
Ellerby 1369 FF

'*Ælfweard*'s farm' *v.* by, and cf. Ellerby (YER), DB *Aluuardebi*.

4. HUTTON MULGRAVE 16 F 9

Hotune, Hotone 1086 DB, etc.

'Farm on the ridge' *v.* hoh, tun. Hutton is near Mulgrave.

BRISCOE

Bircschoke 1279 YI

'Birch wood' *v.* birki, skogr.

CUCKET NOOK [kukit niuk]

Cukewaud 1223 FF; *-wald* 1279 YI, 1301 LS
Kukeswaud 1228 FF
Kokuewald 1265 Whitby   *Cokewalde* 1301 LS

'Cuca's woodland' from the OE pers. name *Cuca*. It closely resembles Coxwold 191 *infra* but the latter probably contains *Cuha* rather than *Cuca*. *v.* w(e)ald.

5. LYTHE 16 E 9

Lid 1086 DB, 1201 Cur, 1210 Abbr
Liz 1181 P
Li-, Lyth(e) 1201 Abbr *et passim* to 1508 Test
Leth 1401 YI   *Lieth* 1623 NR

'The slope' *v.* hlið. The reference is to a slope which borders on the sea-coast north-west of Whitby. For the form *Leth* cf. Upleatham 153 *infra*. The common form [lɑɪð] is from ON *hlíð* (which had a long vowel).

GOLDSBOROUGH

Golborg 1086 DB
Goldeburg(h-e) 1080 DB, 1279 YI, 1301 LS
Goldesburgh 1303 KF, 1402 Test

'Golda's burh' from the OE pers. name *Golda*. For the intrusive -*s*- cf. Blansby 85 *supra*.

MULGRAVE [mɔugriv]

Grif 1086 DB
Mulegrif, -grive 1155–65, 1222–7 Whitby
Mul(e)greve 1224 Pat, 1268 Ebor, 1414 Test, 1415 YI
Mulgref 1303 KF
Mulgrave 1285 (16) KI, 1335 *ForP* 203 *d*
Moulgraue 1577 Saxton
Mowgrave 1577 FF, 1613 NR

'Muli's valley' *v.* gryfja, here applied to the steep-sided valley in which Mulgrave stands. Cf. Mowthorpe 35 *supra*.

SANDSEND

Sandes(h)end(e) 1254 Pat, 1279 YI, 1301 LS
'The end of the sands' *v.* sand, end.

6. MICKLEBY 16 E 8

Michelbi 1086 DB
Miclebi c. 1185–90 YCh 1046
Mikelby 1247 Ch *et passim*

'Large farmstead' *v.* mycel, by. Cf. Norw *Nøkleby* (ONorw *i Myklabœ*), Rygh, *NG* ii. 33, etc., and Swed *Myckleby* (OSwed *Myklaby*), Hellquist, *Svenska ON på -by*, 49.

7. Newton Mulgrave 16 D 8

Newetune, Neutone 1086 DB etc.

It is near Mulgrave.

8. Ugthorpe 16 F 8 [ugθrəp]

Ug(h)etorp 1086 DB
Uggethorp(e) 1161 YCh 619 *et passim* to 1242 P
Ugthorp(e) c. 1180 Percy, 1285 KI, 1665 Visit
Hugethorpe 1262 Guis

'Uggi's village' from the ON by-name *Uggi* (LindBN) and
þorp.

BIGGIN HOUSES

Percybigginge, -byggyng 1262, 1280 Guis

v. bigging. The Percy family held land here (cf. references
cited).

WOOD DALE HOUSE (6″)

Woluedale 12, 13 Guis, 1279, 1293 YI

v. Woodale Beck 135 *supra*.

Hinderwell

1. Hinderwell 16 D 8

Hildre-, Ildrewelle 1086 DB
Hilder-, Hylderwell(e) 1139–48 YCh 906 *et passim* to 1475 Pat
Hildrewell 1347 Pat, 1348 FF, 1404 YI
Hynderwell, Hinderwell 1468 Test, 1490 Ipm, 1573 FF, 1665
    Visit

'Hild's well' *v.* w(i)ella. The name was probably originally
OE *Hildewella*, containing the name of the famous Saint Hild
of *Streoneshalch*, whose monastery was a few miles to the south-
east of Hinderwell. The present form of the name, however,
points to a Scandinavianising of the name on the analogy of ON
Hildr, gen. *Hildar*, found in Hinderskelfe 40 *supra*. There is still
a well at Hinderwell called St Hilda's Well. Cf. also a lost
Hildekelde, fons sancte Hilde (12 Guis) in Guisborough.

RUNSWICK BAY [runzik]

Reneswike, Reneswyk 1273 YI, 1348 FF
Ri-, Rynneswyk 1293 QW, 1407 YI
Remmeswyk 1327 BM
Ryneswyk 1404 YI
Runswick 1577 Saxton

Perhaps 'Rægen's creek' from OE *Rægen* or ON *Hreinn*
which appears as *Ren-* in Rainton 185 *infra*, and vik. On
the phonology of this name *v.* Introduction xxxii.

SEATON HALL

Scetun(e) 1086 DB
Seton 1279 YI *et passim* to 1412 YI   *Seaton* 1571 FF

'Farm by the sea' from OE *sǣ* and tun.

STAITHES [stiəz]

Setonstathes 1415 YI   *Stathes* 1577 Saxton, 1665 Visit
Stease 1686 Marske

v. stæp. Staithes is a little fishing village built in a creek on
the sea-coast.

2.   ROXBY 16 D 7 [rouzbi]

Roscebi, Rozebi 1086 DB
Raucebi 1145–8 Whitby
Rouceby 1285 KI, 1301 LS, 1346, 1425 Pat
Rotseby 1311 Ch
Rouseby 1415 YI   *Rousby* 1577 Saxton
Rokesby 1575 FF

'Rauth's farm' from the ON pers. name *Rauðr*, gen. *Rauz*.
v. Roxby 90 *supra* and by, and cf. Rauceby (L).

SCALING

Skalynge, Skalinge 12 Guis, 1301 LS, 1577 Saxton
Scalingis 1243–73 *Heal* 43 *d*
Estskaling 1415 YI

'Shieling, pastureland, or a roughly built hut (near such a
piece of land).' The etymology of this word is probably ON
*skáling (*v.* NED s.v. *shieling*), a derivative of skali. The
same element is found in Scale Foot 148 *infra*.

Easington

1. EASINGTON 16 D 6

Esingetun, -ton 1086 DB

Esintun 1119, 1129, a. 1199 Guis

Esinton(a) 1154–61 BM, 1160–75 YCh 656, 1228 Lib, 1292 Pap, 1369 FF

Esing-, Esyngton 1154–81 Guis *et passim* to 1371 NCyWills, etc.

Eassington 1575 FF

'Esa's farm' from OE *Ēsa* (*v.* Easingwold 24 *supra*) and ingtun. Easington is found also in YER and Du.

BOULBY [bɔulbi]

Bollebi, -by 1086 DB, 1262 BM, 1279 YI, 1303 KF, 1363 FF

Bolebi, -by 1086 DB, 1204 FF (p), 1285 KI

Bolby 1407, 1412 YI

Bowlby 1575 FF, 1665 Visit

'Bolli's farm' from the ON pers. name *Bolli*, gen. *Bolla* (LindN) and by.

Loftus

1. LOFTUS 16 D 6

Loctus(h)um, Loctehusum 1086 DB

Lofthus 12, 13 Guis (9 X), 1155–65 Whitby *et passim* to 1303 KF

Loftus 1160–75 YCh 656, a. 1199 Guis *Loftous* 1285 KI

Lofthuses, -houses 1295, 1300 Ebor, 1301 LS *Lofthowse, Lofthous* 1316 Vill, 1334, 1339 Guis, 1369 FF, 1464 Test

v. lopthus. The DB form represents the ON dat. plur. *lopthúsum*, as in Lofthouse near Harewood (YWR), DB *Loctushun*. For *Locte- v.* Loft Marishes 95 *supra*.

HANDALE, GRINDALE (lost)

In early times the priory is referred to under both these names; there is no doubt about the identification, for in *Malton* 67 *Grendale* is found and *Ha* is written in the same hand above the *Gr*. The name *Grendale* is possibly preserved in Grinkle, a little distance to the east of Handale in Easington parish.

Handale c. 1180 Percy *et passim*
Litlehandailes c. 1200 Riev
Handale-Abby 1666 Visit

The first element is probably OE *hān* 'rock.' It can hardly be a pers. name *Hana* for in the spellings there is no trace of a medial *-e-* representing the OE gen. sing. *-a(n)*. 'Rocky valley' *v.* dæl.

Grendale 1254, 1280 Guis, 1268, 1296 Ebor, (alias *Handale*) 1315–8 Whitby, 1329 Baildon   *Grendall* 1319 Abbr
Gryndale 1395 Whitby   *Grindell Felde* 1540 Dugd iv. 76

'Green valley' *v.* grene, dæl. If *Grendale* is to be identified with Grinkle the modern form is due to the interchange of *t* or *d* and *k* before *l.* Cf. Kirklington 220 *infra.*

ROSKELTHORPE (lost)

Roscheltorp 1086 DB

'Roskel's village' *v.* þorp. The first element is ON *Hrossketill*, which is found as *Roscytel* the name of one of Alfric's *festermen* (YCh 13), and as *Roschel* in DB.

UPTON

Upton 1442 Test

'High farm' *v.* upp, tun.

WAPLEY HOUSE [wɔːplə uːs]

Walepol' 1226–8 Fees
Walpolhou 1231 *Ass*
Walplehous 1231 Fees
Wapel(h)ou 1287 Ebor, 1301 LS
Wayplay 1540 Dugd iv. 75   *Wapley* 1577 Dugd iv. 75

'Howes near *Walpole*,' which itself probably means 'Britons' pool' *v.* pol, haugr. The first element is OE *W(e)alh*, gen. plur. *W(e)ala* (*v.* IPN 18). On the modern pronunciation *v.* Introduction xxxi; *ey* represents the reduction of unstressed *-hou.*

Liverton

1. LIVERTON 16 D 5

Liuretun 1086 DB
Livertun 1165–75 YCh 890, p. 1180 Whitby

Li-, Lyverton(a) 1175–80 YCh 889, 1181 P *et passim*
Leverton c. 1200 BM, 1300 YI, 1571 FF, 1577 Saxton

With this name cf. Liverpool (Ekwall, *PN La* 117), Liversedge (YWR), DB *Liuresech*, and Livermere (Sf), *Liuremere* 12 BM, *Lyvermere* 1224 ClR. The first element is probably in each case a stream-name which Professor Ekwall connects with OE *lyfrig(-blōd)*, ME *livered* 'coagulated, clotted.' The Norw rivername *Levra*, earlier *Lifr-* 'stream with thick water' (Rygh, *NElv* 145, s.v. *Lifr-*) is a parallel to the stream-name contained in these English place-names. Liverton stands on Liverton Beck. *v.* tun.

WAYTAIL GATE (6")

Waytehil p. 1180 Whitby

'Watch hill' from OFr *wait* 'watch' (cf. Waits House 83 *supra*) and hyll. Waytail is near the sea-coast.

Brotton

1. BROTTON 16 C 5

Broctune, Brotune 1086 DB   *Brocton* 1273 YI
Brotton' 1181 P, 1279 Ch   *Brottun* 1185–96 YCh 667

v. broc, tun. Cf. Broughton (Ryed) 46 *supra*. In this name [χ] from *c* was assimilated to following *t* as in Latton (W) from OE *lac(u)tun*; cf. IPN 113, 5.

SKINNINGROVE

Scinergreve 1273 YI
Skynnergreve 1301 LS, 1404 YI; -*gryf* 1348 FF
Skin(n)ergrive 1273 YI, 1279 Ch
Skinnengref(myll) 1407 YI
Skyningrave, Skynnyngrave 1285 (16) KI, 1579 FF

v. gryfja. Skinningrove is a small valley which runs down to the sea-coast. The first element is the ON by-name *Skinnari* (LindBN) from ON *skinnari* 'a tanner.' The pers. name is found in Norw place-name *Skinnerbogen* (Rygh, *NG* i. 156) and Skinnerthorpe (YWR), *Schinertorp* 1297 LS. Forms with -*in*- for -*er*- are due to the analogy of numerous -*ing*- names.

2. SALTBURN 16 C 5 [sɔːtbən]

Salteburnam 1180–90 YCh 767, 1293 QW

'Salt stream' *v.* s(e)alt and burna. The reference is probably to the alum which is found in this district.

HAZEL GROVE

Heselgrive 13 VCH ii. 401

'Hazel valley' from ON *hesli* 'hazel' and gryfja.

Skelton

1. KILTON 16 D 5

Chiltun, -ton 1086 DB

Chiltona a. 1157 Percy

Ki-, Kylton 1219 *Ass* (p), 1292 Ch, Percy *et passim*

It is very difficult to come to any conclusion with regard to this name and Kildale 166 *infra*. For Kilton Professor Ekwall suggests a Scand form of OE *cilda-tun* (cf. Chilton) *v.* cild, tun, whilst the first element of Kildale he suggests is possibly ON *kíll* 'a narrow bay,' well-evidenced in Norw p.ns. In the latter case it is not quite certain what the semantic development of *kíll* must have been that it could be applied to a place inland. In Norw dialects it has the meaning 'narrow triangular piece' and in Dan *kil* the meaning 'a narrow strip of land.'

KILTON THORPE

Torp 1086 DB, *duas Chiltonas* a. 1157 Percy

K. et Thorp 1257, 1292 Ch, 1292 Percy

Thorpkilton, Kyltonthorp 1406, 1407, 1409 YI

'The hamlet belonging to the village of Kilton' *v.* þorp and cf. IPN 58.

2. GREAT (LITTLE) MOORSHOLM 16 E 5

Morehusum 1086 DB

Mores(h)um 12 Guis, 1328 Banco

(Magna, parva) Morsum 13, 1222–40 Guis, 1257, 1292 Ch, 1273 YI, *(petit)* 1404 YI

(Parva, Little, Great) Morsom 1285 KI, 1301 LS, 1348 FF, 1404 YI

Muressom 1412 YI
Moresham 1610 Speed

'(At) the houses on the mor.' *v.* hus.

AVENS HOUSE, AVENS WOOD

le hauenes 1273 YI

'The havens' from OE *hæfen*; the sense in which the word is used is not clear but it is probably 'refuge, shelter' (cf. NED s.v. *haven*).

GIRRICK, GIRRICK RIDGE

Gren(e)rig(g)e, -ryg 1273 YI, 1280 Ch, 1293 QW, 1407 YI
Gericke 1575 FF   *Girricke* 1616 NR

'Green ridge' *v.* grene, hrycg. The modern form arises from the metathesis of *Grenr-* to *Gern-* with later loss of *-n-*.

HAREDALE (6″)

Hardale 1273 YI

Probably 'rocky valley' *v.* Harwood Dale 113 *supra*.

SKATE BECK (6″)

Skaytebec 1271 YI, 1272 Cl
Sketebec 1271 YI
Skeyte-, Scaitebek 1272 Cl

Lindkvist (135) is probably correct in deriving this name from ON *skøyti*, a mutated form of ON *skaut*. ON *skøyti* is only recorded with the meaning of 'shaft, missile' but it may also have had the meaning of *skaut* 'nook, bend' (cf. Rygh, *NElv* s.v. *skaut-*). Skate Beck is a stream with many twists and turns in its course. 'Twisted stream' *v.* bekkr. We probably have a parallel in *Staitebec* (sic), the name of a tributary of the Wharfe (1310 Ch).

SWINDALE HOUSE

Svyn-, Suindale(wra) 12 Guis

'Swine valley' *v.* swin, dæl.

SWINSOW [swinsə] (6")

Swineswithne 13 Guis

Professor Ekwall suggests 'burnt clearing where pigs are turned out to forage' *v.* swin and *swithen* (EDD).

3. SKELTON 16 C 4

Sc(h)eltun 1086 DB, 1130–5 YCh 671

Later forms are the same as for Skelton (Bulm) 16 *supra*. The interpretation is discussed under that name.

BAG DALE (6")

Bagdalesclose 1407 YI

'Baggi's valley' *v.* dæl. The first element is the ON pers. name *Baggi*.

BOROUGHGATE LANE (6")

Burghgate 1407 YI

'Road to the castle (of Skelton)' *v.* burh, gata, and cf. Birdgate 85 *supra*.

BOOSBECK [biuzbek]

Bosbek 1375 Barbour's *Bruce*

'Stream near the cowshed' from OE *bōs(ig)* and bekkr.

COLD KELD (6")

Kaldekelde 12 Guis

'Cold spring' *v.* cald, kelda. This name is fairly common in Y: it appears as Cawkill (YER), *Caldekelde* 1328 Banco, as the names of places (now lost) in Ampleforth, *Caldkeldhill* c. 1226 *RegAlb* ii. 56, and in Easby, *Caldekeld(e)* 1160 *Easby* 4, 12 *d*, etc.

GLAPHOWE (6")

Glaphou 12 Guis (p) *Galaphoue* 1279 YI *Claphow* 1404 ib.

'Glappa's mound' *v.* haugr. On the OE pers. name *Glæppa*, *Glappa* which enters also into Glapthorn (Nth), *Glapethorn* John BM, Glapwell (Db), DB *Glapewelle*, and OE *Glæppanfelda* BCS 1295, *v.* Redin 96; there is variation between *G*- and *C*- in the OE forms of the pers. name, as also in Glapthorne (Nth).

HALLIGILL COTE (6″)

Halikeld Cote 1301 LS

'Cottage near the holy well' *v.* halig, kelda, cot. Cf. Halikeld wap., Hallikeld House, and Hallikeld Spring 212, 218–9 *infra*. For medial *g* cf. Wigginton 14 *supra*.

HOW LA HAY

Haia, Haya 1129, 1239 Guis

'Mound near the hunting enclosure' *v.* haugr, (ge)hæg. For *la* cf. Barton le Willows 38 *supra*.

MILLHOLME (6″)

Milnholm 1407 YI

'Mill field' *v.* myln, holmr.

RAWCLIFF BANK

Readecliff 1043–60 (12) SD
Roudeclif, Roudclive 1086 DB *Routheclyve, -clive* 1190, 1242 Guis
Rouclif(flat) 1407 YI, *Rocliff* 1582 FF

This name is of great interest as showing what must have repeatedly happened in Yorkshire place-names, viz. the replacement of an OE name by a Scand cognate. The SD form *Readecliff* is from OE read 'red,' whilst later forms show the substitution of ON rauðr. *v.* clif.

SKELTON BECK

Skelton bek 1407 YI

v. bekkr and cf. Skelton 145 *supra*.

WAND HILLS

Wandale(flat) 1407 YI

Cf. Wandales 59 *supra*.

4. STANGHOW 16 D 4 [stæŋɔu]

Stanehou 1273 YI
Stanghou, -houe 1280 Ch, 1293 QW, 1301 LS, 1575 FF
Staynghou 1301 LS

'Howe marked by a pole' *v.* stǫng, haugr. Cf. the lost *Stangerhou* in Ravensmeols (PNLa 250). The spellings *Stane-*, *Stayng-* are due to the influence of OE stan and ON steinn.

AYSDALE GATE

Asadale 1119, 1129 Guis   *Asedale* 1239 Guis
Hasdale 1273 YI

'Asi's valley' from ON *Ási* (LindN) and dæl.

THE BLACK HOWES

tres Hoggae c. 1200 Guis

v. haugr.

CAMEDALE (6″)

Camisedale 1086 DB (? identical)   *Camdale* 1407 YI

If the DB form is to be identified with this place the first element is the ON by-name *Kámsi* or *Kámr* (LindBN). This identification is, however, doubtful and it seems more likely that the first element is OE camb or ON kambr 'comb, crest, ridge' (cf. Cam 196 *infra*). *v.* dæl.

COMBE BANK

The Combes 1407 YI

'The hollows' *v.* cumb.

KATERIDDEN [keːt ridin]

Kateriding 1273 YI   *Cadringe* 1301 LS

'Kati's clearing' from the ON pers. name *Káti* (LindBN) and hryding. The LS form is erratic.

LOCKWOOD

Locwyt 1273 YI

From OE *loc* 'enclosure' and viðr, which was later replaced by OE wudu. Cf. Lockwood (YWR).

SLAPE WATH (6″) [slɛəpwaθ]

Slaipwath 1200–22 Guis   *Slaypewath* 1222 Guis

'Slippery ford' from ON *sleipr* and vað.

TIDKINHOW [tiŋkinɔu]

Tidkinhowe 1575 FF

v. haugr. The first element is a late pet-form of some such personal name as OE *Tydi, Tidi.*

Guisborough

1. COMMONDALE 16 F 4

Colemandale 1273 YI
Colmandale 1539 Dugd vi. 275, (al. *Comondale*) 1583 FF
Colmendall 1573 FF

'Colman's valley' *v.* dæl. The name *Colman* (which is also found in Coldman Hargos *infra*) is of Irish origin, from OIr *Colmán*, a shortened form of OIr *Columbán* (*v. Revue Celtique*, XLIV. 41). *v.* Introd. xxvii.

COLDMAN HARGOS (6")

Colemanergas 1119, 1129 Guis
Col(l)emanhergas 1170–90 YCh 659, a. 1199, 1239 Guis

'Colman's shielings' *v.* erg, and Commondale *supra*.

DIBBLE BRIDGE

Depehil 1119 Guis
Dephil 1129, a. 1199, 1239 Guis, 1170–90 YCh 659
Depilbrigge 1301 LS   *Dybell Brigge* 1539 Dugd vi. 275

'Bridge near the deep pool' *v.* deop, hylr, brycg.

MADDY HOUSE

Mady House 1539 Dugd vi. 275

SCALE FOOT (6")

Schalingthawythe 1301 LS
Skalethwayte 1539 Dugd v. 510
Scalethwayte al. Scaylthat 1573 FF

'Enclosure with a small shed or shieling,' cf. Scaling 139 *supra*, and *v.* þveit. The final element þveit has undergone a dialectal sound-change of *th* to *f* (cf. Garfit 69 *supra*) and popular etymology has connected the word with *foot*.

SKELDERSKEW

Schelderscoh 1119, 1129, a. 1199 Guis, 1170–90 YCh 659
Skelderschog 1239 Guis
Skelderschuthe 1285 KI
Skelderskayg' 1301 LS
Skilderskew 1577 Saxton
Skelderskew 1623 NR

The first element is probably the ON pers. name *Skjǫldr*, gen. *Skjaldar* (LindBN). *v.* skogr.

SLEDDALE

Sleddal Cote 1301 LS   *Sleddalle* 1539 Dugd vi. 275

From OE slæd 'a wide flat valley' and dæl. Cf. Sleddale (HangW) 267 *infra*.

TOD HOWE

Todhou, -how 1200–22 Guis

v. haugr. The first element may be the common word *tod* 'a fox' or it may be the ON pers. name *Toddi* (LindBN). As *haugr* seems to be most frequently coupled with a pers. name the latter alternative is preferable.

WAYWORTH

Wayewathe 1301 LS   *Whawathe* 1539 Dugd vi. 275
Wayworth 1615 NR

'Ford where the road crosses' *v.* weg, vað.

2. GUISBOROUGH   16 D 2 [giːzbrə, gizbrə]

There is variation in the forms of Guisborough between *-burn* and *-burgh*; *-burn* forms predominate but do not seem to be the original ones:

Ghiges-, Gighes-, Chigesburg, -burc, -borc 1086 DB
Gisburham 1104–8 SD
Gisebur(g)h 1130–5 YCh 671 and 9 examples noted before
    1410 Guis
Giseburc(h) 1155–1210 YCh 654, 1189–1214 YCh 564
Gi-, Gysburgh 1285 KI, and 7 examples noted before 1577
    Saxton

Gisseburgh c. 1291 Tax
Gysborow, -borough 1530 Visit

The following references are to *-burn* forms:

Giseborne 1086 DB
Gi-, Gyseburn(e) 1119 Guis, and 27 examples noted before
    1430 *Bodl* a. i. 63
Gisbourne c. 1180 Percy
Gi-, Gysburn 1228 FF, and 7 examples noted before 1483 Test
Guiseburna early 14 Whitby; *Guysborn* 1504 Test; *Guisburne*
    1531 NCyWills

This is a difficult name of which the interpretation is not
made easier by Simeon of Durham's *Gisburham*. There is a
rare ON by-name *Gígr* (LindBN) which would account for the
DB forms, of which a diminutive seems to occur in Giggleswick
(PN YWR 77). If this is correct the second *g* was early lost
from the combination *gsb* and Simeon's form can only be explained as a case of suffixed ham; cf. DB *Breilesfordham* for
Brailesford (Db). For the fluctuating final element *v.* Cheese-
burn, Newburn and Sockburn (PN NbDu s.nn.). Gains-
borough (L) and Scarborough 105 *supra* are further examples
of burh-names compounded with a Scand by-name.

BARNABY
Bernodebi 1086 DB
Bernaldeby 12 Guis, 1155–c. 1170 YCh 752 *et freq* to 1303 KF
Bernaldby c. 1190 (p), 1263 Guis
Barnaldeby 1285 KI, 1412 YI
Barntby al. Barneby 1285 (16) KI

'Beornwald's farm' from the OE pers. name *Beornw(e)ald*
and by.

BELMANGATE (6″)
Belmundegate 12 Guis   *via de Belmund* 13 ib.
Belmangate 1539 Dugd vi. 275

'Road to Belmont' *v.* next name and gata.

BELMONT
Belmund 1185–94 YCh 695, 1230–50 Guis
Baumund 1230–50 Guis

'Beautiful hill' from OFr *bel* and *mont*.

CARLING HOWE

Kerlinghou   12, c. 1170 Guis   *Kerlinhou*   c. 1176 Guis

'Old woman mound' *v.* haugr. ON *kerling* 'old woman' is used in ON as a by-name (LindBN). There is an unidentified place in this township called *Kerlingkelde* 12 Guis, 'old woman spring' (*v.* kelda).

HOLMES BRIDGE (6")

Holmes   c. 1175 Guis

v. holmr, brycg.

HOWL BECK

Holebec   1119, 1129 Guis *et passim*   *Hollebek*   1239 Guis

v. Howl Beck 69 *supra*.

KEMPLAH (6") [kemplə]

Kempclive 13 Guis   *Kempley*   1539 Dugd vi. 275

'Kempi's cliff' from the ON by-name *Kempi* (LindBN) and clif. For loss of final *f* cf. Hamley 80 *supra*.

MOORDALE (6") [mɔdᵊl]

Moridayles   c. 1175 Guis

'Swampy shares of the common field' *v.* deill. *Mori* is the OE adj. *mōrig* from mor.

OLD SLEIGHTS (6")

Adthewaldeslet c. 1175 Guis   *Adalwalslet*   12 Guis

'Athelwald's level-ground' from the OE pers. name *Æþelwald* and sletta. The development to *Old* must have arisen from loss of medial *th* and subsequent assimilation of *Alwald* to *Ald* and [ɔːd].

PERCY CROSS

Percycros   1231 Guis

v. cros. The Percy family held land here (*v.* Guis *passim*).

SCUGDALE

Scuggedale, Skugge- 12 Guis, 1185–95 YCh 695, 13, c. 1230
Guis

'Shady valley' from ON *skuggi* 'shadow' (cf. Björkman,
Loanwords 35) and dæl.

WATERFALL

Waterfal c. 1200 G

WESTWORTH

Westwith 12 Guis, c. 1170 Riev, 1170–80 YCh 662 *et passim*

'West wood' *v.* west, viðr.

3. HUTTON LOWCROSS 16 E 2

Hotun 1086 DB, 1170–85 YCh 695
Hoton(a) 1189 Guis, (*juxta Gis(e)burne*) 1301 LS

'Farm on the spur of land' *v.* hoh, tun and Lowcross *infra.*

LOWCROSS FARM

Loucros 12, 1218–34, 1230–50 Guis

v. cros. Professor Ekwall suggests that the first element is
the ON pers. name *Logi* found also in Lowthorpe (YWR).

4. PINCHINTHORPE 16 E 1

Torp, Oustorp 1086 DB
Thorp 1155–70 YCh 752, 1222–7 Whitby
Pinzunthorp c. 1195–1210 YCh 753
Pi-, Pynchunthorp(e) 12, c. 1230, 1292 Guis, 1303 KF, 1347
Baildon, 1409 YI
Pynchonthorp 1301 LS   *Pynchenthorp* 1316 Vill
Pyncheonthorp 1395 Whitby, 1412 YI
Punchunthorpe 1406 YI
Pi-, Pynchinthorp 1530 Visit, 1577 Saxton

v. þorp. The original form of the name means simply
'village' or 'east village' (DB *Oust-* from ON *austr*). Why
'east' is not clear, unless it was an outlying settlement from
Newton, a mile to the south-east. The first element is the
name of the family of *Pinchun* who held land here in the

12th and 13th cents. (YCh 753). The name is also the first element of *Pinzuncroft* (12 Guis), the name of a lost field in Pinchingthorpe.

5. TOCKETTS 16 D 2 [tɔkits]

Theoscota 1043–60 (12) SD
Toscutun, *Tocstune* 1086 DB
Toucotes c. 1180 Guis (p), 1404, 1412 YI
Tofcotes 1187 P (p), 1202 FF, 1252 *Ass* (p)
Toscotes 1202 FF
Thocotes 1202 FF, 1230–50 Guis, 1279 YI
Tokotes 1301 LS, *Tochotes* 1303 KF, *Tocotes* 1369 FF
Toukotes 1338 Baildon (p)
Tockets 1665 Visit

v. cot. The forms are too conflicting and uncertain in themselves for any satisfactory solution of the first element to be offered.

Upleatham

1. UPLEATHAM 16 C 3

Upelider 1086 DB
Uplyum, *Uplium*, *Uplihum* 1119, 1129, 1230–50 Guis *et passim* to 1310 Ch
Uplithum 1140–54 Whitby, 13 *Easby* 247 *d*, Percy, 1280 Ch, 1308 Whitby
Ouerlidun 1181 P
Uppelithum 1222–40, 1239 Guis
Lyum 1231 *Ass*, 1257, 1292 Ch
Oppelidun 1314 NRS
Uplethum 1285 (16) KI, 1407 YI   *Upleythome* 1581 FF
Upledam 1613 NR   *Up-Leatham* 1665 Visit

'The upper slopes' *v.* upp(e), hliŏ. The DB form represents the ON nom. plur. *hliðir*, whilst the remaining forms are from the dat. plur. *hliðum*. For the P form *Ouer- v.* ufera.

The modern form of the name has arisen as follows:—ME *i* in the open syllable was lengthened to *ī* and lowered to *ē* (written *e*, *ey*) in the 15th cent.: this was raised to [i:] in modern times, as also in Cleveland 128 *supra*, Kirkleatham, Healam, Skeeby, Smeaton 155, 220, 288, 211.

CORNGRAVE

Cornegreve 1273 YI

'Cranes' or herons' pit (or valley)' from OE *corn 'crane, heron' (*v.* Cornbrough 32 *supra*) and gryfja. Corngrave Farm is on the slope of a hill, but the name perhaps referred originally to a small valley which lies 200 yards to the south-west.

DUNSDALE

Dunesdale 1273 YI

'Dun's valley' *v.* dæl.

RAISBECK (locally RAYBECK)

Rabec 12 Guis, 1180–90 YCh 767

From ON ra 'roe-buck' (cf. Raskelf 26 *supra* and Raydale 264 *infra*) and bekkr. The modern form is corrupt.

Marske

1. MARSKE 16 B 3 [mask]

Merscum 1043–69 (12) SD   *Mersch(e)* 1086 DB
Mersc 1086 DB *et passim* to 1223 FF
Mersk(e) 1180 Percy *et passim* to 1401 Test
Mers 1218–34 Whitby
Marske 1285 (16) KI, 1442 Guis, 1677 Marske
Mask(e) 1577 Saxton, 1581 FF, 1665 Visit, 1685, 1714
    Marske

'The marsh(es)' *v.* mersc, and cf. Marske 293 *infra*. The earliest form is in the dat. pl. After DB the forms show the substitution of Scand *sk* for Engl *sh* (cf. Loft Marishes 95 *supra*).

CAT FLATS (6″)

Cateflat 12 Guis, 1180–90 YCh 767

'Kati's field' from the ON by-name *Káti* (LindBN) and flat.

FELL BRIGGS

Alfelebrigge 13 Whitby   *Felebrige* 13 Whitby

The first spelling is erratic. The second and the modern form suggest that the first element is ON *fjǫl* 'a board'; cf. *Felebrigge* (PN La 253) Felbrigg (Nf) and Fell Beck (YWR), *Felebrigebec* 1170–9 *RegAlb* i. 71 *d*, 72. 'Bridge made of planks' *v.* brycg.

GILDERT FLAT (6"), a field

Gyldhousflat 1407 YI

'Field near the guild-house,' from ON *gildi-hús* (Björkman, *Loanwords* 154) and flat. Cf. the lost *Gildhusmor* (e. 14 Whitby) in Middlesborough and *Gildusclif* (1284 YI) in Scarborough.

MICKLEDALES (6")

Mikeldailes 13 Guis   *Mikeldeldes* 1407 YI

'Large shares of the common field' *v.* mycel, deill. The form *deldes* arises in the same way that early English *vilde* comes from *vile*.

MORDALES (6")

Moredeldes 1407 YI

v. mor and preceding name.

Kirkleatham

1. KIRKLEATHAM 16 C 2

Westlidun, -lid(e), Weslide, Westlidum, Westude 1086 DB
Livum 1221 Guis
Lisum 1268 Ebor
Kyrkelidun 1181 P   *Kirkledom* 1491 Sanct

Other forms follow those of Upleatham 153 *supra*.

It is called *Westlidun* from its position in relation to Upleatham and *Kyrkelidun* from its church (of early foundation). For the forms *Lisum* and *Livum* cf. IPN 108 ff. Cf. further Upleatham 153 *infra*.

CRUMBACRE (6")

Crumbaker 1231 Guis   *Crumbacre* 1231 FF

'Crooked field' from crumb and æcer.

GREENWALL (6")

Grenewall(e) 1231 FF, Guis   *Grenewalde* 1401 YI

Probably 'green woodland,' *v.* grene, w(e)ald.

YEARBY [jiəbi]

  Uverby 1174–9 Guis, 1539 Dugd vi. 275
  Overby 1270, 1395 Guis
  Ureby 1579 FF, 1611 NR
  Yerbye 1577 Saxton
  Urierby 1609 BM
  Eureby 1615 NR

'Upper farm' from OE ufera and by. Cf. *Ovrebi* (DB) the name of a lost place in Whitby. The development of *Uverby* to *Ureby* (= [iurbi]) is due to the vocalisation of medial -*v*-. The change of *Ure*- or *Eure*- to *Year*- is normal in the dialect (*v.* Introd. xxxiii).

2. REDCAR 16 B 2

  Redker 1165–75 YCh 768 *et passim* to 1422 YI
  Redeker(re) c. 1180 Percy, 1198 Fount, 1301 LS, 1333 Riev
  Rideker 1271 Ipm
  Redkerre 1353 Percy
  Ridkere 1407 YI
  Readcar 1653 Marske

'Red marshy land' *v.* read, kjarr. The land is low-lying and the rocks are of a reddish hue (cf. Rawcliff Bank 146 *supra*).

EAST COATHAM

  Cotum 1123–8 Guis, (*Est*) 13 BylE 19 *et passim* to 1404 YI
  Oustcotum 1181 P
  Cotun 1165–76 YCh 657
  Cotom 1231 FF, 1443 Test

  v. cot. East (OE east, ON austr) in relation to

WEST COATHAM

  Westcotum 1181 P, 1237 Percy

SALT SCAR

  Salcker in Clyvelond 1281 Pat

  v. s(e)alt, kjarr. A wreck took place here in 1281.

WANDALE

    Wandayles 12, 1230–50 Guis *Wanddayles* 1175 ib. *Wandayll*
      1231 FF
    Wandeldes 1407 YI

    v. Wandales 59 *supra*. For -*deldes* cf. Mickledales 155 *supra*.

WILEY BRIDGE (6″) [wiləbrig]

    the Wylyes 1296 YI (p) *le Wyli*(*g*)*es* 1300 YI, 1301 LS
    Willey 1571 FF

    'The willows' *v.* welig.

VI. LANGBARGH WEST WAPENTAKE

    v. Langbargh East Wapentake 128 *supra*.

Ormesby

1. ESTON 15 H 9

    Astun(*e*) 1086 DB
    Eston(*a*) 1160–72 YCh 772 *et passim*

    v. east, tun. Eston is in the east of the parish.

2. MORTON 15 K 9

    Mortun, -tona 1086 DB

    v. mor, tun.

3. NORMANBY 15 J 9

    Norðmannabi c. 1050 HSC *Northmanby* 1222–40 Guis
    Normanebi 1086 DB *et passim* to 1252 Ch
    Normannesbi 1181 P
    Normanby 1191–9 Guis

    Cf. Normanby (Ryed) 57 *supra*.

4. ORMESBY 15 J 9

    Ormesbi, -by 1086 DB *et passim*   *Ormysby* 1414 Test

    'Orm's farm' from ON *Ormr* and by.

BOTTOMS FARM

> *Midel-*, *Litelbothem* 13 Guis
>
> *v.* botm.

HAMBLETON HILL

> *Hameldune* 13 Guis
>
> 'Scarred hill' *v.* hamel, dun and cf. Hamley 80 *supra*. The
> name Hambleton is a common hill-name in Yorkshire, and
> most of them are characterised by their scars.

HILLBRAITH (lost)

> *Hillebrait* 12 Guis   *Hille-*, *Illebrayth* 13 Guis
>
> This name seems to be one of the "inversion compounds"
> dealt with in the Introduction (xxvii). Hillbraith is 'Breith's
> hill or pool' from the ON pers. name *Breiðr* (LindN) and either
> OE, ON hyll 'hill' or ON hylr 'pool.'

HUNGER HILL (6")

> *Hunggerhil* c. 1250 Guis
>
> *v.* hungor and hyll, and Field-names, 328 *infra*.

LADGATE (lost)

> *Laddegate* 12, 13 Whitby, 13 Guis
>
> *v.* gata. The name occurs elsewhere in this district as
> Ladgate in Skelton (not adduced from early sources) and seems
> to be a regular type of name, parallel to *Wayncarlegate* c. 1175
> etc. Guis, *Walkarlagata* (Ryed) 1154–63 Riev, each containing
> ON *karl*. Here the first element is probably ME *lad* 'lad, boy.'
> This is first found in the OE nickname Godric *Ladda* (KCD
> 1351). It may have had some special meaning in OE besides
> 'boy'; the use of the element with *gata* perhaps indicates that
> a "lad" was one who had to do with driving (cattle or horses).

5. UPSALL 15 J 9

> *Upes*(*h*)*ale* 1086 DB
>
> *Uppesale* 1155–65 Whitby, 1222–40 Guis, 1284 Ebor (p),
>   1412 YI
>
> *Upsale* c. 1170–95 YCh *et passim* to 1498 Test
>
> *Upsall* 1443 Test

This name, like Upsall (Bird) 200 *infra*, is the same as the Swed *Uppsala*, from ON *up-salir* 'high dwellings.' The name is a common Scand type: cf. Norw *Opsal*, earlier *i Vpsalum* (Rygh, *NG* i. 138 *et passim*).

DIBDALE (6″)

Depedale 13 Whitby

Cf. Deepdale 96, 103 *supra*.

6. WILTON 16 C 1

Widtune 1086 DB *Wiltune* 1086 DB, 1155–65 Whitby

Other forms and interpretation are as for Wilton (Pickering) 90 *supra*.

LACKENBY

Lachenebi, Lachebi 1086 DB
Lacnebi, -by 12 Dods xcv. 36 (p), 1308 NRS
Lagenebi 1181 P
Lackenbi, -by 12 Guis, 1202 FF *et passim*
Lackeneby, Lackebi 1208 FF *Lacceneby* 1218–33 BM
Lachaneby 1231 *Ass*
Lakenebi 1297 YI
Lakkingby 1285 KI
Lak-, Lacenby 1310 Ch, 1367 FF, 1406 YI, 1463 YD

v. **by.** The first element is probably a pers. name; there was an ON by-name *Læknir* (LindBN) which may have had a weak form *Lækni*, but from the persistence of *-ene* and *-ane* endings in the first element this etymology is extremely doubtful and a more likely derivation is the OIr pers. name *Lochan* (cf. *Revue Celtique*, XLIV. 49). This pers. name is a diminutive in *-an* (gen. *-ain*) of OIr *loch* 'black' (cf. Welsh *lluig* 'livid'). The appearance of the OIr vowel *o* as *a* in the place-name is not unparalleled and is probably due to the influence of Scandinavians who introduced the name: the OIr pers. name *Colmán*, for example, appears as ON *Kalman*, *Combán* as *Kamban*; the place-name *Stainpapan* (YWR) appears to be derived from a diminutive pers. name *Popan* from OIr *popa* 'teacher' (*loc. cit.* 50, and Ekwall, *Scands. and Celts*, 47). There is, therefore, sufficient evidence to account for the OIr *Lochan* appearing as *Lachan* in Scandinavian Yorkshire. Normally in Ir pers. names introduced by the Norwegians into Yorkshire place-names no trace of the OIr gen. *-ain* is preserved, but Ekwall (*op. cit.* 54, note) cites one or two examples which might well be from this form. The early forms of Lackenby with *-ene* should probably, therefore, be regarded as survivals of the OIr gen. ending *-ain*.

LAZENBY [lɛəzənbi]

Lesingebi, Laisinbia, Lesighebi 1086 DB
Lei-, Leysing(e)bi, -by 1086 DB, 12 *Dods* xcv. 36, 1279–81 QW
Lesingby 1300 YI

'Village of the freedmen' *v.* leysingi, by. Cf. Lazenby (Allert) 210 *infra* and a lost *Laysingcroft* (c. 1180 Percy) in Redcar.

MOORDALE BECK, MOORDALE BRIDGE (6″)

Moredale 1230 Guis

SCRATH (6″)

Scrith 13 Guis

Probably connected with ONorw *skrið* neut. or *skriða* fem. '(land-)slide.' Cf. Rygh, *NG Indledning* 76. The modern form of the place-name is perhaps due to metathesis to *Scirth* > *Scarth*, with later remetathesis to *Scrath*.

Middlesbrough

1. MIDDLESBROUGH 15 H 8 [midəlzbruf]

Mid(e)lesburc(h), -burgh 1114–40 Whitby *et passim* to 1314 NRS
Middelburg(h) 1273 YI, c. 1291 Tax, 1613 Dugd iii. 692
Medellesburghe 1285 KI, *Medils-* 1395 Whitby
Middelesburgh, Middlesbrough 1407 YI, 1665 Visit

v. burh. The first element is the OE pers. name *Midele*, not found independently; cf. Middlesmoor (YWR), *Midelesmore* 1346 Percy, and the name of a lost field *Midelesmar* (Percy) near Scalby.

ARNOLDSTOFT (6″)

Arnodestorp 1086 DB   *Arnaldestoftes* 13 Whitby

'Arnald's homestead' from ON *Arnaldr* and topt. The DB form is probably erratic (cf. Spennithorne 253 *infra*).

AYRESOME (6″)

Arus(h)um 1129 Guis, 1218–34 Whitby, 1160–70 YCh 1851
Aresum 1119, a. 1199, 1222–40 Guis
Arsum 1222–40 Guis, 1285 KI, 1303 KF, 1336 Ch, 1412 YI
Arsham 1577 Saxton

'(At) the houses near the river' *v.* **a, hus**. The original form of the name is ON *í ár-húsum* (*ár* = gen. sg. of *á*, and *húsum* = dat. plur. of *hús*), which is the origin of the Norw place-name Aarus (Rygh, *NG* ii. 23, etc.).

CARGO FLEET

C-, Kaldecotes 12 Whitby *et passim* to 1301 LS
Caldcottes 1288 YI
Cawkers Nab 1624 *Terrier* (*penes* Major R. B. Turton)

For this common type of place-name *v.* **cot**. The identification of Caldecotes with Cargo Fleet was first suggested by Canon Atkinson, and it is made more certain by the last spelling provided by Major Turton. The development of *Cald-* to *Caw-* is quite regular. Cargo Fleet is near the Port of Middlesborough and the change from *Cawker* to *Cargo* arises from the similarity of sound of the two words and from association with the business of the port.

GATERIGG (lost)

Gayteryk c. 1142 Dugd v. 352
Gayteryg, -rig 1160–70 YCh 1851 *et passim* to 1392 BM
Geytrik 1247 Ch

'Goats' ridge' *v.* **geit, hrycg**.

LINTHORPE [linθrəp]

Levingtorp c. 1138, e. 14 Whitby
Leving-, Levyngthorp 1160–80 YCh 1852 *et passim* to 1392 BM
Leuengthorp late H 3 BM

Leventhorp(e) 1301 LS, 1412 YI, 1463, 1482 YD, 1577 Saxton
Leventhrope 1573 FF
Linthropp 1614 NR

'Leofa's village' from the OE pers. name *Lēofa* joined to
þorp by the *ing* found in ingtun.

LONGLANDS (6″)

(*þe*) *Langelandes* 12, 13 Whitby

v. lang, land. An old field-name.

Acklam

1. ACKLAM   15 J 7 [aklǝm]

   Achelu', Aclun 1086 DB
   Aclum   1086 DB, 1129 Guis, 12 *Dods* xcv. 36, 1202 FF,
      1247 Ch
   Acclum c. 1142 Dugd v. 352, c. 1170–80 YCh 703 *et passim*
      to 1404 YI
   Ackelom 1301 LS, 1303 KF
   Acclom 1303 KF *et freq* to 1453 Test
   Acclam 1399 YI

   Acklam is of the same origin as Acklam (YER), *Aclun* 1086
   DB, *Acclum* 1223 *RegAlb* iii. 4, etc.   The origin of both names
   is probably ON *í ǫklum*, dat. plur. of ON *ǫkull* 'ankle,' and later
   'slope.' The word *ǫkull* in the sense of 'slope' is found in
   some Norw place-names (cf. Rygh, *NG Indledning* 28).

Marton

1. MARTON IN CLEVELAND   15 J 8

   Martun(e), -ton' 1086 DB *et passim*, (*in Cliveland*) 1292 Ebor

   Cf. Marton (Bulm) 28 *supra*.

BRACKENHOE (6″)

   Brac(h)anhou 12 Whitby *Brachan(e)hoc* 1160–76 YCh 1848,
      13 Whitby

   'Bracken hill' *v.* braken, hoh.

BURTREE (lost)

Buirtrekelde 1199–1203 Guis   *Birtrestub* 12 Whitby
Buirtrestub 13 Whitby

The first element is found fairly frequently in Y; *burtrecros*
13 *Easby* 81 *d* (a lost place in Hornby, GillE), a lost field in
Monkby 245 *infra* called *Buyrthwait, Burethwaites, Byrthwait* 13
Easby 205, 210, 214, *Byrtre* c. 1180–94 YCh 796, and Burtersett
267 *infra*. The ultimate origin of the element is rather obscure,
but it is certainly identical with NEDial *bottry*, 'aldertree,' Engl
burtree, the earliest recorded instance of which is c. 1450
burtre = *hec sambucus* (NED s.v. *bourtree*); cf. Scots *bourtree*,
'alder.'

NEWHAM

Niwe-, Newe-, Niue-, Neuham 1086 DB   *Newenham* 1201 ChR

Self-explanatory. For *Newen-* cf. Newton 20 *supra*.

PRISSICK FARM

Prestsic 1199–1203 Guis

'Priest stream' *v.* preost, sic.

TOLLESBY [tɔuzbi]

Tolesbi, Tolesby 1086 DB, a. 1199 Guis, 1201 ChR, 1206 FF
Tollesbi, Tollesby 1086 DB *et passim*   *Tollisbi* c. 1130–40
   YCh 686
Toulesbi, Toulesby 1166 P (p) *et freq* to 1310 Ch
Tolebi 1181 P
Towsby 1364 YD   *Towlesbie* 1578 FF

'Toll's farm' from ON *Tollr* (LindBN) and by.

Newton

1. NEWTON 15 K 10

Newetun, Nietona 1086 DB
Newetunie sub Ohtnebercg 1140–53 Whitby
Neuton sub Otneberch 1155–65 Whitby
Castell Neuton 1399 YI

'New farmstead' *v.* niwe, tun. Newton stands under Roseberry Topping (*infra*). The last two spellings refer to an old
castellated house. On the DB form *Nietona v.* IPN 68.

GUNNERGATE LANE

Gunregate 1135 Whitby

'Gunnar's road' *v.* gata. The usual gen. of the ON pers. name *Gunnarr* is *Gunnars*, but a form *Gunnar* is also found (LindN). Dr Lindkvist suggests ON *Gunnvǫr* (f).

ROSEBERRY TOPPING

Othenesberg, Ohensberg 1119, 1129 Guis
Ohtnebercg 1147–53 Whitby
Otheneberg 1170–90 YCh 659, a. 1199, c. 1210 Guis
Outhensbergh 1239 Guis
Ounesbergh c. 1303–18 Whitby, *-burgh* 1409 IpmR
Ouesbergh (sic) 1404 YI
Ounsbery or Rosebery Topping 1610 Camden

The forms with *Ou-* at first suggest that the first element is the ON pers. name *Auðunn* (LindN), but they are not inconsistent with a more interesting derivation, viz. that *Othenesberg* is a Scandinavian parallel to the well-authenticated OE *Wodenesbeorg* (cf. IPN 38) and that this remarkable hill was a centre of the worship of Othin, the Scandinavian equivalent of Woden. There is an exact parallel to the name in the Danish *Onsbjærg* in Samsø, *v. Samsøs Stednavne* 48.

The editor of the Whitby Cartulary (Surt. 69, p. 166 note) says that there was an OAngl name *Hreosabeorh* and that this has given the modern *Roseberry*. There is no evidence at all for this. The change from *Oues-* to *Rose-* is due to metanalysis in the place-name *Newton-under-Ouesbergh* (*v.* Newton 163 *supra*), just as the modern common river-name *Ree* has come from OE *æt þǣre ēa* (*v.* ea), so Roseberry is apparently from the form *under-Ouesbergh*; cf. further under Thornton Riseborough 77 *supra*. For the influence of *rose* on place-names cf. Rosedale 80 *supra*.

LITTLE ROSEBERRY

Parvi Othensberg 12 Guis

The two Roseberrys are large conical hills. It is chiefly of hills of this shape that *topping* (from OE top, 'hill') is used.

Great Ayton

1. GREAT AYTON 15 L 9 [jætn, kæni jætn]

Atun(a) 1086 DB, c. 1175 Guis, 12 Whitby
Aton(a-m) 12 Guis, Whitby, 1129–35 YCh 866 *et passim* to
    1508 Test, (*Magna*) 1300 Baildon, (*in Cleveland*) 1279 Ipm
Etonam c. 1160 Guis
Haiton 1202 FF
Atton' 1226 FF, 1235 Cl, 1252 *Ass*

'Farm by the river' *v.* a, tun, and cf. Ayton (Pick) 100
supra. For [jætn] *v.* Introduction xxxi. The popular appellation "Canny" probably refers to its pleasant situation, as
suggested to us by Sir Alfred Pease.

AIRY HOLME

Ergun 1086 DB *Ergum* 1282 YI

v. erg and cf. Airyholme (Ryed) 49 *supra.*

AYTON SCARTH (6")

Etunescarth c. 1160 Guis   *Etonescarth* 13 Guis
'Hill-pass near Ayton' *v.* skarð.

CLIFF RIDGE

Clyverigg 1350 Ipm
v. clif, hrycg.

LANGBAURGH

Langberg 13 Guis   *Langbarge* 1572 FF

'Long hill' *v.* lang, beorg. This hill, which is a long, high,
narrow ridge, gave its name to the wapentake of Langbargh,
and, being practically in the centre of the wapentake, was a good
meeting place. Cf. 128 *supra.*

LONSDALE (6") [lɔunzdil]

Lonesdale 1263 Guis
Lonsdayll, Lounesdaill 1285 (16th) KI
Lounesdale 1539 Dugd vi. 275

v. dæl. The first element of this place-name is probably a pers. name and is possibly identical with the first element of Londesbrough (YER), *Lodenesburg* 1086 DB, *Lones-, Lonnes-, Lounesburgh* KF, Vill, from the ODan pers. name *Lothaen* (Nielsen), which appears in OE as *Lothan* (on the dial-stone of Edstone Church, *v.* Collingwood, *Anglian and Anglo-Danish Sculpture in the North Riding,* 329) and as *Lothen,* the name of a Danish commander (ASC, MS E, s.a. 1046).

2. LITTLE AYTON   15 L 10

   Atun 1086 DB   *Parva Hatona* 1155–65 Whitby

   v. Great Ayton 165 *supra.*

3. NUNTHORPE   15 K 9 [nunθrəp]

   Torp 1086 DB, 1181 P, c. 1196–1210 YCh 753
   Nunnethorpe 1301 LS, *Nunthorp(e)* 1328 Banco

   v. þorp. Called Nunthorpe from the Nuns of the Church of St James, formerly here (cf. YCh 753).

MAGGRA PARK   (6″) [maːgrə]

   Magerbrigge 1230–50 Guis
   Maugrepark 1407 YI   *Maugrey* 1575 FF

   v. pearroc. The form *Maugre-* possibly indicates that the first element is the OE pers. name *Mæþelgār;* cf. Meagre (PN BedsHu 264).

TUNSTALL   (6″)

   Ton(n)estale 1086 DB   *Tunstall'* 1189 Cur
   v. tun-steall.

Kildale

1. KILDALE   16 F 2

   Childale 1086 DB
   Kildalam, Ki-, Kyldale 1119, 1129 Guis, 1179–90 YCh 659
   et passim
   Kylldayll 1285 (16) KI
   Ki-, Kyldall 1382 Test, 1418 NCyWills

   v. Kilton 143 *supra.*

Ingleby Greenhow

1. EASBY 16 G 1

Esebi, -by 1086 DB *et passim* to 1369 FF
Esby (in Clyveland) 1307 Ch, 1285 (16) KI

'Esi's farm' *v.* by. The first element is ON *Ési* (Nielsen), only found in OEScand (= OWScand *Ási*). Note also Easby (Birdf, GillW) 185, 287 *infra* and cf. OE *Ésa* as in Easingwold 24 *supra*.

2. INGLEBY GREENHOW 16 G 1

Englebi, Engleby 1086 DB, 1203–7 Whitby
(H)engelby 1140–54, 1222–7 Whitby, 1235 Cl
Aengelby 1153–4 YCh 568
Engilby juxta Grenehoue 1285 KI
Ingolby 1291 Ch, *Ingleby juxta Grenhou* 1301 LS, *Ingelby-Grenhowe* 1369 FF

'Village of the English,' from OE *Engle* and by. There are three places in this district so called and they probably all denote isolated survivals of English inhabitants amid a prevailing Scandinavian population. For similar types, cf. Normanby and Danby 57, 117, 157, 226 and 131, 249, 276 *supra*.

BATTERSBY

Badresbi 1086 DB, *Baderesby* 1236 Dugd v. 508
Batersby 1214–22 Whitby
Batherby 1285 KI, *Batheresby* 1301 LS, *Bathersby* 1303 KF, 1369 FF
Bettersby 1577 Saxton

'Bothvar's farmstead' *v.* by. The ON pers. name *Bǫðvarr* (LindN) is from earlier Norse *Baðu-harir* (*v.* Heusler, *Altisländ. Element.* § 167, and cf. OE name element *Beadu-*) and this form without *u*-mutation as in Dan *Bathaer* (Nielsen) occurs in the place-name. Cf. the note by the late Mr C. J. Battersby (a model of its kind) on Battersby in PN YWR 215 ff. The change of *th* to *t* is modern and is found again in Battersby (YWR), *Bathersby* 13 Kirkst, and in the use of the NEDial *t'* for the definite article *the*.

GREENHOW

   Grenehou c. 1175–89 YCh 799

   'Green mound' *v.* grene, haugr.

HAGGSGATE (6″)

   Haggesgata, -gate c. 1175–89 YCh 799

'Road of, or in, the clearing' *v.* hǫgg, gata. The district is still well-wooded.

Kirby in Cleveland

1. GREAT BROUGHTON 15 M 9

   Magna Broctun 1086 DB   *Mekil-Broghton* 1481 Test   *Great Broughton* 1665 Visit

With the same run of forms and meaning as Broughton (Ryed) 46 *supra*.

LITTLE BROUGHTON

   Broctune 1086 DB   *Parva Brocton(a)* 1302 *Bodl* a. i. 32

2. KIRBY 15 M 9

   Cherchebi 1086 DB
   Kirchabi, Kirkabi 1140–54 Whitby, 1149–53 YCh 567
   Ki-, Kyrkeby (in Cliveland) 1149–53 YCh 878 *et passim*

   'Church farm' *v.* kirkja, by.

DROMONBY

   Dragmalebi 1086 DB
   Tromundesbi c. 1150 Godr
   Dromundby c. 1190 Fount
   Dromundebi, -by 1190–1210 YCh 581 *et passim* to 1310 Ch (p)
   Dromondby 1371 Baildon, *Dromonby* 1285 KI, 1665 Visit

'Dromund's farm' *v.* by. The first element is the OWScand pers. name *Drómundr* (LindBN), found as the surname of *Henr. Dromund* (Guis ii. 302) in Y. The normal gen. in ON would be *Drómundar*, so that the above spellings without any trace of the gen. suffix -*r* may arise from OEScand loss of -*r*- before a consonant (*v.* IPN 61–2) in such compounds. Cf. Romanby

210 *infra*. The DB form is curious. It cannot be brought into relation with the later forms. It should not, however, be dismissed as a mere mistake. In BCS 1052 a man named *Dragmel* occurs among other Northern witnesses to a Yorkshire charter of King Edgar. Evidently Dromonby was in the possession of one *Dragmel* before it passed to *Drómundr*. The *Dragmel*[1] may even be identical with the witness named above.

Stokesley

1. GREAT BUSBY 15 N 8
   Buschebi 1086 DB, 1202 FF
   Magna Buskebi(a), *Buskeby* 1180–90 YCh 581 *et passim* to 1327 Fount
   Buskby 1369 FF, *Magna Busbye* 1581 FF
   'Buski's farm' from the ON pers. name *Buski*, a weak form of *Buskr* (LindN) and by.

BLATEN CARR (6″)
   Blatun 1086 DB *Blatonkerr* 1198, 1535 Fount, 1535 VE
   'Bleak farmstead marsh' *v.* blár, tun, kjarr.

2. LITTLE BUSBY 15 N 8
   Buschebi 1086 DB
   v. Great Busby *supra*.

3. NEWBY 15 L 8
   Neubie, *-by* c. 1236 *Heal* 57 (p) *et passim* to 1463 YD
   'New farm' *v.* niwe, by.

4. STOKESLEY 15 M 8 [stɔuzlə]
   Stocheslag(e) 1086 DB
   Stokesle(i), *-le(y)* 1112–22 YCh 559 *et passim*
   Stokelega 1181 P
   Stocheslei 1189–1204 YCh 564
   Stokelay 1254 Ebor
   Stokeslay 1319 Guis, 1359 FF, 1399 YI, 1461 Test
   Stoxelay 1481 Test, *Stoxley* 1530 NCyWills

---

[1] This name may be a by-name from ON *drag-máll*, 'drag-speech,' used of one who speaks with difficulty.

This is a very difficult name. The forms suggest that the first element is OE *stoc* rather than *stocc*, but no local compounds in which stoc forms the first element have hitherto been identified. Further, the element *stoc* is otherwise unknown in this area and a certain difficulty always attaches to genitival compounds of the kind involved in suggesting that Stokesley might mean the leah belonging to some lost *stoc*.

TANTON

> *Tametun*, *-ton(a)* 1086 DB, *Tameton* 1170 P (p), 13 Guis,
> 1208 FF, 1224 Pat
> *Tanton(a)* 1203–7 Whitby, 1285 (16th) KI
> *Tampton* 1243–73 *Heal* 43 *d et passim* to 1418 YI
> *Tamton* c. 1280–90 *Heal* 108, 1312 Ch
>
> 'Farm on the Tame' *v.* Tame, R. 6 *supra* and tun.

Stainton

1. HEMLINGTON   15 K 8

> *Himelige-*, *Himelintun* 1086 DB
> *Hemelington* 1253 Ch, 1301 LS, *Hemillington* 1279 YI
> *Hemling-*, *Hemlyngton* 13 BM, 1285 KI
>
> 'Hemela's farm' *v.* ingtun. Cf. Gate Helmsley 10 *supra*.

COULBY [kɔubi]

> *Colebi* 1086 DB
> *Colleby* a. 1135 Whitby, 1295 YI, 1310 Ch (p)
> *Colby* 1292 *Heal* 166 (p), *et freq* to 1416 YI
>
> 'Kolli's farm' from the ON pers. name *Kol(l)i* (LindN), found also in the Dan place-name *Kulby* (Nielsen), and by.

2. INGLEBY BARWICK   15 K 6

> *Englebi* 1086 DB   *Ingleby* 1463 YD
> including
> *Caldengilbi* (1279 YI), *K-*, *Caldingelby* (1283, 1296 YI),
> *Caudhyngilby* (1516 Sanct) and *Ingelby-Loringe* (1285 KI),
> *Engelby-Lorenge* (1303 KF), *Ingulby Loring* (1407 YI),
> *Ingleby Lawrell* (1575 FF)

v. Ingleby Greenhow 167 *supra.* 'Cold' Ingleby possibly refers to Ingleby Hill rather than to Ingleby Barwick itself. *Loringe* refers to the family of *Lorenge* who held here: the canons of Guisborough held *ex dono Willelmi Lorengie tres bouatas terre et tres toftas in Caldengelby'*. *Barwick* from its nearness to

BARWICK [barik]

> *Berewic* 1086 DB *Berewick super Teysa* 1219 FF
>
> *v.* berewic. It is on the Tees.

3. MALTBY 15 K 7 [mɔːtbi]

> *Maltebi, Malteby* 1086 DB, 1176–86 YCh 673 *et passim* to 1406 YI
> *Mauteby* 1222 FF, 1222–40 Guis, 1239 Ebor, 1240 Cl, 1310 Ch (p)
> *Mahuteby* 1310 Ch (p)
> *Mawtby* 1575 FF
> *Maltby* 1616 NR, 1666 Visit

'Malti's farm' *v.* by. The pers. name *Malti* (Nielsen) is adduced in OEScand only. Cf. Maltby (YWR), two Maltbys in L and Mautby (Nf).

SANDBECK (6″)

> *Sandbec* 1222 FF

4. STAINTON 15 K 7

> *Steintun, Esteintona* 1086 DB

'Enclosure or farm built of stone' *v.* steinn, tun.

STAINSBY

> *Steinesbi* 1086 DB

'Stein's farm'; cf. Stainsacre 123 *supra. v.* by.

THORNTON

> *Torentun, Tornetun* 1086 DB
>
> *v.* þorn, tun.

5. THORNABY 15 J 6

Turmozbi, Thormozbi, Tormozbi(a) 1086 DB
Thormodby 1175–1200 *BylE* 71 *d*, 1312 Guis
Thormodebi, -by 1202, 1231 FF, 1252 Riev, 1262–80 Guis,
    1333 Riev
Thormotebi, -by 1279 YI, 1280 Ch, Guis, 1293 QW
Thormotheby 1285 KI, *Thormothby* 1416 YI
Thormotby 1301 LS, 1369 FF, 1410 Guis
Thornaby 1665 Visit

'Thormoth's farm' *v.* by. The first element is ON *þormóðr*
found also in Thormanby (Bulm) 26 *supra*.

Seamer

1. SEAMER 15 L 8

Semer, Semers (sic) 1086 DB, (*in Clevelande*) c. 1150 Godr
Samara, Samare 1133, 1140–54, c. 1180 Whitby, 1218 FF

With the same run of forms and interpretation as Seamer
(Pick) 102 *supra*. *v.* Addenda xlv.

Hilton

1. HILTON 15 L 7

Hiltun(e) 1086 DB, 1166 P (p), *Hilton(a)* 1086 DB, c. 1180
    Guis (p) *et passim*

Self-explanatory.

Yarm

1. YARM 15 K 5 [jaːm]

Gerou (sic), *Iarun* 1086 DB
Jarum 12 Guis (*passim*), 1198 Abbr *et passim* to 1369 FF
Yarum 1182 Guis, 1198 Fount, 1342 Test (*passim*), 1354 FF,
    1407–19 YI, 1436 NCyWills
Garum 1218 FF
Jarrom 1234 Pat
Yarom 1285 KI, 1429 NCyWills, 1464 Test, 1470 RichWills
Yarm(e) 1300 YI, 1530 Visit

From OE *gearum*, the dative plural of OE *gear* (found in the
compound *mulen-gear* BCS 984), 'a *yair*, a pool for catching
fish' (cf. Ekwall, *PN in -ing* 95 note). Yarm is on the river
Tees and the name denotes 'fish pools.'

Kirkleavington

1. CASTLE LEAVINGTON (6″), identical with CASTLE HILL 15 L 6

Levetona, Lentun(e) 1086 DB

Levinton, Levynton 1230, 1246 Cl, *(Castel)* 1219 *Ass*, 1299 Fine, 1571 FF

Levincthon c. 1275 *Bodl* a. i. 59 (p)

Castellevington 1293 QW, 1299 YI, 1301 LS, 1378 YD

'Farm by the river Leven' (later distinguished by its castle).
v. Leven, R. 4 *supra* and tun.

HOLDENFIELD

Holdene 1270 Pat

v. hol, denu.

2. KIRK LEAVINGTON 15 L 6

Levetona, Lentune 1086 DB

With the same run of forms as for Castle Leavington and first called *Kirkelevingtona* in 1230–50 Guis. Kirk Leavington is distinguished by its church, which stands prominently in the highest part of the village. *v.* kirkja.

3. PICTON 15 M 5

Pike-, Pyketon(a), -tun c. 1200 BM *et passim* to 1310 Ch

Pickton 1285 KI, 1565 FF

Pykton 1301 Abbr, 1354, 1369 FF, 1435 Baildon

'Pica's farm' *v.* tun. The first element is probably the weak form of the OE pers. name *Pīc* (Redin 22), cf. Pickhill 224 *infra* and Pickenham (Nf), DB *Pichenham*.

4. LOW WORSALL 15 L 4 [wɔrsəl]

Wercesel, Wirceshel, Wercheshal(e) 1086 DB

Wi-, Wyrkeshale 1154–81 Guis *et freq* to 1335 Ch, *Estwirke-shala* 1181 P

Werkeshal' 1201 ChR

Wirkesale, Wy- 1285 KI, 1303 KF, 1367 FF, *(Parva)* 1301 LS

Wirkesall 1285 KI, 1316 Vill

Wirsal(e) 1316 (Eliz) Vill, 1369 FF

Parva Worsall 1483 Sanct

The first element is an OE pers. name *Wyrc* not found independently in OE but inferred from numerous place-names. *v.* Warkworth in PN NbDu 207. The second element probably refers to the nook of land enclosed by the river Tees. *v.* h(e)alh.

Appleton Wiske

1. APPLETON WISKE 15 N 4

    Ap(p)elton(a), *Apletune* 1086 DB

    v. æppel, tun. Appleton is on the river Wiske.

Crathorne

1. CRATHORNE 15 M 6

    Gratorne (sic), *Cratorne* 1086 DB, 1279–81 QW
    Crathorn c. 1160–75 YCh 688 *et passim*
    Creythorne 1575 FF

    The second element is þorn. The first element is not certain but it may be ON *krá*, 'nook, corner,' hence, 'thornbush in the corner of land.' It lies by a bend in the Leven.

Rudby

1. HUTTON RUDBY 15 M 7

    Hotun, *-ton* 1086 DB *et passim* to 1412 YI, Guis
    Hottona juxta Rodeby 1204 YCh 787, *Hooton Rudbye* 1582 FF

    'Farm on the spur of land' *v.* hoh, tun. Rudby *infra* is on the opposite bank of the river.

2. MIDDLETON UPON LEVEN 15 L 7

    Mid(d)eltun, *-tone* 1086 DB
    Midetun in Cliveland 12 Dods xcv. 36
    Mydilton juxta Leuene 1218–31 Heal 113, etc.

3. RUDBY 15 M 7

    Rodebi 1086 DB
    Rudebi, *-by* c. 1150 RegDun, 12 Guis, 1189–99 YCh 800,
        c. 1225 BM, 1228 Ch, Cl
    Ruddeby c. 1190 Guis, *et freq* to 1402 Test

Rudby 1285 KI *et passim*
Ruthby 1489 Sanct

'Rudi's farm' *v.* by. There is a rare ON name *Rudi* which
Lind (s.n. *Ruði*) thinks should be spelt *Ruði*.

4. SEXHOW 15 M 7

Sex(h)ou c. 1160–80 YCh 692, c. 1280–90 *Heal* 108 (p),
   Sexhowe 1285 KI, 1303 KF, *Sexho* 1665 Visit
Saxhow 1404 YI, 1478 Test, *Saxo* 1483 Test

'Sek's mound' from ON *Sekkr* (LindBN) and haugr.

5. SKUTTERSKELFE 15 M 7

Codreschelf, Codreschef, Codeschelf 1086 DB
Scuðerschelf 1176 P (p) *Sc-, Skutherskelf* c. 1236 *Heal* 57
   (p), c. 1290 *Heal* 108, 1292 *Heal* 166
Sc-, Skotherskelf(e) 1301 LS, 1303 KF (p), 1316 Vill
Scuherscelf 1310 Ch
Scuderskelf 1310 Ch (p) *Scuþerskeelf* 1350 Pap
Scoterskelf 1285 (16) KI, 1481 Test
Scutterskelf 1529 NCyWills *Scuterskill* 1577 Saxton

The first element is probably the ON by-name *Skvaðra*,
which also had a form *Skoðra* (LindBN). Lind supposes that
this was an old place-name but it seems more likely, as Professor
Ekwall suggests, that *Skvaðra* is an old by-name derived from
skvaðra, in the sense of 'chatter, talk.' The second element is
ON *skjalf*, 'shelf, seat,' *v.* Raskelf 26 *supra*.

BRAWORTH

Breydewad 1240–50 *Bodl* a. i. 88
Brathwaith 1285 KI, *Brathewheyt* 1327 Ipm
Braythwayth 1299 KI, *Braithewath* 1300 YI, *Braythwat*
   1350 Cl

'Broad ford' *v.* breiðr, vað. Braworth lies near a ford across
the Leven. The various forms *waith, wheyt* are due to confusion
with þveit as in Flawith 21 *supra*.

THORALDBY

Turoldes-, Toro(l)desbi 1086 DB
Thoroldeby 1219 *Ass*

Thorald(e)by c. 1280–90 *Heal* 108 d, 1292 *Heal* 166, 1310 Ch
Thoralby 1285 (16) KI

'Thorold's farm' *v. by*. The first element is ON *þorvaldr*
(LindN, Nielsen); cf. Swed *Tolleby* (OSwed *þoralderby*), Hellquist, *ON på -by* 107.

Carlton

1. CARLTON 15 N 8

Carletun 1086 DB

v. karlatun.

Whorlton

1. FACEBY 15 N 8 [fɛəsbi]

Feizbi, Fezbi, Foitesbi 1086 DB
Fayzeby, Fayseby 12 Guis, 1340 Pat
Fayceby c. 1160 Riev *et passim* to 1367 FF
Faicesby 1208 FF
Faceby 1285 KI, 1399 *Archd* 19

'Feit's farm' *v. by*. The first element is derived from ON
feitr 'fat' used as a pers. name in the OIcel place-name *Feitsdal*
(Landnamabók). A weak form of the pers. name, *Feiti*, is
adduced by LindBN.

The DB form *Foites-* is satisfactorily explained by Lindkvist
(43, note 1) as due to a Central French scribe, whose language
would contain OFr *oi* instead of Northern Fr and AN *ei*. The
ON gen. -*s* is preserved in this name (cf. Haxby 14 *supra*).

2. POTTO 15 N 7

Pothow(e) 1202 FF *et freq* to 1385 Baildon
Pottowe 1285 KI, 1354 FF, *Potto* 1548 YChant, 1575 FF

'Hill near the small valley' *v.* hoh and cf. Pott Hall 234 *infra*.

GOULTON [gɔutən]

Goltona, Goutun, Gotun 1086 DB
Gouton 1202 FF, 1301 LS (p), 1303 FF, *Gow(e)ton* 1285 KI,
1548 YChant

Perhaps 'Golda's farm' from the OE pers. name *Golda* and
tun.

3. WHORLTON 15 O 7

Wirveltun(e) 1086 DB
Weruelthun, -ton 1189–99 YCh 800 *et freq* to 1294 Ebor
Qwerlton 1198 Fount
Wheruelton 1202 FF
Wherfletun, Wherfelton 1259 Ass
Werleton 1279–81 QW
Wherleton 1299 YI, 1323 Abbr, 1354 FF
Werelton 1301 LS
Warleton 1285 (16) KI
Whorl(e)ton 1399 Test, 1412 YI, 1470 Test, 1575 FF

'Farm near the Whorl Hill.' No early spellings are adduced for Whorl Hill, but there is no doubt that *whorl* is from OE hwyrfel or ON hvirfill. The Whorl Hill is a high hill with a rounded top. Cf. Whorlton (PN NbDu 215).

HUTHWAITE [iuθwit]

Hogthuet 12 *Cur* No. 46, m. 3 *d, Hogtweit* 1207 FF, *Hothwayt* 1350 Cl

The first element of this name is probably OE hoh and not ON *haugr* or ON *hór* 'high' as suggested by Lindkvist (111). Modern [iu] points to an OE or ON *ō* (*v*. Introduction xxxii) and we are probably right in taking the first element to be OE hoh 'spur of land' for this would normally become [iu] (as in Huby 18 *supra*) and it suits topographically, for Huthwaite is on a long narrow ridge of land overlooking Crook Beck. *v*. þveit.

SCARTH WOOD, LEES etc.

Scarth 1189–99 YCh 800, *Scarthwood* 1616 NR

v. skarð. The scarth here is the long narrow pass running through the Cleveland Hills.

SCUGDALE (6″)

Schugedale 1228 Cl

v. Scugdale 152 *supra*.

SWAINBY

> *Swayn(e)sby* late 13 BM, 1313 Pat
> *Swaneby* 1314 Pat
> *Swainby* 1367 IpmR, 1616 NR

Possibly 'Swain's farm' from the ON pers. name *Sveinn* (LindN) and **by**, but cf. Swainby 225 *infra*.

TRENHOLME

> *Traneholm* 1177 P (p), 1285 KI, 1299 YI, 1323 Abbr
> *Thranholm* 1226 FF
> *Treyneham* 1575 FF, *Traynholme* 1596 Pickhill

'Crane-meadow' *v.* trani, holmr.

Ingleby Arncliffe

1. INGLEBY ARNCLIFFE 15 O 6

> *Englebi, -by* 1086 DB, 1231 *Ass*, *Engelby juxta Erneclyf* 1303 KF

v. Ingleby Greenhow 167 *supra* and Arncliffe *infra*.

ARNCLIFFE

> *Erneclive, Gerneclif, Lerneclif* 1086 DB
> *Ernesclive* c. 1160 Riev
> *Erneclive* c. 1170 Riev *et passim* to 1293 QW
> *Arneclive* c. 1291 Tax, *Arneclyff* 1349 Test, 1474 YD, etc.

'Eagles' cliff' *v.* earn, clif. Arncliffe is a large, steep, wooded bank. The DB forms *Gerne-* and *Lerne-* (*L* is an error for *I*, Zachrisson, *Mélanges de Philologie offerts à M. Johan Vising*, Göteborg, 1925, p. 191) arise from the shifting of the stress in OE *éa* to the second element of the diphthong (cf. Yearsley 193 *infra*).

FOWGILL BECK

> *Fulbroke* c. 1150, c. 1160 Riev   *Fowgill* 1616 NR

'Dirty stream' *v.* ful, broc, gil.

VII. BIRDFORTH WAPENTAKE

Gerlestre wapentac 1086 DB
bruthewrthe scire 1088 *LVD* 50 *d*
wap' de Brud(d)eford' 1166 P *et freq* to 1303 *Ebor* 203
Brideford wap' 1170 P
wap. de Brudesford 1279–81 QW
Birdforth 1612 NR

Gerlestre is undoubtedly the name of the old wapentake meeting-place, but it cannot now be identified with any modern name. After the Conquest the place seems still to have been used as the meeting-place of the Riding court, for there are frequent references in the 13th and 14th cents. to *thrithingum de Yarlestre et wapentagium de Bruddeford* (13 RichReg 122 *d*), *thrythinge de Yarlestre* (1298 YI), *thrithingu' de Yarlestre, thrydyngum de Yarlestr'* (1279–81 QW), and *thrithingum de Yarnestre pro cccccc acris terre in parva Brochton* (which is in Cleveland, 1323 Abbr). In the reorganization after the Conquest the wapentake court met at the village of Birdforth and the court of the North Riding, from which Richmondshire and Allertonshire would now be excluded, met at the old wapentake meeting-place of *Yarlestre*. Possibly *Yerlestre* may be best interpreted as from OE *eorles-trēow*, 'eorl's tree.' Such tree-names are very common in names of ancient moots. The influence of Scand *jarl* would readily account for the development of initial *y*.

For Birdforth, *v.* 190 *infra* and scir.

Kirby Hill

1. ELLENTHORPE 27 A 1

Adelingestorp 1086 DB
Edelyn(g)thorp 1154–89 MaryH 6 *d*, 13 RichReg 106, 1328 Banco
Edelingetorp 1308 Ch
Ellyngthorpe 1523 BM, 1541 Dugd iii. 570, *Ellinthrope* 1574 FF

'Atheling's village' *v.* þorp. The first element may be either OE *æþeling*, 'prince' or a patronymic based on the OE pers.

name *Æþel*. Athelney (So), *Æþelinga eigg* ASC, and OE *Æþelingaden* (ASC s.a. 1001, MS A) both contain the gen. pl. of the OE noun *æþeling*. Perhaps we should not lay too much stress on the DB *s* (cf. the DB form of Brampton Hall *infra*).

2. HUMBURTON 27 A 1

Burtun, -tone   1086 DB, 1300 YI, 1301 LS
Hundesburton   1224–30 Fees, 1283, 1301 YI
Hundeburton   1276, 1307 YI, p. 1290, 1322 YD, 1327 Pat
Hundburton   13 *RichReg* 105 *d*, 1278 BM, 1285 KI, 1295 *For*, 1408 YI
Hunburton(e)   1486 YD, 1546 YChant, 1579 FF

'Hund's burhtun' from the ON pers. name *Hundr* (LindBN) or possibly from OE *Hund* (cf. MLR xiv. 241). Cf. Langthorpe *infra*.

3. KIRBY HILL 26 A 13

Chirchebi   1086 DB
Ki-, Kyrkeby in Mora, super Moram   1224–30 Fees
Kirby under hill   1665 Visit

v. kirkja, by.

4. LANGTHORPE 26 A 13   [læŋθrəp]

Torp   1086 DB
Langliuetorp   12 *RegAlb* i. 36
Langle(i)thorp   1157 *RichReg* 82, 1301 YI, c. 1300 id. 36 *d*
Langathorp   1308 Ch, *Langthorp(e)*   1300 *RichReg* 105 *d*, 1576 FF

v. þorp. The first element is the pers. name *Langlif*, recorded in the later insertions in *LVD* as *Langlif(e)* from the ON woman's name *Langlífr*. The name as a whole is of the same type as Humburton *supra*.

BRAMPTON HALL

Bran(s)tone   1086 DB   *Branton'*   1182 P
Bramton   1235 Ch   *Brampton*   c. 1260 *Malton* 39, (*uppon Swale*) 1536 YChant

'Bramble farm' *v.* brame, tun.

5. MARTON LE MOOR 26 A 13

Marton' 1198 Fount, (*on the Moor*) 1292 Ch, (*super Moram*)
1293 Fount

v. Marton 28 *supra.* For *le, v.* Barton le Willows 38 *supra.*

CALDWELL (lost)

Caldeuuelle 1086 DB   *Caldewell* 1198 Fount

'Cold spring' *v.* cald, w(i)ella.

6. MILBY 26 A 14

Mildebi, -by 1086 DB *et passim* to 1359 FF
Milbye 1557 RichWills

'Mildi's farm' *v.* by. The first element is ON *Mildi* (LindBN).

Cundall[1]

1. CUNDALL 22 J 1

Cundel, Goindel 1086 DB
C-, Kundale 12 *RegAlb* i. 36 *d, et passim* to 1457 Test
Cundall 1418 *Archd* 20

v. dæl. The first element may be from the OE name *Cunda*
or from the ODan pers. name *Kundi* (Nielsen) or from the
OWScand by-name *Kunta.* The assimilation of *d-d* to *d* or
t-d to *d* is paralleled by the assimilation of *t-t* to *t* in Catton
183 *infra.* Another possibility is OE *cūna-dæl,* 'cows' valley.'

LECKBY

Ledebi, -by 1086 DB
Letteby, Lecceby 1301 LS
Lecby 1399 YI   *Letby* 1586 FF

'Let's farm' from ON *Ljótr* (LindN) and by. The appearance of medial -*c*- is bound up with two problems: one is the
problem arising from the difficulty in distinguishing *c* and *t*
in the handwriting of the 14th and 15th cents.; the second
arises from the fact that *c* in medieval orthography was used to
represent ON *z* (= ts), as in the early spellings of Roxby 139
supra. Where *t* is found it seems probable that ON gen. -*s* had

---

[1] A detached part of Halikeld wapentake.

been lost; where *c* is found it may be a mistake for *t* or re-present ON gen. *Ljótz*. The modern form seems to have arisen from the interchange of *k* and *t* in difficult consonant combinations in the dialect. *v.* Addenda xlv.

2. NORTON LE CLAY 21 J 14

    Norton(e) 1086 DB, *(in le Drit)* 1301 LS, *(in the Cley)* 1536 YChant, *(in luto)* 1578 FF

'North farm' *v.* norþ, tun. The affix *drit* is from ON *drit* 'dirt'; Lat. *lutum* = OE *clæg* 'clay'; all these words refer to the clayey, swampy nature of the land round Norton. For *le*, *v.* Barton le Willows 38 *supra*. 'North,' perhaps in relation to Boroughbridge, three miles to the south.

Topcliffe

1. ASENBY 21 H 14 [ɛəzənbi]

    Æstanesbi 1086 DB, *Aistanesbi* 12 *Dods* viii. 154 *d* (p)
    Aystaneby 1157 *RichReg* 82, 1182 Percy, 1244 *Ass*
    Ai-, *Aystenby*, *Eistanby*, *Aystanby* 1198 Fount, *et freq* to 1417 YI
    Estanesby 1244 *Ass*
    Aysynby 1408 Pat, 1539 RichWills, *Aesonbye* 1581 FF

'Eystein's farm' *v.* by. From ON *Eysteinn* (LindN), ODan *Østen* (Nielsen). The forms in *stan* are due to the influence of the corresponding OE name-theme.

BONNY CARR (6″)

    Brunigker 13 Percy

v. kjarr. The first element is not clear, but it may be the pers. name *Bruning*, common in the 11th cent. The modern form arises from metathesis of *Brun-* to *Burn-*, the dialectal pronunciation of which is [bɔrn] or [bɔˑn] (*v.* Introd. xxxii).

2. BALDERSBY 21 G 12

    Baldrebi 1086 DB *Balderbi*, *-by* 1156 Fount, *et passim* to 1576 FF
    Baldersby 1648 Pickhill

v. by. The first element is the OE pers. name *B(e)aldhere*.

3. CATTON 21 G 13

Catune 1086 DB

C-, Katton 1199 FF *et passim*

'Catta's or Kati's farm' *v.* tun. The first element is from ON *Káti* or OE *Catta*, not found in independent use in OE, but *v.* MLR xiv. 237. Cf. Caton (PN La 177) and Catton (Nf), *Catetuna, Cat(t)una* 1086 DB.

SOUTHERBY HOUSE

Southby super Swale 13th, 1333 Percy

'South farm' *v.* suð, by.

4. DALTON 22 H 2 [dɔːtən]

Deltune 1086 DB

Dautona c. 1200 Guis, *Daweton* 1573 FF

Dalton 13 Percy, 1252 *Ass, et passim*

'Valley farm' *v.* dæl, tun.

BROATS HOUSE

Brotes 13 YD

v. Broates in Pickering 86 *supra.*

ISLE BECK

Iselbec 1086 DB, *I-, Yselbec(h), -be(c)k* 13 *BylE* 46, 1285 KI, 1299 YI, 1301 LS, 1334 YD, *Ysilbeke* 1500 Test

Y-, Isebec 1182 P (p), 1247 Ch

Yserbec 1182 P (p), c. 1197 YD, 13 Percy, *Hiserbeck* 13 Percy

Isselbecke 1571 FF

Possibly, as suggested by Mr Bruce Dickins, the original name of this stream was OE *Isel*, cognate with the Dutch river-name *Ijssel*, found in the 9th and 10th cents. as *Is(e)la* (Förstemann, *ON* 1592). *v.* bekkr.

SANDHOLMES

Sandholm 13 Percy

v. sand, holmr.

5. DISHFORTH 21 J 13

Di-, Dysford(e) 1086 DB, 1276 YI, 1285 KI, 1314 Ch, 1327
    Fount, 1403 YI, -forthe 1541 RichWills, 1577 Saxton,
    1578 FF, 1612 NR
Disseford 1157 RichReg 82, 1198 Fount, Di-, Dysceford 1208
    FF, 1298 Abbr, 1301 LS, 1316 Vill, 1328 Banco, 1333
    Percy, 1350 FF
Diceford 1202, 1208 FF
Dichefurthe 1535 Fount
Dishford 1665 Visit

Dishforth is from OE dic and ford. Zachrisson has shown
(Mélanges etc. u.s. p. 179 ff.) that in the form Disford we have
AN influence, whereby OE c became s, as in Diss, Dissington
(Nf, Nb). For the later development of Dis- to Dish-, cf.
Whashton 292 infra and Dishley (Lei), Dislea DB. The
same name Ditchford is found in Blockley in Wo and there the
dic is the Foss Way (PN Wo 98). Here the ford carried an
important road from Boroughbridge to Northallerton but we
do not know that the road was ever called a 'dyke.' More
probably the meaning is that of Ditchford in Hanbury (PN Wo
322), viz. 'ford across the small dic or stream.'

6. ELDMIRE 22 H 1

Elvetemer(e) 1236 Cl, 1246 Ch, 1252 Ass Elvytemere 1301 LS
Eldmer 1500 Test, 1615 NR Elmyer 1573 FF

'Swan pool' from OE elfetu and mere, as in Ellermire 68
supra. Eldmire is by the river Swale.

CRAKEHILL

Crecala 1086 DB
Crakhale 1301 LS Crakhall(e) 1314 Ipm, 1536 YChant

'Craca's nook' v. h(e)alh (which probably here refers to one
of the nooks of land round which the river Swale flows). The
first element is the late OE pers. name Craca (LVD) from ON
Kráki (LindN, LindBN). Cf. Crakehall 237 infra.

7. RAINTON 21 H 13

Reineton, Rainincton 1086 DB
Renyng-, Renington 1157, 1184 RichReg 82, 84 d, et passim to
    1319 Cl

Renningeton 1202, 1208 FF
Reignington 1213 Abbr
Reniton 1219 Percy
Ranyngton 1285 KI, c. 1300 *RichReg* 86 *d*, 1527 Fount
Raynyng-, *Raynington* 1301 LS, 1319 Cl, 1548 Fount
Raynton 1535 Ve

Cf. also DB *Raneuuat* (*Rainincton* superscribed) and *Rainingewat*.

With this name we should compare Rainton and Rennington (PN NbDu s.nn.). The first element is a pers. name *Rægen*, *Rein* which in Rainton (Du)[1] is known to be a shortened form of OE *Rægenwald*.

Rægenwald is commonly taken to be an Anglicising of ON *Rǫgnvaldr*, but it should be pointed out that OE names *Regengar*, *Regnhæg*, *Regenhere*, *Regenweald* and *Regenweard* are found borne by persons of whom some at least cannot be Scandinavian by birth or name and we must assume that this element was in free use in native names. An English name is more likely than a Scand one in an *ingtun* place-name formation.

CANA BARN

Kanehou 1202 FF

v. haugr. The first element is the OWScand by-name *Kani* (LindBN), OSwed *Kani* (Lundgren-Brate), found in DB as *Cane*.

EASBY (lost)

Asebi, *-by* 1086 DB, 1157 *RichReg* 82, 1184 ib. 85 *d*
Esseby 1157 *RichReg* 83
Esebi, *-by* 1190 Fount, 1243 Percy, 13 *RichReg* 106

'Esi's farm' *v.* by. The first element is the ODan pers. name *Esi* (Nielsen), which in some of the above spellings has been influenced by the cognate OWScand *Ási* (LindN). Cf. Easby 287 *infra* and 167 *supra*.

NEWBY ON SWALE (6")

Neuby 1157 *RichReg* 82, (*super Swale*) 1285 KI

'New farm' *v.* niwe, by.

[1] Professor Mawer informs me that Simeon of Durham's *Reiningtun* is Rainton (Du) and not Rennington (Nb) as stated in PN NbDu s.n.

RAINTON CARR (6″)

Reyningtonker 1303 Percy

v. kjarr and Rainton 184 *supra.*

8. SKIPTON ON SWALE 21 G 13

Schipetune 1086 DB   *Skipton' super Swale* 1243 Fees

'Sheep farm' *v.* sceap, tun. The first element is a Scand form of ONb *scip* (= WSax *sceap*), as in Skipton in Craven (YWR), *Scipton(e)* 1086 DB.

9. TOPCLIFFE 21 H 14

Topeclive 1086 DB, 1166 P (p), 1236 Cl, 1251 Percy
Toppecliue 1154–81 *RegAlb* i. 70 *et passim* to 1301 LS
Topclif 1288 Ebor *et passim* to 1371 Fabr
Topleffe 1519 Sanct

'The highest part of the cliff' from OE *topp* and clif. Topcliffe is on the upper edge of a very steep and lofty bank, overlooking the Swale R.

GALLOW GREEN (6″)

Galgholm 1333 Percy

'Gallow field' from ON *galgi* and holmr.

GRISTHWAITE

Grisethwayt(h) 1285 YI, 1334 Pat   *Grystwhate* 1447 Fabr

'Gris's enclosure' from the ON by-name *Griss* (*v.* Gristhorpe 104 *supra*) or 'pig enclosure' from ON griss. *v.* þveit.

10. FAWDINGTON 22 J 2

Faldingtun 1247 Ch
Faldin-, Faldynton 1254 YI, 1404 Fabr, *Falding-, Faldyngton* 13 *BylE* 32 *et passim*
Fawdington 1541 Dugd v. 355

'Falda's farm' *v.* ingtun. The OE pers. name *Falda* is not adduced independently, but it is the base of Faldingworth (L), *Faldingeuurde* 1086 DB, and a cognate form enters into OSwed *Faldunge* from an earlier *Faldungar (Hellquist, *ON på Inge* 25–6).

Sessay[1]

1. HUTTON SESSAY 22 H 3
Hottune 1086 DB
Hotun juxta Tresk 1252 Ch, *Hotton et Cessay* 1316 Vill
'Farm on the spur of land near Sessay' *v.* hoh, tun.

2. SESSAY 22 H 2 [sesi]
Sezai 1086 DB, *Ceszay* 1170–80 YCh 961, *Sezay* 1236,
1304 Ch, *Cezzaye* 1293 *For*, *Cesszay* 1365 FF
Segege 1088 *LVD* 50 *d*
Secey 1182 P, *Cesay* 1283 Ebor, 1376 FF, *Cessay, ey* 1285 KI,'
1295 *For*, 1316 *For*, *Secsay* 1295 *For*, *Sessay* 1483 Test
Probably, as suggested by the form in *LVD*, OE *Secges-ēg*,
'Secg's well-watered land' *v.* eg. The later forms represent
AN attempts to deal with these unfamiliar sounds.

Thirsk

1. CARLTON MINIOTT 21 F 14
Carletun, -ton 1086 DB
Karleton juxta Tresk n.d. YD *Carleton Mynyott* 1579 FF
v. karlatun. The family of Miniott held land here in the
14th cent. (VCH ii. 63).

2. SAND HUTTON 21 F 13
Hot(t)une 1086 DB
Hoton 1202 FF, (*Sande-*) 12 *FountA* 52 *Sand-Hutton* 1665
Visit
v. Sand Hutton (Bulm) 38 *supra*.

3. SOWERBY 22 F 2
Sorebi 1086 DB *Sourebi, -by* 1228 FF *et passim*
With same run of forms and meaning as *Sowerby* 128 *supra*.

THORPEFIELD
Petithorp juxta Thresk c. 1142 Dugd v. 352
campo de Thorp 1243 *BylE* 81 *d*, *Thorpfeld* 1303 KF
'The land belonging to Thorp' *v.* þorp, feld. Thorp was
probably a *petit* or small hamlet belonging to Thirsk.

---

[1] A detached part of Allerton wapentake.

4. THIRSK 22 F 2 [θɔsk, θrusk]

> *Tresch(e)* 1086 DB, c. 1150 RegDun, Godr, c. 1285 *Malton* 99
> *Thresca* 1145–53 *Leon* 35
> *Trescke* 1178 YCh 1114, 1281 Ebor
> *Tresc* 1086 DB, c. 1150 RegDun, c. 1160 JohHex
> *Tresk(e)* 1198 Fount, 1200 Cur *et passim* to 1333 Riev
> *Threske* 1243–8 Guis *et freq* to Sanct 1492
> *Thirsk, Thyrske* 1403, 1491 Test, 1413 *Heal* 157 d
> *Thriske* 1473 Test
> *Tryske, Thersk* 1536 YChant
> *Thrusk(e)* 1580 Cai, 1733 Kirklington

Professor Ekwall suggests that we have here an Anglo-Scand form of OSwed *thræsk*, Swed *träsk* 'fen, lake.' Thirsk is in a low-lying well-watered situation. The same element is possibly found in Threshfield, for the forms of which *v.* PN YWR 190.

DOWBER LANE (6″) [duːbə leːn]

> *Doutheburghe* 1243–8 Guis

'Duthi's burh.' Cf. the OSwed pers. name *Dudhi* (Lundgren-Brate).

NORBY

> *Northebi* John BM, *Norbyeng* 1243–8 Guis

'North village' (i.e. in relation to Thirsk) *v.* norð, by. The final element in the second form is ON eng 'meadow.'

STONYBROUGH (6″)

> *Steinhouberg* 1243–8 Guis

'Hill with the rock mound' *v.* steinn, haugr, berg. For the modern form cf. Stony Keld 305 *infra*.

WOODHILL FIELD (6″)

> *Wodhall* 1285 KI   *Wodehalfeld* 1407 YI

'The land near Woodhall' (i.e. the hall in or near the wood) *v.* wudu, h(e)all, feld.

Kirby Knowle[1]

1. BAGBY 22 F 3

Baghebi 1086 DB
Bagebi, -by 1086 DB, 1224–30 Fees, 1285 KI, 1301, 1400 YI
Baggaby 1158–66 YCh 175   *Baggebi, -by* 12 *Leon* 66 *d et passim* to 1344 Pap

'Baggi's farm' *v.* by. Cf. Bag Dale 145 *supra*.

SPITAL MOOR

Spitel More 1313 YD

For *spitel v.* Spital Bridge 123 *supra*. Note also *spitel lonyng*, a lane in Bagby (1313 YD).

2. BALK 22 F 3 [bɔːk]

Balc(h), Balk(e) 12 YD, 1192–9 Riev, 13 *BylE* 70 *d*, 1226 FF, 1575 FF
Bawke 1622 NR

From OE *balca*, the meaning of which is 'ridge, bank.' Balk stands in the valley bottom on Balk Beck, but originally the name must have been applied to the ridge of land between Balk Beck and Hood Beck, now occupied by Balk Wood.

BALK BECK

Balkesbec 13 *BylE* 84

MONK PARK

le Monkepark' 1300 YD

Thirkleby

1. THIRKLEBY 22 G 3

Turchilebi 1086 DB
Thurkillebi, -by 1202 FF, 1224 Pat, 1231 *Ass* (*passim*)
Thirtleby 1202 FF
Turkelby 1224–30 Fees

Further forms are without interest.

'Thurkel's farmstead' *v.* by. Cf. ODan *Thurkil* (Nielsen), ON *þorkell* (LindN).

[1] A detached part of the parish.

HOOD BECK

Hodesbec 13 *BylE* 84, *riuulus de Hode* 1243 *BylE* 81 *d*

v. Hood 195 *infra* and bekkr.

MENCLIFFE (6″)

Mel(e)clyue 1243 *BylE* 81 *d*, 1246 *BylE* 53 *d*

v. clif. The first element is probably ON melr, hence 'sandy hill.' For *n* cf. Hinderskelfe and Hinderwell 40, 138 *supra*.

OSGOODBY

Ansgotebi 1086 DB

With the same run of forms and interpretation as Osgodby (Pick) 104 *supra*.

Husthwaite

1. BIRDFORTH 22 H 3 [budfəθ]

    Brudeford 1199 Pap, 1219 FF, 1244, 1252 *Ass*, 1253 Ch, 1279–81 QW, 1293 *For*, QW
    Burdeford 1226 Pat
    Bruddeford 1286 YI, 1291 Fine, 1301 LS
    Brouddesforth 1296 YI
    Birdford 1485 Test, *-furth* 1537 Dugd vi. 199
    Burdforth 1564 FF
    Bridforth 1577 Saxton

    v. also Birdforth wapentake 179 *supra*, where there is earlier evidence for the name than there is here.

    The origin of the first element is obscure, for there is no pers. name like OE *Brudda* recorded or otherwise known from place-names. Such a name might, however, have existed; probably as a hypocoristic form of such an OE dithematic name as *Burgheard* with later metathesis from *Burda* to *Brudda*. The ON by-name *Brúðr* (LindBN) is also a possibility; ð (which is found in the 11th cent. form of the wapentake name) was changed to *d*, perhaps by analogy with OE *brȳd* 'bride'; cf. also ON *kið* and ME *kid* 'kid.'

2. CARLTON HUSTHWAITE 22 H 4

    C-, Karleton 1086 DB *et passim*, *Carlton Husthwat* 1516 Fabr
    v. karlatun. It is near Husthwaite *infra*.

3. HUSTHWAITE 22 H 4 [ustwit]

Hustwait, -twayt(e) 1167 P *et passim* to 1581 FF
Husthweyt, Husthwayt 1169–93 YCh 790, 1283 Ebor

'þveit with houses built on it' *v.* hus and cf. Norw *Hustveit* (NG).

BAXBY (6")

Basche(s)bi, Bachesbi 1086 DB
Baxeby 1169–92 YCh 790, 13 *BylE* 8 *d*, 1230 Cl, 1247 Ch,
     1262 YD, 1292 *For*, 1310 Ch
Baxseby 1227 FF, 1285 KI *Baxby* 1301 LS

'Bak's farm' *v.* by. The first element is probably the rare ON pers. name *Bak* (LindN).

RUDDINGS (6")

This is the name of an enclosed piece of land (*v.* hryding) which seems to have included *Gamelridding, Normanridding, le Suterridding*, and *Wluerikridding* (13th, 1346 YD), deriving respectively from the ON pers. names *Gamall, Sútari* (LindBN) and the OE *Norðman*, 'Norwegian.' For the last-named we have the name of one *Ulric* who held a ridding here c. 1217 (YD). On the modern form, cf. Ruswarp 125 *supra*.

Coxwold

1. ANGRAM GRANGE 22 G 4

Angrum 1252 Ch, 1293 QW, 1327 Banco, 1333 Riev
Angrame Graunge 1538 Riev

v. anger and cf. Angram Cote and Angram 249, 272 *infra*.

2. COXWOLD 22 G 5 [kukud]

Cuha-walda 757–8 BCS 184
Cucualt 1086 DB
Cukewald' 1154–89 *MaryH* 6 *d et passim* to 1304 BM
Cukwald 1196 Dugd v. 353, 1243 *BylE* 81 *d*, 1406 YI
Cukewaud' 1231 *Ass*
C-, Kokewald 1284 Baildon *et passim* to 1443 YD
Cucawald 1308 Ch

Cookwold 1545 BM

Cuckwould 1577 Saxton, *Cuckoldie* 1579 Cai, *Cockwould* 1665 Visit

The letter which contains the earliest form (BCS 184), though hardly to be accepted in its present shape, undoubtedly contains ancient and authentic matter, and there is no reason to mistrust the form *Cuhawalda*. It suggests that the first element of this name is an otherwise unknown OE pers. name *Cuha*. The development to later *Cuk-* has its parallel in Cockfield (Sf) from earlier *Cohhanfeld* (KCD 685). The *s* is pseudo-genitival. *v.* w(e)ald.

SUNLEY WOOD

Sonoluetre 1243 *BylE* 81 *d*

v. treow. For the pers. name element cf. Sunley Hill 66 *supra*

3. NEWBURGH 22 H 5

Nouo Burgo 1199 Pap, *Newburg* c. 1250 *Malton* 166, *Neuburgh* 13 *BylE* 81

'New burh.'

BRINK HILL

Brinke 1376 Dugd v. 348

v. brink.

4. OULSTON 22 H 5 [ɔulstən, ɔustən]

U-, V-, Wluestun, -ton 1086 DB, 1167 P, *et passim* to 1440 YD

Vlfeston 1176 P

Uulveston 1286 *For*

Ulston 1498 Test, 1613 NR

Owlston 1572 FF, *Owston* 1577 Saxton

'Ulf's farm' *v.* tun. The first element may be a Scand form of the common OE pers. name *Wulf* (cf. Ovington 299 *infra*) or it may be the ON cognate *Úlfr*.

5. THORNTON ON THE HILL 22 J 5

Torenton 1167 P *Thorenton on the Hill* 1275 YI

v. þorn, tun.

6. THORPE LE WILLOWS 22 H 6

Torp 1086 DB   *Thorp* c. 1142 Dugd v. 352 *et passim*
v. þorp.

7. WILDON GRANGE 22 G 4

Wildon, Wyldon 1138 Dugd v. 350, 1224 FF *et passim*
Wildun 1247 Ch

The first element is probably of the same origin as that of Wilton (Pick) 90 *supra*. The second is dun; hence 'wild hill.'

8. YEARSLEY 22 H 6 [jaːzlə]

Eureslage 1086 DB
Euereslei 1176 P, *-ley(a)* 13 BylE 36, 1303 Var
Euersle, -legh, -ley 1204 ChR *et passim* to 1304 Var
Yeveresleye 1304 Var   *Yeuersley, -lay, Yhevereslay* 1327 Banco, 1399, 1406 YI
Yearesley 1577 Saxton, 1613 NR

'Eofor's forest-clearing' *v.* leah. Forssner is uncertain whether *Eofor-* existed in OE as a name-theme (the only independent example of the name in OE is in *Beowulf*), but *Eofor* seems to be a native theme in *Eoforhuaet* and *Eofuruulf* (LVD), *Euerwacer* (KCD 811), etc. (*v.* Müller, *Namen des nordhumbrischen Liber Vitae*, 80). As a patronymic it enters into Everingham (YER), *Euringham* 1086 DB. It is from OE *eofor* 'wild boar' (cf. Everley 115 *supra*). For the development of prosthetic *y-*, through stress-shifting in the OE diphthong, *v. Anglia*, xxxiv. 293 ff.

IRTON (lost)

Iretone 1086 DB

v. Irton 101 *supra*.

PEEL WOOD

Yearesley Pele 1613 NR

Peel is from OFr *pel-* (from Latin *pāl-us* 'stake'; cf. 12th cent. Latin *pēlum*, Du Cange), and was used in English of 'a palisade of stakes, a stockaded enclosure' (NED).

Kilburn

1. BYLAND ABBEY 22 G 5

Beghland(a) 1142–3 *BylD* 15 *d*, 1140–60 YCh 1827 *et passim*
to 1231 FF
Beiland(a), Beyland c. 1150 Riev, 1167 P *et passim* to 1242 Cl
Bellalanda 1153 *Jerv* 20 *et passim* to 1287 Ebor
Beland' 1162 P *et freq* to 1354 FF
Begheland 1225 Pat, 1228, 1237 Cl
Bellaund 1285 KI
Biland(a), Byland 1285 KI, 1375 Barbour's *Bruce, et passim*

'Bega's land' *v.* land. The OE pers. name *Bēga* or *Bēaga*
enters also into Bayham (Sx), Baydon (W), and Beeley (Db),
Begelie 1086 DB.

On the spellings *Beland*, *v.* Zachrisson, *Studier i modern
språkvetenskap* v. 16. The form *Bellalanda* is Latin and shows
confusion of the first element with OFr *bel*, 'beautiful.'

BURTIS WOOD

Burtofts a. 1196 Dugd v. 353, 1376 ib. v. 348

A similar name is Burtoft (L), which appears as *Burtoft* in
OE (BCS 331, KCD 520, 1086 DB). The meaning is 'messuage
attached to a storehouse' from ON *búr* (cf. OE bur) and topt.
Cf. OSwed *burtomt* (Lindkvist).

CAMS HEAD

Cambisheved 1376 Dugd v. 348

'Head of the ridge' *v.* heafod and camb, though it is possible
that we have here the ON cognate *kámbr* rather than the
OE *camb*.

LUND (6″)

Lounde 1541 Dugd v. 354
v. lundr.

NEWSTEAD

Newestede 1541 Dugd v. 354

Cf. Oldstead 196 *infra* near by; *v.* niwe, stede.

WASS [wæs]

Wasse 1541 Dugd v. 355

Zachrisson (*Eng PN* etc. 41 ff.) has suggested that this is OE *wāse*, 'mud,' but no such dialectal form of 'ooze' is on record. Wass lies where three streams meet, and has two fords, one to the north and the other to the west of the village, so the name is probably ME *wathes*, 'fords.' Cf. vað. For such a sound-development cf. Newlass 73 *supra* and Smallways 292 *infra*. For such a name cf. Ford (Sx) which in earlier days was always used in the plural.

2. HOOD GRANGE 22 F 4 [ud]

Hod(e) 12 *BylE* 42 *d*, 1138 Dugd v. 350, 1172–80 *Dods* vii. 149, 1218 ClR, 1293 QW, 1332 Pat, 1376 Dugd v. 348

Cf. Hood Beck 190 *supra*. The origin of this name is uncertain but the element is probably found again in Hotham (YER), *to fastan hode* 963 (14) *RegAlb* i. 57, *Hode, Hodhum* 1086 DB, *Hodum* 1166 P, *Hothum* 1285 (16) KI, and in the names of two lost places in YNR, called *Bakerhod* 1278 *Malton* 243 *d* (in Huttons Ambo) and *Sculphode* 13 *Easby* 121 (in Scotton). Actually the word may be OE *hōd*, 'hood,' used in a topographical sense of either 'the top of a hill' or 'a hood-shaped hill.'

Professor Ekwall would prefer to take OE *hōd* as a lost word which is to be associated with OE *hēdan*, 'to protect,' in the same way that we have Germ *hüten* (vb) and *hut* (noun). In that case the word in place-names would mean 'shelter.' Dr Schram notes that the corresponding MLG *hoede*, beside its abstract sense 'protection, custody,' has developed the concrete sense 'place under military protection, fortress,' the kind of meaning that is required here. (Cf. Verwijs en Verdam, s.v. *hœde*.)

3. KILBURN 22 G 4

Chileburne 1086 DB
Killebrun(na) 12 Riev (p), 1209 FF, *-brunne* 1224 FF, 1231 Ass, *-burna* 13 *BylE* 52 *d*
Ki-, Kylebrunn(e) 1233 Cl, 1239 Ch, 13 YD, *-burne* 1293 *For*

Kilibrunn 1245 Cl

Ki-, *Kylburne* 1249 Baildon, 1285 KI, 1301 LS, 1399 YI

'Cylla's stream' *v.* **burna, brunnr.** Cf. Kilburn (Db), *Killeburn* 1236 Ch.

OUSEY CARR (6")

Wlsiker 13 *BylE* 52 *d*

v. **kjarr.** The first element is the OE pers. name *Wulfsige*. Loss of initial *w-* may be due to the influence of Scand pers. names in *Ulf-*. Cf. Ovington 299 *infra*.

ROSE HILL (6") [ro:zil]

Roseberg(h)(a) 13 *BylE* 52 *d*, 1246 ib. 53 *d*, 1247 Ch, 1249 Baildon, 1376 Dugd v. 348

v. **berg.** The first element is difficult but it may be compared with Rosedale 80 *supra*. It probably had a short vowel in ME to give NEDial [o:], so that we may have here a form of ON *Rossi* (LindBN). 'Rossi's hill.'

STOCKING HOUSE

Stocking a. 1196 Dugd v. 353

v. **stocking.**

TRENCAR (6")

Traneker 1231 *Ass*, 13 *BylE* 52 *d*

'Crane marsh' *v.* **trani, kjarr.** Cf. Trenholme 178 *supra*.

4. OLDSTEAD 22 G 5

veterem locum 1247 Ch   *Oldsteade* 1541 Dugd v. 355

v. **(e)ald, stede** and cf. Newstead 194 *supra*.

CAM, COLD CAM

Camb(e), *Kambe* 1138, a. 1196 Dugd v. 350, 353, 1376 ib. v. 348, 1371, 1385 Baildon

Camp' 1293 QW

v. **camb** and Cams Head 194 *supra*. Cam is at the northern end of a ridge.

Old Byland

1. OLD BYLAND 22 E 5

The spellings follow closely those of Byland Abbey. We may note *Begeland* 1086 DB, *Veteri Bella Landa* 1293 QW, *Old Bylande* 1541 Dugd v. 355. *v.* Byland Abbey 194 *supra.*

ASHBERRY HILL

   Escheberch 1135–46 Riev *Eskebergam* 1143 *BylD* 15 *d*, 1181 *BylE* 103 *d*

   'Ash-tree hill' *v.* eski, berg.

NETTLE DALE

   Netteldala 1241 *BylE* 28 *d*

OXENDALE

   Oxedale c. 1300 *BylE* 36

2. COLD KIRBY 22 E 5

   Carebi 1086 DB
   Kerebi, -by 1170 Riev, 1185 P (p) *et passim* to 1343 YD
   Kerby 1143 *BylD* 15 *d*, 1257 Ch, 1269 Ebor, 1393 Test
   Kareby, Kairebi 1209 FF
   Kyerby 1541 Dugd v. 353   *Keirby* 1581 FF

Lundgren-Brate (158) presuppose an OSw *Kærir*. This name cannot well be represented here as there is no sign of the strong gen. inflexion. They quote from Nielsen (56) a pers. name *Petrus Kæreson*. This points to the possibility of a weak *Kæri* side by side with the strong *Kærir* (cf. *þori* and *þorir*). This would satisfactorily explain the various forms assumed by the present name. *v.* by.

BLACKAMORE (lost)

   mora de Blachou c. 1160 Guis
   Blakemore 1301 LS
   Blakoumore, Blakeowe More 1343 YD, 14 Horn Childe (line 110)
   Bla(c)kamore 1421 YD, 1571 FF
   'Black howe moor' *v.* blæc, haugr, mor.

HAMBLETON HILLS

>*Hamelton(a)* c. 1160 Riev, 1350 FF, 1452 Test
>*Hameldon'* 1301 LS, *Hamylden* 1431 Test

v. Hambleton Hill (LangW) 158 *supra.* There was early confusion of the suffixes tun and dun.

Felixkirk

1. BOLTBY 22 E 3 [bɔutbi]

>*Boltebi, -by* 1086 DB *et passim* to 1399 YI
>*Bolthebi* c. 1155, 1160 Riev
>*Boutebi, -by* 1176, 1181 P, 1209 FF, 1230 Ebor, 1271 Ch
>*Boltby* 1316 Vill

'Bolt's farm' *v.* by. *Bolt* is from ON *Boltr* (LindBN), with gen. form *Bolt.*

HAGGIT HILL (6")

>*Haichoved* c. 1180 Riev

'Oak hill' *v.* eik, hǫfuð, and cf. *Aykhouth* (a lost place in Hudswell) 13 *Easby* 205. For voicing of intervocalic -*k*- cf. Wigginton 14 *supra.*

HESKETH GRANGE

>*Hesteskeith, Hesteskeid* 1153–9, 1154–63 Riev
>*Heyscayth* 1268 Ch
>*Heskayth* 1273 Riev, 1293 QW *Hesketh* 1538 Riev, 1579 FF

v. hestr, skeið and IPN 90

RAVENSTHORPE MANOR [reːnzθrəp]

>*Rauenstorp* 1086 DB
>*Rauenestorp* 1086 DB, 1189 Riev, 1230 Ebor, 1248 Riev, 1252 Ch
>*Ravenet(h)orp* 1086 DB, 1271 Ch
>*Revenesthorb* 1088 *LVD* 51
>*Raven(e)sthorp(e)* c. 1155 Riev *et passim* to 1412 Test
>*Rawynsthorpe* 1507 Test
>*Ranethorppe* 1578 FF

'Raven's village' from the ON pers. name *Hrafn* and þorp.

2. FELIXKIRK 22 E 3

Fridebi 1086 DB

Ecclesia S. Felicis 1210 FF

Felicekyrke, -kirk 1293 QW, 1316 Vill, *Feliskirk* 1410 NCyWills

Fillyxchurche 1578 FF

Fridebi appears from the topographical arrangement of DB to be in the parish of Felixkirk and may represent what was later known as Felixkirk. It is of the same origin as Firby 237 *infra*.

Felixkirk is 'the church dedicated to St Felix' *v.* kirkja. Cf. Oswaldkirk 55 *supra* and Romaldkirk 309 *infra*.

MARDERBY GRANGE

Martrebi 1086 DB

Marther(e)by 1170–83 *Dods* vii. 148 *d*, 13 *BylE* 66, 1285 KI

Mardarbye 1546 YChant

v. by. The first element is ON *morðr*, 'marten,' gen. *marðar* used as a pers. name as in Norw *Malerod, Marstad* (Rygh, *Gamle Personnavne* s.n.). 'Marth's farm.'

3. SUTTON UNDER WHITESTONE CLIFFE 22 F 3

Sudtune, Sudtone 1086 DB

Sutton subtus Whitstanclif 13 *BylE* 68

Sutton is in the extreme south of this parish. *v.* Whitestone Cliffe *infra*.

GORMIRE LAKE

Gormyr' 1243 *BylE* 82

'Dirt marsh' from OE gor and myrr.

WHITESTONE CLIFFE

Whitstanclyff 13 *BylE* 49 *d*

Wystan 1301 LS   *Whistoncliffe* 1613 NR

4. THIRLBY 22 E 3 [θɔrlbi]

Trillebi(a), Trylleby 1189, 1248 Riev, 1226 FF, 1252 Ch, 1285 KI

Thirleby 1271 Ch, 1316 Vill, 1399 YI, 1579 FF

Thrilleby 1273 Riev, 1301 LS

The forms point to an ON *prilli* or *prylli*. No such name is on record, but it is a conceivable weak diminutive of the pers. name element *þrýð-* found in ON *þrýð-rikr*. If so, the name means '*prylli's* by.'

KELMER GRANGE

Keldithemar 1243–8 Guis

This is probably a compound of *mar* (*v.* Marton 28 *supra*) and ON keld-hliþ 'spring-hill.' For this last name *v.* Kellet (PN La 186). Hence, 'marsh by *Keldlith*.'

South Kilvington

1. SOUTH KILVINGTON 22 E 1

Cheluintun, Chelvinctune 1086 DB
Ky-, Kiluinton 1185–95 BM, 1257 Ch
Ki-, Kylvington' 13 BylE 50, 1219 *Ass, et passim*
Suth Kiluingtona H 3 BM

The persistence of *Kil-* forms reduces the value of the DB forms with *Chel-*, especially as *e* in that source is frequently written for *i*, so that the name may be taken as 'Cylfa's farm' from the OE pers. name *Cylfa*, not found in independent use but inferred from OE *Cylfantun* (BCS 553) and Kilvington (Nt), *Chiluinton, Cheluinctone* 1086 DB. *v.* ingtun.

2. THORNBROUGH 22 E 2

Thorn(e)bergh, -berge 1185–95 *Add* 19922

'Thorn hill' *v.* þorn, berg. The name occurs several times in the North Riding.

3. UPSALL 22 D 2

Upsale 1086 DB   *Uppesale* 1185–95 *Dods* vii. 68

With the same run of forms and interpretation as Upsall (LangW) 158 *supra*. It is on the upper slope of a fairly steep hill.

Kirby Knowle

1. KIRBY KNOWLE 22 D 3

Chirchebi 1086 DB, (*under* (*sub*) *Knol*) 13 RichReg 122 d
v. kirkja, by and Knowle Hill 201 *infra*.

KNOWLE HILL (6")

Cnol c. 1217 YD

v. cnoll. This hill is a high round-topped hill. Cf. Norw *Knoll* (NG ii. 192, etc.).

Cowesby

1. COWESBY 22 C 3 [kɔuzbi]

Cahosbi 1086 DB
Cousebi, -by 1199 Cur *et passim* to 1407 NCyWills
Causeby 1202 FF, 1227 Pat, Ebor, 1333 Riev
Couesby 1228 Ebor *Coosby by Trysk* 1476 Pat

'Kausi's farm' *v.* by. Cf. ON *Kausi* (LindBN), found in a number of Norw place-names such as ONorw *Kausærut*, Norw *Kausebøl* (NG i. 31, etc.).

Over Silton

1. KEPWICK 22 C 3 [kepik]

Capuic, Chipuic 1086 DB
Chepewic 1166 P (p)
Kepwic, -uuic, -wyche 1202 FF, 1208–10 Fees, 1234 Guis
Kepewyk, -wick 1224–30 Fees, 1240 Riev, 1285 KI, 1298 Abbr, 1301 LS, 1348 Baildon
Keppewic, -wyk 1310 Ch, 1316 Vill
Kepyk, Kepec 1451 Test, 1505 Sanct

On topographical grounds this name cannot reasonably be connected with OE *cēap*, 'market,' with Scandinavianised initial consonant. A pers. name is far more probable. There is an OSwed p.n. *Kæplinge* which Hellquist (*ON på -inge* 86) connects with the pers. name *Kappe assumed by Lundgren-Brate (146) to lie behind certain Swedish p.n.'s. A mutated derivative *Kæppi* formed from the name would explain the forms of Kepwick. The possibility then is that the name means 'Kæppi's **vik**' or 'nook in the hills.'

2. OVER SILTON 22 B 2

Silftune, Siluetun(e) 1086 DB, 12 Riev (p)
Silton 1204 Ass, (*Parva*) 1301 LS, (*Over*) 1316 Vill

v. tun. The first element is probably the pers. name found in Silpho 115 *supra*. Cf. also Nether Silton (Allerton) 207 *infra*.

GREYSTONE FARM

    Grastan c. 1217 YD

Hawnby

1. ARDEN 22 G 4

    Ardene 1086 DB, 1327 Banco

    Erdene, Erden(a) 1160 Riev, 1286 Ebor *et passim* to 1436 Baildon

    Arden 1201 ChR *et passim*

    v. denu. The first element of Arden is probably the same as that of Ardleigh (Ess), *Ardeley* 1185 RotDom, from the OE pers. name *Earda*, not found in independent use in OE; it is a hypocoristic form of such an OE pers. name as *Eardwulf, Eardhelm*, etc.

BLACK HAMBLETON

    Hameldon 1290 Dugd iv. 285

    v. Hambleton Hill (LangW) 158 *supra*.

POTTERKELD (6″)

    Potterkeld 1290 Dugd iv. 285

    v. kelda. The first element is OE *pottere*, 'a potter.'

STEEPLE CROSS

    Stepingecrosse 1290 Dugd iv. 285

    The first element may possibly be OE *Stēapinga* (gen. pl.) 'dwellers on the slope' (cf. PN BedsHu 84, s.n. Steppingley); hence 'cross of the hill-dwellers.' The second element is cros.

2. BILSDALE WESTSIDE 22 C 6

    v. Bilsdale (Ryed) 67 *supra*.

3. DALE TOWN 22 D 5

    Dal 1086 DB, *Dale* 1170 Riev *Daile* 1470 Test

    v. dæl, dalr. The simplex ON *i Dale* is very common in Norw place-names (cf. NG i. 12, ii. 45 *et passim*).

GOWERDALE [jɔuwǝdil]

Yowirdale 1387 YD *Yowerdalle* 1434 YD

Possibly 'boar valley' from ON *jǫfurr*, 'wild boar,' and dalr. The spelling *G-* is probably modern and perhaps arose by analogy with OE *geat*, written *gate* but still pronounced as [jæt] in the local dialect.

4. HAWNBY 22 D 5 [ɔːmbi]

Halm(e)bi, -by 1086 DB *et passim* to 1301 LS
Halmbi, -by 1170 Riev, 1200 FF, 1201 ChR, 1219 *Ass*, 1301, 1399 YI
Halmiby 1200 FF
Haunneby 1285 KI, *Hawnbye, Haunby* 1538 Riev
Halneby 1316 Vill

'Halmi's farm' from the ON by-name *Halmi* (LindBN) and *by*. One may also compare the Swed place-name *Halmby* (Hellquist, *Svenska ON på -by*), which is derived from ON *halmr*, 'straw,' and refers to 'a straw-thatched farm.' The persistence of *-e-* in the early spellings of Hawnby points, however, to the pers. name *Halmi*.

BLOW GILL

Blawathgila 1170–2 BylE 109

'Ravine with the dark ford' *v.* blár, vað, gil.

LADHILL BECK

Laddedale c. 1160 Riev, 1170–85 YCh 1845
Laddale 1200 FF *Laddelle* 1538 Riev

v. dæl. On the origin of the first element *v.* *Ladgate* (LangW) 158 *supra.* 'Ladda's valley.'

5. MURTON 22 D 5 [muǝtǝn]

Mortun, -ton(a-m), -tonie 1086 DB *et passim* to 1376 Dugd v. 348
Murton 1541 Dugd v. 355

Farm on the mor' *v.* tun.

CONYGARTH (6″)

   le Conygarth 1533 Riev

'The king's enclosure' from konungr and garðr.

6. SNILESWORTH 22 B 4

   Snigleswath 1150–70 YCh 1846, 1243 *BylE* 109
   Snygheleswath 1186–9 *Dods* vii. 107
   Sniles-, Snyleswath 1230 FF, 1247 Ch (*corrigenda*), 1290
      Dugd iv. 285, 1376 ib. v. 348
   Snailesworthe 1575 FF

'Snigel's ford' *v.* vað. The first element is probably a by-name based on ON *snigill*, 'a snail.' Medial -*g*- was palatalised in such positions before the Scandinavian settlements took place in England.

MILEY PIKE [milə paik]

   Milehowe 1290 Dugd iv. 285

'Milla's mound' from ON *Milla* (LindBN) and haugr. Cf. Norw *Millehaugen* (Rygh, *NG* iii. 374).

RYE HEAD (6″)

   Rihened (corr. -*heued*) 1290 Dugd iv. 285

'Head of the valley of the Rye' *v.* heafod. This is the source of the river Rye.

WHITESTONES

   Wytstayndale 1290 Dugd iv. 285

v. hwit, steinn, dalr and cf. Norw *Hwitstein* (Rygh, *NG* ii. 6).

VIII. ALLERTON WAPENTAKE

   Aluretune Wapentac 1086 DB
   Aluertone scire 1088 *LVD* 50 *d*, 1242 P
   Alverstonsir(a) 1217 Riev, 1237 Cl
   Libertatem de Alverton' 1233 Cl, (*de Allerton*) 1401 YI

The liberty (originally a wapentake) takes its name from Northallerton 210 *infra*, the county town. *v.* scir.

Thornton le Street

1. NORTH KILVINGTON 22 E 1

Chelvintun 1086 DB *Keluintune* 1088 *LVD* 51
North Kilvyngton 1292 Baildon

Later forms all have *Kil-*. For the history of this name
v. South Kilvington 200 *supra*.

2. THORNTON LE STREET 22 E 1

Torentun 1086 DB *Thorinton in via* 1208 ChR

The place is variously referred to as *in Strata* 1268 Ebor,
in le Strete c. 1291 Tax

v. þorn, tun. Thornton stands on a supposed Roman road
(6″ OS 87 NE 3); *v*. stræt and Barton le Willows 38 *supra*.

SANDPOT (6″)

Sandpot 1227 FF

'Sand hole' *v*. sand. On the second element *v*. Pott Hall
234 *infra*.

Leake

1. BORROWBY 22 D 1 [bɑrəbi]

Ber(g)(h)ebi, -by 1086 DB *et freq* to 1333 Riev

With the same run of forms and interpretation as Borrowby
(LangE) 136 *supra*.

WANDALES (6″)

Wandailam 1170–88 YCh 1849
v. Wandales (Ryed) 59 *supra*.

2. COTCLIFFE 22 C 1 [kɔtlif]

Koteclyf 1285 KI *Cotcliffe* 1581 FF
'Bank by the cottage' *v*. cot, clif.

3. CROSBY 21 C 14

Croxebi, Croxbi 1086 DB
Crossebi 1153–7 YCh 952 *et passim*, *Crossbye* 1153–94 Riev

Possibly 'farm by the cross' *v.* **cros, by.** In that case the DB form is an error. Perhaps, however, one should take the name to be 'Krok's by,' from ON *Krókr*, with later assimilation of *ksb* to *ssb* and consequent association with ON *cros*.

4. KNAYTON 22 D 2 [neːtən, niːətən]

> *Keneuetun, Cheneuetone, Cheniueton, Chennieton* 1086 DB
> *Cheuetune* 1088 *LVD* 50 d
> *Cneveton* 1233, 1235 Cl
> *Knayveton(e)* 1279 Ebor, 1280 *Ass*, 1285 KI, 1301 LS
> *Knayton* 1354, 1372 FF   *Knaton* 1562 NCyWills

v. **tun.** The first element here, as in Kneeton (Nt) and Kniveton (Db), is OE *Cēngifu*, a woman's name; for shifting of the accent cf. Knowsley (PN La 113) from *Cēnwulf*, and Fringford (O), DB *Feringeford*.

BRAWITH [brewiθ]

> *Brai-, Braythwath* 1231 *Ass*, 1301 LS

'Broad ford' *v.* **breiðr, vað.**

5. LANDMOTH 22 C 1 [lanməθ]

> *Landemot(e)* 1086 DB, 1088 *LVD* 51, a. 1157 Percy, 1208 FF, Fees, 1285 KI, 1313 Whitby (p)
> *Landmot* 1231 *Ass*, 1359 FF
> *Landemoth* 1291 Riev
> *Lamouth* 1506 Sanct
> *Lanmouth* 1577 Saxton, 1616 NR
> *Lamoth* 1614 NR

'District meeting-place' *v.* **land, (ge)mot.** Landmoth is on the top of a steep hill overlooking Cod Beck and near to the main road from Thirsk to Stokesley. The final element is found again in Skirmett (PN Bk xvii. 180) and as the first element of OE *gemotbeorh* (Ha), BCS 392, and in such compounds as " *Sancti Petri wapentacmot nec Tredingmot nec schiresmot* " (1316 Abbr 334). Landmoth is not far from either Northallerton or Fingay Hill 213 *infra* and this contiguity is paralleled by that of Skirmett and Fingest in Bk (*loc.cit.*). They are probably alternative Riding or wapentake meeting-places. For a similar group *v.* PN Wo 166 s.n. Stoulton.

On the development of the last element to *-moth* cf. Catterick 242 *infra*.

6. LEAKE 22 C 2 [liːk]

Lece 1086 DB
Leche 1086 DB, 1088 *LVD* 51
Leic, Leyk 12 *RegAlb* i. 67 *d*, 1239, 1272 Ebor, c. 1291 Tax
Lecc c. 1150 Godr, 1154–81 Riev, 1160–80 YCh 954
Lek(e) 1200 FF *et passim* to 1562 NCyWills
Leek' 1291 Ebor, 1328 Banco, 1508 Test
Leake 1665 Visit *et passim*

'Brook' *v.* lœkr.

7. NETHER SILTON 22 C 2

Silftune 1086 DB
Silton Paynill 1285 KI,(*Paynel*) E 1 BM,(*Nether*) 1298 Abbr

Other forms and interpretation as for Over Silton 202 *supra*.
Isabell *Paynell* held land here in 1231 (*Ass*).

North Otterington

1. NORTH OTTERINGTON 21 D 13

Otrin(c)tun(e), -tona 1086 DB, 1088 *LVD* 50 *d*, 12 *RegAlb* i. 68
Otheringeton' 1208 ChR
Ot(e)rington' 1208–10 Fees, 1219, 1231 *Ass*, 1254 Ebor, (*North*) 1292 ib.
Oterinton 1227 Ebor

The form *Ostrinctune* for South Otterington 208 *infra* suggests that we have here an OE pers. name *Ōhthere*, but that is only on record as King Alfred's anglicising of ON *Óttarr* and as the name of a Swedish king in *Beowulf*, and it would be difficult to explain the later forms on the basis of initial *Oht-*. These should have given *Ought*[1]. More probably *Oter* is the

---

[1] Possibly *Ohthere* lies behind Oughtrington (Ch) but unfortunately no forms for this have been found.

right form and is an OE pers. name derived from *otor*, 'otter,' which lies behind Otteringham (YER), DB *Otringeham*, and the lost *Oteringhithe* (Nf), DB *Otringeheia*. This name was identical in form with the common Anglo-Scand name *Oter* derived from *Óttarr*. Confusion with this *Oter* and knowledge that its OE equivalent was *Ohthere* might lead to the spelling of the first *Oter-* name as *Ostr-*. *v.* ingtun.

2. SOUTH OTTERINGTON[1] 21 D 13

    Ostrinctune 1086 DB
    Sonotrinctune 1088 *LVD* 51
    Otheringeton' 1208 ChR (and as in North Otterington *supra*)

    Son- in the second form is probably from OWScand *sunnr*, 'south,' an assimilated form.

3. THORNTON LE BEANS 21 C 14

    Gri(s)torentun 1086 DB
    Grisethorntune 1088 *LVD* 51
    Thorinton super vivarium 1208 ChR
    Thorn(e)ton in Vivar' 1285 KI

The place is also distinguished as *in le Beyns*, *in Fabis* 1534 VE; *in the Beanes* 1577 Saxton; *in lez Beanes* 1613 NR, etc.

    v. þorn, tun. The earliest spellings point to a name of the same type as Humburton 180 *supra*: 'Griss's *þorntun*' from the ON pers. name *Griss* (*v.* Gristhorpe 104 *supra*).

The various suffixes indicate the position of Thornton. The *vivarium* or fish pond is mentioned in 1208 ChR *vivario juxta Thorinton'*. *Fabis* is from Latin *faba*, 'horse-bean,' and is equivalent to the more common affix *Beans* from OE *bean*. Horse-beans must have been a staple commodity of the district. For *le v.* Barton le Willows 38 *supra*.

CROSBY COURT or CROSBY COTE

    Cotun 1086 DB   *Cotem* 1088 *LVD* 51
    Crosseby et Cotunam 1252 Ch

    '(At) the cottages' from the OE dat. plur. *cotum*; *v.* cot. The Ch scribe has mistaken *Cotun* for a common OE *tun*-name.

---

[1] A detached part of Birdforth wapentake.

4. THORNTON LE MOOR 22 D 13

Torentona 1114–23 YCh
Thorinton' in mora 1208 ChR
Thornton in the More 1327 Banco

v. þorn, tun. For *le* v. Barton le Willows 38 *supra*.

Northallerton

1. BROMPTON 21 B 13

Bruntun, Bruntone 1086 DB
Bromtune 1088 *LVD* 50 *d*, c. 1130 SD

With the same forms and interpretation as Brompton (Picker) 96 *supra*. This interpretation is rendered more certain in this case by the form from SD, who frequently gives names in their OE form.

In the 12th cent. the place is distinguished as

Moderbruntun c. 1121–8 YCh 936
Materebrinton' 1158 (1204) ChR
Mathrebruntona 1153–c. 1160 YCh 937

The prefixed pers. name is probably OE *Mǣðhere*. The name-type is similar to that of Humburton and Thornton le Beans 180, 208 *supra*.

2. DEIGHTON 14 J 13 [diːtən]

Dictune, -ton 1086 DB, 1088 *LVD* 50 *d et passim* to 1285 KI
Dichton 1198 Guis, 1231 FF
Di-, Dyghton 1316 Vill *et passim* to 1536 YChant

'Farm surrounded by a ditch' v. dic, tun. A large moat is marked on the map by the side of the village; probably this is the *dic*. The name is of common appearance (e.g. Deighton YER, Nf, YWR), and is found as OE *Dictun* (KCD, index). The development of *-ct-* in this name is similar to that in Broughton (*passim*): OE *c* became χ before *t* and [iχ] then followed the normal development of OE *ih*, as in dialect *leet* from OE *liht*. Cf. Dinsdale 279 *infra*.

3. LAZENBY 21 A 12 [lɛəzənbi]

Leisenchi, Leisinghi (sic) 1086 DB
Lai-, Laysingbi, -by 1088 *LVD* 50 *d*, (*by Northalverton*)
  1301 Ch
Lei-, Leysingebi, -by 1203 FF, 1204 Ass (p), 1219 FF

With the same run of forms and interpretation as Lazenby
(LangW) 160 *supra*.

4. NORTHALLERTON 21 B 13

Aluretune, Aluertun(e), Alverton(e) 1086 DB, 1088 *LVD* 50 *d*,
  (*North*) 1301 LS *et passim* to 1444 NCyWills
Auuerton' 1231 *Ass*
Northallerton 1371 FF

'Alfhere's farm' *v*. tun. The first element is the common
OE pers. name *Ælfhere*. The gen. *-es* has been lost except in
two instances of the wapentake name 204 *supra*.

BULLAMOOR

Bullehoumore 1314 Dunelm

v. haugr, mor. The first element is probably the OEScand
pers. name *Bulle* (cf. ZEN 26).

5. ROMANBY 21 B 12

Romundrebi 1086 DB
Romundabi 1088 *LVD* 50 *d*
Romundebi, -by 1086 DB *et passim* to 1316 Vill
Romundby 1347 Baildon, 1348 IpmR
Romanby 1398 Pat

'Romund's farm' *v*. by. The name *Romund* (DB, P) is from
ON *Hrómundr*, gen. *Hrómundar* (LindN). The ON gen. *-ar* is
found in the DB spelling, but was dropped at an early date.
The mere fact that it does appear in the early form shows that
its loss cannot be due to the OEScand loss of *-r-* before a
voiced consonant as in Dromonby 168 *supra*.

Birkby

1. BIRKBY 14 J 11 [bɔrkbi]

Bretebi 1086 DB
Brettebi, -by 1088 *LVD* 50 *d et passim*
Brytheby 1230 Pat
Bret-, Briteby 1249 *Heal* 127, 1285 KI
Brytteby 1373 Test
Birtbye 1577 Saxton
Berkby 1316 (16) Vill, *Byrkbye* 1581 FF

'The Britons' village' from ON *Breta-býr.* Such a name might arise if any men of British descent from the north-west accompanied Viking settlers in their movements into Yorkshire. The term *Brötar* is used for British Celts in Scandinavian sources (cf. Zachrisson, *Romans, Kelts, etc.* 46–7).

2. HUTTON BONVILLE 14 J 12

Hotune, -ton 1086 DB, (*Bonevill*) 1316 Vill

v. hoh, tun. It was held t. Henry III by Robert de *Boneville* (VCH i. 496).

3. LITTLE SMEATON 14 H 12

Smidetun(e), Smitune 1086 DB
In litle Smithetune 1088 *LVD* 50 *d*
Parva Smitheton 1199 ChR, 1316 Vill
Smedeton 1200 Abbr
Smiton parva 1285 KI
Litill Smeton 1530 Visit

'The smiths' farm' *v.* tun. The first element is OE *smiđ.* The modern form arises from lengthening of OE *i* in an open syllable as in Upleatham 153 *supra*, with subsequent lowering to [eː] and raising to [iː]. Cf. Great Smeaton 281 *infra.*

Kirby Sigston

1. KIRBY SIGSTON 22 B 1

Kirchebi 1088 *LVD* 50 *d*, 51
Kirkeb', -by 1208–10 Fees, (*Si, Sygeston*) 1244 Ebor

v. kirkja, by and Sigston 212 *infra.*

SIGSTON

> *Sig(h)estun* 1086 DB
> *Siggestune, -ton* 1088 *LVD* 50 *d*, 51 *et passim* to 1474 YD
> *Si-, Sygeston(a)* 12 *RegAlb* i. 67 *d*, c. 1291 Tax, 1414 YI
> *Sicgeston'* 1204 ChR, *Siggheston* 1208–10 Fees

'Sigg's farm' *v.* tun. *Sigg* is probably from an ON name
Siggr, corresponding to the weak form *Siggi* (LindN).

2. SOWERBY UNDER COTCLIFFE 22 B 1

> *Sourebi, -by* 1086 DB, 1088 *LVD* 51
> *Saurebi* 1240–50 *Bodl* a. i. 58 (p)
> *Suleby sub Koteclyf* 1285 KI

v. saurr, by, *Sowerby* and Cotcliffe 128, 205 *supra*.

3. WINTON 21 A 14

> *Winetun(e)* 1086 DB   *Winton* 1578 FF

'Wina's farm' from the OE pers. name *Wina* (Redin 57)
and tun.

HALLIKELD HOUSE

> *Halikeld* 1226 FF, 1314 Dunelm   *Halykell* 1575 FF

'Holy spring' *v.* halig, kelda.

STANK HOUSE

> *Stanke, Wyntonstank*, 1571, 1575 FF

'Winton pool' from ME *stank*, 'pool, pond.'

Osmotherley

1. ELLERBECK 22 A 2

> *Elrebec* 1086 DB
> *Alrebec* 1086 DB, 1088 *LVD* 50 d, 51

'Alder stream' *v.* elri, bekkr. Later forms as for Eller Beck
and Ellerburn 82, 88 *supra* and Eller Beck 233, 266 *infra*

2. WEST HARLSEY 22 A 1

> *Herlesege, Herelsaie, Herselaige, Erleseie* 1086 DB
> *Herleseie, -ey, -ay* 1088 *LVD* 50 *d*, 1175–89 YCh 962, 1206
>   ChR, (*West*) 1316 Vill
> *West Harlesay* 1365 FF

'Herel's eg.' *Herel(e)* is not adduced in independent use in OE, but there is good evidence for its existence; it enters into Herleshow near Ripon (YWR), *Herelesho* c. 1030 *Gosp*, Herringfleet (Sf), DB *Herlingaflet*, Harlingham (Nf), *Herlingaham* KCD 1339, *At Herlinge* Thorpe 582, Harlesthorpe (Db), *Harlethorp* 1324 Ipm, Harlington (YWR), *Herlintune* 1086 DB. It is a diminutive form of a hypocoristic pers. name derived from OE *Herebald*, etc., and corresponds to OHG *Herilo*; it is probably found as an early ME surname in *Rann' herel, Symund' herel* (*LVD* 60 *d*, line 16).

Fingay Hill

Thynghou c. 1250 Riev, *Thyngowe* 1508 Guis

'Hill where the *thing* met' *v.* þing, haugr. Fingay Hill is a round-topped hill standing out prominently from the level land of the parish. As the name shows, it was formerly a district meeting-place, possibly of the Riding Court (cf. Landmoth 206 *supra* and VCH Y ii. 134).

The change of *th-* to *f-* in this name is well evidenced as a dialectal change all over the country. It is found in initial *Thing-* in Fingest (PN Bk 176) and in Finedon (Nth), *Tingdene* 1086 DB, *Thyngdon* 1327 Banco. Cf. Throxenby 110 *supra*.

3. Osmotherley   22 A 2 [ɔzmələ]

Asmundrelac 1086 DB
Osmunderle, -ley(e), -lai(e) 1088 *LVD* 50 *d*, 1219 *Ass*, 1281 Ch
  et passim to 1418 YI
Osmundeslay 12 *RegAlb* i. 67 *d*
Osmundelai, -leye 1220 *Ass*, 1231 Ebor
Osemunderl' 1280 Cl, c. 1291 Tax
Osmondirlay 1398 Pat
Osmoderl(a)y 1536 YChant, 1558 RichWills
Osmoth'ly 1577 NCyWills

'Asmund's clearing' *v.* leah. The first element is from ON *Ásmundr*, gen. *Ásmundar*; on forms with *Os-* *v.* Osgodby (Pick) 104 *supra*. For *-lac* *v.* Helmsley 71 *supra*. A hybrid formation with a Norse inflexion of the first element suggests very intimate association of the Norse and Anglian speech.

MOUNT GRACE, formerly BORDELBY

Bordlebi, Bordelbia 1086 DB
Bordelesby 13 Riev
Bordelby 1243 Fees, 1303 YI, 1310 Ch, 1405 Riev
Bordilbi 1297 YI
Borthelby 1301 LS, 1323 YD, 1366 BM
Brodeby 1508 Guis

'Bordel's farm' *v. by*. The name *Bordel* is probably OE in origin; cf. the lost Y stream-name *Bordelbrunn(e)* 1227 Baildon, Guis. It is a diminutive of the OE pers. name *Borda* (Redin 73). Cf. further Bordesley (PN Wo 365).

Monte Grace 1413, 1467 Test
Mountgrace, Monte(m) Graciae 1414, 1430 Test

The name is of French origin and refers to the priory which was set up at Bordelby (*v*. VCH ii. 28).

OAK DALE [jagdil]

Aikedale 1208 FF, *Hayckedale* 1234 Riev, *Eykedal* 1339 Pat

'Oak valley' *v*. eik, dalr. The modern spelling shows substitution of the modern English *oak* for ON *eik*, just as the local pronunciation shows dialectal [jæk] for OE *āc*.

4. THIMBLEBY 22 B 2 [θiməlbi]

Timbelbi, Timbelli (sic) 1086 DB
thémelebi 1088 *LVD* 51
Thimilby c. 1160 Riev
T(h)imelebi 1182, 1184 P
Thimilisbi 1208 FF
Timleb' 1208–10 Fees
Thi, Thymelby 1233 Cl, 1234 Riev, 1247 Ebor, 1301 LS, 1316 Vill
Thimmelby 1293 QW
Themelby 1329 YD
Thimbelby 1359 FF

v. by. The first element is a pers. name which is also contained in Thimbleby (L), *Timleby* LindsSurv, *Thymelby*, *Themelby* RH, and Themelthorp (Nf), *Thimeltorp, Tymelthorp*

1267, 1269 Ch, *Thimilthorp* 1289 BM. There is a scantily attested ON *þumall* (LindN) from ON *þumall*, 'thimble,' and a by-name (LindB) *þumli* from the same source. In these place-names we must have a mutated by-form *þymill (with mutation of *u* by the suffix as in OE *þȳmel*, 'thimble') or the ON name has been altered under the influence of OE *þȳmel* itself.

FOXTON

Fo(u)stune 1086 DB
Foxtun(e) -ton(a) 1088 *LVD* 50 *d et passim*
Focston 1233 Ebor
Fosceton 1349 Test

v. fox, tun.

SCRATHOWES (6″)

Scrathowe, -hou 1388 YD   *Scrattey* 1610 NR

'The devil's mound' *v.* haugr. *Scrat* is a common Y name for the devil (EDD). It is derived from ON *skratti*, 'wizard, goblin'; cf. the p.n. *Skrattasker* in the Heimskringla.

East Harlsey[1]

1. EAST HARLSEY 15 O 5

Herlesege 1086 DB, *Esteharlsay* 1536 YChant

v. West Harlsey 212 *supra*.

BRUNTCLIFFE

Brunneclive 1333 Riev.

v. clif. The first element is probably brunnr, 'spring.' A stream rises just by Bruntcliffe, hence 'cliff by the stream.'

MORTON (6″)

Morton 1293 QW, 1301 LS

v. mor, tun.

---

[1] A detached part of Birdforth wapentake.

SIDDLE

Syfthehylle, Syvehill c. 1250 Riev
Sithill 1303 YI, *Sythell'* 1508 Guis
Scithill 1412 Ad iii

v. hyll. In view of the first two spellings the first element
may possibly be derived from OE *sifeða*, 'siftings, bran, tares.'

STADDLE BRIDGE

Stathelbrig' 1508 Guis

NEDial *staddle* is used of a wooden platform on which hay-
ricks are built. Staddle Bridge crosses the river Wiske near its
source where the river is narrow and the ground flat. The
bridge could, therefore, originally have been a "staddle"
thrown across the stream. *v.* brycg.

2. WELBURY 15 O 5
Welberga 1086 DB
Welleberg(e), -berga 1086 DB *et passim* to c. 1291 Tax
Welleberc, -berh 1198 Guis, 13 YD, etc.
Welleberyg 1301 LS
Wel(le)byry 1310 Ch, 1344 FF
Welbery 1400 Pap, 1403 YI, 1508 Guis

'Spring hill' *v.*w(i)ella, berg. Welbury is built on the NE side
of a hill (to which the name originally applied) and on the top
side of the village on the hill slope is a spring known as *Hali
Well* (6").

SAWCOCK (6") [sɔːkɔk]
Salecohc 1190–1200 YCh 721
Salkok 13, 1323 YD, *Salcok* 1243 Fees, 1508 Guis, *Salcock*
1301 LS

The origin of this name is not quite certain. OE *coc* is not
recorded in any sense which would suit the final element.
There are, however, in this district indications of Irish influence
of the same type as that found in Ryedale and Cleveland (*v.* Airyholme (Ryed) and Coldman Hargos and Lackenby 49, 148, 159
supra). Irish pers. names found about here in the 11th and 12th
cents. are *Dughel, Malgrin, Melmidoc,* and *Ghilemichel* (*v. Revue*

Celtique, xli. 45); Irby 218 *infra* and the lost *Irton* in Birdforth 193 *supra* point to Irish-Norwegian influence, whilst Blow Gill (Bird) is an indication of Norwegian influence which is usually associated with Irish names in Y.

Bearing this in mind, an Irish-Norwegian origin of the name Sawcock is not out of the question. Indeed, the best solution of the name is to assume that it is an example of the Irish-Norw reversal of the order of elements, as in *Hillbraith* 158 *supra*. Sawcock would then mean 'Cock's hall' from ON *salr* (as in Upsall 158, 200 *supra*) and a pers. name *Coc*. This pers. name is itself a difficulty; it appears in the later additions to *LVD* as *Cocus de Coldigham* (60 *d*, l. 11), and, although it might ultimately be connected with OE *cocc*, 'cock(bird),' it seems in this case better to derive it from the well-evidenced OIr pers. name *Coc(h)*, a woman's name, or OIr *Cocca*, *Cocha*, identical with Welsh *coch*, 'red' (cf. Smith, *loc.cit.* 55), and the OBrit pers. name *Coccos* (Förster 105).

Rounton

1. WEST ROUNTON 15 N 5

> *Runtune* 1086 DB, 1088 *LVD* 51
> *Rungtune, -ton* 1128–35 YCh 944, 1170–5 YCh 945, 1483 Test, 1508 Guis
> *Rungheton* 1208–10 Fees
> *Rungeton(e)* 1218 FF, 1276, 1281 Ebor, 1285 KI, 1291 Ebor, 1301 LS, (*West*) 1328 Banco, 1330 Pap
> *Ringeton* 1218 FF
> (*West*) *Rongetone* 1281 Ebor
> *Rongton* 1285 KI
> *Westruncton* 1562 NCyWills, 1612 NR
> *West Rounckton* 1614 NR

The name is of the same origin as Runcton (Nf), *Runget'* 1185 RotDom, *Rongeton* 1495 BM, and East Rounton 218 *infra*. The first element in each case is OE *hrung*, 'rung, staff, pole,' and the meaning of the name would be 'farmstead enclosed with poles' (from OE *hrunga-tūn*), or 'farm marked by a pole' (from OE *hrungtūn*); a parallel meaning is found in Stapleton 283 *infra*. *v.* tun.

IRBY MANOR [ɔrbi]

   Irebi 1086 DB, 1088 *LVD* 51

'Farm of the Irishman or Irishmen' *v.* by. On the first element *v.* Irton (Pick) 101 *supra* and cf. Sawcock 216 *supra*.

2. EAST ROUNTON 15 N 5

   Rontun, Rantune 1086 DB, *Estrungeton* 1324 Abbr

   v. West Rounton 217 *supra*.

IX–XIII. THE HONOUR OF RICHMONDSHIRE

   shira de Richmond 1174 HCY, *Richemundesir(a)* 1198 Fees
   honore de Ri-, Rychemund 1218 Pat
   Richemondskyre 1252 YI

   v. scir and Richmond 287 *infra*. At the time of the DB survey the wapentakes of Hang and Gilling, probably corresponding to the two great lordships of Catterick and Gilling belonging to Earl Eadwine, formed *terra Alani Comitis*, later known as Richmondshire from the new castle built and named by Earl Alan himself. On the origin of Richmondshire and its status as a separate county *v.* Stenton, *William the Conqueror*, 324. The wapentake of Halikeld was in DB counted as part of the West Riding, but in all subsequent records (including that portion of *RichReg* which is a digest of DB) it forms part of the Honour of Richmond.

IX. HALIKELD WAPENTAKE

   Halichelde 1086 DB
   Halikeldshir 1157 *RichReg* 82 d

   The wapentake takes its name from Hallikeld Spring 219 *infra*, which was probably the wapentake meeting-place. *v.* halig, kelda, scir.

Hutton Conyers

1. HUTTON CONYERS[1] 21 J 11

   Hot(t)on(e) 1086 DB   *Hotune* 1086 *LVD* 50 d
   Hotonconyers 1198 Fount, *(Coigners)* 1316 Vill
   Howton Coniers 1530 Visit

   [1] Detached part of Allerton wapentake.

'Farm on the spur of land' v. hoh, tun. The Conyers family were enfeoffed of land here between 1099 and 1133 (VCH i. 393).

HALLIKELD SPRING (6″)

fontium de Halikeld' 1202 FF

'Holy spring' v. halig, kelda. v. 218 supra.

2. MELMERBY 21 H 12

Malmerbi, Malmerby 1086 DB, 1200 Cur (p), 1243 Ch
Melmerby 12 FountA 236 d et passim

'Farm on sandy ground' v. by. Lindkvist's suggestion (13) that the first element is from ON *málmr*, gen. *málmar*, 'sandy field,' is certainly borne out by the geological characteristics of the district and the name is paralleled by the Swed *Malmby* from OSwed *malm* (Hellquist, *ON på -by* 10). The form of the name has been influenced by Melmerby (HangW) 255 *infra* which is of different origin.

3. MIDDLETON QUERNHOW 21 G 12

Middeltun(e) 1086 DB, *Medelton* 1208 FF

Distinguished as *in the Mire* 15 VCH i. 392, *in the Myers* 1578 FF, *Whernehow* 15 VCH i. 392.

'Middle farm' v. middel, tun. It is the centre of a number of *tuns*.

For Quernhow v. Quernhow 224 *infra*. The affix *in le Mire* is the same as that in Ainderby Mires 239 *infra* and refers to the marshy nature of the land (v. myrr).

4. NORTON CONYERS[1] 21 H 11

Nortun(e), -ton(e) 1086 DB, 1088 *LVD* 50 d et passim

The affix is first found as *Coniers* in 1316 Vill

'North farm' v. norð, tun, probably so-called from its lying to the north of Ripon (YWR). For the manorial name v. Hutton Conyers 218 *supra*.

5. WATH 21 H 11 [waθ]

Wat 1086 DB, 1239 Pap, 1249 Ebor
Wath 1184 RichReg 84 d et passim
Waz 1253 Ch

'The ford' v. vað.

[1] Detached part of Allerton wapentake.

Kirklington

1. HOWGRAVE 21 G 11 [ɔugriv]

Hograve 1086 DB, 1088 *LVD* 50 *d*
Hogram, Hogrem 1086 DB
Holgrave 1128–35 YCh 944, 1170–5 *Dods* cxiii. 184, 1198
Fount
Hougrave 1184 *RichReg* 84 *d*, 1208–10 Fees, 1285 KI, 1332,
1362 FF, *Howegrave* 1403 YI, 1536 YChant

'Grove in the hollow' *v.* hol, graf.

2. KIRKLINGTON 21 F 11

Cherdinton 1086 DB
Chirtlintuna 1145–53 *Leon* 35
Kirtlyngton, Kirtlington 12 *RichReg* 80 *d,* 84 *d et freq* to
1449 Test
Ki-, Kyrtelington 1198 Fount *et freq* to 1301 Ebor, LS
Kertlinton 1207 Abbr, 1208 FF, 1231 *Ass*, 1239 Ebor
Kirclinton, Kirklinton 1230 Ebor, 1575 FF
Kirkelington, -lynton 1276 *RegAlb* ii. 18 *d*, 1368 FF, 1396 Pap

Kirklington is of the same origin as Kirtlington (O), *Kyrt-lingtun* ASC s.a. 977, *Chertelintone* 1086 DB, and Kirklington (Nt), and means 'Cyrtla's farm' *v.* ingtun. For the pers. name *Cyrtla* cf. *on cyrtlan geat* (Crawf i. 19, ii. 10), now Curtlake in Crediton (D)[1], and Kirtling (C), *Chertlinge* 1086 DB. On the interchange of *t* and *c* before *l* cf. Stittenham 33 *supra*.

HEALAM HOUSE, HEALAM BECK [i:ləm]

Hilum 1257 YD *Healam Bridge in Watlinge Streete* 1613 NR

'(At) the pools' from ON hylr, dat. plur. *hylum*. The modern form shows that the original vowel *-i-* was short and was lengthened in an open syllable in ME; cf. Upleatham 153 *supra*. The country round about is flat and the name probably refers to pools formed by Healam Beck. On Watling Street cf. Leeming Lane 1 *supra*.

[1] *Ex inf.* Mr J. E. B. Gover.

UPSLAND

Opsala, Upsale 1086 DB
Oppeslunde 1184 *RichReg* 84 *d*
Upselund 1280 *Ass*
Uppeslunde 1285 KI, (*-lounde*) 1301 LS, (*-lond*) 1406 YI
Uppislande 1556 FF *Upesland* 1571 FF

The DB form *Upsale* means 'upper hall' (*v*. Upsall 158 *supra*). The first element of the later spellings can hardly be from ON *ups*, 'steep cliff,' which is common in Norw place-names (Rygh, *NG Indledning* 83), for though the house is on the top of a small hill there is no cliff or steep bank in the neighbourhood. Probably it is really *Uppes(ale)lund* from the name of the place mentioned in DB and lundr.

YARNWICK (6″) [jaːnik]

Gernuic 1086 DB
Yarnewik(e) 12 *RichReg* 80 *d*, 105 *d*, 1198 Fount, 1270 YI
Jarnewik 1184 *RichReg* 84 *d*, (*-wyke*) 1301 LS
Yarnewyk(e) 1296 Ch, 1298 YI, 1316 Ch, 1544 FF

v. wic. The first element offers some difficulty; it is probably a pers. name *Georna* not found in OE but derived from OE *georn*, 'willing, eager.'

3. SUTTON HOWGRAVE 21 G 11

on Suptune c. 1000 *LVD* 43 *d*, *Sud(t)one* 1086 DB
Sutton 1157 *RichReg* 83, (*Rugemond*) 1280 YI, (*Hougrave*) 1285 KI

'South farm' *v*. suð, tun. It is to the south of Howgrave 220 *supra*, and Ralph de *Rougemond* held one-third of a fee here in 1280 YI.

4. EAST TANFIELD 21 G 10

Tanefeld 1086 DB, 1184 *RichReg* 84 *d*, 1204 Ass, 1279–81 QW, 1283 *Rich* 28, c. 1291 Tax
Danefeld, Danefelt 1086 DB
Estanfeld(e) 1157 *RichReg* 83, 1396 Pap, 1579 FF
Tannefeld(e) 1198 Fount, 1301 Ebor
Est Tanefeld 1280 *Ass*, 1292 Ch
Esttanfeld 1327 Banco, etc.

The first element of this name offers difficulty. Redin (110, 137) adduces a number of pers. names from DB such as *Tone* (Y), *Tonne* (L, Wa), and suggests that as the distribution of the name is in Scand England it is derived from OEScand *Tonne, Tonna*. There is, however, a certain amount of evidence which points to an OE pers. name *Tona* or *Tana*. A pers. name *Ton* (possibly OE) is adduced from MHG ii. 634, and another form of this strong pers. name is found in OE *in tanes bæce* (Staunton on Arrow, He) BCS 1040, Tansley (Db), *Tanysleg* E 1 BM, *Tanesley* e. 14 BM, and Tansor (Nth), *Tanesoure* 1316 BM. A weak form *Tana, Tona* is possibly the first element of Thanington (K), OE *Taningtune* BCS 404, and Tanworth (Wa), *Taneworth* 1229–43 BM, *Thanewurth* 1251 Ch, *Toneworth(e)* 1316 FA, 1340 BM. As a name-theme it is found in OE *Tonberct* (LVD) and it is connected by Müller (*Die Namen des nordhumbrischen Liber Vitae* 112) with OHG *-zan* in the pers. names *Donazan, Grazan*, and *Zanvidus*.

Professor Ekwall suggests that in the case of East and West Tanfield we may explain the name by metanalysis as from *ēast* (*west*) *ānfeld*, with *t* of *east* (*west*) transferred to an earlier and unrecorded *Anfeld*. *v*. feld.

West Tanfield

1. WEST TANFIELD   21 G 10

   Tanefeld(e) 1086 DB   *Westanfeld(e)* 1282 YI, 1396 Pap

BINSOE [binsə]

   Binzhou c. 1190 *Dods* cxx. 3
   Bishou (? for *Bīs-*) 1202 FF
   Binzhou 1257 YD
   Bynshu 1301 LS   *Bynsoo* 1536 YChant

This is a difficult name but one is probably right in assuming that the various forms all go back to *Binteshou*. This would point to a strong pers. name *Binte* corresponding to the weak *Binta* which lies behind Bentworth (Ha), *Binteorde* Ric 1 Ch, *Bintewurd* 1222 Pat. This may be cognate with OHG *Binizo*, *Binzo* (Förstemann, *PN* 307). *v*. hoh.

NOSTERFIELD

Nostrefeld 1204 Ass (p) *Nostreffeld* 1245 Cl
Nosterfeld 1257 YD, 1282 YI, 1285 KI, 1298 YI, 1301 LS,
1521 FF

This name is probably a case of metanalysis of the final
sound of the ME inflected definite article *then* with the beginning of the place-name itself. Nosterfield goes back to the
OE name formula *æt ðæm eowestrefelda*, 'at the sheepfold field,'
ME *at then (e)ostrefelde*, which before the recorded instances
of the name became *(atte) Nostrefelde*. A name of similar
origin is Nosterfield (C), *Nostresfelda* c. 1080 Skeat (PN C).
Cf. Napleton, PN Wo 146.

The name is ultimately derived from OE *ēowestre*, 'sheep
fold,' and feld, whilst the compound *ēowestrefeld* in addition to
the two Nosterfields is also found in Austerfield (YWR), which
appears as OE *Ouestraefelda* in Eddi's *Life of St Wilfrid*[1],
Oustrefeld in 1086 DB. For Austerfield, *v.* Bradley in EHR
xxxvi. 299.

THORNBROUGH

Thorn(e)bergh 1198 Fount *et freq* to 1399 YI
Thorn(e)bargh 1536 YChant, 1541 FF
Thornbrough 1654 Pickhill

'Thorn hill' *v.* þorn, berg.

Pickhill

1. AINDERBY QUERNHOW 21 F 12 [ɛəndəbi kwaːnə]

Aiendrebi, Andrebi 1086 DB
Endreby, Enderby 1207 Abbr, 1208 FF
Ai-, Aynderby 1208 FF, *(juxta Querenhou)* 1301 LS, *(Vis-
compt)* 14 RichReg 87
Einderby 1231 Ass
Anderby (vesconte) 1280 YI, *(Whernhowe)* 1578 FF

The name Ainderby occurs three times in the district
(Ainderby Mires, Ainderby Steeple 239, 275 *infra*). All three
are derived from the ON pers. name *Eindriði* (LindN), ODan

---

[1] The identification is made by Goodall in PN SWY 63.

Endridhi (Nielsen). *v.* by. The forms with *Ender-* are due to the Scand sound-change of *ei* to *e* before *n* + a consonant (cf. Noreen, *Altisländ. Gram.* 123). Forms with *Ander-* are to be explained, as by Lindkvist (39), as due to the influence of a Scand by-form *Andriði.*

QUERNHOW

In addition to the spellings in the preceding name the following may be noted:

Quernhowe 1327 Banco   *Whernehowe* 15 VCH   *Whernou* 1536 YChant, 1578 FF

Quernhow is a small mound on the Roman road (Leeming Lane or Watling Street), which forms the boundary between the parishes of Ainderby and Middleton Quernhow. *v.* haugr. The first element is ON *kvern*, 'mill stone' (cf. cweorn), which also enters into a similar Norw p.n. *Kvernehaugen* (NG i. 79).

2. HOLME 21 F 12 [ɔum]

Hulme 1086 DB, 1128–35 YCh 944, *Hulmo* 1252 *Ass*
Holm(e) 1088 *LVD* 50 *d et passim*
Houm 12 *Dods* viii. 154 *d*, 1208–10 Fees

v. holmr. On the significance of the name *v.* Introd. xxv.

3. HOWE 21 F 12 [ɔu]

Hou 1086 DB, 1157 *RichReg* 83, (*upon Swale*) 1294 Ch
Hau c. 1204 *FountA* 27   *Haw* E 1 BM
How(e) 13 *RichReg* 105 *d*

v. haugr. Howe probably takes its name from Howe Hill, a small hill in the west of the township.

4. PICKHILL 21 E 12

Picala 1086 DB, 1301 Pap,   *Picale* 1184 *RichReg* 84 *d*
Pichal(a) 1158–66 YCh 175, H 2 *Leon* 3 *d*, 1289 Ebor
Pi-, *Pykehal(e)* 1207 Abbr *et passim* to 1328 Banco
Pikehall 1280 *Ass*, 1396 Pap
Pykel 1327 Fount
Pykall 1536 YChant, *Picoll* 1625 Kirklington, *Pickhill* 1718 ib.

'Pica's nook of land' *v.* h(e)alh. On the pers. name *v.* Picton 173 *supra.*

NESS

Nes 1158–66 YCh 175   *Ness(e)* 1399 YI
Ness is a tongue of land near the river Swale. *v.* næss.

ROXBY HOUSE

Rokeby 1198 Fount, 1280 *Ass*, 1327 Fount
Rokesbi, -by 1210 Abbr *et passim* to 1328 Banco
Rokysby 1252 *Ass*
Rowcesby 1285 KI   *Rukesby* 1554 RichWills
'Rook's farm' from the ON pers. name *Hrókr* and by.

5. SINDERBY 21 F 12 [sinəbi]

Senerebi 1086 DB
Sindarebi 1170–88 Leon 228 (p)
Sinderbi, -by 12 Dods xcv. 34 *d et passim*
'Sindri's farm' *v.* byr. ON *Sindri* is adduced by LindN and
enters into a lost place called *Sinderberg* (12 *Easby* 27) in Burrill
237 *infra.*

6. SWAINBY 21 E 12 [swɛənbi]

Suanebi 1086 DB
Suenebi 1111–22 *Mary Y* 229
Swayneby 1184 *RichReg* 84 *d et passim* to 1560 RichWills
Suanes-, Suanisby 1196 Guis, 1313 Pat
Sweinesby 1349 (H 3) Dugd vii. 920

This name is parallel to OSwed *Swenaby* (Hellquist, *Svenska
ON på -by*, 72 ff.) and denotes 'farm of the young men,' from
ON *sveinn*, the Scand cognate of OE swan. The first form has
been influenced by that word itself, the last ones by the pers.
name *Sveinn*. Cf. Swainby 178 *supra.*

ALLERTHORPE HALL

(H)erleuestorp 1086 DB
Arleythorp(e) 1184 *RichReg* 84 *d*, 1508 Test
Arlethorp(pe) 1224–30 Fees, 1270, 1298, 1418 YI, 1508 Test
Arlagh(e)thorp c. 1300 *RichReg* 86 *d*, 1349 Dugd vii. 921
Allerthorp 1665 Visit
'Herlef's village' from ON *Hjǫrleifr* or *Herleifr* (LindN),
ODan *Herlew* (Nielsen), OSwed *Hærlef* (Lundgren-Brate) and
þorp.

Burneston

1. BURNESTON 21 E 11 [bɔnistən]

Brennigston 1086 DB

With the same run of forms and meaning as Burniston 107 *supra*.

2. CARTHORPE 21 E 11 [ka:θrəp]

Caretorp 1086 DB, *Karethorp* 1246 YI *et freq* to 1322 Abbr
Carthorp, Karthorp 1161–70 *Mary Y* 231 *d et passim*
Carethropp 1558 RichWills

'Kari's village' from the ON pers. name *Kári* (LindN) and þorp; cf. Caythorpe (YER), *Caretorp* 1086 DB.

NORMANBY (lost)

Normanebi 1086 DB

v. Normanby (Ryed) 57 *supra*.

3. EXELBY 21 D 10 [eʃəlbi]

Aschilebi 1086 DB
Aschelebi 1161–70 *Mary Y* 231 *d* (p)
Eskelby 12 Easby 139 *d et passim* to 1316 Vill, *Eskilby* 1199 FF
Exkilby 1372 FF
Exil-, Exylby 1419 YI, 1468 Pat

'Eskel's farm' from the OEScand pers. name *Eskel* (Lundgren-Brate 312) and by. The two earliest spellings contain the OWScand equivalent *Áskell* (LindN), found also in Asselby (YER), *Aschilebi* 1086 DB, though the persistence of *Esk*-forms makes ultimate derivation from the OEScand certain. This should be considered in connexion with Holme 224 *supra* and Introd. xxv. In the case of this name and Asselby (YER) *sk* underwent metathesis to *ks* (*x*), which became *s* in the dialect (*v.* Introd. xxxii). In Exelby this has further developed to *sh* as in Dishforth 184 *supra*.

CROSBY HOUSE (6″)

Crosby 1184 *RichReg* 85 *d*

v. cros, by.

LEEMING

aquam de Lemyng 13 *Easby* 142
on Leming, -inc 1154–89 ChR, 1231 *Ass*
pontem de Lemming 1202 FF
Lemyng(e) 13 *RichReg* 10, (*by Eskelby*) 1300 Ch, 1363 FF,
    1400 YI, 1428 *Archd* 26, 1516 FF
Magna Lymynge 1576 FF

As the earlier forms show, Leeming was originally a river-
name, derived from Brit **lemanio*; this is ultimately from a
Brit word cognate with OIr *leamh* 'elm-tree' and is paralleled
by the name of the river Leam (Wa); cf. RNY 16.

LEEMING WATH   (6″)

Lemingeford 1154–66 Marrick

'Ford across the river Leeming' *v.* ford. This element was
later replaced by ON **vað** 'ford.'

NEWTON PICOT

Neuton(e) 1086 DB, (*on Leminc*) 1154–89 ChR, (*Pygot*)
    1301 LS
Niwetune 1088 *LVD* 50 *d*
Scab(b)ed Newton 13 VCH, 1574 FF

'New farm' *v.* niwe, tun. NEDial *scabbed* is used of land
having 'a thin, bare, gravelly soil interspersed with rocks, etc.'
(EDD), and this suits the site. The land of Leeming through
intermarriage passed to the family of *Picot*, Randel *Pigot* holding
it in 1502 (VCH).

4. GATENBY   21 D 11 [gɛətənbi]

Ghetenesbi, Chenetesbi 1086 DB
Gaitaneby 1184 *RichReg* 84 *d*
Gaitenebi 1228 Dugd v. 576
Geytenby, Gaytenby 1270 YI, 1285 KI, 1298 YI
Gaytanby 1316 Vill
Gaittyngby 1542 RichWills   *Gatonby* 1563 FF

The name Normanby 226 *supra* indicates that there were
occasional settlements of Norwegians in this district and it is
probable that Gatenby also points to Norwegian influence of the

Irish type. Lindkvist (53) suggests that the name is from ON *geita-nes-býr* 'farm on the goats' tongue of land,' but this can hardly be correct, for we should in this case expect *nes* to preserve its identity later than DB. More probably Gatenby means 'Gaithan's farm' from the OIr pers. name *Gaithen* (Annals of the Four Masters) and by. Forms with *-ene* in the p.n. are traces of the use of the OIr gen. form *Gaithain*. Cf. *Revue Celtique*, xliv. 48 and Lackenby 159 *supra*.

5. THEAKSTON 21 E 11 [θiːkstən]

> *Eston* 1086 DB
> *Texton(e)* H 2 *Leon* 3 *d*, Hy 3 Dugd vii. 920, 1158–66 YCh 175, 1208 FF, 1270 YI
> *Thekeston* 1157 *RichReg* 83, 13 ib. 104, 1285 KI
> *Thexton* 1184 *RichReg* 84 *d*, 1298 YI, 1301 LS, 1307 Dugd
> iii. 562, 1409 YI

v. tun. The first element in this name is probably a pers. name in the poss. case and Professor Ekwall suggests either a strong-form *þēofoc*, corresponding to the weak-form *þēofeca* found in *þeofecan hyl* (BCS 1237) or a diminutive *þēoduc* formed from the common pers. name element *þēod*. For the early reduction of such names, cf. Tewkesbury (Gl), DB *Teodechesberie*, 1218 Pat *Theokesbir'*, 1233 Lib *Thekesbury*.

X. HANG EAST WAPENTAKE

The old wapentake of Hang embraced the whole of the valley of the river Ure and the south side of Swaledale. In the 13th cent. it was divided into two separate wapentakes, Hang East and Hang West.

> *Hangeschire* 1157 *RichReg* 82 *d*
> *In wap' de Langerschire* (sic) 1167 P
> *Hang'* 12 *RichReg* 82, 1229 Cl *et passim*
> *Hange* 1231 *Ass*, 1242 P, 1301 YI
> *Hengest* 1280 YI
> *wapentach de Hanger* 1290 Abbr
> *Hangest, Hangwest* 1283 *Rich* 34, 1367 *ForP* 413 *d*, 1610 Speed

The wapentake takes its name from the site of its old meeting-place, Hang Bank—a small hill in Hutton Hang (HangW) 248 *infra*, approximately in the centre of the combined wapentakes of Hang East and West. *v.* scir.

The P form *Langer* and the Abbr forms *Hanger* represent OE hangra 'a wooded slope'; as in Langstrothdale (YWR), *Langestrother*, *Langestroth* 13, 14 Percy, final *-er* was lost, though in some cases the diacritic ' should perhaps be interpreted as *-er*.

Well

1. SNAPE 21 E 10

   Snape 1270 YI, 1283 *Rich* 25 *et passim*
   Snap 1386 NCyWills

   'Winter pasture' from ME *snape*, a word of Scand origin (*v.* PN La 17).

THORP PERROW [θɔːp pɔrə]

   Torp 1086 DB, *Thorp* 1184 *RichReg* 84 *d*, (*Pirrow(e)*) 1285 KI
   v. þorp. The lords holding the tenure of Thorp were lords of *Pir(n)hou* in Ditchingham (Nf); thus in 1285 Helewise de *Perrow* held two carucates of land here (KI). For [pɔrə] *v.* Introduction xxxii.

2. WELL 21 F 10

   Welle 1086 DB *et passim*

   'The spring' *v.* w(i)ella. The name refers to certain springs in the township now known as The Springs, St Michael's Well and Whitwell. Cf. also *Welskough* 1536 YChant, 'the wood near Well' from skogr.

FAIRWOOD FIELDS (6")

   Fagherwall 1257 YD; *-wald(e)* 1285 KI, 1319 *RichReg* 112 *d*
   Faverwald c. 1300 Dugd iii. 562
   Fayerwald 1349 Dugd vii. 921 (p), *Fayrewald* 1410 *RichReg* 114 *d*

   'Fair woodland' *v.* w(e)ald. The first element is from ON fagr 'fair' (which with ME vocalisation of *-g-* gave the form *Faver-*), but it has been replaced by ME *fair* (from OE fæger); for the development of OE *wald* to *wood* cf. the local pronunciation of Easingwold 24 *supra*.

Mashamshire

This district is conterminous with Masham parish.

Mashamshire, -shyre 1142–96 Dugd v. 596, 1327 Banco
Massamshire c. 1150 Dugd v. 572, e. 14 *RichReg* 87 *d*
Massamsir' 1224–30 Fees *Masshamshire* 1468 Fount
v. Masham 234 *infra* and scir.

1. BURTON ON URE 21 F 8

Burton(e) 1086 DB, *(super Yor)* 1270 YI
Little Burton (on Yore) 1368 FF, 1483 Test

v. burhtun. Burton stands on the river Ure near Aldburgh
infra, and takes its name from "the old burh."

ALDBURGH [ɔːdbrə]

Aldburgh H 2 BM, 1535 Fount
Aldeburg(h) .1155, 1180–90, c. 1190, 1198 Fount, 1271
    Baildon, 1279, 1327 Fount
Audeburg 1231 *Ass*

v. (e)ald, burh. There are now no traces of fortifications at
Aldburgh, but it occupies a position of importance above the
river Ure. Cf. Burton *supra*.

NUTWITH COTE

Nuttewith, Nutewyth 1198 Fount, 1305 Baildon
Notewiht c. 1190 Fount
Nuttweth 1535 VE *Nuthwith Cote* 1540 Fount

'Nut wood' *v.* hnutu, viðr. The first element may be ODan
*hnuta (= OWScand *hnot*) or OE *hnutu*. *Cote* is a late addition.
v. cot.

2. COLSTERDALE 21 F 5 [kɔustədil]

Colserdale 1301 LS
Costerdale 1330 Ch
Kwustardhall 1416 YI
Cowsterdale 1616 NR
Colsterdale 1705 Pickhill

A clue to the interpretation of this name is furnished by a reference in 1330 (Ch) to "the grant of the said Joan of free passage through all Mashamshire to Costerdale, so that no one coming to Costerdale to the mine of the said monks for coals (*carbonibus*)...shall be held to bail." The first element of the name may well be ME *colster*, 'one who has to do with coals.' For the wide application of the suffix *ster*, *v*. Jespersen in MLR xxii. 129 ff.

BACKSTONE BECK (6")

> *Bacstainbek* 1314 Fount

'Stream from which *backstones*, i.e. bake-stones, were obtained' ME **bakstain* < ON steinn and bekkr. Cf. Baxterwood and *Backstonerigg* PN NbDu s.nn.

3. ELLINGSTRING 21 F 7

> *Elingestrengge* 1198 Fount
> *Elingstring* 1279–81 QW, 1316 Vill
> *El(l)ynstrynge, Elling-, Ellyngstring(e)* 1285 KI, 1361 FF, 1369 BM, 1571 FF

The first element is an OE *Elling*, a derivative of the OE name *Ella* found in Ellington *infra*, or the name may be formed from *Ella* with the same use of *ing* to link the pers. name to the suffix, as in the ingtun names. The second is ON *strengr* 'water-course,' which enters into the Norw p.n. *Strengen* (NG i. 17, 91, etc.). The form *-string* arises from the ME sound-change of *eng* to *ing* (cf. the forms of Ingleby 167 *supra*).

4. ELLINGTON 21 E 8

> *Ellintone* 1086 DB
> *Elling-, Ellyngton* 12 RichReg 84 d et passim
> *Eling-, Elyngton* 1219, 1231 Ass, 1279–81 QW, 1280 Ass, 1285 KI

'Ella's farm' *v*. ingtun. *Ella* (Redin 65) is the ONb form of WSax *Ælla*. Cf. also Ellingstring *supra*.

SWARTHORPE (lost)

> *Siuuar-, Siwartorp* 1086 DB
> *Swarthorp'* 1184 RichReg 84 d

Smartorp' (sic) 1207 FF, *Siwardthorp* 1226 FF
Swartrups 17 *Tithe Apportionment*

This place is of interest as in it Mr T. S. Gowland has, with
the aid of the Tithe Award, discovered the site of the lost DB
vill. The name means 'Siward's village' from the OE pers.
name *Sigeweard*. *v.* þorp.

5. FEARBY 21 F 7 [fiəbi]

Federbi 1086 DB
Fetherby 1184 *RichReg* 84 *d*
Feherbi 1193 *Studley Royal MS.* (box 10, No. 172)
Fe(g)herbi, -by 1204 Ass (p), 1231 *Ass*, 1285 KI, 1291 Ch,
1301 LS, 1316 Vill
Faireby 1231 *Ass*
Feryby 1279–81 QW
Fegtherby 1301 LS
Foyerby 1361 FF
Feyerby 1369 BM
Fethirby 1406 YI
Fearby 1537 FF

There are two types of spellings, *Fether-* and *Fegher-*. It
seems most likely that the *Fether-* spellings are original and
that the forms *Fegher-*, *Feher-* arise from AN loss of *th* and the
insertion of a hiatus-filling *gh* (*v.* IPN 109, 111). Professor
Ekwall suggests that the first element may be OScand *fioðer*,
fiædher, 'four.' If such a compound is possible, this name
presumably contains *by* in its original sense of 'dwelling' and
the name would have some such meaning as 'four farms.'
Cf. Sevenhampton (PN Wo 356). *v.* by.

6. HEALEY 21 G 7 [i:lə]

Helagh 1279–81 QW, 1327 Banco *Helaugh* 1406 YI
Healey 1561 FF

'High forest clearing' *v.* heah, leah.

LEIGHTON [li:tən]

Suthleghton 14 VCH *Lighton* 1540 Fount
v. leactun.

SOURMIRE

Surmire 1314 Fount   *Sourmyremore* 1330 Ch

v. saurr, myrr, mor.

SPRUCE GILL BECK [sprius gil]

Spronesgilbek (leg. *Sproues-*) 1330 Ch

v. gil, bekkr. The first element of this name is the same as that found in Sprucedale (Darrington, YWR), *Sprouesdale* c. 1190, c. 1200 Pont, and must be the OE name *Sprow* of which there are three examples before the Conquest.

SUTTON

Su(d)ton(e) 1086 DB   *Sutton* 1184 *RichReg* 84 *d et passim*

v. suð, tun. 'South' probably in relation to Ellington.

7. ILTON 21 G 7

Hilchetun, Ilcheton 1086 DB

I-, Ylketon 1184 *RichReg* 84 *d et passim* to 1535 VE

Ilkton 1581 FF, *Ilton* 1558 RichWills

v. tun. The first element is an OE pers. name *Ylca*, derived from the rather rare OE pers. name *Ylla* (LVD) extended by the suffix *-(i)ca*. Cf. Elkham (Sx), with early forms *Ulkeham*, *Elkeham* which in that county must go back to OE *Ylcanham*.

AUTHERLANDS

Aldolflund 1314 Fount

'Aldulf's wood' from the OE pers. name *Aldwulf* (LVD) and lundr. For the phonology *v*. Introduction xxxi.

CRAWL SIDE (6″)

Crawell 1314 Fount

Cf. Crow Hill (Halifax, YWR), *Crowelschais* 1562 Halifax Wills, and *Crowallsike*, a lost place in Fixby, Goodall, *PN SWY* 114 all from OE crawe and w(i)ella.

ELLER BECK

Elrebec Hy 2 BM

'Alder stream' *v*. elri, bekkr.

GRIMES DALE (6")

Grymesdalebek 1314 Fount

'Grim's valley' from ON *Grímr* and **dæl**.

POTT BECK

Pozbek 1314 Fount

POTT HALL

Pott(e) 12 VCH, 1314 Fount, 1535 VE   *Pot* 1301 LS

Pot is used in Cu and We of 'a deep hole or cavity, especially in the bed of a river, a pool; a moss hole from which peats have been dug' (EDD). In the YNR it is used of 'a rift in the limestone' (as here and in Crackpot 271 *infra*). The word is probably of Scand origin; cf. Swed dial. *putt, pott* 'water hole, abyss' and Potto and Sandpot 176, 205 *supra*.

8. MASHAM 21 F 8 [mæsəm]

Massan 1086 DB
Masham 1153 Jerv 20 *et freq* to 1328 Ch
Massham 1163 YCh 82 *et freq* to 1468 Fount
Mesham 1233 Cl
Masseham 1251 Ch, 1271 Baildon, 1279–81 QW
Massam 1286 Ebor *et freq* to 1530 Visit

'Mæssa's homestead' v. ham. For *Mæssa*, v. Marsworth (PN Bk 98), OE *Mæssanwyrð*, KCD 721.

9. SWINTON 21 G 8

Suinton 1086 DB

Cf. Swinton 47 *supra*.

TWISLEBROOK (lost)

Tuislebroc 1086 DB   *Tuisebrok* 1184 RichReg 84 *d*

Mr T. S. Gowland informs us that the name *Twistlebro* occurs in a 17th cent. list of field-names in this township, and places fairly accurately the site of the DB vill. The name means 'fork stream' from OE **twisla** which is used in the topographical sense of 'the fork where two streams meet,' and **broc**.

WARTHERMARSKE [waːðəmask]

Wardonmersk 1198 Fount, 13 VCH, 1542 Fount
Wardermarske 16 VCH i. 328, 1606 NR; -*maske* 1535 Fount
Wardon Marske 1540 Fount

'The marsh below the watch-hill' *v.* weard, dun and mersc.

Thornton Watlass

1. CLIFTON ON URE 21 E 8
   Clifton 1086 DB

2. ROOKWITH 21 E 8 [riukwiθ]
   Rocvid, -uid 1086 DB
   Rokewyk 1184 *RichReg* 84 *d*, 1283 *Rich* 30, 1290 Ch
   Rokkewyt 1280 YI, 1283 *Rich* 34
   Rok(e)wyth(e) 1536 YChant, 1539 Dugd v. 578
   Rookwith 1561 RichWills

   'Rook wood' from OE *hroc* (or ON *hrókr*) and viðr. The
   forms with final -*k* are due to the scribe misreading -*wit* as -*wic*.
   (For this error cf. Leckby 181 *supra*.)

3. THIRN 21 E 8 [θɔrn]
   Thirn(e) 1086 DB, 1184 *RichReg* 84 *d et passim*, 1328 Ch,
      1551 FF
   Thirun 12 *MaryH* 37 *d*
   Thryn 1406 YI
   Therne 1576 FF

   v. þyrne. For *Thryn* cf. Thrintoft 276 *infra*.

4. THORNTON WATLASS 21 E 9
   Thornton and Watlass were separate vills until the 13th cent.
   when Watlass was absorbed by Thornton. After this the names
   also were combined.

   Torreton, -tun 1086 DB
   Thorn(e)ton 1184 *RichReg* 84 *d et passim*
   Thorenton 1230 Pat

   v. þorn, tun.

Watlass appears either alone or (in later spellings) in combination with Thornton as:

Wadles 1086 DB
Watlos 12 *MaryH* 37 *d*, 1208 FF, 1435 IpmR
Watlas(s) 1263 Pap, 1665 Visit
Watlous 1269 Ipm *et passim* to 1555 RichWills
Wattelaws 1376 *Archd* 12
Watlows 1406 YI, 1424 Pat, 1430 *Archd* 27, *Watloose* 1576 FF

This name is fully discussed by Lindkvist (165), who derives it from ON *vatn-lauss* adj. 'waterless.' Cf. Westley Waterless (C).

Bedale

1. AISKEW 21 D 10 [ɛəskiu]

Echescol 1086 DB
Ai-, *Aykescogh* 12 *RichReg* 79 *d*, 1318 ib. 107; -*scouk* 1279–81
    QW; -*scoch'* 1283 *Rich* 26; -*schogh* 1352 FF
Ayscough, *Aiscogh* 1285 KI, 1400 YI
Askew(e) 1516 FF, 1665 Visit   *Ascugh* 1576 FF

'Oak wood' *v.* eiki, skogr; cf. Aiskew 294 *infra.* The DB form -*col* is due to confusion of -*og*- and -*ol*- by French scribes at the time when OFr -*l*- was vocalised (and still written -*l*-) and ON -*g*- was vocalised in ME after back vowels, producing a diphthong similar to the OFr diphthong. Cf. Swinesale 110 *supra.*

LITTLE LEEMING (6″)

Lemyng(e), -*ing* 1285 KI, (*Little*) 1516 FF
Parva Lymynge 1576 FF

v. Leeming (Halik) 227 *supra.*

2. BEDALE 21 D 9 [biːdəl]

Bedale 1086 DB, 1281 Abbr *et passim*
Bedhal 1256 Abbr
Bedehale 1504 Dugd iii. 603
Bedel 1514 Sanct, 1530 NCyWills, *Bidell* 1564 Cai

Probably 'Beda's nook of land' *v.* h(e)alh. The pers. name is OE *Bēda* (Redin 60). The absence of early -*hale* forms is probably due to the influence of ME *dale* with which the second element seems to have been confused, though -*ale* often appears for -*hale* in ME spellings, as in Pickhill, Strensall, Finghall, etc.

3. BURRILL 21 D 9 [bɔril]

Borel(l) 1086 DB, 1184 *RichReg* 84 d, 1285 KI
Burel(l) 12 *Easby* 27, 1282 YI, 1283 *Rich* 26, 1316 Vill, 1400 YI, 1572 FF
Burrell 1568 FF

This, as Professor Ekwall suggests, may be a compound of OE burh and hyll. Cf. Burghill (He).

COWLING [kɔulin]

Torneton 1086 DB
Thorneton Collinge, -ynge 1270 YI *et freq* to 1328 Banco
Collyng(e) 1400 YI, 1538 FF
Cowling(e) 1572 FF, 1666 Visit

v. þorn, tun. *Cowling* was originally a feudal addition like Picot in Newton Picot 227 *supra*. Later the first element was lost. The name *Colling* appears in DB, Riev, and P (1185), and is a patronymic derived from OE *Cola* (*v.* Redin 46, 166).

4. GREAT and LITTLE CRAKEHALL 21 D 9

Crachele 1086 DB
K-, Crakehale 1157 *RichReg* 83 *et freq* to 1298 YI
Crachall 1204 Ass (p)
Crakehall (parva) 1231 *Ass*, 1285 KI, 1318 *RichReg* 106 d, 1396 Pap
Crac-, Crakhale 1276 *RegAlb* ii. 18 d *et freq* to 1331 Ch
Crakall 1364 FF, *Crakell* 1663 Pickhill
Craykall 1418 YI

'Craca's nook of land' *v.* h(e)alh. Cf. Crakehill 184 *supra*.

KIRKBRIDGE

Kirkebrigge 13 *Easby* 142 d
'Bridge leading to the church' *v.* kirkja, brycg.

5. FIRBY 21 E 10 [fɔrbi]

Fredebi 1086 DB
Fritheby 1184 *RichReg* 84 d, 1252 *Ass*
Frytby 1282 YI, 1283 *Rich* 26

Fryth-, Frethby, Frithby 1285 KI, 1352 FF, 1400 YI
Fi-, Fyrthby 1485 Test, 1566 FF, *Fyrby* 1566 FF

'Frithi's farm' *v.* by. Cf. *Fridebi*, the old name of Felixkirk, and Fryton 199, 50 *supra*.

HOL BECK (6")

Hol(e)bec c. 1150 Dugd v. 572

Cf. Howl Beck 69 *supra*.

6. LANGTHORNE 21 C 9

Langetorp 1086 DB
Langethorn(e) 1086–1112 *Dods* lxxvi *et freq* to 1350 FF
Langthorne 1285 KI, 1514 Sanct, 1562 RichWills

'(At) the tall thorn tree' *v.* lang, þorn. The DB form *-torp* is erratic as in Spennithorne 253 *infra*.

7. RAND GRANGE 21 D 9

Randes 12 *Easby* 27
Rand(e) 1285 KI, 1319 *RichReg* 112 *d*, 1328 Banco

OE rand, ON rǫnd 'border, edge.'

Scruton

1. SCRUTON 21 C 11 [skriutən, skruːtən]

Scurueton, Skurveton 1086 DB, 1210 Abbr, 13 *RichReg* 122 *d*,
    1270 Ch, 1289 Ebor, 1370 *Archd* 8, 1396 Pap
Sc(h)orveton 1184 *RichReg* 84, 1252 Ch, 1280 YI
Scurfeton' 1231 *Ass*
Scrurueton (sic) 1285 KI, 1356 FF
Scrowton 1470 RichWills
Screwton 1611 NR

'Scurfa's farm' *v.* tun. *Scurfa* (ASC) is the name of a Scand jarl. Björkman (*NP* 124) identifies it with OWScand *skurfa*, 'scurf, scab,' found also as the ON by-name *Skurfa* (LindBN). The name of the same man probably enters into the name of Scurf Beck, a local stream (6"). For a possible OE parallel, *v.* Sheraton, PN NbDu 176.

Kirkby Fleetham

1. AINDERBY MIRES 21 C 9

Endrebi 1086 DB
Andrebi 1198 FF, *Anderby in le Myers* 1563 FF
Enderdeby 1280 YI
Aynderby in le Myre 1498 AD
Anderby Miers 1740 Pickhill

v. Ainderby Quernhow 223 *supra.* The terminal *Mires* denotes the swampy nature of the ground. *v.* myrr, and cf. Barton le Willows 38 *supra.*

HOLTBY [ɔutbi]

(H)eltebi, Holtebi, Boltebi 1086 DB

With the same forms and interpretation as Holtby (Bulm) 9 *supra.*

2. KIRKBY FLEETHAM 21 B 10

Originally there were two places here, but nothing remains of Kirkby but the name and a church at Kirkby Hall. A combination of the two names is now used of this parish as of Kirby Ravensworth 290–2 *infra.*

Chirchebi, Cherchebi 1086 DB
Fletham et Kirkeby 13 Leon 67 *d*, *Ki-, Kyrkeby (cum) Fletham*
   1289 Ebor

'Farm by the church' *v.* kirkja, by.
Fleetham by itself appears as:

Fleteha(m)' 1086 DB, 1086–c. 1112 *Dods* lxxvi, 1285 KI,
   14 *RichReg* 87 *d*
Fletham 1270 Ch *et freq* to 1400 YI

'Homestead by the stream' *v.* fleot, ham.

GREAT and LITTLE FENCOTE

Fencotes 1270, 1280 YI *et passim*

v. fen, cot.

Hornby

1. HACKFORTH 21 B 9
   Acheford(e) 1086 DB
   Akeford 1142–53 *RegAlb* ii. 72
   Hac-, *Hakford* 1184 *RichReg* 84, 1204 FF, 1285 KI, 1305 Ch, 1350 FF
   Ha(c)keford 1276 *RegAlb* ii. 18 *d*, 1282 Ipm, 1283 *Rich* 34
   Hacceford 1283 *Rich* 25
   Hackfourth 1565 FF

   Despite the two earlier spellings, initial *H-* is organic (cf. Zachrisson, *Some Yorkshire Place-Names* in *Språkvetenskapliga Sällskapets förhandlingar*, 1925–7, p. 37). The first element is probably OE *hæcc* used of 'a hatch, a floodgate or sluice'; and the whole name may be descriptive of a ford at which there is a *hatch* to stop animals from being carried down stream. For possible further examples of this name *v.* Hackford (PN NbDu 98).

2. HORNBY 21 B 8
   Hornebi, -by 1086 DB *et passim* to 1361 FF
   Hornby 1469 RichWills

   'Horni's farm' *v.* by. According to Ekwall (*PN La* 180) the Scand pers. name *Horni* is adduced in OEScand sources only; cf. however Björkman, *ZEN* 47, n. 3.

Patrick Brompton

1. ARRATHORNE 21 C 7 [arəθɔːn]
   Ergthorn 13 Marrick 117
   Erchethorn, Erg(h)ethorn Hy 3 BM, 1259 Ass, 1278 Baildon, 1285 KI
   Erethorn 1285 KI
   Arrowthorne 16 VCH i. 334   *Arathorne* 1581 FF

   'The thornbush near the shieling' *v.* erg, þorn.

2. PATRICK BROMPTON 21 C 8
   Bruntun, -ton(e) 1086 DB
   The affix appears as
   Pateryke Hy 2 *MaryH* 6 *d*, *Patric(k)*, *-ryk* 1280 *Ass*, 1285 KI, *Petrick* 1577 Saxton

With the same run of forms and interpretation as Brompton (Pick) 96 *supra*. The affix *Patrick* is a feudal name and it is derived from the OIr pers. name *Patric*; it was probably introduced by Norwegians who had come from Ireland (*v*. Introd. xxviii). It is also found in *Paterik-keld* (13th Marrick 113), the name of a lost spring in Spennithorne 253 *infra*, Patrick Pool (York), *Patrikepole* 1311 Leon 134 *d*, etc. (cf. *Revue Celtique*, XLIV. 50). Irish influence in this district is also betokened by the names Arrathorne 240 *supra* and *Miregrim infra*.

3. HUNTON 21 C 7

Hunton(e) 1086 DB *et passim*

'Huna's farm' from the OE pers. name *Hūna* and tun.

MIREGRIM (lost)

Myregrim 13 Marrick 114

'Grim's marsh' from myrr and the ON pers. name *Grímr*. This name is an example of Irish-Norwegian reversal of the order of elements (cf. *Hillbraith* and Sawcock 158, 216 *supra* and *v*. *Revue Celtique*, u.s.).

4. NEWTON LE WILLOWS 21 D 8

Neuton 1086 DB, (*in le Wilughes*) 1300 Ebor 31, (*in le Wilighes*) 1344 Ebor 9

'New farm' and later distinguished as 'where willows abound' *v*. niwe, tun, and Barton le Willows (Bulm) 38 *supra*.

RUSWICK [ruzik]

Risewic(k) 1086 DB, 1145–55 *Mary Y* 250 *et passim* to 1293 QW

Rysewyk Hy 2 *MaryH* 6 *d*, 1285 KI

Ryswyk(e) 1535 Dugd v. 577, 1539 ib. 578

'Corner of land in the hills overgrown with brushwood' *v*. hris, vik. On the modern form cf. Ruswarp 125 *supra*.

Catterick

1. WEST APPLETON 21 B 8

Westapelton 1142–53 *RegAlb* ii. 72, *Mikelapleton* 14 VCH, i. 304, etc.

EAST APPLETON

Apleton, Apelton 1086 DB, (*Est*) 1142–53 *RegAlb* ii. 72, (*Parva*) 1205 FF

v. æppeltun.

2. BROUGH HALL 21 A 8 [bruf]

Burgh 1184 *RichReg* 84 *et passim* to 1665 Visit

v. burh. Brough is near the actual site of the Romano-British station of *Cataracton* (*v.* Catterick *infra*).

3. CATTERICK 21 A 9 [kætrik, kæθərik]

καταρρακτων 2nd cent. (c. 1200) Ptolemy

Cataractone, -i 4th cent. (8th) AntIt

Cataractam uicum, Cataractone uico 8 Bede

Cateracta(*m*), *Ceteracte* c. 1130 SD

Cetrehttun, Cetrihtun, Cetreht worþig(*n*)*e* 10 BedeOE

Catrice 1086 DB, Hy 2 *MaryH* 6 *d*

Catherick 12 *FountC* 317

K-, Cateriz 1198–1208 YD, c. 1200 *Easby* 97 *d*, 1289, 1301 Ebor

Catrich 1238 Pap

Cheteriz 1241 Ch

C-, Katerik 1283 *Rich* 33, 1285 KI, 1305 *MaryY* 248, 1396 Pap

Caterich 1295 Abbr

Katrici 1308 Ch

Catrik 1362 *Archd* 5 *d*, 1400 Test, 1441 BM

Catteryke 1396 Pap

Catheryk 1536 YChant; *-ick*(*e*) 1556 RichWills, 1586 Pickhill

It has been suggested (IPN 23) that Catterick is a Celtic name probably of the same origin as Chatteris (C); some of the spellings such as *Cateriz, Cheteriz* certainly support this.

There was at Catterick during the Roman occupation an important station and the extant site of the encampment is near Watling Street, the great Roman road running through the North Riding. It seems possible that the name, therefore, is ultimately connected with Welsh *cader*, OIr *cathair* 'hill fort,' which enters into Catterton (YWR), *Cadretone* 1086 DB, etc., in the old kingdom of Elmet. The Brit form of this element would be *catar-*, which is cognate with Lat. *caterva* 'a troop of soldiers,' and *-t-* did not undergo Brit "mutation" to *th* as it did in Catterton.

The second part of the name is not clear, but Sir John Morris Jones suggests that the original Brit name had two forms, *Caturacto*, gen. *Caturactonos*, and a derivative form *Caturact-on*, gen. *-ion*; this was read by the Romans as Lat *cataracta* 'waterfall,' which, curiously enough, is apt, as near this point the river Swale has a very swift flow.

Noteworthy is the rendering of Bede's *vicus* by the alternative tun and worþig in the OE Bede.

The modern form *Catheryck* is due to the local sound-change of ME *-t-* to NEDial *-th-*; *v.* Introduction xxxii.

ORAN

    Archorouen e. 12 Dugd iii. 603   *Archorhouen* 13 *Easby* 197

This name is not clear, though it seems probable that the first element is ON erg 'shieling' and that the second element is a pers. name of obscure origin, the whole name being a case of Irish-Norwegian reversal of elements (cf. *Miregrim* 241 *supra*).

4. COLBURN 21 A 7 [kɔubən]

    Corburne 1086 DB

    Colebrun(n) 12 *Leon* 66 *d*, 1208 Ass (p), 13 *Easby* 130, *-burn'*
        1198 Cur, 1219 *Ass* (p), 1260 *Easby* 131 *d*, *-bron* 1280 YI

    Colburn(e) 13 *RichReg* 82 *et passim*

    Cowburne, -born 1574 FF, 1577 Saxton

The name was originally a river-name referring to Colburn Beck; *v.* burna (brunnr). The first element is probably OE col 'cool' or OE col, ON *kol* 'coal,' the latter being an allusion to the dark colour of the water, as in the Norw river-name *Kola*. Colburn, therefore, means either 'cool stream' or 'coal-black stream.' For the DB form *v.* IPN 106.

WINTYLOW [wintəlɔu]

    Wintuneoves 12 YD

    Wintun houes 1198–1208 YD

    Wyntonhowes c. 1200 *Easby* 97 *d*

v. haugr. The first element of this name is a lost place-name *Winton*, which is of the same origin as Winton 212 *supra*. On the change of *-n-* to *-l-* cf. Skiplam 65 *supra*.

5. HIPSWELL 21 A 7

Hiplewelle 1086 DB
Hippleswell 12 *Easby* 114
Hippeswell(e) 1184 *RichReg* 84, 12 *Easby* 5, 1228 ib. 113,
    1285 KI, 1316 Vill, 1328 Banco, 1396 Pap, 1561 FF
Hippeleswell(e) 1260 *Easby* 131 *d*, 1300 Ebor
Hipleswelle c. 1270 *Easby* 165
Hippliswell 1301 LS
Hipsewell 1545 RichWills

v. w(i)ella. No satisfactory pers. name can be suggested for the first element, and it is probably a lost *hӯpels* (Angl *hēpels*), a derivative of OE *hēap* 'heap,' used of a hill as in Heape (PN La 61). If so we have very early shortening of *ē* to *ĕ* and raising to *ĭ*. Cf. Redmire 257 *infra*. There is an isolated hill on the west side of the village which might well be so called. Hence, 'hill stream or spring.'

RISEDALE and RISEDALE BECK

Risedalebec c. 1200 *Easby* 152
Ri-, Rysedale 1262 *Easby* 155 *et passim*
Risdale 1577 Saxton

'Valley overgrown with brushwood' *v.* hris, dæl, bekkr, or else 'Risi's valley' from the ON pers. name *Hrísi* (LindBN).

WAITHWITH

Watewith 1204 Ass, *-wyth* 1290 Baildon
Watwith 1206 *Easby* 154 *d*, 155
Wathwith 1262 *Easby* 155
Waitwith 1562 FF, 1577 Saxton

Professor Ekwall suggests that the first element is ON *vátr*, 'wet' and the second viðr, hence 'wet wood.' Cf. Weetwood (PN NbDu 210). The change from *t* to *th* is probably due to common confusion with the suffix *thwaite*.

6. HUDSWELL 14 J 6

Hudreswelle, Undreswelle 1086 DB
Hud(e)leswell e. 12 Dugd iii. 602
Hudeswell 12 *Easby* 5 *et passim* to 1403 YI
Huddeswell 1184 *RichReg* 84 *et passim* to 1519 FF
Hutleswell 1204 Ass
Hoddeswell 1280 *Ass*, 1316 Vill
Hoteswella 1308 Ch
Huddiswell 1556 RichWills

'Hudel's well' *v.* w(i)ella. OE *Hudel* may be inferred from Huddleston (YWR), OE *Hudelestun* c. 1030 *Gosp.* It is a diminutive in *-ela* of the OE name *Huda* (Redin 98); an *r*-derivative of the same name enters into Huddersfield (YWR). For the DB form, cf. IPN 107.

KIRKGATE WOOD (6")

Kirkegat(h)e 1198–1208 YD, c. 1200 *Easby* 97 *d*
'Church road' *v.* kirkja, gata.

MONKBY (lost)

Munkeby 13 *Easby* 200 *Monkby* 1540 Dugd iii. 606
'The monks' farm' from OE *munuc* and by.

SAND BECK

Sandbe(c)k(e) e. 12 Dugd iii. 603

THORPE UNDER STONE

Torp 1187 P *Thorp* 13 *Easby* 167, 1577 Saxton
Thorpesgill 13 Dugd iii. 603

v. þorp, gil (referring to the ravine in which Thorpe lies).

7. KILLERBY 21 B 9

Chiluordebi 1086 DB

With the same run of forms and history as Killerby (Pick) 103 *supra.*

8. Scotton 21 B 7

Scot(t)une 1086 DB
Scotton(a) 1199–1210 *Easby* 109 *d et passim*
Schotton 1184 *RichReg* 84, 1295 YI

This is probably from OE *Scotta-tun*, 'farm of the Scots or Irish,' with early loss of the inflexional syllable between the two *t*'s, cf. Catton 183 *supra*. A similar explanation may hold for Scotton (L), LindsSurv *Scottuna*, etc. *v.* tun.

9. Tunstall 21 B 8

Tunestale 1086 DB
Tunstale 1157 *RichReg* 82 *et passim*

v. tunst(e)all.

The Mount

Michelmunt e. 12 Dugd iii. 603

'Large hill' from ME *michel* (OE micel) and OFr *munt*.

Thieves Gill

Theuesgill 12 Dugd iii. 603

v. gil and cf. Thieves Dikes 116 *supra*.

XI. HANG WEST WAPENTAKE

v. Hang East Wapentake 228 *supra*.

Wensleydale [wenslədil], the valley of the Ure

Wandesleydale 1142 Dugd v. 568, 1153 *Jerv* 20
Wandelesdale c. 1146 (14th) Dugd v. 570
Wendeslei-, -ley-, 1199–1210 Abbr, 13 *RichReg* 121, 1218 FF
Wendeslacdale 1275 *Easby* 163 *d*
Wendeslaidale 1307 Ch
Wandeslaghdale 1315 Riev
Wenslawdale 14 *RichReg* 87 *d*, 1421 YI
Wensladale 1451 Test, 1564 FF

v. Wensley 257 *infra* and dæl.

Finghall

1. AIKBER 21 C 7

Akeberga 1160 YCh 1119
Aykebergh 1279–81 QW, 1289 ChR, *Aykbergh* 1342 IpmR
Aykebargh 1539 Dugd v. 578

'Oak hill' *v.* eiki, berg. Cf. Norw *E(i)keberg* (NG i. 6, ii. 52, 114, etc.). The earliest spelling suggests OE *āca-beorg*, with later Scandinavianisation.

HESSELTON

Heselton' 1137–46 *Easby* 321 *et freq*
Hesiltone 1228 Dugd v. 576

'Hazel-tree farm' *v.* OE hæsel or ON hesli and tun.

2. CONSTABLE BURTON 21 C 6

Burton 1279–81 QW *et passim*

v. burhtun. Burton probably takes its second name *Constable* from the Constables of Richmond. Stephen, Earl of Richmond, granted it to his constable, Roald, c. 1100 (VCH i. 233). The feudal addition first appears as *Conestabel(l)* in 1279–81 QW.

STUDDAH [studə]

Stodhage, -hag(h) c. 1200 *Easby* 159, 1210 FF, 1219, 1231 *Ass*
Stodehawe 1301 LS
Studhowe 1561 FF, *Studdowe* 1575 FF

'Stud enclosure' *v.* stod, haga and cf. Stody (Nf).

3. FINGHALL 21 D 7 [fiŋgəl]

Finegal(a) 1086 DB
Fingala, -ale, Fyngale 1086–c. 1112 *Dods* lxxvi *et freq* to 1406 YI
Fi-, Fynyngale 1157 *RichReg* 83, 1291, 1300 Ebor
Fi-, Fyning-, Fynynghal(e) 1184 *RichReg* 84 *d*, 1236 Pat, 1300 Ebor
Fynkall 1285 KI
Fi-, Fynegale 1289 Ebor, 1290 Ch
Fynighale c. 1291 Tax

Fenegale 1301 LS
Fynghall 1361 FF　*Fyngell* 1548 RichWills, 1574 FF

Bugge's suggestion that Finghall (YNR) is identical with the Irish p.n. Fingall (co. Dublin) is quoted by Ekwall (*Scands. and Celts* 87, IPN 34) as an example of Irish influence. This is an interesting solution of the name, but the fact that spellings with *Fining-* are not infrequent and the fact that the greater number of local p.n.'s in that area are of Anglian origin points to an Anglian origin for this name.

The first element is probably an OE pers. name. The name *Finn* is only on record in the Heroic poems but the forms of Finghall suggest that the name had a single *n*. More probably we should therefore presume the same OE name *Fin* which Ekwall finds in Finningham (Sf), DB *Finingaham* (*PN in -ing* 313) and in Fyning (Sx). This is found in the derivative form *Finca* in Finkley (Ha) and the pers. name *Fynke* recorded in Berkshire in the 12th cent. Cf. also OGer *Fino, Finich* in Förstemann (*PN* 506). Hence, 'nook or corner of Fin's people,' *v.* h(e)alh.

HANG BANK (6")

A hill on the SW boundary of the township, just north of Hutton Hang *infra*. This was the wapentake meeting-place. *v.* Hang Wapentake 228 *supra*.

4. HUTTON HANG 21 D 7

Hotun(e) 1086 DB
Hohton' 1231 Ass
Hoton Hang(e) 1280 YI *et passim* to 1328 Banco
Hunton (sic), *Hanger, Hutonhang* 1535–9 Dugd v. 577–8
v. hoh, tun. It is just south of Hang Bank.

Thornton Steward

1. THORNTON STEWARD 21 D 7

Tornenton(e), -tune 1086 DB
Thorneton 1157 RichReg 83, (*Dapifer*) ib., (*Steward*) 1252 Pap
v. þorn, tun. Before the Conquest Thornton was held by Gospatric and he was succeeded by Wymar, *dapifer* or *steward* of the Earls of Richmond (Dugd iii. 601–2).

DANBY ON URE

Danebi, -by 1086 DB *et freq*
Danby on Yore 1358 FF; *of Yeure* 1530 Visit

v. Danby 131 *supra* and Introduction xxv.

MARRIFORTH (Fm)

Mariford 1301 LS   *Mar(r)yforth* 1439 Dugd v. 578 etc.

v. ford. The first element is probably the woman's name
Mary or *Marie*.

ULSHAW BRIDGE [ulʃə, ɔusə]

Wolueshowe 1158 *RichReg* 83 *d*
Ulveshowe 1246 FF, 1285 KI, e. 14 *RichReg* 87
Ulschowe 1319 *RichReg* 112
Ulsogh 1427 *Archd* 25 *d*, *Ulsey* 1605 NR
Howsey 1614 NR
Ulsa al. Owsa 1623 NR

'Ulf's mound' from ON *Úlfr* and haugr. There are still
traces of an earthwork at Ulshaw. The first form suggests OE
Wulf. Cf. Ousey Carr 196 *supra*.

East Witton

1. EAST WITTON 21 E 6

Witun(e), Witone 1086 DB, (*Est*) 1204 ClR, 1396 Pap
Wittun, -ton c. 1150 Dugd v. 572, 1201 FF, 1268 Abbr,
    1298 YI
E(a)stwitton 1156 Dugd v. 573
Est Wotton 1316 FA

'Farm in the wood' *v.* tun. The spelling *Widtun* (West
Witton 255 *infra*) shows that Witton is derived from PrOE *widu*
(later OE wudu = ON *viðr*), and that *-dt-* was assimilated to
-tt-. This PrOE form *widu* is found in some early p.n. forms
such as *Widutuun* 723 BCS 157 (Wootton Wawen, Wa), though
it is usually later replaced by *wudu*.

ANGRAM COTE (6″)

Angrum 1280 *Ass*

v. Angram Grange 191 *supra* and Angram 272 *infra*.

BRAITHWAITE

>*Brathoit* c. 1190 *Dods* cxx. 3
>*Braytwayt* 1301 LS
>*Brathewait(e)* 1354 FF, 14 VCH
>*Braythwhayte* 1563, 1575 FF

'Broad clearing' *v.* breiðr, þveit. Cf. Norw *Bredtvedt* (ONorw *Breiðaþveit*), NG ii. 107. On the first form cf. Faceby 176 *supra*.

JERVAULX [dʒaːvis, dʒəːvou]

>*Jorvalle* 1135–54 (late MS) Dugd v. 568
>*Jorevall(e)* 1142–96 Dugd v. 569 *et passim* to 1361 *Archd* 5
>*Joresuals* 1162 P
>*Joraualle* 1177 BM
>*Gereuall(e)* 1196, 1218 FF, 1244 *Ass*, 1253 Baildon
>*Gervaus* 1200 Cur, 1241 Pat, 1283 *Rich* 30
>*Gerwalle* 1209 Pap
>*Geravaus* 1249 Baildon
>*Gir(e)vall(e)* c. 1200 BM, 1224 Pap, 1225 Pat, 1227, 1235 Cl, 1274 Ebor
>*Gyrovall'* 1242 Cl, 1243 Fees, 1283 *Rich* 33
>*Jer(e)vall* 1224 FF, 1236 Cl, 1249 Baildon
>*Jerovall(e)* 1253 Ch, 1289 Ebor, 1435 *Archd* 31 *d*
>*Yorevall* 1312 Ch
>*Jervax, Gervax* 1400, 1480, 1508 Test
>*Jorovall* 1427 NCyWills
>*Gerveis, -veys* 1530 Visit, 1536 YChant
>*Jarvaux* 1539 Dugd v. 578
>*Geruis* 1577 Saxton

'The valley of the Ure' from OFr *vals*. Like Rievaulx 73 *supra*, Jervaulx is the name of a Norman monastic foundation.

The phonetic problems connected with this name and that of the river Ure (*v.* spellings 7 *supra*) are the same, but some of these have been partly explained in *Anglia*, XLVIII. 291 ff. The above spellings at first sight suggest that *Jorevall* is the earliest type; Zachrisson accepts this and tries to show that the *Jerevall* forms are derivatives of this (ANInfl 63)[1]. But most of these

---

[1] Professor Zachrisson has recently expressed a different view in MLR XXI. 362. He also holds that OE *Earw* was not the Ure; but the relationship of *Earp* and Ure is certainly more than coincidence.

early *Jorevall* forms are from late MSS and it seems preferable to regard the *Jerevall* forms as being, if anything, the earlier. The OE form of the river-name was *Earp* (*v.* RNY 17) and according to certain ME sound-changes (cf. Yearsley 193 *supra*) *earu* could become ME *yere-*, or with Scand influence *yore-* (which is on record for the river-name). The *Jerevall* forms apparently contain this unrecorded form, *yere-*, of the river-name. *Jorevall* forms contain the well-evidenced *Yore*. By an AN sound-substitution of [dʒ] for [j] (*v.* IPN 104), *Yerevall* became [dʒerəval], from which the modern form is descended. There is, of course, some difficulty in the interpretation of the initial consonants of the spellings given above. According to Zachrisson (*ANInfl* 62), *g*, *ȝ*, *j* represent [dʒ], whilst *y* and sometimes *i* represent initial [j]. This cannot be accepted as being regular, for *ȝ* is often used for [j], and *j* and *i* are often indistinguishable in the court hand of the period when most of these instances occur. It is doubtful, therefore, if any of the *Jorevall* forms were ever pronounced with initial [dʒ], for it will be noticed that *Gor-*, which would indicate such a pronunciation, is never found.

It seems probable, therefore, that *Jerevall*, *Gerevall*, *Girevall* are the original forms of the p.n., derived from ME *yere-, an unrecorded form of the river-name Ure, and this form of the p.n. underwent an AN sound-substitution of [dʒ] for [j], as indicated by spellings with *g*. At a later date, when *Yore* was the regular form of the river-name, this was substituted for *Jere-*, giving the forms *Jorevall*; in this last case there is nothing to prove that the initial consonant was pronounced as [dʒ] as in the case of the *Jerevall* forms which have given the modern form [dʒaːvis]. This fact supports the idea that *Jore-* forms arise from substitution of the current form of the river-name.

The usual modern pronunciation of the name is [dʒɜːvou]; this is simply a spelling pronunciation. The dialectal pronunciation [dʒaːvis] is rapidly passing into disuse; it is the regular development of ME *Gerevals*.

KILGRAM GRANGE

Kelgrimhou 1228 Dugd v. 576, *Kylgramhowe* 1539 Dugd v. 578

'Kelgrim's mound' *v.* haugr. *Kelgrim* is found in Kellamergh (PN La 151), and Björkman (*ZEN* 53) suggests that its ultimate origin is an unrecorded ON *Kelfgrímr* or ON *Ketilgrímr*.

NEWSTEAD

> *Newestede* 1301 LS
>
> *v.* niwe, stede.

Middleham

1. MIDDLEHAM 21 D 5

> *Medelei, Medelai* 1086 DB
> *Mid(d)elham* 1184 *RichReg* 84 *et passim*
> *Midilham(e)* c. 1380 SurvDu, 1400, 1481 Test, 1459 Sanct
> *Midelam* 1530 Visit

'Middle homestead' *v.* middel, ham. The significance of *middel* here is obscure.

Spennithorne

1. BELLERBY 21 C 5

> *Belgebi* 1086 DB
> *Belgerby* 12 *Easby* 94 *d*, 1244 *Ass*
> *Beleherebi* 1166 P (p)
> *Beleg'bi* 1167 P
> *Belgre-, Belleherby* 1231 FF
> *Bellierby* 1235 *Easby* 190 *d*
> *Bellerby* 1285 KI *et passim*

'Belg's farm' *v.* by. *Belg* is from the ON by-name *Belgr* (gen. *Belgs*), derived from ON *belgr*, gen. *belgjar* 'bellows,' and then 'withered, dry old man.'

2. HARMBY 21 D 5

> *Hernebi, -by* 1086 DB, 12 *Leon* 66 *d et passim* to 1404 YI
> *Ernebi* 1086 DB
> *Harneby* 1519, 1574 FF

v. by. The first element is probably the OWScand by-name *Hiærne* (LindBN), inferred also by Lundgren from Swedish p.n. material.

3. SPENNITHORNE 21 D 5

Speningetorp 1086 DB
Spinithorn c. 1150 Godr
Spennigthorn 1289 Ebor
Spening-, -yngthorn(e) 1184 *RichReg* 84 *d et freq* to 1457
RichWills
Spenigthorne 1301 LS
Spenythorn(e) 1285 (16) KI, 1347 FF, 1396 Pap, 1410
RichReg 30
Spennithorne 1614 Pickhill

v. þorn. This name offers great difficulty. It clearly contains
the same first element as Spennymoor (PN NbDu 186), earlier
Spennyngmore, and both are probably to be connected with the
word which lies behind Spen (ib.), 1312 *le Spen*, but the significance of this word is very doubtful. The name as a whole is
probably an *inga*-formation (*v.* ing).

Coverham

1. CALDBERGH 21 E 4 [kɔːdbə]

Caldeber 1086 DB; *-bergh* 1184 *RichReg* 84 *et passim* to
1311 Ch
Caudeberg(h) 1269 Ch, 1293 QW

v. cald, berg.

EAST SCRAFTON

Sc(h)rafton 1184 *RichReg* 84, 1270 YI *et passim*

v. West Scrafton 255 *infra*.

2. CARLTON IN COVERDALE 21 E 3

Carleton (in Coverdale) 1086 DB *et passim*

v. karlatun.

ARKLESIDE

Arkelsit 1240 VCH i. 222, *-sat* 1270 YI

'Arkel's pasture' from the ON *Arnketell*, *Arnkell*, ODan
Arkil, OSwed *Arkil* (Björkman, *NP* 8). *v.* sætr.

BRADLEY
>   *Bradeleie* 1270 YI
>   'Broad clearing' *v.* brad, leah.

FLEENSOP, FLEEMIS GILL
>   *Flemmishope* 1240 VCH i. 222   *Flemmeshope* 1270 YI
>   *v.* hop, gil. No satisfactory explanation of the first element
can be offered.

GAMMERSGILL
>   *Gamelscale* 1388 IpmR   *Gamylscale* 15 VCH i. 222
>   'Gamel's hut,' from ON *Gamall* and skali.

HINDLETHWAITE, sometimes HINDLEYTHWAITE
>   *Hyndeletheyt* 1269 Ipm
>   *Hyndelaythwayt* 1388 IpmR, 1405 Pat
>   This p.n. contains an older p.n., *Hindelei* 'forest clearing for
hinds' from hind, leah, as in Heindley (PN YWR s.n.) and þveit.

SWINESIDE
>   *Swinesate* 1240 VCH i. 222, 1270 YI   *Suyneset* 1301 LS
>   'Swine pasture' *v.* swin, sætr.

WOODALE
>   *W(u)lvedale* 1223 FF
>   *v.* wulf, dæl and Woodale Beck (LangE) 135 *supra*.

3. COVERHAM 21 E 4 [kuvərəm, kɔurəm]
>   *Covreham* 1086 DB, *Coverham* 12 Cov 141 *et passim*
>   *Couerhaim* 1177 P (p)
>   'Farm on the river Cover' *v.* ham. The P form contains
ON heim. Cf. also *Coverhede* (1405 AD i), now Cover Head.

AGGLETHORPE
>   *Aculestorp* 1086 DB
>   *Acalthorp* 1184 *RichReg* 84
>   *Akolfthorp* 1244 *Ass*
>   *Akelthorp* 1285 KI, 1301 LS
>   *Aglethorp(e)* 1311, 1328 Ch *et passim*
>   'Aculf's village' from OE *Ācwulf* and þorp. On the later
forms cf. Wigginton 14 *supra*.

COTESCUE PARK [koːtskiu]

Scotescogh, Scoteskew 15 VCH i. 248, 1610 NR
Cotescough, -scugh, Coteskewe 1606 NR, 16 VCH ib.

v. skogr. The first element may be ON *skot* 'shooting,' which occurs in several Norw p.n.'s such as *Skotsberg* (NG i. 184), *Skattebøl* (ib. 120), *Skotbu* (NG ii. 35), etc. Professor Ekwall suggests the possibility of OE *Scotta*, from some early encounter with the Scots. The loss of initial *s-* is late and probably arose from the difficulty of pronouncing the combination *Scoteskew*.

4. MELMERBY 21 E 4

Melmerbi 1086 DB, 1202 FF
Melmor(e)by 1184 *RichReg* 84, 1219 *Ass et passim*

This name is, as the early forms show, of different origin from Melmerby 219 *supra*. It is 'Melmor's farmstead' from the OIr pers. n. *Maelmuire* (Annals of Ulster, Four Masters) which was borrowed in OWScand as *Melmor*. Cf. *Revue Celtique*, XLIV. 49.

5. WEST SCRAFTON 21 F 4

Sc-, Skraftun, -ton 1086 DB *et passim*, (*West*) 1285 KI
Scalftun 1086 DB

The first element of this name and East Scrafton 253 *supra* is OE *scræf* 'a cave, a hollow place in the earth, a miserable dwelling,' with Scandinavianising of the initial consonant. *v.* Shrawley (PN Wo 78). There is nothing in the local features of Scrafton to suggest a preciser meaning than 'a depression or hollow in the earth.' *v.* tun.

West Witton

1. WEST WITTON 21 D 3

Witun 1086 DB   *Widtona* 1166 P
West Witton 12 *RichReg* 82
v. East Witton 249 *supra*.

DOVE SCAR

Duuesker 1202 FF, *Douuesker* 1270 YI

'Dove cliff' from ON *dufa*, ME *duve* and ON *sker* 'rock, scar.'

LAYRUS (6″) [lɛərəs]

Leiragh 1202 FF

'Muddy enclosure' *v.* leirr, hagi. Presumably there was an alternative plural form giving final *s*.

PENHILL

Penle 1202 FF   *Penhill* 1577 Saxton

Probably the same as Pendle Hill (La), in which the first element is from a Brit word connected with Welsh *pen* 'head.' *v.* hyll.

SWINITHWAITE

Swiningethwait, Swiningtweit 1202 FF
Suiningetheyt 1220 *Ass*, etc.
Swynigt(h)wayt 1295 YI, 1301 LS
Swynythwayt 1315 Riev (p)

The first element may be the patronymic found in OSwed *Swiningæ* (Hellquist, *ON på -inge* s.n.) or a noun found in the ONorw p.n. *Svinningen* from ON *sviðningr* (cf. ON *sviða* 'to burn,' NG i. 71), hence 'place cleared by burning.' Cf. Swinsow 145 *supra. v.* þveit.

Wensley

1. CASTLE BOLTON 21 C 2

Bodelton(a), -tun 1086 DB, 1173 Riev, 1252 Ch
Boeltun 1160 Riev, 1201 ChR, 1208 FF
Bouelton 1240 Riev, 1252 *Ass   Bolton* 1396 Pap *et passim*

v. booltun. A castle was built here by Richard le Scrope in 1379 (Pat).

LOW BOLTON

Estbouelton 1231 FF

ELLERLANDS (6″)

Ellerlund 14 YD (a wood)

'Alder wood' *v.* elri, lundr. Cf. Sutherland 79 *supra*.

2. LEYBURN 21 C 5 [leːbən, leibən]

Leborne 1086 DB
Layburn(e) 12 RichReg 82, 1252 *Ass et passim* to 1519 FF
Laibrunn 1208 Ass
Lei-, Leybroun 1208 ChR, 1301 LS
Labrun 1319 Abbr

Possibly, 'stream by the forest clearing' *v.* leah, burna.
Forms with *-brun* are due to the influence of ON brunnr.

MILL BECK (6")

Milnebec c. 1180 Riev
v. myln, bekkr.

3. PRESTON UNDER SCAR 21 C 3

Prestun, -ton 1086 DB *et passim, (undescar)* 1568 FF
v. preost, tun and ON *sker* 'scar.'

4. REDMIRE 21 C 3 [redmaː]

Rid(e)mare 1086 DB, 1173 Riev (p)
Ridemere 1166 P (p), 1203 FF *et passim* to 1403 YI
Ry-, Ridmer 1184 RichReg 84, 1285 KI, 1410 RichReg 114
Redmar' 1243 Cl
Redmire 1665 Visit

Professor Ekwall suggests we may have OE hreod, 'reed,'
and mere. For early *i*-forms, cf. the history of Redmarley
(PN Wo 86, 156) and Tripsdale, Hipswell *supra* 69, 244.

APEDALE

Apedale c. 1175 Riev
'Api's valley' from the ON by-name *Ápi* and dalr. Cf.
Bergh Apton (Nf).

5. WENSLEY 21 D 4

Wendres-, Wentreslaga 1086 DB
Wandesle(i), -ley, -legh 1199 Cur, 1201 Abbr *et passim*
Wendesle(y), -lay 1201 Cur, 1205 Abbr *et passim* to 1396 Pap
Wenselawe 1363 FF   *Wenslaugh* 1536 YChant

'Wændel's forest-clearing' *v.* leah. The first element is from
an OE pers. name *Wændel*, for the use of which in p.n.'s *v.*
Wensdon (PN BedsHu 114). On the DB forms *v.* IPN 107.

GALE BANK

Gailbanc 1293 YD

v. geil, bank.

KELD BECK (6")

Keldebec 13 YD

v. kelda, bekkr.

MOUTHWAITE (6")

Muset(h)wayt(h) 1253 Ch, 1301 LS
Mousethwayt 1307 Ch
Musethoutland c. 1200 Riev (probably identical)

'Musi's enclosure' *v.* þveit. The first element is the ON pers. n. *Músi.*

Aysgarth

1. HIGH ABBOTSIDE 20 B 10

'The hill held by the Abbot (of Jervaulx)' *v.* sid.

CAMS HOUSE

Camb 1218 FF, 1308 Ch   *Cambehous* 1301 LS

'House on the ridge' *v.* camb, hus and Cams Head 194 *supra.*

COTTERDALE [kɔtədil]

Cottesdale 1266, 1267 Pat
Cotterdale 1280 YI, 1283 *Rich* 33, 1608 NR
Coterdale 1301 LS

v. dalr. The first element is probably identical with the Norw p.n. *Kaater* (ONorw *Kotar*) from ON *kot* neut. 'hut, cottage'; the plural form is that of the feminine (*v.* NG i. 362). We should have expected. ON *Kotadalr*, with gen. pl. *kota*, but Cotterdale may be a comparatively late formation from the *Cotter* of Cotter End Fm in the neighbourhood. Unfortunately no early forms of this name have been found. The first form *Cottesdale* suggests an alternative English plural form *Cotes.* *v.* cot.

FOSSDALE [fɔsdil]

> *Fossedale* 1280 YI, 1283 *Rich* 33
> *Foresdale* 1301 LS, *Forsdalethwayt* 1307 Ch
> 'Waterfall valley' *v.* fors, dalr, þveit. The earliest spelling is
> from the OWScand assimilated type *foss.*

HARDROW [aːdrə]

> *Hardrawe* 1606 NR
> 'Shepherd's dwelling' from OE (Angl) *herde* and raw.

HELL GILL BECK

> *Helebec* 1201 OblR, 1252 Ch
> *Helbec, -bek* 1307 Ch *et passim*
>
> *v.* bekkr. The first element of this name is probably ON
> *hella* 'flat stone,' as in the p.n.'s Helwith, Helwath (*passim*); this
> is reasonable on topographical grounds, for the bed of the
> stream is made up of great flat boulders.

HELL GILL

> *Helgill* 13 *RichReg* 126 *d*
> *v.* Hell Gill Beck *supra* and gil.

HOW BECK BRIDGE (6″)

> *Holebech* 1220 FF *Holbeck* 1301 LS
> *v.* hol, bekkr and Howl Beck 69 *supra.*

LITHERSKEW

> *Litherskewe* 1606 NR
> 'Wood of or on the slope' *v.* hlið (gen. *hlíðar*), skogr. Cf.
> Litherland (La) and OIcel *hlíðarlond.*

LUNDS

> *Lund* 1208 FF *Hel-, Holbeclundes* 1253 Ch *et passim* to
> 1610 Speed
> *Lounes* 1613 NR
> 'The woods' *v.* lundr.

17-2

LUNDS BECK (6″)

Lundesik 1307 Ch

v. Lunds *supra* and sic, later replaced by bekkr.

SEDBUSK

Setebu(s)kst(e) 1280 YI, 1283 *Rich* 33
Sedbuske 1611 NR

'Bush near the shieling' *v.* sætr, buskr.

SHAW

S(c)hal(l) 1218 FF, 1301 LS

This may be an Anglicised form of ON skali 'shieling' or an AN form of sc(e)aga 'wood' (*v.* Swinesale 110 *supra*).

SIMON STONE

Simoundstane 1301 LS, *Symonstayn* 1307 Ch

'Sigemund's rock' *v.* stan, steinn.

THWAITE

Arkeltwayt 1301 LS   *Thwaite* 1607 NR

'Arkel's clearing.' Cf. Arkleside 253 *supra* and þveit. On the loss of the first element cf. Waites House 135 *supra* and Keld 272 *infra*.

URE HEAD

Yore(s)heued 13 *RichReg* 126 *d*, 128

'Head (i.e. source) of the river Ure' *v.* heafod.

2. LOW ABBOTSIDE 20 B 12

v. High Abbotside 258 *supra*.

FORS (lost)

The original site of the Abbey which was afterwards removed to Jervaulx. Its location on the 6″ OS is 66 NE 7:

Fors(e) 1086 DB *et passim* to 1228 Dugd v. 576

'The waterfall' *v.* fors.

MEER BECK (6″)

Merbek 13 *RichReg* 126 *d*

v. (ge)mære, bekkr. This is one of the bounds of the ancient Forest of Wensleydale.

SKELL GILL

Skalgayl 1301 LS

'Hut ravine' *v.* skali, geil.

STAGS FELL

Staggesffell 13 *RichReg* 126 *d*

3. ASKRIGG 20 C 14

Ascric 1086 DB, *-kric* 1330 Ch, *-cryk* Hy 2 *MaryH* 6 *d*
Askerik, -yk 1198 Fount, 1228 Dugd v. 576
Askerich 1218 FF, 13 *Easby* 277
Askerigg 1285 KI *et passim*

v. askr. The second element is almost certainly hrycg. Cf. *Gaterigg* 161 *supra*, which is a *hrycg*-name, and shows forms in *-ryk* and *-rik* in the 12th and 13th cents. Note also Girrick 144 *supra* and Marrick 294 *infra*. 'Ash-ridge.'

COGILL [kɔgil]

Cottkeld 13 *RichReg* 126 *d*

'Spring near the cottage' *v.* cot, kelda. The name probably became *Cokkeld* and so Cogill on the analogy of names in *gill*.

INGS BECK (6″)

Ingusbec 12 *Easby* 249

In the Wolley Charters (ix. 6) we have the attestator Willelmus fil. *Inguse* in the 13th cent. This is one of a series of difficult names which end in *-us* or *-usa*, including *Edus, Sigus* and *Hacus*. The first two of these are beyond question feminine and the person bearing the first of them is also called *Ēadgifu*. *Ingus* may well be short for ON *Ingiriðr*. Hence 'Ingus' stream.'

NAPPA

> *Nappay, -ey* 1251 Ch, 1279–81 QW *et passim* to 1610 Speed
> *Naphay* 1577 Saxton   *Nappa* 1665 Visit

Probably, 'turnip field' from OE *næp* and (ge)hæg. Cf.
Nappa (PN YWR 136).

NEWBIGGIN

> *Neubigging* 1228 Dugd v. 576 *et passim*
> *v.* niwe, bigging.

WOODHALL

> *Le (La) Wodehall(e)* 13 Easby 278

This is an ancient hall, *v.* wudu, h(e)all.

4. AYSGARTH 21 D 1 [ɛəzgaːθ, eːska]

> *Echescard* 1086 DB
> *Aykescart(h), Ai-, Aykeskarth* 12 Easby 249 *et passim* to
>   1420 YI
> *Ayksc(h)arth* 1317, 1330 Ch
> *Aykesgarth* 1374 *Archd* 9 d, 1388 IpmR
> *Ayskarth(e)* 1400 Pat *et passim* to 1574 FF
> *Asegarth* 1687 Grinton

'Open space marked by oaks' *v.* eik, skarð. Aysgarth was
in the centre of the Forest of Wensleydale and it is noticeable
that a large number of p.n.'s in this wapentake indicate the
wooded nature of the country.

HIGH GILL, LOW GILL

> *le Gill(e)* 1319 *RichReg* 112
> *v.* gil.

5. BAINBRIDGE 20 D 13 [beːnbrig]

> *Bainebrig(g), Beynebrigge* 1219 FF *et passim* to 1285 KI

'Bridge across the river Bain' *v.* brycg.

ADDLEBROUGH

> *Otholburgh* 1153 Dugd v. 573
> *Authelburi, Authelburgh* 1283 Dugd v. 575, 1307 Ch

'Authulf's burh' from the ON pers. n. *Auðulfr*. Roman remains have been found here as at Brough Hill *infra*. On ON *au* becoming *a* cf. Laskill 72 *supra*, Marsett 264 *infra* and Scratby (Nf), *at Scroutebi* BCS 1017.

BARDALE [baːdil]

Beredale 1280, 1285 YI, 1283 *Rich* 33

Possibly 'Bera's valley' *v.* dæl. The OE pers. name *Bera* may be assumed from Barbury (W), *Beranbyrg* (ASC). OE bere seems impossible in this high country.

Professor Ekwall suggests that a probable etymology is ON *bjórr* 'a beaver,' giving an ON *Bjóra-dalr*, or perhaps still better, a stream-name *Bjórá* (derived from *bjórr*).

BLEAN, BLEAN BECK

Blayngbek 1153 Dugd v. 573, 1280 *RichReg* 126 *d*
Blainbec 1218 FF
Bleing, Bleyng 1253 Ch, 1301 LS, 1307 Ch

Professor Ekwall derives Blean (together with Bleng (Cu)), from ON *blæingr*, used of a 'dark stream.'

BROUGH HILL [bruf]

Burg 1218 FF   *murum de Burgh* 1283 Dugd v. 575

v. burh. Roman remains and fortifications have been found here.

COUNTERSETT [kuːntəsit]

Constansate 1280 YI, 1283 *Rich* 33
Cuntellatte (? *Cuntessatte*) 1285 YI

v. setr. The first element is a pers. n., OFr *Constance* from MedLat *Constantius*. *Constantin* is found in the Danelaw in the 12th cent.

CRAGDALE [krægdil]

Cragdal 1218 FF   *Crakedale* 1307 Ch

ME *crag* (from Ir *creag*, Ekwall) 'crag, rock' and dæl. The second spelling shows influence of ME *krake* in such p.n.'s as Crakehall. The valley is rocky and scarred. It is possible however that the forms should be taken the other way round, and that the true meaning is 'Kraki's valley,' with later voicing of *k* to *g* before *d*.

GREEN SCAR MIRE

> *Grenesker* 1153 Dugd v. 573, *-scher* 13 *RichReg* 126 *d*

'Green (grassy) precipice' *v.* grene. The second element is ON *sker* 'scar.'

KELD BOTTOM, KELD SCAR (6")

> *Keldebothem* 1153 Dugd v. 573

v. kelda, botm.

MARSETT [maːsit]

> *Moursette* 1285 YI   *Mouressate* 1283 *Rich* 33

With this name should go *Mouresgate* 1280 YI, unless this is an error for *Mouressate*.

v. sætr. Lindkvist suggests that the first element is ON *maurr* 'an ant,' probably used as a pers. n. For the development of ON *au* to *a*, cf. Addlebrough 262 *supra*.

RAYDALE

> *Radale* 1307 Ch

'Roebuck valley' *v.* ra, dæl.

SEMER WATER [seməwætə]

> *Semerwater* 1153 Dugd v. 573, 1283 *Rich* 33
> *Semar* 13 *RichReg* 126 *d*
> *Semmerwater* 1280 YI *et passim*

The origin of the name of this natural lake is the same as that of Seamer (Pick, LangW) 102, 172 *supra*.

SEMERDALE

> *Semmerdale* 1218 FF

STALLING BUSK [stɔːlin busk]

> *Stalunesbusc* 1218 FF   *Stalunbusk* 1283 *Rich* 33, etc.

v. busk. The first element is probably *stalun*, 'a stallion' (OFr *estalon*).

STONE RAISE

la Staynrayse 1307 Ch

v. steinn, hreysi. There is a cairn here.

WINDGATE (6″)

Weingate 1218 FF *Wyngate* 1607 NR

'Wagon road' from OE *wægen* and gata.

WORTON

Werton 1086 DB, *Wirton(a)* 1152 *Jerv* 20 *et passim* to 1307 Ch

'Vegetable enclosure, garden' *v.* wyrt, tun.

6. BISHOPDALE 21 E 1

Biscop(p)edale 1202 FF, c. 1230–50 BM, 1279–81 QW
Bis(s)hopdale 1289 *RichReg* 124 *et passim* to 1519 Sanct
Bishdale 1589 Cai

'Bishop's valley,' probably from the OE pers. n. *Bisceop*, of which there are two examples from Anglian territory in the 7th cent., and dæl.

HOWGILL

Hol(e)gil 1218 FF, 1338 Pat, *Howgill* 1607 NR

'Hollow ravine' *v.* hol, gil.

KIDSTONES

Kidderstanes 1301 LS *Kidstons* 1613 NR

v. stan. The first element is obscure.

7. WEST BURTON 21 E 2

Burton 1086 DB, *(West)* 1284 *Bodl* 133 *a*

v. burhtun.

WALDEN [wɔːdən]

Walden(e) 1270 YI, 1301 LS, 1536 YChant
Waledene 1321 Dugd vii. 921
Wawden 1574 FF

Probably of the same origin as Walden (Herts), earlier *Wēaladene*, *v.* weala, denu.

8. CARPERBY 21 D 1 [kaːpəbi]

Chirprebi 1086 DB

Kerperby(a) 1137–46 *Easby* 321, 1218 FF *et passim* to 1420 YI

Professor Ekwall suggests that the first element is OIr *Cairpre*, later *Cairbre*, a pers. name meaning 'charioteer.' *v.* by.

BEAR PARK

Bearpark 1540 Dugd iv. 247 *Beryparke* 1544 Dugd iv. 248

v. pearroc. The first element is possibly beorg 'hill' which would explain the two forms.

WEST BOLTON

(*Little*) *Boulton* 1296, 1312 Ch, 1316 Vill

v. boðltun and Castle and Low Bolton 256 *supra*.

ELLER BECK (6″)

Ellerbech 13 *Easby* 278   *Elrebek* 1291 YD

'Alder stream.' *v.* elri, bekkr.

TEWFIT (6″)

Thuue-, Thufwath 13 *Easby* 278

'Thufa's ford' from the ON pers. n. *þúfa* (LindN) and vað.

THACKTHWAITE BECK (6″)

Thacthwet 1203 FF

v. þveit, bekkr. The first element is ON *þakk*, NEDial *thack* 'long coarse grass, rushes.'

THORESBY

Toresbi 1086 DB

Thoresby 1184 *RichReg* 84

'Thor's farm' from ON *þórr* and by.

9. HAWES 20 D 11 [tɔːz]

Hawes 1614 NR
the *Hawes* 1666 Visit

The village is only of recent growth. The meaning of the name is 'neck, pass between the mountains' *v.* hals.

APPERSETT

Appeltresate 1280, 1285 YI, 1283 *Rich* 33
Aperside 1577 Saxton, 1610 Speed; *-set* 1661 Grinton

'Shieling near the appletree' *v.* sætr. The first element is
OE *æppeltrēow.*

BURTERSETT [bɔtəsit]

Beutresate 1280 YI, 1283 *Rich* 33
Birtresatte 1285 YI (YAS xii. 225 n.)
Butterside 1577 Saxton
Burtersett 1608 NR

'Shieling near the alder tree' *v.* sætr and *Burtree* 163 *supra.*

GAYLE, SLEDDALE

Seldalegile 1280 YI
Sleddalgayle, Sledalegayle 1285 YI, 1423 Baildon
Ga(y)le, Sleddall 1606 NR

'Sleddale ravine' *v.* geil. Sleddale is from slæd and dæl as
in Sleddale (LangE) 149 *supra.*

MOSSDALE

Mussedale 1280 YI, 1283 *Rich* 33
Mos(e)dale 1285, 1298 YI *et passim* to 1607 NR

'Bog-valley.' From ON *mosi* and dalr.

SNAIZEHOLME [sneːzəm]

Snaysum 1280, 1285 YI, 1283 *Rich* 33
Snaysome 1423 Baildon

From ON *sneis* 'a twig' (dat. plur. *sneisum*), found in the
Norw p.n. *Sneis* (NG ii. 66); cf. Rysome (YER) and Lealholme
133 *supra* with practically the same meaning.

WIDDALE and WIDDALE BECK

Withdale 1217 FF, *Wyddale* 1307 Ch, (*-bec*) 1218 FF
Wy-, Widal(l) 1404 Pat, 1423 Baildon

'Wood-valley' *v.* viðr, dalr.

10. NEWBIGGIN 21 E 1

Neu-, Newbigging(e) c. 1230–50 BM

v. niwe, bigging.

WHIT BECK (6″)

Wythebec 12 *Easby* 249, 1268 ib. 280

'White stream' *v.* hwit, bekkr.

11. THORALBY 21 E 1

Turo(l)desbi, Toroldesbi 1086 DB

With the same run of forms and interpretation as Thoraldby (LangW) 175 *supra.*

CROOKSBY (6″) [kriuksbi]

Croc(he)sbi 1086 DB, 1189 *RichReg* 84, 13 ib. 77 *d*
Crokesby c. 1280 *RichReg* 77 *d*

'Krok's farm' from ON *Krókr* and by.

HEANING GILL (6″)

the Hyghnyng' 1298 YI

v. haining, gil.

SWINACOTE

Swynewathco... 1298 YI

'Cottage near the swine ford' *v.* swin, vað, cot.

12. THORNTON RUST 20 D 14

Torentun, Toretun 1086 DB
Thorneton Ruske 1153 Dugd v. 573, *Rust* 12 *RichReg* 77 *d*
et passim

v. þorn, tun. The suffixed feudal element can best be explained if we think that the manor was at one time held by an Anglo-Scand owner called *Hrosskell*, a name which appears in the Yorkshire DB as *Roschil* and *Ruschil*. *Rusk* would be a regular shortened form of this, and *Rust* a folk-etymologising perversion of it. There is nothing definitely to connect Thornton with a man of this name, but it is at least a curious coincidence that DB records a *Roschil* among the pre-Conquest owners of land in Richmondshire.

BRINDLEY (6")

Brendele 1218 FF

'Clearing in a wood caused by fire' *v.* **brende** and **leah**.

GREENBER (6")

Greneberghe 1153 Dugd v. 573

v. grene, beorg.

Swaledale

The remaining parishes of this wapentake are in Swaledale.

Sualadala 1128–32 BM

Svaledale 1155 P, *Swaledal(e)* 1159 P, 1200 ChR, 1207 OblR, 1251 Ch etc.

Swaldale c. 1180–5 YCh 1140 *et passim* to 1401 YI

Swawdall 1538 Riev, *-dell* 1574 FF

The local pronunciation is [swɔːdil]. Cf. Swale R. 6 *supra*.

Hauxwell

1. BARDEN 21 B 6

Bernedan 1086 DB

Berdene 1184 *RichReg* 84 *d et passim* to 1285 KI

Barden 1552 FF

'Beorna's valley,' with early loss of *n* from the cons. group
rnd. v. denu.

2. GARRISTON 21 C 6 [gaːrᵊstən]

Gerdeston(e) 1086 DB

Gertheston 1184 *RichReg* 84 *d*, 1301 LS, 1328 Ch, 1406 YI

Gareston, Garristonne 1521, 1582 FF

'Gerth's farm' from ON *Gerðr* and tun.

3. HAUXWELL 21 C 6

Hauoc(he)swelle 1086 DB

Houcheswell 1166 P (p)

Hou-, Haukeswella, -e 1177 P (p), 1184 *RichReg* 84 *d et passim* to 1362 *Archd* 5 *d*

Hauekeswell 1219 FF

'Hawk's well,' but whether from OE *Heafoc* or ON *Haukr*
it is difficult to say. For the use of OE *heafoc* as a pers. name
cf. MLR xiv. 239. *v.* w(i)ella.

Downholme

1. DOWNHOLME 21 A 5 [duːnəm]

   Dune 1086 DB
   Dunum 12 *Marrick* 120, 1184 *RichReg* 84, 1231 *Ass*, 1292 Ch
   Dounoum 1314 Ch   *Downhum* 1535 FF

   '(Amongst) the hills' from OE *æt þǣm dūnum*. *v.* dun. The
   DB form is from the dat. sing.

2. ELLERTON ABBEY 21 A 4

   Elreton 1086 DB, 1228 Pat, 1230 Ebor, 1268 Abbr
   Ellerton(a), *-tun* 1184 *RichReg* 84 *et passim*

   'Alder enclosure' *v.* elri, tun.

3. STAINTON 21 A 4

   Steintun 1086 DB

   'Enclosure made of stone' *v.* steinn, tun.

4. WALBURN 21 B 5 [wɔːbən]

   Walebrun(e), *-burne* 12 *Easby* 95, 1222 FF, 1295 YI, 1301 LS
   Walbro(u)n 1270 YI, 1314 Ch
   Walburn 1285 KI *et passim*

   v. burna 'stream' (influenced by ON brunnr). The first
   element is probably OE W(e)ala (*v.* Walden 265 *supra*).

Grinton

1. GRINTON 21 A 3

   Grinton 1086 DB *et passim*
   Grenton(e) c. 1180–5 YCh 1140, c. 1291 Tax *et passim* to
      1397 *Archd* 18 *d*

   'Green enclosure' *v.* grene, tun. On the modern form *Grin-*
   cf. the forms of Ingleby 167 *supra*.

COGDEN

> *Cockeden* Hy 3 BM   *Cogden* 1661 Grinton

Of the same origin as Cockden (PN La 85), from cocc and denu.

CRACKPOT

> *Crakepot(e)* 1298 YI, 1301 LS, R 2 *RichReg* 89 *d*

'*Pot* where crows abound' *v.* kraka. For the topographical use of *pot v.* Pott Hall 234 *supra*.

RAWCROFT [ro:krɔft]

> *Ruck(c)roft* 1274 YI, 1563 FF   *Rowcroft* 1564 FF
> 'Rough pasture' *v.* ruh, croft.

STUBBING (6″)

> *Stubbynge* 1568 FF

ME *stubbing* 'clearing of land' (*v.* Ekwall, *PN in -ing* 26).

2. MELBECKS 13 J 13

> *Melbecks* 1676 Grinton

'Sand-bank streams' *v.* melr, bekkr and cf. Melbecks (Cu).

FEETHAM [fi:təm]

> *Fytun, -on* 1242 P (p), 1274, 1298 YI
> *Fethom* 1645 Grinton

ON *fit* 'meadow,' dat. plur. *fitjum*, found frequently in Norw p.n.'s, such as *Fetten, Steifet,* etc. (NG *passim*); cf. the lost *Fithum* in Faceby (1333 Riev) and Fitts 127 *supra*. For the long vowel cf. Upleatham 153 *supra*.

GUNNERSIDE [gunəsit]

> *Gunnersete* 1301 LS
> *Gonersete* R 2 *RichReg* 89 *d*
> *Gonnerside* 1655 Grinton

'Gunnar's pasture' *v.* sætr. The first element is ON *Gunnarr*.

KEARTON

> *Kirton* 1298 YI   *Kerton* 1301 LS, 1646 Grinton

The forms are too late for any certainty.

OLD GANG

Old gang 1687 Grinton

OE *gang* is still a dialect word for a road. Old Gang leads up to a disused mine. Cf. Upgang 126 *supra.*

SMARBER (6")

Smerbergh 1298 YI

From ON *smjǫr* 'butter' (*v.* smeoru) as in the common Norw p.n. *Smørbergh* (NG *passim*) and berg.

3. MUKER 20 A 12 [miukə]

Meuhaker 1274 YI
Muaker 1577 Saxton
Mewacre 16 VCH i. 242
Mewker 1606 NR

'Small cultivated field' *v.* akr. The first element is ON *mjór* adj. 'thin, narrow, small' which enters into the Scand p.n.'s *Mjovidale* (Landnamabók) and *Mjøvik* (NG ii. 41).

ANGRAM

Angram 1195–1200 Guis   *Angrom(e)* 1367, 1551 FF, etc.

'(At) the pastures' *v.* anger. and cf. Angram Grange and Cote 191, 249 *supra.*

BIRKDALE

Birkedale 1301 LS

IVELET [aivlət]

Ivelishe (sic) 1298 YI   *Iflythe* 1301 LS

'Ifa's slope' *v.* hliŏ. For the pers. name *v.* Ivinghoe (PN Bk 96).

KELD

Appeltrekelde 1301 LS   *Keld(e)* 1538 Riev, 1577 Saxton

'Spring near the appletree' from OE *æppeltrēow* and kelda.

OXNOP

Oxenhop(e) 1301 LS, 1605 NR   *Oxhoppe* 1538 Riev

'Oxen valley' *v.* hop. The first element is OE *oxa*, gen. plur. *oxena*, as in Oxenhope (YWR).

SATRON

Saterom 1301 LS (p)   *Satteron* 1664 Grinton
'Wood cleared for pasture land' *v.* sætr, rum.

STONESDALE

Sconesdale (sic) 1298 YI   *Stonedale* 1577 Saxton
v. dæl. The first element is obscure.

4. REETH 21 A 2 [ri:θ]

Rie 1086 DB
Reyth in le Swale c. 1170 Marrick 101
Ri-, Ryth(e) 1184 *RichReg* 84 *et passim* to 1575 FF
Reth(e) 1401 YI *et passim* to 1581 FF
Ree 1414 Test, 1515 Sanct
Reeth 17 Grinton (*passim*)

'(At) the stream' from OE *æt þæm rīðe, v.* rið. On the DB
form *Rie* cf. IPN 109 and Ryther (YWR), *Rie* DB, and on the
later change to *Rethe v.* Upleatham 153 *supra.*

BROUGH [bruf]

Borch 1086 DB   *Burgh* 1184 *RichReg* 84 *et passim*
v. burh. Earthworks exist here (VCH i. 302).

FREMINGTON

Fremin(g)-, -yngton 1086 DB *et passim* to 1348 BM
Freminton 1086 DB
Fremmingeton 1251 Ch
Fremigton 1301 LS
Fremynton 1562 FF

'Frema's farm' *v.* ingtun. *Frema* is not recorded in OE, but
it is a possible derivative of the OE pers. n. *Fram* (Redin 13)
which enters into Framingham (Nf), and Framlingham (Sf),
and Framlington (Nb). It is apparently found in the similar
name Fremington (D), DB *Framintona,* c. 1120 AD *Fremigtun,*
Framigton.

HEALAUGH [i:lə]

Hale 1086 DB
Helagh 1200 ChR, (*in Swaldale*) 1281 Ipm *et passim* to
1402 Test

Helag(e) 1219 FF, 1274 YI, *Helach* 1283 *Rich* 26
Helawe 1279–81 QW, 1298 YI, *Healaughe* 1531 FF

'High forest clearing' v. heah, leah. The various forms point to an OAngl form *lǣh*, which may be noticed in the spellings of Helmsley and Wensley 71, 257 *supra*.

XII. GILLING EAST WAPENTAKE

The southern part of Gilling East is in Swaledale, the northern in Teesdale. It formed part of the original wapentake of Gilling, which in DB is simply called (along with Hang) *terra comitis Alani.*

Gillyngschire 1157 *RichReg* 82 d
Gillyng, -yng wap 1157 *RichReg* 82
Gillyngest, -west c. 1300 *RichReg* 97

The wapentake takes its name from Gilling 288 *infra*, its meeting-place. Zachrisson (*Some Yorkshire PN's*, 45) draws an unnecessary conclusion from the form *-schire* in holding with Moorman (*PN YWR*) that *Gillyngschire* was used for the whole North Riding. OE scir was used here, as elsewhere in YNR, for a wapentake or any smaller district such as Mashamshire 230 *supra*.

Kirby Wiske

1. KIRBY WISKE 21 E 13
   Chi(r)chebi, Cherchebi 1086 DB
   Kirkebi, -by 1086 DB, (*Wisc*) 1176–82 YCh 673 *et passim*
   v. kirkja, by. The village is on the Wiske R.

SWALE BRIDGE
   Sualebrig c. 1205 *FountA* 25

2. MAUNBY 21 E 12 [mɔːnbi]
   Mannebi, Mannesbi 1086 DB
   Magnebi, -by 1157 *RichReg* 82 *et passim* to 1301 LS
   Maghen(e)by 1198 Fount, 1328 Banco, 1344 YD
   Maun(e)by 1310 Ch, 1362 AD, 14 *RichReg* 87 d
   'Magni's farm' from ON *Magni* and by.

3. NEWBY WISKE 21 D 13

Neuby 1157 RichReg 82, (*super Wisk*) 1285 KI

v. niwe, by.

SOWBER HILL, SOLBERGE [sɔubəril]

Solberg(h)e 1086 DB *et passim* to 1285 KI
Sollebergh 1422 YD
Sowbar 1578 FF, *Sowber Hill* 1666 Grinton

From ON *solberg* 'sunny hill,' common in Norway in the
form *Solberg* (NG i. 11, ii. 31, 189 *et passim*). *v.* berg.

4. NEWSHAM 21 E 13

Neuhuse 1086 DB; *Neu(e)husum* 1086 DB, 1088 *LVD* 51
Neusum 1231 *Ass et passim*

v. niwe, hus. There was also in this par. a place called
Westhuse 1086 DB.

BRECKENBROUGH

Bracheberc 1086 DB
Brac-, Brakanberg 1208, 1228 FF
Brakenberg(h) 1316 Vill *et passim*

'Bracken hill' *v.* braken, berg. Cf. *Brakanberg* in Brompton
on Swale (12 *Easby* 13 *d*) and Brackenborough (L).

Ainderby Steeple

1. AINDERBY STEEPLE 21 C 12

Eindre-, Andrebi 1086 DB (and as in Ainderby Mires and
Ainderby Quernhow 223, 239 *supra*), (*Fourneux*) 1285 KI,
(*w(i)th, wythe Stepil(l)*) 1316 Vill

v. Ainderby Quernhow 223 *supra*. In 1316 (Vill) John de
Furneis was certified lord of "Aynderby wythe Stepil." The
church tower stands out prominently from the surrounding
country. *v.* Addenda xlv.

2. MORTON UPON SWALE 21 C 11

Mortun(e) 1086 DB, (*on Swale*) 1281 Ch

'Farm on the mor' *v.* tun.

3. THRINTOFT 21 C 11

   T(h)irnetoft(e) 1086 DB *et passim* to 1562 RichWills
   Tirnetoste 1086 DB
   Thirntoft 12 *Mary Y* 261, 1439 IpmR
   Thorntoft 1304 Ch   *Thrumtoft* 1597 Pickhill
   'Thorn-bush messuage' *v.* þyrne, topt. *Thrin-* by a common
local metathesis.

4. WARLABY 21 C 12 [wɔːləbi]

   Warlauesbi, Werlegesbi, Wergeḷesbi 1086 DB
   Warthelbi 1227 FF
   Warlauby 1283 *Rich* 34, 1328 Banco
   Warlow(e)by 1344 Dugd iii. 567, 1396 Pap
   Worleybye 1550 RichWills
   Possibly 'Wǣrlaf's by' from the OE pers. name *Wǣrlaf.*
The spellings in DB and FF are difficult. Something of the
same problem arises in the name Theddlethorpe (L), where
early forms vary between *Thedlac-, Tedlaue-, Tedolf-* and
Dedlonc- in the first element. In any case the pers. name seems
to be English. Compounds of such with *by* are not common.

Danby Wiske

1. DANBY WISKE 21 A 12

   Danebi, -by 1086 DB, (*super Wiske*) late 13 BM
   v. by and Danby (LangE) 131 *supra.*

BROCKHOLME

   Brokholme 1382 YD
   'Field where badgers are found' *v.* brocc, holmr.

LITTLE DANBY

   Parua Daneby 1161–70 *Mary Y* 252

REDHOLME

   Redeham 13 *RichReg* 101 d, *Redham* 13 AD ii, 1285 KI *et*
     passim to 1558 FF
   Redam al. Redholme 1583 FF
   'Homestead amongst the reeds' *v.* hreod, ham. Cf. OE
hreodham (K) BCS 227 and Reedham (Nf).

2. YAFFORTH 21 B 12

Eiford 1086 DB, 13 VCH i. 174
Iaforde, Iaforbe 1086 DB
Jaford(e) 1198 FF, 1280 YI
Jafford 1280 *Ass*, 1316 Vill
Yafford 1283 *Rich* 34 *et passim* to 1530 Visit
Yafforthe 1574 FF

'Ford across the river (Wiske)' *v.* ea, ford. On the development of *ēa-* to *ya-* cf. Yearsley 193 *supra*. The DB form *Iaforbe* is corrupt.

Langton on Swale

1. GREAT LANGTON 21 A 10

Langetun, -ton 1086 DB *et passim*, *(magna)* 1285 KI, *(Mekyl, apon Swaylle)* 1536 YChant

'The long farm' *v.* lang, tun.

LITTLE LANGTON

Langeton (parua) 1292 Ch

Bolton on Swale

1. BOLTON UPON SWALE 21 A 9

Boletone 1086 DB
Bo(h)eltona 1184 *RichReg* 83 *d*, 1280 *Ass*
Bolton c. 1300 *RichReg* 83 *d*, *(oppon Swale)* 1403 YI

v. boðltun.

2. ELLERTON (ON SWALE) 21 A 9

Alreton 1086 DB
Ellerton 1184 *RichReg* 83 *d*, *(upon Swale)* 1314 Ch *et passim*

'Alder enclosure' *v.* alor (elri), tun and cf. Ellerton Abbey 270 *supra*.

LAYLANDS

Leylands 1559 FF
v. læge, land.

3. KIPLIN 21 A 10

Chipeling 1086 DB
Kypplyng 1184 *RichReg* 83 *d*, 1285 KI, c. 1300 *RichReg* 101
Kepling 1205 OblR
Ki-, Kyplyng 13 *Easby* 144, 1269 ib. 146, 1328 Banco
Ki-, Kypeling 1301 LS, 1408 YI
Kyplin 1576 FF

Probably 'the settlement of the Cippelings' from an OE *Cippelingas*, though one would have expected forms in *inges*, but cf. Lilling 32 *supra*. The pers. n. *Cippela* (not adduced in independent use) is probably a diminutive formed by the suffix *-ila* from OE *Cippa*, a pers. n. found in Chippenham, etc. *v.* ing. One should perhaps compare *Cippelinges* 1336 *ForP* 205 *d*, the name of a lost place in Goathland. See further Ekwall, *PN in -ing* 95.

STANHOWE

Staynhou 13 *Easby* 36 *et freq*
Stangehawe 1556 FF

v. steinn, haugr.

4. SCORTON 14 J 9

Scorton(e), -tona 1086 DB, 12 *FountA* 317 *et passim* to 1665 Visit
Schorton 1184 *RichReg* 84

Professor Ekwall suggests that the first element is ON *skor*, 'ravine,' here used as in 'the *fosse Syrithescore*' (*Bridlington Cart.* 137), of a 'ditch,' possibly Scorton Beck.

5. UCKERBY 14 J 9

Ukerby 1198 Fount
Huckerby c. 1250 *Easby* 74
Ukkerby 1285 KI, c. 1300 *RichReg* 86, 1400 YI *et passim*

Professor Ekwall tentatively suggests that the first element of this difficult name is an ON pers. name *Út-kári* formed from ON *út* 'out' and *Kári* in the same way as *Útsteinn* was formed from *út* and *Steinn*. *v.* by.

6. WHITWELL 21 A 10

Witeuuella 1086 DB   *Wittewell* 1201 Cur, 13 *Leon* 67
Whitwell(e) 1285 KI *et passim*

v. hwit, w(i)ella and Whitwell (Bulm) 39 *supra*.

GREENBERRY

Greneberg(e) c. 1190, 1198 Fount *et freq*
Gren(e)berry 1456, 1535 Fount

v. grene, beorg.

Girsby[1]

1. OVER DINSDALE 14 F 12

Digneshale, Dirneshale 1086 DB
Dineshale 1086 DB, 1196 FF
detnisale 1088 *LVD* 51
Dinneshall 1128–35 YCh 944
Dydensale 1170–5 YCh 945
Ditneshal(l) c. 1174–90 YCh 950, 1208–10 Fees
Ditensala 1184 *RichReg* 83 *d*
Diteneshall' 1231 *Ass*
Dytenshale 1301 LS
Dit(t)ensale 1333 Riev, 1435 Test
Dynsda(i)ll 1555 RichWills, 1570 NCyWills

The first element of this name is difficult. The forms given should be supplemented by those for Lower Dinsdale just across the Tees (PN NbDu 63–4) which tend to confirm the genuineness of the *t* and *n* of the early forms. It may be an unrecorded pers. name *Dihten* derived by the addition of an -*n* suffix (*v.* IPN 171) to the stem of OE *dihtan* 'to prepare' and its various derivatives such as *dihtere* 'governor,' *dihtnere* 'steward,' a pers. name which possibly enters into Deightonby (YWR).

Professor Ekwall makes an interesting suggestion that the first element might be an OE *Dīctūn*. There is no phonological difficulty in this, except the very early appearance of -*tun* as -*ten*; one can, however, compare Swinston 303 *infra* for an early

---

[1] Detached part of Allerton wapentake. This and the following parishes are in Teesdale, earlier *T(h)esedale*, 12, 13 Guis, Riev.

example of this reduction of *tun* when followed by another element. What does lend weight to Professor Ekwall's suggestion is that Dinsdale is a detached part of Allerton wapentake separated from the township of Deighton (209 *supra*) only by Great Smeaton township. Dinsdale, therefore, is probably best explained as 'the nook of land belonging to Deighton' *v.* h(e)alh, used here (as in Dinsdale, Du) of a piece of land almost encircled by the Tees R.

2. GIRSBY 14 G 12 [gɔrzbi]

    Grisebi, -by 1086 DB, c. 1130 SD, 1196 FF *et passim*
    Grisibi 1088 *LVD* 50 d
    Grysby 1128–35 YCh 944, etc.

    v. by. The first element ON *Gríss* (cf. Gristhorpe 104 *supra*).

STAINDALE

    Staynedalerig 1303 KF etc.

    v. steinn, dæl, hrycg.

3. HIGH WORSALL 14 F 13

    Wirceshel, Wercesel 1086 DB

    For forms and interpretation *v.* Low Worsall 173 *supra*.

Great Smeaton

1. ERYHOLME 14 G 11 [erium]

    Argun 1086 DB, *Argum* 1179 P
    Erg(h)um 12 Easby 250 *et passim* to 1346 Test
    Eryom 1285 KI *et passim* to 1404 YI
    Eriholme 1665 Visit

    v. Airyholme (Ryed) 49 *supra*.

2. HORNBY 14 H 12

    Horenbodebi 1086 DB
    Hornbotebi 1088 *LVD* 50 d
    Hornebi, -by 1199 ChR *et passim* to 1367 FF
    Hornby 1421 YI *et passim*

'Hornbothi's farm' *v.* by. The first element is probably an ON dithematic pers. n. *Hornbọði* composed of the ON name-themes *Horn(i)* and *boð* (cf. Naumann, *Altnordische Namen-studien* 25). The name is possibly on record in ON, cf. Lind s.n. *Holdboði*. Probably it was shortened to *Horne-* to bring it in line with Hornby (HangE) 240 *supra*.

3. GREAT SMEATON 14 H 12

on smiþatune 966–72 *LVD* 43 *d*
Smidetune, Smideton, Smet(t)on 1086 DB
Smithetuna, -ton 1088 *LVD* 51 *et passim*, (*Magna*) 1231 *Ass*
Smetheton 1157 *RichReg* 82 *d et passim* to 1366 *Archd* 7
Smittun' 1166 P (p)
(*Great*) *Smeton* 1541 Dugd iii. 572, 1665 Visit

v. Little Smeaton (Allert) 211 *supra*.

Cowton

1. EAST COWTON 14 H 11 [kuːtən]

Cudton 1086 DB
C-, Kuton(a) Hy 2 BM *et passim* to 1243 Ebor
Coutona 1184 *RichReg* 83 *d*, (*Est*) 1314 Ch, (*Temple*) 1316 Vill

'Cow farm' *v.* cu, tun, and cf. such names as Swinton, Cawton, Shipton, etc. The Knights *Templars* held land here (VCH i. 160).

COCKLEBERRY

Cokelbergh 1241 FF
v. be(o)rg. The first element is OE *coccel* 'cockle.'

COWTON MOOR

Coutonemore 1145 Fount etc.

2. NORTH COWTON[1] 14 H 10

Coutona 1184 *RichReg* 83 *d*, (*Magna*) 1273 Ebor, (*North*) 13 Fount

v. East Cowton *supra*.

[1] North and South Cowton (282 *infra*) form a detached part of Gilling West wapentake.

3. SOUTH COWTON 14 J 10

  Couton 1158 *RichReg* 82 *d*, (*Suth*) 13 *Easby* 134
  Atloucouton 1158 *RichReg* 82 *d* etc.

  v. East Cowton 281 *supra*. It is frequently called *At(t)elou-couton* from Atley Hill *infra*.

ATLEY HILL

  Atlou 1157 *RichReg* 82 *d*, 1269 Marrick 111
  At(t)elou 1301 LS, 1316 Vill
  Atley 1544 Dugd iv. 248, 1582 FF

  'Atla's hill' from the OE pers. n. *Ætla* (*v.* Redin 147), as in Attleborough (Nf), earlier *Atleburc* 1185 RotDom, and hoh.

WHINHOLME

  Qwhinholm 1198 Fount   *Wyneholme* 1547 FF
  'Meadow overgrown with gorse' *v.* whin, holmr.

Croft

1. CROFT 14 F 10

  Croft 1086 DB, (*super Teyse*) 1252 *Ass*
  Crofst 1086 DB
  v. croft.

CLOW BECK

  Cloubeck 1285 KI *et passim*
  'Stream in the deep valley' *v.* cloh, bekkr.

HALNABY HALL [ɔːnəbi]

  Halnathebi, -by 1170–88 *Leon* 228 (p), 1193–9 *RegAlb* iii.
    41 *d*, 13 *Easby* 35
  Alnatheby 1219, 1231 *Ass*
  Halnathby 1301 LS *et passim*
  Halnaghby 1316 Vill
  Halnaby 1577 FF
  Hawnaby 1577 Saxton

  Col. Parker (YAS 62) has suggested that Halnaby took its name from one *Halnath* who lived there c. 1218. The above spellings antedate this by a considerable period and we must assume either that *Halnath* was long-lived and early gave his name to the place or that he had an ancestor called *Halnath* (of whom nothing is known). *v.* **by**. The name *Halnath* is probably an anglicised form of the continental name *Halanant* found in the Suffolk DB.

JOLBY [dʒoubi]

Jo(h)eleby 1193–9 *RegAlb* iii. 41 *d*, 1219 *Ass*, FF, 13 *Easby* 34*d*
Jol(l)eby 1231 *Ass*, 1301 LS *et passim* to 1403 YI

'Joel's farm' *v.* **by**. From the OFr pers. n. *Johel*, well evidenced in early ME records (e.g. *Jo(h)el* 1226 Lib). Colonel Parker suggests (*u.s.*) that this place is named from a *Joel* who lived here c. 1170. These two names form the only definite evidence in the North Riding of the survival of **by** as a living place-name element after the Norman Conquest.

WALMIRE [wɔːmɑ]

Walemire 12 *Easby* 61 *d*, 13 ib 62 *d*, 1301 LS etc.
Walemur 1205 ChR, OblR
Walmire 1316 Vill *et passim*

v. weala, myrr. The two forms with *mur* possibly indicate that the original final element was OE mor rather than ON myrr which later replaced it. 'Moor of the wealas.'

2. DALTON UPON TEES 14 G 10

Dalton super Tese 1221–6 *RegAlb* iii. 24

v. dæl, tun.

3. STAPLETON 14 F 9

Staple(n)dun 1086 DB
Stapeltun, -ton 1166 P (p), 12 *Easby* 39

'Farm marked with a pole' *v.* stapol, tun and cf. Stapleton (Lei), *stapelton* BCS 409.

BORNESSES (6″)

Burghanes 13 VCH i. 163

The history of this name is that given by Ekwall (*PN La* 85) for Burwains, from OE **burgæns* 'burial place,' in which he shows that it is cognate with OE *byrgan* 'bury' and identical with the common dialectal *borrens, borwens. v.* 325 *infra,* s.v. *burgæsn.

Cleasby

1. CLEASBY 14 E 9 [kliːzbi]

   Clesbi, -by 1086 DB, 1314 Ch
   Clesebi, -by 1184 *RichReg* 83 *d et passim* to c. 1300 *RichReg* 102 *d*
   Cleysby(e) 1545, 1562 RichWills

   Perhaps from ODan *klēss* (ONorw *kleiss*) 'inarticulate in one's speech,' used as a pers. n. *v.* by.

Manfield

1. CLIFFE 14 E 8

   Ileclif c. 1130 SD   *Ylcliue* 13 *Leon* 18 *d*
   Ycliffe HistDunelmScriptores (append. 427)
   Clive 1086 DB   *Clif(f)* 1234 Cl *et passim*

   'Ylla's cliff' from the OE pers. n. *Ylla* (cf. Ilton 233 *supra*) and clif.

2. MANFIELD 14 E 8

   Mannefelt 1086 DB, *-feld* 1202 FF
   Manefeld(e) 1086 DB, 12 *Easby* 5 *d et passim* to 1280 YI
   Manafeld 1146–54 BM, 1294 Ch
   Manfeld 1310 Pap *et passim*

   'Manna's expanse of land' from the OE pers. n. *Man(n)a* and feld.

GRUNTON

   Grendon' 13 *Easby* 40 *d*   *Grounton* 1561 FF
   'Green hill' *v.* grene, dun.

PINKNEY CARR

   Pynchinhou c. 1250 *Easby* 74 *d, Pynkinhou* 13 *Easby* 86 *d*

   This is probably from OE *Pincinghoh(e),* i.e. 'Pinca's spur of land.' There is an isolated hoh to the east of Pinkney Carr. For ing, *v.* ingtun.

Barton

1. BARTON 14 G 8

Barton 1086 DB, 1184 *RichReg* 83 *d et passim*

v. beretun. Cf. Barton le Willows 38 *supra*

BRETTANBY MANOR

Bretanebi, -by 12 *Easby* 5 *d*, 1219 *Ass*, FF, 1260 *Easby* 160 *d*
Brethaneby 1220 *Ass*   *Breteneby* 1228 Ebor
Bretanby 1285 KI *et passim*

v. by. The first element is the OIr pers. n. *Brettan* (*v. Revue Celtique*, xliv. 46), which also perhaps appears in *Bretonenges* (1206 *Easby* 154 *d*), a field-name near Brettanby.

GRASS KILN HEAD SPRING (6")

Cresekeld 1193–9 *RegAlb* iii. 40 *d*
Cressekeldheved 13 VCH i. 150
Creskeld 1271 *Easby* 63

'Well overgrown with cress' *v.* cærse, kelda.

KNEETON HALL [niːtən]

Naton 1086 DB
C-, Kneton 1157 *RichReg* 82, 1193–9 *RegAlb* iii. 40 *d et passim*

v. tun. The first element is OE *cnēow* or ON *kné* 'knee'; the significance of the word in this name is explained by the fact that Kneeton Hall stands close to a point where a main road branches off from Watling Street at an angle of about 45°.

2. NEWTON MORRELL 14 F 9

Neuton(e) 1086 DB, (*Morell*), 1157 *RichReg* 82

v. niwe, tun. *Morell* was the name of a family of landowners here (VCH i. 150).

Middleton Tyas

1. MIDDLETON TYAS 14 H 8

Midelton 1086 DB
Middeltun, -ton 1086 DB, 1177 HCY *et passim*
Mi-, Medilton Tyas 14 *RichReg* 87 *d et passim*

v. middel, tun. *Tyas* is a Norman French name known elsewhere in Yorkshire but no evidence of any connexion of the family with Middleton has been noted.

WOODHOUSE

Wodehuses 1280 *Ass*

2. MOULTON 14 H 8 [mɔutən]

Moltun 1086 DB
Muleton' 1176–1182 P (*passim*), 1219, 1220 *Ass*
Moleton 1241 Ch
Multon 13 *RichReg* 73 *et passim* to 1441 BM
Mowton 1577 Saxton, 1613 NR

'Mula's farm' from the OE pers. n. *Mūla*, found in OE *Mulantun* (KCD 759), a weak form of OE *Mūl* (*v.* Redin 21). Cf. Mowthorpe 35 *supra*.

XIII. GILLING WEST WAPENTAKE

v. Gilling East Wapentake 274 *supra*.

Easby

1. ASKE HALL 14 H 7

Has(s)e 1086 DB, *Ask(e)* 1157 *RichReg* 82

'Ash-tree.' The DB form may represent OE æsc rather than ON askr.

2. BROMPTON ON SWALE 21 A 8

Brunton 1086 DB, 1231 FF
Brumton(a) 1160 *Easby* 2 d, 12 ib. 149
Brumpton (*on Swale*) 1184 *RichReg* 83 d *et passim*

v. Brompton (Pick) 96 *supra*.

BROMPTON BECK (6″) and BROMPTON BRIDGE

Brumtone becke 1238 *Easby* 231 d, *Brumton brigge* 13 ib.
229

3. EASBY 14 J 7

Asebi, -by 1086 DB, 1276 *RegAlb* ii. 18 *d*
Esebi, -by 1151 *Easby* 2 *et passim* to 1400 Pap
Esseby 1231 FF
Easby 1557 RichWills

'Esi's farm' *v.* by. The first element is the ODan pers. n. *Esi*, which is equivalent to OWScand *Ási*. Cf. *Easby* (Birdf) 185 *supra* and *Eslundes* (c. 1240 *Easby* 9 *d*) 'Esi's woods,' the name of a lost place in this township.

WATH COTE [waθkoːt]

Warth 1137–46 *Easby* 231   *Warthe Cote* 1301 LS

'Cottage near the heap of stones' *v.* varða. The *varða* probably refers to the earthwork called Scots Dyke by which the cot stands.

4. RICHMOND (a borough) 14 J 6, 7

The site of Richmond was called *Hindrelac* in DB and *Hindeslak* in 1184 *RichReg* 84 (a digest of DB). The elements of this name are not clear from the scanty material.

After the Conquest Earl Alan considered the fine strategic importance of the place and built himself a castle which he called *Richemund(e)* (1108–14 YCh 25, c. 1130 SD, c. 1155 BM *et passim*, *Richemunt* 1176 *et passim* P, etc.) on the top of a lofty precipice overlooking the Swale R. The name was probably transferred from some well-known site in France where there are many examples of the name. Here it means 'strong hill,' and for this meaning of OFr *riche v.* Godefroy s.v.[1]

---

[1] Minor and street names of Richmond are: Ankriche (lost), *Ankirkirk* (1479 Sanct), *The Ankriche* (1610 Speed), from OE *ancra* 'anchorite' and cyrice; Leland says that it was the chapel of a woman-anchorite, cf. Ankerchurch (Db). Bargate Street, *Beregate* (1275 *RichReg* 124 *d*), *Bargate* (1536 YChant, 1610 Speed) used of a road along which barley was led, *v.* bere, gata and cf. PN BedsHu 52. Frenchgate, *French Gate* (1536 YChant), from ME *Frenshe* and gata. Gallowgate, Gallowfields: reference to the gallows (*v.* gealga) is found in *Galowbrawghe* (1523 VCH i. 21) 'the brow where the gallows stand,' *Gallowe Felde* (1536 YChant), *Gallowgait close* (1586 YD). Newbiggin Street, *Newbiggen* (1610 Speed) *v.* bigging and cf. *Aldbyggyng Strete* (1536 YChant) also in Richmond.

WHITCLIFFE MILLS

 Hwittecliff 1275 *RichReg* 124 *d*

 There is a white limestone scar here, *v.* hwit, clif.

5. SKEEBY 14 J 7 [skiːbi]

 Schirebi 1086 DB
 Schittebi 1187 P
 Sc-, Skytheby 12 *RichReg* 83 *d et passim* to 1301 LS
 Sch-, Skiteby 1205 OblR, 1231 *Ass*
 Sketeby 1396 Pap
 Sketheby 1421 YI
 Skebye 1565, 1574 FF

'Skithi's farm' from the ON pers. n. *Skiði* and by. On the
modern form cf. Upleatham 153 *supra.*

Gilling

1. GILLING 14 H 7

 Ghelling(*h*)*es, Gellinges* 1086 DB
 Gellynghes 12 *RichReg* 73
 Gwyllingues[1] 1137–46 *Easby* 321
 Gillinge, -ynge 1202 FF, 1220 Ebor, 1396 Pap
 Gi-, Gylling 13 Easby 32, 1237 Cl *et passim*
 Gillinges 1241 Ch

The author of an article in VCH (i. 72) pointed out that
Bede's *Ingetlingum* (HE iii. 14) was usually identified with this
Gilling, but "that the scene of Oswiu's death and the site of
the expiatory monastery raised by Eanfled has now been shown
to be Collingham, 6 miles from Barwick in Elmet, WR. Yorkshire." On topographical grounds there is nothing against this
view, for Bede simply says that Oswiu took refuge at *Uuilfaraesdun* which was about 10 miles west of *uico Cataractone*
(i.e. Catterick) and from *Uuilfaraesdun* he fled to *Ingetlingum*
where he was killed. *Uuilfaraesdun* was probably a hill in
Marrick, but Bede himself gives us no information as to the
position of *Ingetlingum.*

---

[1] *Ex inf.* Professor F. M. Stenton. The author regrets that, through an
error, this form was given to Professor Zachrisson as *Givelingues* and suggested to him a line of interpretation which the correct form does not support.

The spellings of this name are of the same type as those of Gilling in Ryedale 53 *supra*, and probably the name is of the same origin. The spelling *Gwyll-* is an AN spelling for ME *Gyll-*.

GATHERLEY MOOR

> *Gaiterlac* 13 Easby 143
> *Gatirlemore* 1512 Sanct
> *Gayterley* 1536 YChant

The first element may be OE *gāte-treow*, 'gaiter-tree, wild dogwood,' with partial Scandinavianising by substitution of ON *geit* for OE *gāt*. The second is leah. Cf. Gatherick (PN NbDu 93).

HARTFORTH

> *Herfort, -ford* 1086 DB
> *Hertford(e)* 1157 *RichReg* 82 *d et passim* to 1328 Banco
> *Hereford* 1206 OblR, 1208 Ass (p), 1316 Vill
> *Hert-, Hartforth* 1539 Dugd v. 578, 1577 Saxton

'Hart ford' *v.* heorut, ford. Cf. Hertford (Herts), OE *Heorutford* (BCS 30) and Harford (Gl), OE *Heortford* (BCS 165), DB *Hurford*.

HIGH SCALES, LOW SCALES

> *Scales* 1137–47 *Easby* 321

'The shielings' *v.* skali.

SEDBURY PARK

> *Sadberge* 1157 *RichReg* 82 *d*, 13 *Easby* 32 *d*
> *Satberg* 1257 Ch
> *Saddeberge* 1285 YI
> *Sadbery* 1301 LS, 1328 Banco, 1406 YI
> *Sedbury* 1519 FF

Sedbury should be compared with Sedbergh (YWR) which is from ON setberg 'seat-hill.' Sedbury like Sadberge (PN NbDu) is probably a parallel formation, with Norw *sate* 'a small flat piece of ground on a hill' or even sætr 'shieling,' as in Sedbusk 260 *supra*.

Kirby Ravensworth

Kirkeby Raveneswath(e) 1280 YI

This is the name of the parish in which Kirby Hill and Ravensworth (292 *infra*) are situated.

1. DALTON 14 G 5 [dɔːtən]

There were at first two Daltons (*Daltun, altera Daltun* DB, *Daltona et alia Daltona* 1184 *RichReg* 84), but later we find three mentioned and distinguished as *Dalton Trauers* (1258 *Easby* 92), *Dalton Michel(l)* (1259 Ass), *Dalton Norreys, -eis* (1285 KI), *le norys* (1572 FF). Later references to Dalton are

Dalton in le Dale 1420 NCyWills, *in le Gayles* 1559 FF
Dawtons 1577 Saxton

'Valley farm' *v.* dæl, tun. The affixes arise from the names of tenants of land in the locality: John *Norris* was a tenant in 1285 (KI 167); Dalton *Michel* (also called Dalton *Ryel* in the 14th cent. VCH i. 90) was called *Ryel* from the tenants of the lords of Ryle (Nb) who possessed land here in 1231; the first of these tenants was called *Michel* (ib.); the *Travers* family held land here as early as 1186 (ib.).

Dalton is called *in le Gayles* from its position in a narrow glen (*v.* Gayles *infra*).

2. GAYLES 14 G 5

Austgail 1258 *Easby* 93
Gales 1534 FF, 1577 Saxton, 1665 Visit
Gailes 1576 FF, 1606 NR

'The ravines' *v.* geil. The first form refers to the eastern one of several ravines in the township (*v.* austr).

3. KIRBY HILL 14 G 5

Kirkebi, -by 1154–66 *Marrick* 221, (*super moram*) 1379 Archd 13 d
Kirkby on the Hill 1534 FF

'Church farm' *v.* kirkja, by.

PRIEST GILL

Prestegile, -gill 13 Marrick 222, 1324 ib. 223

4. NEW FOREST, a moor (6")

in noua foresta 1201 ChR   *The new forest* 1577 Saxton

EASEGILL COTE (6")

Esgilecote 13 *Easby* 28 d

v. gil, cot. The first element may be a pers. n. (OE *Ēsa*, ODan *Esi* = OWScand *Ási*). Cf. *Easby* 185 *supra*.

HELWITH

Helwath(e) 1280 YI, 1283 *Rich* 32   *Helwith* 1577 Saxton

v. Helwath Beck 117 *supra*.

HALLGATE (6") and HOLGATE

Hallegate 1280 YI   *Holgate* 1283 *Rich* 32

'Road to the hall' and 'in the hollow' *v.* h(e)all, hol, gata.

KEXWITH

Kexthwayt 1280 YI, 1283 *Rich* 32, *Kextwayte* 1301 LS

The first element is the ME plant name *kex* (PromptParv), Dial *kex, kecks,* used in YNR of the teazle. 'Enclosure overgrown with teazles' *v.* þveit.

WAITGATE

Thwaiteȝate 13 *RichReg* 127 d

v. þveit, geat.

5. NEWSHAM 14 F 5

Neuhuson 1086 DB, *Neusom(e), (in Broghton Lith)* 1336 YD

v. Newsham (Ryed) 45 *supra*.

BROUGHTON LYTHE (lost)

Broctun(e) 1086 DB

Broghtonlyth(e) 1184 *RichReg* 84, 1289 Abbr

'Slope by the farm on the stream' *v.* broc, tun and hlið.

HAWSTEAD (6″)

Halsteds, -stedmyre 1336 YD   *Hallested* 1406 Marrick 224

'The hall site' *v.* h(e)all, stede.

LANGLANDS (6″)

Langelandes 13 Easby 29 d

SMALLWAYS BRIDGE

Smalwathes 1336 YD

'The narrow fords' *v.* smæl, vað. Cf. Wass 195 *supra*.

6. RAVENSWORTH 14 G 6

Ravenesu(u)et 1086 DB
Rafneswad 1154–66 Marrick 221
Ravenswat 12 Marrick 221, 1283 *Rich* 28
Raven(e)swath 1184 *RichReg* 84 *et passim* to 1427 NCyWills
Raveneswad(e) 1201 ChR, 1257 Marrick 222, 1308 Ch

'Hrafn's ford' *v.* vað.

PARK WALL (6″)

The wall of the dike of the old park of Ravensworth still remains and is referred to as *le Parkedyke* in 1406 Marrick 224, *v.* pearroc, dic.

7. WHASHTON 14 H 6 [waʃtən]

Whasingatun 1154–66 Marrick 221
Whassingetun 1154–69 Marrick 224
Wassingtun, -ton 1208 FF, 1257 Marrick 222, 1316 Vill
Wassinton' 1219 Ass
Quassyng-, -ington 1285 KI, 1301 LS
Qwhassyngton c. 1300 *RichReg* 86
Qwaston 1492 Sanct
Whaseton 1562 RichWills
Whassheton 1574 FF

Professor Zachrisson (*PN in* *vis, *vask 49) explains this name as a geonymic meaning 'the homestead of the marsh-dwellers' from OE *wāse* 'mud, marsh.' On the phonetic difficulties of this explanation *v.* PN Wo 176 s.n. Washbourne. On topographical grounds it is impossible; Whashton is on a steep hillside, the gradient of roads leading up to the village being in some cases steeper than 1 in 7.

More probably the first element is a pers. name. OE names in *Hwæt-* are early and well recorded—there are four in LVD alone. An OE *Hwætsige* would almost inevitably give rise to a pet form *Hwassa* and this p.n. is probably to be interpreted as '*tun* of the people of Hwassa' *v.* ing, tun. On the development of *-s-* to *-sh-* cf. Dishforth 184 *supra*.

Marske

1. MARSKE 14 J 4 [mask]

   Mersche 1086 DB

   With the same run of forms and interpretation as Marske 154 *supra*.

APPLEGARTH

Apalgard 1154–63 Riev, *Ap(p)elgarth(e)* 1154–63 Riev, 1205 OblR *et passim*

'Field with an appletree' *v.* æppel, garðr. Cf. OSwed. *apaldagardher* (Hellquist, *ON på -by* 5).

CLINTS

Clynte 1543 FF

'The rocky cliff' *v.* klettr (klint).

FELDOM

Feldon(e) 12 VCH i. 102, 1228 Dugd v. 576, 1231 *Ass*
Feldun, Fildon 1228 FF
Feldom c. 1300 *RichReg* 100 *d*, 1301 LS, 1539 Dugd v. 578

'(At) the expanses of unenclosed land' from the OE *æt ðæm feldum, v.* feld.

SKELTON

Sc-, Skelton' 12 *Easby* 94 *d*, 1260 ib. 161 *et passim*

v. Skelton (Bulmer) 16 *supra*. The meaning here is possibly 'farm on the shelving terrain of land.'

Marrick

1. MARRICK 21 A 4

Marige 1086 DB, 1252 Riev
Marrich c. 1150 Godr
Marrig(g) 1157 *RichReg* 82 *d et passim* to 1400 Test
Maryg' 1283 *Rich* 34
Marrik(e), *-yk* 1301 LS, 1328 Banco, 1393, 1483 Test

'Horse ridge' from ON *márr* 'horse, steed' which enters into
a number of Norw p.n.'s such as *Mardal, Marvik* (Rygh, *NG
Indledning* 67) and hryggr (*v.* hrycg).

AISKEW (6")

Aichescou 1154–66 Marrick 221

With the same run of forms and meaning as Aiskew 236 *supra*.

COPPERTHWAITE

Cowpertwaht 1566 RichWills

'The cooper's field' from ME *coupare* and þveit.

ELLERS

Hygh Ellers 1567 FF

'The alders' *v.* elri.

HURST

Hirst 1539 FF

v. hyrst.

OWLANDS [ɔuləndz]

Ulvelundes 13 Marrick 103
Ullunde 13 Marrick 104   *Ullands* 1540 Dugd iv. 247

v. lundr. The first element is probably the gen. pl. of ON
ulfr 'wolf.' Cf. Sutherland 79 *supra*.

RAY GILL (6")

Reylgaile c. 1170 Marrick 101

v. geil. The first element is obscure.

Arkengarthdale

1. ARKENGARTHDALE 14 H–J 1

Arkillesgarth, -gardh 1199 VCH, 1201 ChR
Arkil, Arkelgarth 13 RichReg 121 *et freq*
Arclegarthdaile 1557 RichWills
Archengarthdale 1671 Grinton

'The valley of Arkil's enclosure' *v.* dæl, garðr. On the
change of *l* to *n* cf. Hinderskelfe and Arkleside 40, 253 *supra*.

ARKLE BECK and ARKLE TOWN

Arkelbek 1226 FF   *Arkilton* 1476 VCH i. 37

These two names are probably back-formations from the
parish name *supra*. *v.* bekkr, tun.

BOOZE [buːz]

Bowehous 1473 VCH i. 37   *Bouze* 1662 Grinton

'House by the bow or curve' possibly referring to the curving
hill between Slei Gill and Arkle Beck. Cf. such names as
Bow Hill. From OE *boga* 'bow' and hus.

ESKELETH

Exherlede 1280 YI   *Eskerlythe* 1342 VCH

The forms of the name are too late to make any certain
suggestion as to the first element. The second is clearly hlið.

FAGGERGILL

Fagardegile 1280 YI, 1283 *Rich* 32
Faggardglle 1285 YI
Fawgargill 1473 VCH i. 37

v. gil 'ravine.' Professor Ekwall suggests tentatively that the
first element is ON *fár-garðr* 'sheep enclosure,' with early and
easily explicable loss of the first -*r*-.

KITLEY HILL

Kydalehowe 1285 YI

'Hill near the cow valley' from ON *kýr* and dalr, haugr.

LANGTHWAITE

>*Langethwait* 1167 P *et passim* to 1341 IpmR
>
>*v.* lang, þveit.

STORTHWAITE HALL

>*Stirkthwayt* 1281 YI, 1283 *Rich* 32
>*Sterthwaytte, Stirthwait* 1284, 1341 IpmR
>*Storthwate* 1575 FF
>
>'Bullock field' from ME *stirk* (OE *styric*) and þveit.

WHAW

>*Kiwawe* 1280 YI, 1283 *Rich* 32
>*le Kuawe* 1285 YI
>*Quagh* 1342 VCH
>
>'Enclosure near the fold' from ON *kví* 'pen, fold (where sheep are milked)' and hagi. Cf. ON *kvíagarðr* 'a pen.' For *wh-* *v.* Whenby 30 *supra*.

WILLIAM GILL

>*Williamgill* 13 *RichReg* 127 *d*

Stanwick

1. ALDBROUGH 14 F 7 [ɔːdbrə]

>*Aldeburne* 1086 DB
>*Aldeburg(h-e)* 12 *Easby* 33 *d*, 90 *et passim* to 1556 FF
>*(H)audeburg* 1231 *Ass*, 1281 Ch
>*Awldeburgh* 1558 RichWills, *Awdbrough* 1606 NR

'The old fortification' *v.* (e)ald, burh. Aldbrough is by Watling Street and there are in the parish a large number of ancient entrenchments, the most important of which is Scots Dyke, a long earthwork stretching north for several miles. The *burh* probably refers to one of these.

2. STANWICK PARK 14 F 7

>*Stenwege, -weghes, Steinueges, Steinwege* 1086 DB
>*Staynwegga* Hy 2 *Leon* 4, 1206 *Easby* 154 *d*, 1221 ib. 290 *d*
>*Stanweg'* 1219 *Ass*
>·*Stein-, Stainwegges* 1228 FF, 1232 Ebor, 1301 LS

Steinweg 1226 Ebor
Stayneweges 1279 Ebor
Stain-, Staynwigges 1285 KI, 1302 *Ebor* 201, 1348 Pat
Staynwyks 1421 YI
Estanwik 1460 BM
Stanwyx 1542 RichWills
Stanwick 1665 Visit

'Stone walls' *v.* steinn. The second element is ON *veggr* 'a wall.' Its significance in ODan *veg* is extended to 'boulder' and ONorw *veggr*, used in p.n.'s mostly with the plural form, also meant 'a mountainous wall' and so 'an abrupt steep cliff.' The reference in this place-name, however, seems to be to some ancient rock entrenchments found in the township (cf. Aldbrough 296 *supra*). Cf. Stanwix (Cu), with a similar run of forms, which lies by the Roman wall.

CARLTON GREEN

Cartun(e) 1086 DB
K-, Carleton 1157 *RichReg* 82 *d et passim* to 1396 Pap
v. karlatun.

Melsonby

1. MELSONBY 14 G 7

Malsenebi 1086 DB
Melsanebi 1154–69 Marrick 227, 1208 FF, 13 *Easby* 43 *d*, 1310 Ch
Malsambi 1182 P
Melsambi, -by 1189–98 YD *et passim* to 1400 YI
Melsanby 1198 Fount, 1268 Abbr, 1280 *Ass*
Melsenbi 12 *FountC* 317, 13 *Easby* 54 *d*
Melsamebi 1202 FF
Melsonbye 1540 RichWills

The first element is probably a shortened form of the OIr pers. n. *Maelsuithan*, gen. *Maelsuithain*, which appears in OE as *Mælsuþan*, the name of a moneyer to Eadgar and Eadward II (Searle) and as *Mæglsoþen, -sowen* in BCS 951. The name as it is in the p.n. was probably introduced by Norwegians from Ireland. ON *Mylsan* (LindBN) may be a short form of the same name. Cf. *Revue Celtique*, XLIV. 49.

DIDDERSTON GRANGE, DIDDERSLEY HILL

> *Di(r)dreston* 1086 DB
> *Didereston* 12 Easby 59 *d*, 1170 P (p)
> *Didreston* 1184 *RichReg* 84, 1285 KI
> *Dideristone* 1228 Dugd v. 576
> *Dyderston, Didirston* 1352 FF, 1400 YI

'Dyder's farm' *v.* tun. The origin of the first element is difficult to decide upon. It may be a mutated derivative of the widely-spread theme *Dud-* extended by an *-r* suffix (cf. Pickering 85 *supra*, and the history of Kettering (Ekwall, *PN in -ing* 89)).

HANG BANK

> *Hangandebank* 13 VCH i. 150

'Hanging or steep bank' *v.* banke. The first element is the northern present participle form. It is used elsewhere to denote 'steep, overhanging ground' as in Hanging Heaton (YWR), Hanging Chadder (La).

Forcett

1. BARFORTH HALL 14 D 6 [baːfəθ]

> *Bereford(e)* c. 1130 SD *et passim* to (*super Teise*) 1314 Ch
> *Berford* 1184 *RichReg* 83 *d et passim* to 1396 Pap
> *Bereforth* 1420 NCyWills
> *Barforth* 1502 Sanct, 1579 FF

'Ford which would carry a load of corn' *v.* bere, ford, and for a full discussion of this name *v.* PN BedsHu 50 ff. (s.n. Barford).

2. EPPLEBY 14 E 7

> *Aplebi* 1086 DB
> *Appelbi, -by* 1157 *RichReg* 82 *et passim* to 1285 KI
> *Appilbi, -by* c. 1204 Marrick 224, 1440 Test
> *Eppilby* 1421 YI

'Farm with an appletree' *v.* æppel, by. Cf. Swed *Apelby* (Hellquist, *ON på -by* 5).

3. FORCETT 14 F 7

Forset(a) 1086 DB, (*in Richemundshyr*) c. 1150 Godr, 1176 P
et passim to 1367 *ForP* 413 *d*
Forsed 1086 DB
Forseth(e) 1280 YI, 1301 LS
Forsett(e) 1285 KI *et passim* to 1519 FF

'Shieling by the waterfall' *v.* fors, sætr.

CARKIN

Kerkan 1157 *RichReg* 82, 13 *Easby* 140, c. 1300 *RichReg* 98 *d*
Kercham 1280 YI
Kirkam 1344 Dugd iii. 567
Kirkan 1396 Pap
Carken 1540 Dugd iv. 247
Carkyn 1556 FF

No solution of this name can be offered.

SANDWATH

Sand(e)wath(e) 1292 YI, 1528 FF

'Sandy ford' *v.* sand, vað.

4. OVINGTON 14 E 5 [ɔuvintən]

Ulfeton 1086 DB
Olueton 1184 *RichReg* 83 *d*
Ulvington 1251 YI, 1301 LS, 1343 FF
Ouinton, Ovington 1577 Saxton, 1665 Visit

'Wulfa's farm' *v.* ingtun. The loss of initial *w* is here
probably due to the influence of the ON pers. n. *Úlfr*. On
forms without *-ing* cf. Lockton 91 *supra*.

Stanwick[1]

1. CALDWELL 14 E 6 [kɔ:dwel]

Caldewell 1086 DB
Caudwell 1564 FF

'Cold spring' *v.* cald, w(i)ella. Cf. *frigidum fontem* 1186–1205
YCh 1821. Leland says that Caldwell "is so caullid from a
lattle font or spring, by the ruines of the old place, and so
rennith into a beke halfe a quarter of a mile off."

[1] A detached part of Stanwick parish 296 *supra*.

2. EAST LAYTON 14 F 6 [leːtən]

Latton 1086 DB, *Estlatton* 1256 Pat   *Laghton* 1346 Test
(*Est*) *Laton* 1184 *RichReg* 83 *d et passim* to 1530 NCyWills
Est Leiton 1256 Pat   *Estlayton* 1492 Sanct

This is probably from OE leactun, which develops in
later English, sometimes to *Laughton*, at others to *Leighton*.
This name was clearly developing into *Laughton*, but ultimately
Leighton forms prevailed.

Hutton Magna

1. HUTTON MAGNA 14 F 5

Hotton 1086 DB
(*Magna*) *Hoton* 1157 *RichReg* 82, (*Longuillers*) 1157 *RichReg*
   82 *d*, (*in Richemundsire*) 1252 Ipm

v. hoh, tun. The land was held by Johannes de *Lungeviler*
in 1224–30 (Fees 1460).

2. WEST LAYTON 14 F 6

Lastun, Laston 1086 DB   *Latton'* 1200 Cur

Other forms are as for East Layton *supra*.

Wycliffe

1. WYCLIFFE 14 E 5 [wiklif]

Witclive 1086 DB
Wigeclif c. 1130 SD
Wittecliff 1275 *RichReg* 124 *d*
Wycliff 1285 KI *et passim*

'White cliff (or bank overlooking the Tees R.)' *v.* hwit, clif.

GIRLINGTON HALL [gɔrlintən]

Gerlin(g)ton 1086 DB, 1184 *RichReg* 83 *d*
Girling-, Girlyngton 1251 YI, c. 1300 *RichReg* 98 *d*, 1301 LS

The modern pronunciation points to a medieval form *Girling-*;
the name probably, therefore, means 'Gyrla's farm' *v.* ingtun.
The pers. n. *Gyrla* is not found at all in OE, but besides

entering into this name it is probably the first element of Girlington (YWR) and cognate with OSwed p.n. *Gyrlinge* which Hellquist (*ON pd -inge* 42) connects with the somewhat doubtful *Gurilf* inferred by Förstemann (*PN* 713) from *Gurilfesheim* (8th cent.).

LITTLE HUTTON

> *Parva Hoton'* 1136–46 *Easby* 321
>
> *v.* Hutton Magna 300 *supra.*

THORPE HALL

> *Torp* 1086 DB   *Thorp(e)* 1184 *RichReg* 83 *d*
> *Thrope near Tease* 1574 FF
>
> *v.* þorp. Probably an outlier of Wycliffe.

Rokeby

1. EGGLESTONE ABBEY 14 E 3

> *Eghistun, -ton* 1086 DB
> *Egleston* 1157 *RichReg* 82, 1204 Ass, 1275 *RichReg* 124 *d*,
>   1285 KI, 1400 Test
> *Egliston* c. 1200 *BylE* 31, 1398 Pap, 1408 Fount, 1421 YI
> *Eggleston* 1226 FF, 1234 Cl
>
> *v.* tun. The first element is probably an OE pers. name *Ecgel*, found in *Ecgeles stiele* (Hist. Abingd. i. 420).

2. ROKEBY 14 E 3

> *Rochebi* 1086 DB
> *Rokeby* 1184 *RichReg* 84 *et passim*
>
> 'Hroca's farm' *v.* by. For this pers. name *v.* MLR xiv. 241. ON *Hrókr* with loss of gen. *-s* is also possible.

MORTHAM [mɔːtəm]

> *Mortham* 1086 DB, c. 1185 *RichReg* 83 *d et passim*
> *Morthaim* c. 1150 Godr
> *Mortam* 1536 YChant
>
> 'Morta's homestead' *v.* ham and heim. The OE pers. name *Morta* is found in OE *Mortancumb* (BCS 479), and in Morthoe

and Murtwell (D). Interchange between *ham* and *heim*, common in L, is very rare in the North Riding. Cf. Coverham and Levisham 254, 92 *supra*.

Brignall

1. BRIGNALL 14 F 3 [brignəl]

Bringenhale, Bringhale 1086 DB
Brigenhal(e) 12 *Leon* 17 *d*, 1184 *RichReg* 83 *d*, 1241 Cl, 1264–5 Ch, 1283 *Rich* 28, 1289 Ebor, 1292 Ch
Bry-, Briggenhal(e) 1227 FF, 1301 LS, 1335 BM, Ch
Bringenhale 1280 Ipm
Brigenale 1281 Ebor, 1285 KI
Briginhale 1300 Ebor
Brygnell 1544 RichWills

The forms of the first element of this name are difficult. The DB and Ipm forms may indicate a ground-form *Bring-hale* which underwent an unparalleled metathesis to *Briggen-hale*. Stiltons 73 *supra*, similarly, underwent an otherwise unknown metathesis.

If this is the case we may have here an OE *Bryninga-* (cf. Burniston 107 *supra*) reduced to *Bringe-* (cf. Finghall 247 *supra*); hence 'nook of land belonging to the Brynings' *v.* h(e)alh. Or we may have, as Professor Ekwall suggests, a Scand name composed of the elements ON *bringa* 'breast' used topographically with the sense 'slope' (as in the cognate OSwed *bringher*, Icel *bringr* 'a small hill') as in such Norw names as *Bringa, Bringedal* (NG xi. 38), and ON *hali* 'a tail' (cf. *NG Indledning* s.v.). In either case the first element underwent the curious metathesis, which may to a certain extent have been due to analogical transformation with Northern Engl. *brigg* 'bridge.'

Barningham

1. BARNINGHAM 14 F 4

Berningha(m), Bernyngham 1086 DB *et passim* to 1406 YI
Bernigeham 1214 FF
Barnyngham 1491 Test

'The settlement of the people of *Beorna*' *v.* ing, ham. Cf. Barningham (Sf), *Bernincham* DB.

HAYTHWAITE

> *Haithwait* 1172–80 *Dods* vii. 149
>
> 'Hay field' from heg (or ON *høy, hey*) 'hay' and þveit.

2. HOPE 14 G 2

> *Hope* 13 *RichReg* 121 *et passim*
> *Hoppe* 1285 KI
> *Est, West Hop* 15 VCH i. 41.
>
> *v.* hop. The meaning here is 'small secluded valley.'

3. SCARGILL 14 F 3 [ska:gil]

> *Seachregil* (sic), *Scracreghil* (sic) 1086 DB
> *Schachelgilla* 1146–61 *Mary Y* 39 d
> *Scakregill'* 1172 P (p)
> *Sca(c)kergill'* 1173, 1177 P (p), 1294 Ch
> *Scargell, Skargill* 1282 YI, 13 *RichReg* 121
>
> 'Skakari's ravine' from the ON by-name *Skakari* (Lind)
> and gil.

RUTHERFORD

> *Rotherforde* 1332 VCH i. 39   *Rudderforth* 1608 NR
>
> 'Ford where the oxen pass' *v.* hryðer, ford. The form with
> *-u-* is to be explained in the same way as Ruswarp 125 *supra*.

SELEY HEAD (6″)

> *Selyhede* 13 *RichReg* 127 d
>
> 'Willow head' from ON *selja* (as in Selley Bridge 90 *supra*)
> and heafod.

SWINSTON

> *Swintenhowe* 1285 KI   *Swynton Howe* 1301 LS
>
> 'Mound near the pig farm' *v.* swin, tun, haugr.

Startforth

1. BOLDRON 14 E 2 [bɔurəm, bɔudrən]

> *Bolrum* 1175–88 *Leon* 22 d, 13 ib. 23
> *Bolerum Scletes* 1204 FF, (*sletes*) 1258 *Easby* 93
> *Bulrun* 1280 YI, 1283 *Rich* 32

Bolron 1285 KI, 1302 *Leon* 22, 1577 Saxton
Boldron 1285 YI
Boleron 1301 LS (p)
Bolerom 1316 Vill
Bolrun 1349 FF
Boldram 1564 FF

'Forest-clearing where steers were kept' from ON *boli* 'steer' and rum. This name is identical with Bowerham (PN La 174–5). Here, as in that name, there is variation between forms with final *n* and *m*. Professor Ekwall (*loc. cit.*) suggests for the La p.n. that the suffix is ON *runnr* 'brake, thicket' and that the final *m* is due to assimilation to the initial labial or to association with names in -*ham* and -*rum*.

2. STARTFORTH 14 D 3 [staːtfəθ]

Stradford 1086 DB
Stredford(e) c. 1130 SD, 1280 YI, 1283 *Rich* 32; *Estred-* 1392 Test
Stretford c. 1130 SD, 1259 Ass, 1301 Ebor, 1316 Vill
Straford 1175–85 *Leon* 22 d *et passim* to 1302 *Leon* 22 d
Stratford(e) 13 *Leon* 23, 1233 Cl, 1399 *Archd* 19 d, 1563 FF
Stretteford 1301 LS
Starforde 1563 FF

'Ford where Watling Street crosses the river Tees' *v.* stræt, ford. On the earlier forms with *Strad-*, *Stred-* *v.* Förster, *Keltisches Wortgut* 118.

Bowes

1. BOWES 14 E 1 [bɔuz]

Castelli de Bogis 1172 P
Boghas 1175–85 *Leon* 22 d
Boues 12 VCH i. 42, 1228 Pat, 1237 Cl, 1267 Ch
Boghes 12 VCH i. 42 *et passim* to 1333 YD, *Bohes* 1295 Ch
Bouys 1241 Ch
Bogues 1267 Ch
Bowes 1283 *Rich* 32 *et passim*
Boughes 1327 Banco, 1347 FF, 1367 *ForP* 413 d

This name is from OE *boga* or ON *bogr* 'bow,' and its meaning is 'the river-bends.' Cf. the Norw p.n.'s *Bogen*, *Boger* (NG i. 81,

ii. 41 etc.). When *Bowes* is used as a surname in medieval deeds it is often translated as *D'arc* or *de arcubus* (Lat *arcus* 'a bow, anything arched or curved').

KILMOND

Kinemund 1175–85 *Leon* 22 *d*

Professor Ekwall suggests that this name should be compared with the well-established Scottish hill-names *Kinmont, Kinmonth* (cf. Watson, *Celtic PNs of Scotland*, 400 ff.). Watson translates it 'head of the hill' from Gael *cenn* 'head' and *monadh* 'hill'—an interesting case of Gaelic influence.

MIRK FELL (6″)

Mirkfell 13 *RichReg* 127 *d*

'Dark mountain' from ON *myrkr* and fell.

RERE or REY CROSS

Rerecros 1301 *Leon* 22

v. cros. The stone cross is still standing. For the explanation of this name, *v.* Addenda xlvi.

SLEIGHTHOLME [sliːtəm]

Slethholm 1254 Pat

With forms and interpretation as for Sleightholme (Ryed) 62 *supra*.

SPITAL

hospital' de Staynmore 1283 *Rich* 32
the Spyttel 1540 Dugd iv. 247

v. Spital Bridge 123 *supra*.

STAINMORE (partly in We)

Steinmor c. 1230 Roger of Wendover
Steyne-, Staynemore 13 *RichReg* 127 *d*, 1352 Pat, 1540 Dugd iv. 247
Steynmor, Stainmore 1279–81 QW, 1487, 1506 Sanct

'Rocky moor' *v.* steinn, mor.

STONY KELD

Staynhoukeld(e) 1257 Ch

'Spring by the rocky mound' *v.* steinn, haugr, kelda.

2. GILMONBY 14 E 1

> *Gil(le)maneby* 1146–61 *Mary Y* 36 *d*
> *Gilmanby* 1301 LS, 1541 Dugd iii. 572, 1577 Saxton

'Gilman's farm' *v.* by. *Gilman* is a pers. n. from ON *gilmaðr* 'a libertine' and it is found independently in English as *Gillemon* c. 1217 YD and *Gylleman* 1249 *Easby* 174.

Romaldkirk

1. COTHERSTONE 14 C 2

> *Codrestune, Codreston* 1086 DB
> *Cothereston*   1184 *RichReg* 84,   1279–81 QW,   1281 Abbr,
>   1354 FF
> *Cud(e)reston* 1201 ChR, 1226 FF
> *Cotherston* c. 1250 YD *et passim*

'*Cūðhere's* farm'[1] *v.* tun.

BALDERSDALE

> *Baldersdale* c. 1250 YD, 1479 Sanct, 1578 FF
> *Bauderdale* 1577 Saxton

'B(e)aldhere's valley' *v.* dæl. *Balder* is from OE *B(e)aldhere*. Cf. Balder R. 2 *supra*.

BLACKTON

> *Blakedene* 1301 LS

'Black valley' *v.* blæc, denu.

BRISCOE [briskə]

> *Byrscogh* c. 1250 YD, *-scoyg* 1301 LS
> *Birscou* 1251 Ch, 1577 Saxton
> *Bursco(gh)* 1400 YI, 1545 FF

'Birch wood' *v.* birki, skogr.

---

[1] This place has been identified with the *Cuthbertestun* mentioned in the *Historia de Sancto Cuthberto* but the order of the names as given in that document suggests that *Cuthbertestun* was nearer the Wear than the Tees. Further, *Cuthbertestun* was part of the patrimony of St Cuthbert, whilst Cotherstone was part of the fee of Richmond. One must, therefore, abandon the old identification.

LOUPS [lɔups]

> *Loupesoulis* c. 1250 YD

The name is possibly composed of the elements ON *hlaup* 'flood' and ON *súla* 'hollow or scar' (*v.* NG Indledning 28).

MERE BECK (6″)

> *Merbec* c. 1250 YD

'Boundary stream' *v.* (ge)mære, bekkr.

NABY

> *Naby* 1562 FF, 1612 BM   *Nateby* 1612 BM

v. by. The forms are late but the name is probably identical with Nateby (PN La 164).

WEST PARK

> *Westparke de Cothereston* 1292 Abbr

2. HOLWICK 13 A 12

> *Holewic, -wyk* 1251 Ch, 1279–81 QW   *Holwick* 1577 Saxton

'Ravine in the hollow' *v.* hol, vik.

CROSSTHWAITE

> *Crosthwait(e)* 1201 ChR

'Field near the cross' *v.* cros, þveit.

LONTON [luntən]

> *Lontun(e), -ton(e)* 1086 DB *et passim* to 1301 LS
> *Lunton(e)* 1184 *RichReg* 83 *d*, 1577 Saxton

'Farm near the Lune' *v.* Lune 4 *supra* and tun. The difference in pronunciation between the river-name and the p.n. is due to vowel shortening of OE *lōn-* in the p.n., whereas in the river-name it developed spontaneously to [iu]. On the etymology of Lune *v.* RNY 11.

3. HUNDERTHWAITE 14 C 1

> *Hundredestoit(h)* 1086 DB
> *Hundresthuait* 1184 *RichReg* 83 *d*, 1302 Pat
> *Hunderthuait, -thwayt* 1208 Ass (p), 1316 Vill, 1352 FF

Hundrethwaite 1285 KI, c. 1300 *RichReg* 97
Hundredthwaite 1316 IpmR
Hondirthwayt 1400 YI

Lindkvist suggests that the first element is OE *hundred* (ON *hundrað*) 'a hundred, a land division,' but if this is correct we have here the only reference to a 'hundred' in YNR.

We are told, however, that in 1070 an infinite multitude of Scots under Malcolm assailed Teesdale and laid it waste, slaying several English nobles at a place 'called in English *Hundredeskelde*, in Latin *centum fontes*' (SD). *Hundredeskelde* may be identical with Hunder Beck (now in Cotherstone parish); at any rate the first element is identical with that of Hunderthwaite and despite the Latin *centum fontes* it is probably a pers. n. ON *Hun(d)rað* or *Hunrøðr* or less probably OE *Hūnrēd*. An intrusive unetymological *-d-* is evidenced also in OIcel *Hundólfr* by the side of *Húnólfr* (*Orig. Island.* i. 219, 271). *v.* þveit.

4. LARTINGTON 14 D 2

Lertinton 1086 DB
Lyrting-, -yngton c. 1130 SD, 1184 *RichReg* 84 *et passim* to 1327 Banco
Lertinctona 1154–69 Marrick 231
Lirthinton' 1252 Pat
Lirtington 1283 *Rich* 28, 1289 Ebor (p), 1301 Ch, LS
Lertington 1403 Test

'Lyrta's farm' *v.* ingtun. There is no recorded pers. n. *Lyrta* or *Lyrti* in OE, but, as Professor Ekwall suggests, we may have a mutated form of the pers. n. found in *Lortan hlæw* (BCS 705) and *Lortinges bourne* (ib. 279 A). Cf. also *Lortelegh* in Cottingham (1281 Ipm).

5. LUNE DALE 13 C 13 [liundil]

v. Lune R. 4 *supra*.

BOWBANK

Bowbanck(e) 1561, 1571 FF

The first element (OE *boga*, ON *bogr*) is here used with the sense 'bent, steep' (cf. Bowes 304 *supra*); *v.* banke.

SKYER BECK·

Skyrbeck Hy 2 *MaryH* 6 *d*

'Bright clear stream' *v.* skirr, bekkr.

THRINGARTH

Thyrnegarth 1251 Ch, 1301 LS, *Thryngarth* 1561 FF

'Thyrni's enclosure' *v.* garðr. The first element is the ON pers. n. *þyrni* or simply þyrne, hence 'thorntree enclosure.'

WEMMERGILL

Wymundergil 1265 Ebor

'Wymund's ravine' from the ON pers. n. *Vigmundr*, gen. *Vigmundar* (suggested by Lindkvist on the evidence of the OSwed runic name *VikmuntR*) and gil.

6. MICKLETON 13 B 14

Micleton 1086 DB

'Large farm' *v.* micel, tun.

7. ROMALDKIRK 14 C 1

Rumoldesc(h)erce 1086 DB
Rumbald(e)kirke 1184 *RichReg* 83 *d*, 1285 KI, 1343 FF
Rombalekirk 1479 Sanct
Romerkirk, -kyrke 1576 FF, 1606 NR

Other forms are Latinised, 'ecclesia St Rum(b)aldi,' as in 1244 *Ass*.

'Church dedicated to St Rumold' *v.* kirkja. For the early veneration of *Rumwald* cf. the reference to his resting-place at Buckingham in the 11th cent. document commonly known as *Saints*. Whytford's *Martiloge* (ed. Procter and Dewick, London, 1893) under Nov. 3rd, p. 173, states: "In englond also the feest of Saynt Rumwold the kynges sone of northumberlond that forthw't whan he was borne cryed w't lowd voyce sayeng thre tymes togyder these wordes, 'I am a chrystyan,' and than required the Sacrament of baptym and after to haue masse and was communed and than he made a noble sermon w't meruaylous good eloquence and lyued thre dayes and so departid and lyeth in buckyngham ful of myracles."

THE ELEMENTS, APART FROM PERSONAL NAMES, FOUND IN NORTH RIDING PLACE-NAMES

This list confines itself for the most part to elements used in the second part of place-names or in uncompounded place-names. Under each element the examples are arranged in three categories, (*a*) those in which the first element is a significant word and not a pers. name, (*b*) those in which the first element is a pers. name, (*c*) those in which the character of the first element is uncertain. Where no statement is made it may be assumed that the examples belong to type (*a*). Elements which are not dealt with in the *Chief Elements used in English Place-Names* are distinguished by an (n) after them.

a *Aymot*, Ayresome, Ayton (4). ac Acomb.
æcer, ON akr (a) Crumbacre, Muker, (b) Stainsacre.
æppeltun Appleton (5).
*anger Angram (3).
askr Aske, Askrigg. austr East Coatham, Gayles.
balca OE (n) Balk. banke Bowbank, Gale Bank, Hang Bank (2).
bekkr (a) Backstone Beck, Beck House, Blean and Bloody Beck, Boosbeck, Brocka Beck, Clitherbeck, Clow and Cod Beck, *Colebeck*, Ellerbeck (4), Hell Gill, Hol (2), How, Howl (2) and Isle Beck, Keasbeck, Keld, Lythe and Meer Beck, Melbecks, Mere, Mill and Moss Beck, Raisbeck, Sandbeck (2), Skate, Skyer, Whit, (b) Arkle, Ings, William and Yarna Beck.
be(o)rg Barugh, Bear Park, Caldbergh, Cockleberry, Greenber, Greenberry, Riseborough, Smarber, Thornbrough (2), Welbury.
beretun Barton (3). berewic Barwick.
berg (a) Aikbar, Ashberry Hill, Borrowby (2), Breckenbrough, Sedbury, Sowber Hill, (b) Hatterboard, Rook Barugh, Roseberry, Rose Hill.
bigging (a) Newbeggin, Newbegin, Newbiggin (3), (b) Biggin Houses.
blar Blaten Car, Blawath, Blea Wyke, Blow Gill, Bluewath.
boga (n) Booze, Bowbank, Bowes. boð Beedale.
*boðl Beadlam. *boðltun Bolton (4).
botm, botn Bottoms Farm, Botton Cross, Hawsker Bottoms, Keld Bottom.
breiðr Braithwaite (2), Brawith, Braworth, Braygate.
brekka *Breck*, Hang Bank. brinke Brink Hill.
broc Brotton, Broughton (4), Cop Keld Brook, *Twislebrook*.

brocc-hol Brocka Beck, Brock Hill.

broti ON (n) Broates, Broats.   **bru** (n) Stoup Brow.

brunnr Bruntcliffe, Ellerburn.   *v.* burna.

brycg (a) Bainbridge, Bridge Holme, Briggswath, Brompton Bridge, Dibble Bridge, Fell Briggs, Howe Bridge, Kirkbridge, Selley Bridge, Spital Bridge, Staddle Bridge, Swale Bridge, Thornton Bridge, (b) Foulbridge.

burh (a) Aldbrough, Aldburgh, Birdgate, Boroughgate, Brough (3), Burrill, Newbrough, Newburgh, Stonybrough, (b) Addlebrough, Benningbrough, Dowber, Goldsborough, Guisborough, Middlesborough, Scarborough, (c) Cornbrough.

burhtun (a) Burton (4), (b) Humburton.

burna (a) Colburn, Ellerburn, Hayburn, Iburndale, Leyburn, Saltburn, Sandburn, Walburn, Welburn (2), (b) Corburn, Kilburn.

buskr Sedbusk, Stalling Busk.

by (a) Birkby, Borrowby (2), Dalby (2), Danby (4), Eppleby, Fearby, Huby, Ingleby (3), Irby Manor, Kir(k)by (10), Lazenby (2), Melmerby (Halik), Mickleby, *Monkby*, Newby (4), Norby, Normanby (4), *Prestby*, Southerby, Sowerby (4), Swainby, Westonby, Whenby, Yearby, (b) Ainderby (3), Aislaby (2), Amotherby, Asenby, Bagby, *Baldby*, Baldersby, Barnaby, Barnby (2), Battersby, Baxby, Bellerby, Blansby, Boltby, *Bordelby*, Boulby, Brandsby, Brawby, Brettanby, Busby Great and Little, Carperby, Cleasby, Coulby, Cowesby, Crooksby, Crosby (?), Crosby House, Dromonby, Easby (3), Ellerby, Exelby, Faceby, Farmanby, Firby, *Fridebi*, Gatenby, Gilmonby, Girsby, Grimsby, Halnaby, Harmby, Hawnby, Haxby, Helperby, Holtby (2), Hornby (2), Jolby, Killerby (2), Cold Kirby, Lackenby, Leckby, Maltby, Marderby, Maunby, Melmerby (Hang W), Melsonby, Milby, Moxby, Naby, Ormesby, Osgodby, Osgoodby, Rokeby, Romanby, Roxby (3), Rudby, Scalby, Sinderby, Skeeby, Skewsby, Slingsby, Stainsby, Stakesby, Stearsby, Swainby, Thimbleby, Thirkleby, Thirlby, Thoralby, Thoraldby, Thoresby, Thormanby, Thornaby, Throxenby, Tollesby, Uckerby, Ugglebarnby, Warlaby, Whitby, Wragby.

camb Cold Cam, Camedale (?), Cams Head, Cams House.

clif (a) Arncliffe, Arnecliff, Bruntcliffe, Cleveland, Cotcliffe, Crosscliff, Crunkly, Hamley, Mencliffe, Rawcliffe (3), Stone Cliff, Topcliffe, Whitcliffe, Whitestone Cliffe, Wycliffe, (b) Cliffe, Kemplah, Musley, Raincliffe.

cloh Cloughton, Clow Beck.   **cnoll** Knowle.

copp Cop Keld.   **corn** Cornbrough (?).

cot(e) (a) Cargo Fleet, Coatham, Cod Beck, Cogill, Cotcliffe,

Cotterdale, Crosby Court, Easegill Cote, Fencote, Halligill Cote, Stonehouse Cote, Swinacote, Wath Cote, (b) Muscoates, (c) Tocketts.

*cramb (n) Buttercrambe, Crambe.

croft (a) Croft, Rawcroft, West Croft, (b) Ellis Croft.

cros (a) Botton Cross, Crosby (?), Crosscliff, Crossdale, Cross Sike, Crossthwaite, Lilla Cross, Rere Cross, (b) Lowcross, Percy, Ralph, Steeple, Swarthoe and William's Cross.

cumb Combe, Cooms, Darncombe, Horcum.

dæl, dalr (a) Camedale (?), Colsterdale, Dale, Dales, Dalton (3), Deepdale, Deep Dale, Dibdale, Drakedale, Esk Dale, Farndale, Flaxdale, Fylingdales, Givendale, Glaisdale, *Grindale*, Grinkle, Handale, Hard Dale, Haredale, Harwood Dale, Hawdale, High Dales, Iburndale, Langdale (3), Little Dale, Lune Dale, Moordale, Mossdale, Nawtondale, Nettledale, Newton Dale, Oxendale, Ramsdale, Raydale, Ryedale, Semerdale, Sleddale (2), Swaledale, Teesdale, Thornton Dale, Tripsdale, Wardle, Welldale, Wensleydale, Westerdale, Wheeldale, Whisperdales, Woodale (2), Wood Dale, (b) Baldersdale, Bardale, Bishopdale, Bungdale, Cundall, Dunsdale, Ladhill, Smiddales, Yedmandale, (c) Stonesdale.

dalr (a) Arkengarthdale, Baysdale, Beedale, Birkdale, Cotterdale, Cragdale, Crossdale, Dalby (2), Fossdale, Gowerdale, Helredale, Kildale, Kirkdale, Kitley, Oak Dale, Scugdale (2), Staindale (3), Widdale, Wydale, (b) Apedale, Aysdale, Bag Dale, Bilsdale, Bransdale, Commondale, Fangdale, Grimesdale, Gundale, Lonsdale, Raisdale, Risedale, Rosedale, Troutsdale.

deill Anserdale, Mickledales, Moredale, Mordales, Wandales (3).

denu (a) Blackton, Cogden, Holdenfield, Scackleton, Walden, (b) Arden, Barden.

dic Cowldyke, Deighton, *Dic wap.*, Dishforth, Friar's Ditch, Green Dyke, Park Wall, Thieves Dikes.

dun Downholme, Grunton, Hambleton (3), Warthermarske, Wildon.

*dympla (n) Dumple Street. ea, eu (b) Lastingham.

eg (a) Breaday, (b) Harlsey, Helmsley Gate and Upper, Sessay.

eik Aikbar, Aiskew (2), Aysgarth, Haggit Hill, Oak Dale.

ekla ON (n) Swinacle. elfitu (n) Eldmire, Ellermire.

elri Aldercarr, Ellerbeck (4), Ellerburn, Ellerlands, Ellers, Ellerton (2).

ende Sandsend. eng Preston Ing.

eowestre Nosterfield.

erg (a) Airy Hill, Airy Holme, Airyholme, Arrathorne, Eryholme, (b) Coldman Hargos, (c) Oran.

eski Ashberry Hill.

fall (b) Yorfalls. **feax** (n) (c) Bellyfax.

feld (a) Broadfields, Feldom, Northfield, Nosterfield, Suffield, Thorpefield, Woodhill Field, (b) Manfield, (c) Tanfield.

fell Mirk Fell, Stags Fell. **fit** ON (n) Feetham, The Fitts.

flasshe Waterflash.

flat (a) Cock Flat, Flat Howe, Gildert Flat, (b) Cat Flats.

flor ON (n) Flowergate.

ford (a) Ampleforth, Barforth, Bowforth, Brafferton, Dishforth, Hackforth, Leeming Wath, Hartforth, Rutherford, Startforth, Yafforth, (b) Birdforth, Marriforth.

fors, foss Forcett, *Fors*, Fossdale.

fyrhþ(e) The Firth Wood. **gang** (n) Old Gang, Upgang.

garðr (a) Applegarth, Conygarth, Faggergill, Garfit, Thringarth, (b) Arkengarthdale, Hawsker.

gata (a) Bargate, Belmangate, Birdgate, Boroughgate, Braygate, Cartergate, Church Street, Flowergate, Frenchgate, Greengate (2), Haggsgate, Hallgate, Gate Helmsley, *Holegate*, Holl Gate, How Gate, Kirkgate, *Ladgate*, Postgate, Saltergate, Sandgate, Stonegate, Windgate, (b) Gunnergate.

gear Yarm. **geat** Waitgate, Yatts.

geil Gale Bank, Gayle, Gayles, Skell Gill.

gil (a) Blow Gill, Faggergill, Fowgill, Gill, Hell, How, Priest, Thieves and West Gill, (b) Easegill, Scargill, Spruce Gill, Wemmergill, William Gill, (c) Ray Gill.

gnipa Gnipe Howe. **graf(a)** (a) Howgrave, (b) Stonegrave.

grip ME (n) (b) Hill Grips.

gryfja (a) Corngrave, Griff, Hazelgrove, (b) Falsgrave, Mulgrave, Skinningrove.

hæcc Hackforth, Heck Dale. **hæfen** Avens House.

(ge)hæg (a) How la Hay, Nappa, Scalby Hay, (b) Broxa.

haga, hagi Layrus, Studdah, Whaw.

haining Heaning Gill.

halig Halikeld, Halligill, Hallikeld (2).

hals Hawes.

ham (a) Coverham, Fleetham, Middleham, Newham, Newholm, Redholme, (b) Levisham, Masham, Mortham. *v.* **ingaham.**

*hamel Hambleton (3), Hamley.

hangra Hang Bank, Hutton Hang.

*har (n) Hard Dale, Haredale, Harland, Harome, Hartoft, Harwood Dale.

haugr (a) *Blackamore*, The Black Howes, Blakey, Carling Howe, Coldy, Fingay, Flat Howe, Greenhow, How la Hay, Howe

(Halik), Kitley, Ling Hill, Moor Howe, Quernhow, Rowe Howe, Scarf Hill, Stanghow, Stanhowe, Stonybrough, Stony Keld, Swinston, Urra, Wapley, Wintylow, Woof Howe, (b) Bullamoor, Cana Barn, Glaphowe, Kilgram, Leaf Howe, Lilla Howe, Loose Howe, *Maneshou*, Miley, *Scograinhowes*, Scrathowes, Sexhowe, Shunner Howe, Sil Howe, Silpho, Simon Howe, Sunley Hill, Tidkinhow, Tod Howe, Ulshaw, William Howes.

heafod Breaday Heights, Cams Head, Dry Heads, Middle Head, Moorside, Murk, Rye, Seley and Ure Head.

h(e)alh (a) Dinsdale, (b) Bedale, Bossall, Brignall (?), Crakehall, Crakehill, Finghall, Pickhill, Strensall, *Streoneshalch*, Worsall.

h(e)all (a) Hallgate, Hawstead, Woodhall, Woodhill, (b) Bownhill.

heim Coverham, Levisham, Mortham. **heope** Shipton.

hella ON (n) Hell Gill, Helredale, Helwath, Helwith.

here Harton (?). **hlaða** Newlass, Whitby Laithes.

hlidgeat Lidyyate Way.

hliþ, hlið (a) Bainley, *Holdlythe*, Kirkleatham, Litherskew, Lythe (2), Pickering Lythe, Upleatham, (b) Ivelet, (c) Eskeleth.

hofuð Haggit, Middle Head.

hogg Abbot Hag, Hagg (2), Haggsgate.

hoh (a) Brackenhoe, Hawthorn Hill, Howe (Ryed), Howe Bridge, Huby, Huthwaite, Hutton (17), Potto, (b) Atley, Binsoe, Hancow, Pinkney.

holegn Hollins.

holmr Bridge Holme, Brockholme, Gallow Green, Holme (3), Holmes Bridge, Keldholme, Millholme, Sandholmes, Sleightholme (3), Trenholme, Waterholmes, Whinholme.

hop (a) Hope, Oxnop, (b) Fryup, (c) Fleensop.

hreyrr ON (n) Rere Cross.

hreysi Stone Raise.

hris Foulrice, Galtres, Rice Lane, Riseborough, Ruswarp, Ruswick.

hrost (n) Ruston. **hrung** (n) Rounton.

hrycg, hryggr Askrigg, Cliff Ridge, *Gaterigg*, Girrick, Lease Rigg, Marrick, Rigg, Shawm Rigg, Wardle Rigg.

hryding (a) Ruddings (Pick), (b) Kateridden, Ruddings (Birdf).

hus Ayresome, Beck House, Booze, Cams House, Hunt House, Husthwaite, Moorsholme, Newsham (3), Stonehouse Cote, Waits House, Woodhouse. **hweol** Welldale, Wheeldale.

hwyrfell, hvirfill The Whorl Hill, Whorlton.

hyll (a) Burrill, Hawthorne Hill, Hunger Hill, Potter Hill, Scarf Hill, Siddle, Warthill, Waytail Gate, Wrelton, (b) Hawkshill, *Hillbraith*.

hylr Healam Beck, Dibble (?).
hyrst Hurst.
ing (b) Benningbrough, Easingwold, Ellingstring, Huntington, Pinkney.
inga Finghall, Steeple Cross, Stonegrave, Westonby, Whashton.
ingaham Barningham, Hovingham, Lastingham.
ingas Fylingdales, Gilling (2), Kiplin, Lilling East and West, Pickering.
ingtun (a) Sinnington, (b) Easington, Ellington, Farlington, Fawdington, Fremington, Girlington, Hemlington, Kilvington, Kirklington, Lartington, Lockton, Nunnington, Otterington, Ovington, Rainton, Stillington, Terrington, (c) Snainton.
iw Iburndale. karlatun Carlton (7).
kelda *Caldkeld*, Cogill, Cold and Cop Keld, Grass Kiln Head Spring, Halikeld, Halligill Cote, Hallikeld (2), Keld (3), Keldholme, Kelmer, Potterkeld, Stony Keld.
kiarr (a) Alder Carr, Crumbcarr, Elliker, Rainton Carr, Redcar, Ruswarp Carr, Salt Scar, Trencar, Whitecarr, (b) Bonny Carr, Ousey Carr.
kirkja (a) Church Street, Cock Flat, Crosslets, Kir(k)by (10), Kirkbridge, Kirkdale, Kirkgate, Kirkleatham, Kirkless, Kirk Leavington, (b) Felixkirk, Oswaldkirk, Romaldkirk.
klint Clints. konungr Coneysthorpe, Conygarth, Rice Lane.
kraka Crackpot, Crakethorn. kringla Cringle Carr.
læla (n) Lealholm. læs Lease Rigg.
(ge)læte Esklets.
lagr Laskill, Lowdales.
land (a) Clevelands, Harland, Landmoth, Langlands, Laund, Laylands, Longlands, (b) Byland, Goathland.
launde Lawn of Postgate, Danby Lawns. leactun Layton, Leighton.
leah (a) Barley, Bradley, Brindley, Elliker, Everley, Flock Leys, Gatela, Gatherley, Healaugh, Healey, Hindleythwaite, Hipperley, Kirkless, Thirley Cotes, (b) Bickley, Dunsley, Helmsley, Hildenley, Osmotherley, Pockley, Wensley, Yearsley, (c) Stokesley.
leirr Larpool, Layrus. leysingi Lazenby (2).
lœkr Leake. lopt ON (n) Loftmarishes, Loskay.
lopthus Loftus.
lundr (a) Blakey Topping, Ellerlands, Lund (3), Lund Forest, Lunds, Lunds Beck, Owlands, Stockland, Upsland, (b) Autherlands, Sutherland.
(ge)mære Meer Beck, Mere Beck.
marr ON (n) Kelmer, Marishes, Marton (4).
melr Melbecks, Mencliffe.

mere Bulmer, Eldmire, *Lexmere*, Redmire, Seamer (2), Semer Water.

mersc (a) Little Marish, Loftmarishes, Marske (2), Warthermarske, (b) *Edymarsh, Kekmarish*, Marishes.

micel, mikill Mickleby, Mickledales, Mickleton.

mor (a) *Blackamore*, Bullamoor, Cold Moor, Cowton Moor, Stainmore, (b) Fadmoor, Gillamoor, Pilmoor.

mos (a) *Cranberry Moss*, Moss Beck, Mossdale, (b) May Moss.

(ge)mot *Aymot*, Landmoth.

mund, OFr (n) Belmangate, Belmont, Grosmont, The Mount, Mount Grace, Richmond.

mynni *Niddermyn*.

myrr (a) Ainderby Mires, Ellermire, Gormire, Rudmoor, Sourmire, Walmire, (b) *Miregrim*.

(ge)myðe Myton-on-Swale.

næss, nes (a) Ness (3), (b) Hackness.

nos (n) Hackness. **okull ON (n)** Acklam.

omstr ON (n) Anserdale.

pæð Roppa. **pol** (a) Wapley, (b) Waterpool.

*pot ME (n) Crackpot, Pott (2), Potto, Sandpot.

poyla ON (n) Larpool. **pytt** Sandpits.

ra ON Raithwaite. Rey Cross. **rand** Rand.

rauðr Rawcliffe (3), Roppa.

raw Hardrow, Row. **riþ** Reeth.

rod (b) Biller Howe. **rum** Boldron, Satron.

sæ (n) Seamer (2), Seaton, Semerwater.

sænget (n) Saintoft.

sætr (a) Appersett, Burtersett, Forcett, Satron, Sedbury (?), Sedbusk, Swineside, (b) Arkleside, Countersett, Gunnerside, Marsett.

salr ON (n) (a) Upsall (2), Upsland, (b) Sawcock.

sceort (n) Short Waite. **scipen** Skiplam.

scir Allertonshire, Birdforth, Bulmer, Gilling and Hang waps., Mashamshire, Richmondshire.

scylf OE, skjalf ON (n) (a) Raskelf, (b) Hinderskelfe, Skutterskelfe.

selja Seley Head, Selley Bridge. **setberg** Sedbury (?).

sic, sik Cross Sike, Midsyke, Prissick, Thack Sike.

side Abbotside, Esk Dale Side.

skali (a) Laskill, Scales, Skell Gill, (b) Gammersgill.

*skaling ME (n) Scale Foot, Scaling.

skarð Aysgarth, Scarf Hill, Ayton Scarth, Scarth Wood.

skeið Hesketh.

sker ON (n) (a) Dove, Green, and Killing Nab Scar, Preston under Scar, (b) Ravenscar.

skirr Skyer Beck.

skogr (a) Aiskew (2), Briscoe (2), Busco, Cotescue, Litherskew, Loskay, (b) Skelderskew.

skor (n) Scorton. skrið ON (n) Scrath.

sletta (a) Crosslets, Sleightholme (3), Sleights, (b) Old Sleight.

smeoru, smjǫr Smarber. snape ME (n) Snape.

sneis ON (n) Snaizeholme. spring Derwent Head.

stæþ Staithes.

stan (a) Graystone, Greystone (2), Whitestone, (b) Simon Stone, (c) Kidstones.

stede Hawstead, Newstead (3), Northstead, Oldstead.

steinn Staindale (3), Stainmore, Stainton (3), Stanhowe, Stanwick, Stone Cliff, Stonegate, Stonegrave (?), Stonehouse, Stone Raise, Stonybrough, Stony Keld, Whitestones.

sticol Stittenham. stiepel Ainderby Steeple.

stig Hunters Sty. stigu Swinesale.

stirc Storthwaite. stocking Stocking (3).

stǫng Stanghowe.

stræt Barton-le-Street, Startforth, Thornton-le-Street, Watling Street.

strand Whitby Strand. strengr ON (n) (b) Ellingstring.

tang Tang. þing Fingay. þing-vǫllr Thingwall.

þorn (a) Arrathorne, Cawthorne, Crakethorn, Crathorne, Langthorn (2), (c) Spennithorne.

þorp (a) Coneysthorpe, Ellenthorpe, Fyling Thorpe, Howthorpe, Kilton Thorpe, Nunthorpe, Sneaton Thorpe, Thorpefield, Thorpe (3), Thorp Perrow, (b) Agglethorpe, Allerthorpe, Carthorpe, Easthorpe, *Etersthorpe*, *Fornthorpe*, Ganthorpe, Gristhorpe, *Kettlethorpe*, Kingthorpe, Langthorpe, Laysthorpe, Linthorpe, Mowthorpe, Pinchinthorpe, Ravensthorpe, *Roskelthorpe*, *Scawthorpe*, *Swarthorpe*, Tholthorpe, Towthorpe, Ugthorpe, Wigginthorpe, (c) *Roberthorpe*.

þveit (a) Braithwaite (2), Copperthwaite, Crossthwaite, Fossdale-(*thwaite*), Garfit, Greenthwaite, Haythwaite, Hilla Thwaite, Hindle(y)thwaite, Husthwaite, Huthwaite, Kexwith, Langthwaite, Raithwaite, Rhumbard Snout, Scale Foot, Short Wait, Storthwaite, Swinithwaite, Thackthwaite, Waitgate, Whyett, (b) Dowthwaite, Gristhwaite, Hunderthwaite, *Inglethwaite*, Kelsit, Mouthwaite, Thwaite, Waits House.

topt (a) Burtis, Hartoft, Saintoft, Thrintoft, (b) Allan Tops, *Alwaldtofts*, Antofts, Arnoldstoft.

treo(w) (a) Appersett, *Burtree*, Burtersett, Gatherley Moor, (b) *Yarlestree wap*.

trog Trough.

tun OE, ON (a) Appleton (5), Brafferton, Brampton, Brompton

(4), Brotton, Broughton (4), Castleton, Cawton, Clifton (2), Cloughton, Coulton, (*Thornton-*)Cowling, Cowton (3), Cropton, Dalton (3), Deighton, Ellerton (2), Eston, Foxton, Grinton, Hawthorn Hill, Hesselton, Hilton, Hutton (17), Kilton, Kneeton, Langton, Leavington (2), Linton, Liverton, Lonton, Malton, Mickleton, Middleton (4), Misperton, Morton (4), Murton (2), Myton on Swale, Newton (11), Norton (2), Overton, Preston (2), Rounton, Ruston, Ryton, Salton, Scorton, Scotton, Scrafton, Seaton, Shipton, Sinnington, Skipton on Swale, Smeaton, Stapleton, Stockton, Sutton (4), Swinston, Swinton (2), Tanton, Thornton (12), Upton, *Walton*, Whorlton, Wilton (2), Witton, Worton, Wrelton, (b) Allerston, Burneston, Burniston, Catton, Cayton, Cotherstone, Didderston, Ebberston, Edstone, Egglestone, Egton, Foston, Goulton, Habton, Harton, *Hoveton*, Hunton, Ilton, Knayton, Lebberston, Lockton, Moulton, Northallerton, Picton, Stilton, Theakston, Tollerton, Wide Open, Winton, Wintylow, Wombleton, (c) Kearton. *v.* beretun, *booltun, burhtun, -ingtun.

tun ON (a) Ayton (4), Blaten, Layton, Marton (4), Scawton, Skelton (3), Spaunton, Stainton (3), (b) Arkle Town, Claxton, Fryton, Garriston, Grimston, Irton (2), Nawton, Oulston, Scruton, Sigston, Silton, Sneaton, Sproxton, Wigginton, Youlton, (c) Flaxton. *v.* karlatun.

tunst(e)all Tunstall (2).

val(s), OFr (n) Jervaulx, Pickering Vale, Rievaulx.

varp ON (n) Ruswarp. varða, varði Warthill, Wath Cote.

vað (a) Blawath, Blow Gill, Bluewath, Brawith, Braworth, Briggswath, Farwath, Flawith, Grundstone Wath, Helwath, Helwith, Sandwath, Slape Wath, Smallways, Swinacote, Wass, Wath (2), Wayworth, (b) Ravensworth, Snilesworth, Tewfit.

vatr ON (n) Waithwith.

veggr Stanwick.

vik (a) Blea Wyke, Holwick, Ruswick, Saltwick, (b) Catwick, Kepwick, Ravenswyke, Runswick.

viðr Lockwood, Nutwith, Rookwith, Waithwith, Westworth, Widdale, Wydale.

w(e)ala Walburn, Walden, Walmire, *Walton*, Wapley, Wardle Rigg.

w(e)ald (a) Fairwood Field, Greenwall, (b) Coxwold, Cucket Nook, Easingwold.

(ge)weorc Aldwark.

wic (a) Wykeham (Ryed), (b) Earswick, Osbaldwick, Yarnwick.

wicham Wykeham (Pick).
w(i)ella (a) Caldwell (2), Crawl, Hipswell, Well, Whitwell (2),
  (b) Hauxwell, Hinderwell, Hudswell.
wilde Wildon, Wilton (2). worþ Heworth.
wudu (a) Harwood, Plockwoods, Witton, Woodhouse, (b)
  Thurtle Wood.

NOTES ON THE DISTRIBUTION OF
THESE ELEMENTS

A few notes on the distribution of certain p.n. elements may
be given, but as the comparative material for other counties is
not (except in one or two cases) complete as yet, the remarks
can to some extent be only tentative.

bekkr. As a stream-name it is far more frequent than either
burna or broc, which to a large extent it must have supplanted.
In this, the Riding agrees with the Northern parts of the West
Riding and with We, but not with Du, where *beck* is of recent
introduction, and where burna is correspondingly more frequent.

be(o)rg is found much more frequently than hyll.

burh is found fairly frequently, whereas ceaster is not found
at all.

by. There are over 150 examples, of which over 100 are compounded with pers. names. There are roughly twice as many
in YNR as YER, and it is comparatively rare in YWR. Although
many of the original farmsteads have become villages, a great
many still remain farms and small hamlets, as in the case of
YWR examples. The element was in living use after the Conquest (cf. Halnaby, Jolby).

cros, it is interesting to note, is found only in those districts
where the Irish-Norwegian element is strong, and this probably
indicates that the word was used in YNR by Norwegians who
had come from Ireland.

dæl, dalr is extremely common, whilst denu is rare; in YWR
the reverse is the case, *dale* being there of comparatively recent
introduction. The differences in topography rule out com-
parison with YER. Of the 104 examples (against 7 denu) 30 are
compounded with an OE element, 37 are definitely ON whilst
the remainder are either OE or ON. The distribution seems
to show that the frequency of its use is due to ON influence.

erg. *v.* Introd. xxii, n. 1. The element is not so common as in
YER, but except for the Craven district it is commoner than in
YWR. Its use is analogous to that found in We, Cu, North La.

feld is rare in YNR and YER but common in YWR and Du and Nb, as in the case of land and worþ.

gata seems to have displaced weg, which is only found once, as a first element.

ham. Apart from ingaham there are nine examples of ham of which six are compounded with early pers. names. As in the case of YER this suffix seems to have passed into disuse at an early date. It is rarer in YWR than in YNR.

haugr is fairly common and YNR is thus distinct from YWR. In many cases the tumulus to which the name refers is still extant.

ing, ingaham. *v.* Introd. xvii, xviii.

ingtun. These names belong with one or two exceptions to the Vale of York and Upper Teesdale.

land is rare in YNR and YER, but common in YWR and Du.

leah. There are 23 examples in YNR, more than in YER, but nothing like so frequent as in YWR and La. They are chiefly found in two districts, one centering round Hackness and the other in Wensleydale, both old forest regions (the Forest of Pickering and the Forest of Wensleydale). It is curious that no examples are known from Bulmer (the Forest of Galtres).

lundr is about twice as common as wudu.

rand, rarely found outside the ECy, is found once.

sætr. Most are found in Wensleydale, though one or two are found in Swaledale.

þorp. *v.* Introd. xxiv. There are 36 examples, but there are about twice as many in YWR and three times as many in YER, and this distribution is roughly in inverse proportion to the distribution of by. The difference is due to the fact that the character of the YNR was such as facilitated the settlement in *bys* or small isolated farms or rather prevented the formation of groups of farms or *thorps*, whereas in the YER the opposite conditions prevailed.

þveit. There are 31 examples, far more than in YER, but not so many as in YWR, or the Lake District. Very few of these are mentioned in DB and the distribution in YNR seems to follow that of the Norwegian settlement. It is commonest in the parts adjacent to We and the Sedbergh district of YWR where they are common.

tun. There are about 250 examples, of which only 44 are distinctively Scand. The distribution is general and follows that of the neighbouring counties.

vað. This is more common than ford, and it seems to have displaced that word after the Conquest.

worþ. *v.* Introd. xviii.

PERSONAL NAMES COMPOUNDED IN
NORTH RIDING PLACE-NAMES

Names not found in independent use are marked with a single asterisk if their existence can be inferred from evidence other than that of the particular place-name in question. Such names may be regarded as hardly less certain than those which have no asterisk. Those for which no such evidence can be found are marked with a double star.

(i) *Old English*

Ācwulf (Agglethorpe), *Ælfhere* (Allerston, Northallerton), *Ælfsige* (Ellis Croft), *Ælfweard* (Ellerby), *Æþelric* (Earswick), *Æþelw(e)ald* (Old Sleights), *Ætla* (Atley), *Aldwine* (Antofts), *Aldwulf* (Autherlands), *Bē(a)ga* (Byland), *B(e)aldhere* (Baldersby, Baldersdale), *Bēda* (Bedale), *Benna* (Benningbrough), *Beorna* (Barden, Barningham), *Beornw(e)ald* (Barnaby), *Bera* (Bardale (?)), *Bica* (Bickley), **Binte* (Binsoe), *Bisceop* (Bishopdale), *Bordel* (Bordelby), *Bōt* (Bossall), *Brocc* (Broxa), **Brudda* (Birdforth), *Brūn* (Bungdale), *Brūning* (Bonny Carr), *Brȳning* (Burneston, Burniston), *Būna* (Bownhill), *Cǣga* (Cayton), *Catta* (Catton), *Cēngifu* (f) (Knayton), *Cēolfrith* (Killerby (2) (?)), *Cippela* (Kiplin), *Coc(c)a* (Cock Mill), *Corta* (Corburn), *Cuca* (Cucket), **Cuha* (Coxwold), *Cunda* (Cundall (?)), *Cūðhere* (Cotherstone), *Cylfa* (Kilvington), *Cylla* (Kilburn), *Cyna* (Kingthorpe), *Cyrtla* (Kirklington), *Dun* (Dunsdale, Dunsley), **Dyder* (Didderston), *Ēadbeorht* (Ebberston), **Ēaden* (Edstone), *Ēadgifu* (f) (*Edymarsh*), *Ēadmund* (Yedmandale), *Earda* (Arden), *Ecga* (Egton), *Ecgel* (Egglestone), *Ella* (Ellingstring, Ellington), *Eofor* (Yearsley), *Ēsa* (Easington, Easingwold), *Fadda* (Fadmoor), *Fœrela* (Farlington), *Falda* (Fawdington), *Fīn* (Finghall), *Fōt* (Foston), *Frema* (Fremington), *Frīga* (Fryup), *Fygela* (Fylingdales, Fyling Thorpe), **Georna* (Yarnwick), **Getla* (Gillamoor, Gilling (2), *Ingetlingum*), *Glæppa* (Glaphowe), *Gōda* (Goathland), *Golda* (Goldsborough, Goulton (?)), **Gyrla* (Girlington), *Hab(b)a* (Habton), *Hac(c)a* (Hackness), *Haneca* (Hancow), *Heafoc* (Hauxwell), *Helm* (Helmsley), *Hemela*, *-le* (Hemlington, Gate Helmsley), *Herele* (Harlsey), *Herra* (Harton (?)), *Hild* (f) (Hill Grips, Hinderwell), *Hilding* (Hildenley), **Hof(a)* (*Hoveton*, Hovingham), *Hroca* (Rokeby), *Hūdel* (Hudswell), *Hūna* (Hunton), *Hunta* (Huntington), *Hwassa* (Whashton), *Īfa* (Ivelet), **Lāst* (Lastingham), *Lēodbeorht* (Lebberston), *Lēofa* (Linthorpe), *Lēofgēat* (Levisham), *Lilla* (Lilla Howe, Lilla Cross, Lilling), **Loca* (Lockton), *Luda* (The Park), ***Lyrta* (Lartington), *Mæssa* (Masham), *Mæþelgār* (Maggra), *Mann* (*Maneshou*), *Man(n)a* (Manfield), **Midele* (Middlesborough), **Morta* (Mortham), *Mūla* (Moulton), *Nunna* (Nunnington), *Ogga* (Waites House), *Ōsb(e)ald* (Osbaldwick), *Ōsw(e)ald* (Oswaldkirk), **Otor* (Otterington), **Pīca* (Pickhill, Picton), **Pīcer* (Pickering), **Pīla* (Pilmoor), *Pinca* (Pinkney), **Poc(c)a* (Pockley), **Rǣgen* (Rainton), *Rūmbeald* (Rhumbard Snout), *Secg* (Sessay), *Sigemund* (Simon Howe, Simon Stone), *Sigeweard* (*Swarthorpe*), *Sprow* (Spruce Gill Beck), *Stān* (Stonegrave (?)), **Strēon* (Strensall, Streoneshalch), **Styfela* (Stillington), ***Tana* (Tanfield (?)), ***Tēofer* (Terrington), **þēofoc* (Theakston), *Til(l)i* (Stilton), ***Tollere* (Tollerton), *Wædel* (Waterpool), **Wændel* (Wensley), *Wǣrlāf* (Warlaby (?)), *Wina* (Winton, Wintylow), *Wineb(e)ald* (Wombleton), *Wipped* (Wide Open Farm), *Wulfa* (Ovington), *Wulfsige* (Ousey Carr), **Wyrc* (Worsall), **Ylca* (Ilton), *Ylla* (Cliffe).

(ii) *Scandinavian*

Arkil (Arkengarthdale, Arkleside, Thwaite (HangW)), *Arnaldr* (Arnoldstoft), *Ásgautr* (Osgodby, Osgoodby), *Ási* (Aysdale), *Áskell* (Marishes), *Áslákr* (Aislaby (Pick)), *Ásmundr* (Osmotherley), *Ásúlfr* (Aislaby (WhitbyS)), *Auðúlfr* (Addlebrough, Marishes), *Baggi* (Bagby, Bag Dale), *Bákr* (Baxby), *Baldi* (*Baldby*), *Belgr* (Bellerby), *Bergúlfr* (*Berguluesbi*), *Bildr* (Bilsdale), *Bili* or *Bil* (f) (Biller Howe), *Bjarni* (Barnby (2)), *Blǫndu* (Blansby), *Bolli* (Boulby), *Boltr* (Boltby), *Bǫðvarr* (Battersby), *Bragi* (Brawby), *Brandr* (Brandsby, Bransdale), *Breiðr* (*Hillbraith*), *Bulle* (OEScand) (Bullamoor), **Buski* (Busby), *Drómundr* (Dromonby), *Dūdhi* (OEScand) (Dowber), *Eindriði* (Ainderby (3)), *Eitri* (*Etersthorpe*), *Ési* (ODan) (Easby (3), Easegill), *Eskel* (ODan) (Exelby), **Fangi* (Fangdale), *Farmann* (Farmanby), **Feitr* (Faceby), *Flak* (Flaxdale (?), Flaxton), *Forni* (*Fornthorpe*), *Frithi* (ODan) (Firby, *Fridebi*, Fryton), *Fulke* (OEScand) (Foulbridge), *Gálmr* (Ganthorpe), *Gamall* (Gammersgill, Ruddings (Birdf)), *Geóla* (AScand) (Youlton), *Gerðr* (Garriston), *Gígr* (Guisborough), **Gilmaðr* (Gilmonby), *Grímr* (Grimes Dale, *Grimsby*, Grimston, *Miregrim*), *Gríss* (Girsby, Gristhorpe, Gristhwaite), *Gunnarr* or *Gunnvǫr* (f) (Gunnergate Lane, Gunnerside), *Gunni* (Gundale), *Hákr* (Haxby), *Halmi* (Hawnby), *Hattr* (Hatterboard Hill), *Haukr* (Hawkshill, Hawsker), *Hjǫrleifr* or *Herleifr* (Allerthorpe), *Hildr* (f) (Hinderskelfe), *Hjærne* (Harmby), *Hjálmr* (Shawm Rigg (?)),

Hjalpr (f) (Helperby), *Holti* (Holtby (2)), **Hornboði* (Hornby (GillE)), *Horni* (OEScand) (Hornby (HangE)), *Hrafn* (Raincliffe, Ravenscar, Ravensthorpe, Ravensworth, Ravenswyke), *Hreinn* (Runswick), *Hrísi* (Risedale), *Hrókr* (Rook Barugh, Roxby (Halik)), *Hrómundr* (Romanby), *Hrossketill* (*Roskelthorpe*), *Hun(d)ra* (Hunderthwaite), *Hvalr* (Falsgrave), *Hvíti* (Whitby, Whyett Beck), *Ingólfr* (*Inglethwaite*), *Ingus* (AScand) (Ings Beck), *Íri* (Irby Manor, Irton (2)), *Járnólfr* (Yarna Beck), *Jarpr* (Easthorpe), *Jórekr* (Yorfalls) (?), **Kæppi* (OEScand) (Kepwick), **Kæri* (OEScand) (Cold Kirby), *Kámr* (Camedale (?)), *Kani* (Cana Barn), *Kári* (Carthorpe), *Káti* (Cat Flats, Catwick (?), Kateridden), *Kausi* (Cowesby), *Kekkja* (*Kekmarish*), **Kel(l)e* (Kelsit), *Kempi* (Kemplah), **Ketilgrímr* (Kilgram), *Ketill* (*Kettlethorpe*), *Klak* (ODan) (Claxton), **Klēss* (Cleasby), *Kol(l)i* (Coulby), *Kráki* (Crakehall, Crakehill), *Krókr* (Crooksby, Crosby), *Kyle* (Killing Nab), *Leikr* (Laysthorpe), *Ljóti* (Leckby), *Logi* (Low Cross), *Lothaen* (ODan) (Lonsdale), *Lúsi* (Loose Howe), *Magi* (May Moss), *Magni* (Maunby), *Mákr* (*Maxude*), *Malti* (ODan) (Maltby), **Maurr* (Marsett), *Mildi* (Milby), *Milla* (Miley), **Moldr* (Moxby), **Mǫrðr* (Marderby), *Múli* (Mowthorpe, Mulgrave), *Músi* (Mouthwaite, Muscoates, Musley Bank), *Nagli* (Nawton), **Náti* (Naby), *Qlvaldi* (*Alwaldcotes*), *Ormr* (Ormesby), *Øymundr* (Amotherby), *Øysteinn* (Asenby), *Rauðr* (Roxby (2)), *Rossi* (Rose Hill), **Røyð(i)r* (Raisdale), *Rudi* (Rudby), *Russi* (Rosedale), *Sekkr* (Sexhowe), **Siggr* (Sigston), *Sile* (ODan) (Sil Howe), *Sindri* (Sinderby), *Sjónr* (Shunner Howe (?)), *Skagi* (*Scawthorpe*), *Skakari* (Scargill), *Skalli* (Scalby), *Skarði* (Scarborough), *Skinnari* (Skinningrove), *Skiði* (Skeeby), *Skjǫldr* (Skelderskew), **Skóga-Hreinn* (*Scograin-howes*), *Skógr* (Skewsby (?)), *Skurfa* (Scruton), *Skvaðra* (Skutterskelfe), **Slengr* (Slingsby), **Snigill* (Snilesworth), *Snjō* (ODan) (Sneaton), **Sprok* (Sproxton), *Stáki* (Stakesby), *Steinn* (Stainsacre, Stainsby), *Stýrr* (Stearsby), *Sunnólfr* (Sunley Hill, Sunley Wood), *Sútari* (Ruddings (Birdf), Sutherland), *Svarthǫfði* (Swarthoe Cross), *Sveinn* (Swainby (LangW)), *Sylve* (ODan) (Silpho, Nether and Over Silton), **Þjokka* (Marishes), *Þórkell* (Thirkleby, Thurtle Wood), *Þórmóðr* (Thormanby, Thornaby), *Þórólfr* (Tholthorpe), *Þórr* (Thoresby), *Þórsteinn* (Throxenby), *Þórvaldr* (Thoralby, Thoraldby), ***Þrylli* (Thirlby), *Þúfa* (Tewfit), **Þymill* (Thimbleby), *Þyrni* (Thringarth (?)), *Toddi* (Tod Howe), *Tōfi* (ODan) (Towthorpe), *Tollr* (Tollesby), *Trútr* (Troutsdale), *Uggi* (Ugthorpe), **Uglubarði* (Ugglebarnby), *Úlfr* (Oulston, Ulshaw Bridge), **Útkári* (Uckerby), *Vigmundr* (Wemmergill), *Víkungr* (Wigganthorpe, Wigginton), *Wraghi* (ODan) (Wragby).

(iii) *Old Irish*

Brettan (Brettanby), *Cairpre* (Carperby), *Cocca* (Sawcock), *Cólman* (Coldman Hargos, Commondale), *Dubhan* (Dowthwaite Hall), *Gaithen* (Gatenby), *Lochan* (Lackenby), *Maelmuire* (Melmerby (HangW)), *Maelsuithan* (Melsonby).

(iv) *Continental*

Alain (OFr) (Allan Tops), *Constance* (Countersett), *Halnath* (Halnaby), *Johel* (Jolby), *Marie* (Marriforth), *Radulphus* (Ralph Crosses), *Willelm* (William Gill, William Howes, William's Cross).

FEUDAL NAMES

Ainderby Steeple, Appleton le Moors, Brompton (Allert), Patrick Brompton, Constable Burton, Carlton Miniott, Cowling, Dalton (GillW), Humberton, Hutton Bonville, Hutton Bushell, Hutton Conyers, High Hutton, Low Hutton, Hutton Magna, Sheriff Hutton, Ingleby Barwick, Langthorpe, Middleton Tyas, Newton Morell, Newton Picot, Norton Conyers, Pinchinthorpe, Nether Silton, Sutton Howgrave, Thornton le Beans, Thornton Rust, Thornton Steward, Thorp Perrow.

FIELD AND OTHER MINOR NAMES

In collecting material for the interpretation of place-names (i.e. those found on the O.S. maps), a good deal of material has been gathered in the form of field and other minor names. It is impossible to deal with these exhaustively because they are too numerous and many are without interest, whilst interpretation is often impossible without a succession of forms.

An analysis of these elements follows, with illustrations of their use. Those elements which have been fully illustrated in the major place-names are for the most part left unnoticed.

æcer is fairly common: as in *Stubacre* (13th), *Lang-*, *Shorthalf-acres* (1341) etc.; ON akr as in *Gailaker* (13th) from geil, *Scayfacre* (12th) from ON *skeifr* 'awry, twisted'; *Gaitacre* (1204) suggests that the element was not invariably used of arable land.

ærs, ears (n), as in *Trollesers* (1335) in Lockton (ON *troll* 'a troll'); *v.* PN Wo 389.

*bæc-stan (n), Dial. *backstone* 'a baking stone' is found from the 12th cent. as in *bacestaingrave* (c. 1170), *Bacstanberks* (1230–50), *Bakestanbrec* (13th), *Bakstandaleflat* (1407).

balca OE (n) is found twice, *Austbalca* (1202) in W. Witton and *Balkendes* (c. 1250) in Bilsdale.

banke is found occasionally, as in *Scoredbanke* (1271) from ME *scored* p.p. of ME *score* 'cut, score' (ON *skora*).

be(o)rg is found occasionally as in *Windeberg* (13th) 'windy hill,' *Galheberh* (13th) 'gallow hill.'

bondi, as in *Bondehoxganges* (13th) as distinct from *Tunhoxganges*, *Bondeflatmire* (1193–9).

boð is rare, as in *Bothum* (c. 1190–1214) in Ebberston.

brade ME (*v.* PN BedsHu 292) enters into *Gayre-*, *Garebrad* (1198, 1294) from gara.

brekka appears in *Hertebrekes* (1333) in Greenhow, *Hangabrec* (1154–69) in Melsonby, *Hungrebrekes* (1316) in W. Bolton, *Endebrec* (13th) in Guisborough, and *Bakestanbrec* (13th) in Tocketts. *v.* Introduction xxvii.

*burgæsn, *burgæns OE (n) 'burial place' is found frequently but only in Richmondshire, as *borchanes* (13th) in Crakehall, *burwanes* (13th) in W. Layton, *Bourhans* (c. 1200) in E. Appleton, *Borhanes* (12th) in Burrill, *Borghanes* (12th) in Harmby, and *Fordanborghanes* (1336) in Newsham in Gilling West. Cf. Bornesses 283 *supra*.

butte ME (n) used of a short strip ploughed in the angle where two furlongs meet at right-angles is noticed several times as *Buttes* (1290–1300, etc.), *Cotumbuttes* (1231) in Coatham, *Crummorbuttes* (13th), *Le Crocbut* (1268), *Scortbuttes* (c. 1230).

*bysc OE, buskr ON. One may note *Wyntrebusc* (12th), *Mapelbusc* (13th), *Tuabusche* (13th) 'two bushes.'

clos ME (n) 'an enclosure' is found occasionally in early times as in *Byrkeclos* (1407), *Ercedekneclos* 'archdeacon close' (1317), and is common in the 17th cent. and after.

croft is very common. When not compounded with a pers. name it is usually combined with a word denoting the crop as in *Barlicroft* (4) from OE *bærlic* 'barley,' *Bygcroft* from bygg, *Henepcroft* from OE *henep* 'hemp,' *Lincroftes* (2), *Ricroft*, *Waythcroft* from ON *hveiti* 'wheat.'

dal is common as *dale*, and so is difficult to distinguish from dæl and dalr. One may note *Barlicdale* (13th) and *Lindale* (1252), *Bosedale* (1160) from OE *bōs* 'cowhouse,' and *Mawyngedale* (1260) from OE *māwan* 'to mow grass.'

deill is common as in *Uvere-*, *Netherdeile* (1218), *Langedayle* (1250), *Chutdayll* (1244), etc.

eng is a very common element in field-names, as in *Constabil-henge*, *Kingeshenge* (c. 1240), *Dernynge* (13th) from d(i)erne, *Slecthenges* (1199–1203) from sletta, *Windmillenheng* (1404), etc.

feld is of rare occurrence in field-names, as in *Benefeld* (1155–70) in Spaunton.

fell, fjall though now fairly common is rare in early times, as in *Swartfell* (13th) in Hawes.

flat is exceedingly common. Usually it is combined with another p.n. as in *Bonnesdale flatte* (1336), *Briggebothemflat* (1320), *Hirdegaileflat* (1193–9), *Graystaynflath* (13th), or with a significant word denoting a neighbouring feature as in *Crosflat* (1407), *le Halleflat* (1341), *Kirkeflat* (1167), *Cotheflat, Briggeflath* (13th), *Galweflath* (1248). In the remaining instances it is distinguished by the owner's name, as in *Bondflat* (1193–9) from bondi, *Marscalflath* (1238), its nature as *Stainiflat* (1210), *Waterflat* (1250), *Morflattes* (13th), *Marleflatte* (1236), *Laynde-flath* (13th) from ON *leyndr* 'hidden,' *Cryngelflath* (1232) from kringla, or its use as *Goseflat* (13th), *Herteflath* (1230–50), and *Wreckeflatte* (1236) in Fylingdales 'flat where the wreck was thrown up from the sea.'

furlang is found occasionally as in *Damfurlanges* (1294) near the Ouse R. (from dam, *v.* PN Bk 257) and *Morefurlang* (1341) from mor.

garðr is fairly common as *Cunyngarth* (1407), *le engegarth* (1406), *Halgarth* (1298). Usually the first element is a significant word denoting animals as in *Hertegarth* (1294), *Ragarth* (2), *Suinegarth* (1193–9), or crops as in *Apelgarth* (2), *le Haygarth* (1311), and *Lingarth* (c. 1223).

gata is very common compounded with a pers. name or a word denoting ownership or use as in *Levedygate* (13th), *Wayncarlegate* (c. 1175) from OE *wægen* 'waggon,' *Scotgate* (13th) from *Scot* 'a Scotsman.' In other cases the significant word denotes some object to which the road leads as in *Birgate* (1227) from byre, *Marketesgathe* (13th), *Kirkegate* (1210) etc. One may also note *Meregate* (c. 1160) from (ge)mære 'a boundary road' and *Blingate* (1193–9) from *blind*, probably indicating a cul-de-sac.

geil is not common: *Hirdegail* (13th) in Jolby, *Westegayl* (13th) in Hutton Lowcross, *Austgail* (1204) in Dalton on Tees.

gil is compounded with a pers. name or more frequently with a significant word as *Wythegil* (c. 1200) in Hauxwell (from viðr), *Leveracgille* (13th) in Ruswick (from lawerce), *Wantegile* (1176) in Castle Bolton (from ON *vánt, vátn* 'bad water'), *Thwertlang-gille* (1306) in W. Bolton (ON *þver-t* neut. 'across, transverse'), *Burstadgile* (1177–89) in Suffield, *Waterslakgille* (c. 1265–78) in Thirley Cotes, etc.

gote ME (n) 'a water channel,' as in *Quenhilgote* (c. 1300) in Carthorpe.

grein 'a fork in the valley of a river,' as in *Grayne* (13th) and *Ricolvegreines* (1333) both referring to the Riccal R., *Grundalegreynes* (1335) in Allerston, *le Wester Grayne* (1286) in Hackness.

grene used substantivally of a grassy spot occurs several times from the 12th cent. as in *le Spitelgrene* (12th), *Boulandegrene* (e. 13th), *Cotegrene* (1241), *le Southgrene* (1341), etc.

hafri occurs several times in field-names, as in *Hauerland*, *-thweit* (2), *-holm*.

haining is found once as *Heynnyng* (12th) in Baysdale.

hals is found once in *Grenhals* (13th) in Loftus.

haugr is frequently compounded with a pers. name. In other cases the first element signifies a neighbouring feature of the mound, as in *Aschou, Thornhou* (12th), *Stapelhowe* (1333) from stapol; the material of which the mound is made, as in *Lairhou* (13th) from leirr, *Moldhowe* (12th) from OE *mold* 'earth,' *Stainhou* (13th), *Warthou* (c. 1300) from varða 'a heap of stones.' Also noteworthy are *Colledhou* (13th) 'mound with its top knocked off' (from ME *collen*, OSwed *kulla* 'to behead'), *Trunhou* (13th) from OE **trun* 'round' (*v.* Ekwall, *PN La* 158 s.n. Trunnah), *Cuenhou* (13th) from OE *cwēn* 'a woman,' and *Drechowe* (1336) from ON *dreki* 'dragon.'

heafod is fairly common in field-names.

hǫfuð appears once as *haved* in *Tofteburhavedes* (13th), frequently as *houed* as in *Houedlandes, Buscohoved*, and later as *houth*, as in *Byrk-, Hayk-, Kirkhouth* (1335–8).

holmr is one of the commonest field-name elements; usually it is compounded with a significant word indicating its position or size as in *Dernholm* from d(i)erne, *Braidholme* from breiðr; the crop or plants grown on it as in *Haverholm* (2), *Lockeholme* (12th) from ON *lok* 'a weed, fern,' *Redholmes* (1241) from hreod, *Wedholmes* (1241) from OE *wēod* 'weed'; or the animals found there as in *Raholm* (2), *Oxhenholm* (1258) and *Brocholme* (13th) from brocc.

horn is found only in *Stubbehorn* (13th) in Great Ayton and *Hornlandes* (13th) in Scorton.

hryding is found several times as *le Ridding* (13th), *Akridding* (1326), *Hellepotriding* (13th).

hungor is fairly common in field-names denoting poor pasturage as in *Hungerhil* (6), *Hungrebrekes* (1316), *Hungerrigges* (14th), *Hungerscotes* (14th), etc.

hyrst is rare, as in *Heselhurst* (1223), *Huhyrst* (1257).

intake (n) used of 'a piece of land enclosed from a moor,' though now common, is rare in ME; the earliest example is *Langintake* (1409) in Skelton (Bulmer).

kelda is commonly coupled with an adjective as in *Breithekelde* (1202), *Caldekeld* (3), *Fulkelde* (13th), *Mosykelde* (c. 1200), or less frequently with a substantive as in *Wlfekelde* (1260), *Buirtrekelde* (1200–2) from *burtree* 'alder,' *Skitekelde* (c. 1230–40) from ON *skíta* vb. 'cacare,' *Thruhkelde* (1231) which seems to contain OE *þruh*, ON *þró* 'coffin,' the whole name probably indicating 'a well made of or in the shape of a stone coffin.'

kjarr is fairly common, as in *Hassokker* (1302) from hassuc, *Redker* (1226–9) from hreod, *Crumbker* (1337) from crumb, *le Potker*, cf. Pott Hall 234 *supra*, *Turfker* (1205) from OE *turf*.

klint is extremely rare, as in *Crafclynt* (1376) in Byland.

krokr is found in *le Crok'* (1285), *Le Crocbut* (1268), *Crokeland* (1316), *Foxcroke* (1406).

kros, cros ON (n) 'cross' (*v*. Förster, *Keltisches Wortgut*) is common as the first element in field-names, as in *Crosseflatte* (1336) in Hutton Hill, *Crosflat* (1407) in Upleatham, *Crostweit* (1201) in Dale, *Crosseker* (13th) in Marton in Cleveland. As a suffix it is usually combined with a pers. name, but noteworthy are *Spelcros* (c. 1175) in Guisborough from ON *spjall* 'speech,' and *Houthloscrosse* (13th) in Great Brompton 'headless cross' from hǫfuð and ON *lauss* 'less.'

land is very common. The shape is described in *Hornlandes* (13th), *Langelandes* (4), *Wranghelandes* (c. 1200 *et freq*) from wrang. Reference to crops is found in *Barliclandes* (13th) from OE *bærlic*, *Baunelandes* (2) from ON *baun* 'bean,' *Ben(e)landes* (2) from bean, *Haverland* (1316) from hafri, *Peselandes* (c. 1230) from pise, to animals in *Swinelandes* (13th), to soil etc. in *Claylandes* (13th) from clæg, *Blalandes* (2) from blar, *Morelandes* (13th) from mor. Noteworthy are *Sueinlandes* (1193–9) from ON *sveinn*, *Dryngland* (1407) from dreng, and *Selandes* (1304) on the sea-coast in Loftus from OE *sæ*.

leirr is found in *Lairhou* (13th), *Lairberg* (1198–1208), *Layre-berch* (1316), *Lairbeck* (13th), *Layrsic* (c. 1250).

lundr is found as in *Berklound* (1320), *Rokelund* (1286), *Sot-lounde* (1358) and several times compounded with a pers. name.

lyng is fairly common, as in *Lings* (1154–89), *Lingberhou* (13th), *Lingstanflat* (1193–9), *Lingthwaite* (1372).

marr ON (n) 'marsh' (*v.* Marton 28 *supra*) is found chiefly in Pickering Lythe wap., as in *Moldewarpmar* (1244) from ME *moldwerp* 'mole,' *Hassokmar* (1244) from hassuc, *Oustecotmarre* (13th) from austr, cot, *Rosshowmarre* (1407), etc.

mold OE (n) 'earth' is found once as in *Swartemolde* (1250) in Guisborough.

myrr is common. Apart from pers. name compounds it is used with bird names as in *Haffokemire* (1236) from heafuc, *Tranemyre* (1335) from trani, and *Tywythmire* (13th) which probably contains the name *tewit* (*v.* EDD s.v.) 'peewit.' Note-worthy also are *Turfmire* (1185–95) from OE *turf*, *Redmire* (1193–9) from hreod, and *Kerlingmire* from ON *kerling* 'an old woman' (possibly here a reference to a ducking pond).

ofnam ME (n) is used of a piece of land 'taken from' the common land and is derived from OE *ofniman* or ON *afnima* 'to seize' (*v.* Whitby Cartulary, ii. 440 n.): *les ofnames* (1190–1227) in Cayton, *Ofnam* (1160) in Allerston, *Houenam* (12th) in Middlesborough, *Ovenham* (13th) in Ormesby, Newton Morell and Fylingdales, *Ovenamwithrane* (1336) in Newsham (GillW).

oxgang (n), a measure of land varying from 10 to 25 acres of land according to the nature of the soil (*v.* EDD s.v.); *Bondehoxganges* (13th) from bondi, *Flatoxganges* (14th) from flat, *Tunhoxanges* (13th) from tun.

pol is rare, as in *Brinepol* (12th) in Croft 'brine pool,' *Rossepol* (c. 1250) from ON *hross* 'horse.'

pot (n) is found in *Fulepotte* (1335) in Allerston and *Potteker* (1175–88) in Marton in Cleveland.

pytt is rare, as in *Ellerpittes* (1226–9) in Haxby.

ran 'a boundary strip' (*v.* PN Bk 55 s.n. Rhon Hill) appears frequently as in the simplex *le Ranes* (13th) or in combination with a significant word as in *Austkeldrane* (13th), *Blaberyrane* (13th), *Goderan* (12th), *Haverlandesrane* (1290), *Heselrane* (14th), *Hinderbergrane* (13th), *Huwerranes* (13th) from ON *hverr* 'cauldron, boiler,' *Langeran* (13th), *Nordrane* (1329). The first element in these examples seems to bear out the suggestion that the word was used of a boundary.

rod is not common; not more than six examples have been noticed, including *Thretyrodes* (1252), *Fourtenerode* (13th).

sætr, setr is found chiefly in Richmondshire combined with a pers. name.

sand is used of the silt banks of the Tees R. in *Scortesandes* (c. 1230) in Ormesby.

sic is frequently compounded with either a pers. name or a descriptive adjective, as in *Grenesic* (c. 1167), *Blachesic* (1290), *Layrsic* (c. 1250). *v.* grene, blæc, leirr, *Golsic* (13th) from ON *gull* 'gold.'

skali occurs several times as in *Scalorig* (1198–1208) in Hudswell, *Scalebec* (12th) in Liverton, *Scalestedes* (1230–50) in Tocketts, (13th) in Wensley, *Skaleflat* (1274) in Feetham, *Stainschale* (13th) in Upleatham and *Raufscales* (12th) in Baysdale.

skarð is found as *le Scarth* (1337) in Seamer in Pickering Lythe, *Scharth* (12th) in Guisborough, etc.

sker ON (n) 'skerry, rock,' as in *le Sker* (1326), *Fallenskerre* (1335).

skogr is found a few times, as in *Haukescou* (12th), *Lagheschogh* (1308), *Rysscogh* (1333). *v.* lagr, hris.

slakki is rare, as in *Waterslakgille* (c. 1265–78) in Thirley, *Westslak* (1335) in Kingthorpe, *Hyndeslak* (1335) in Thornton Dale.

stank ME (n) 'a stagnant pool,' as in *le Stank* (1305) in Howthorpe, *le Stanke*, *Stankenge* (1538) in Rievaulx.

stocking is rare, as in *Stokkyng* (1409) in Skelton (Bulmer).

stodfald occurs thrice in that form, (1407) in Marske on Sea, (13th) in Brompton on Swale and in Kirkdale.

swithen (n) used in YNR of 'a moor which has been cleared by burning' (cf. Swinithwaite 256 *supra*), as in *Estsnithen* (sic, 12th), *Swythenes* (1232).

þveit is a common element in field-names. Usually the first element is descriptive of size, shape, etc., as in *Mickel-, Smale-twaytes* (13th), *Cringeltheit* (c. 1200) from kringla, *Brounthwayt* (1335) from brun, *Stayntuait* (1282); the name of a neighbouring feature as *Eskebriggethwoyt* in Danby (1242) 'bridge across the Esk,' *Setwait* (1155–65) in Hawsker near the sea (OE *sæ*), *Burethwaites* (13th) near the bur, *Crostweit* (1201) near the *kros*; the name of the crop, plants, etc., as in *Thorntwait* (1293), *Burbladthwayt* (1318) (cf. We dialect *burblek* 'bog rhubarb'), *Hauerthwait* (1317) from hafri, *Lingthwaite* (1372) from lyng, *Nettelthwayth* (1292) from netel, *Brakenthwayth* (1300) from braken; and a few indicating possession such as *Karlethwoyt* (1242) from ON **karl**, and pers. names.

topt is not common, as in *le Toftes* (1380), *Gildhustoftes* (13th), *Bruntoft* (1193–9).

vað is common; noteworthy are *Straumeswat* (13th) from ON *straumr* 'stream,' *Stayn-*, *Braythe-*, *Sandwath* (12th–13th), *Weltewath* (12th) from ON *velta* 'overturn,' probably referring to a ford which was likely to cause carts to overturn.

vra is fairly common; it is sometimes combined with a significant word as in *Pesewra* (1335) from pise, *Merswra* (1335) from mersc, but more often with a p.n. as in *Westmyrewra* (14th), *Wykescroftwra* (12th), *Souregatewra* (12th), etc.

wandale ME (n) (*v.* Wandales 59 *supra*) is fairly common as a field-name, as in *Wandayla* (c. 1160) in E. Ayton, *Wandeles* (12th) in Guisborough, *Wandailes* (12th) in Middlesborough, *Wandayles* (13th) in Swinton in Ryedale, etc.

Amongst other minor names there is an interesting group in which the first element is a ME present participle formation in -*and*, as in *Boulandsike* (1185–95) from ME *bollen* 'to swell,' *Hengendebriggam* (1333), *Hengandehill* (1244), -*kelde* (2), -*nese* from ME *hengen* (ON *hengja*) 'suspend' (used in p.n.'s in the sense 'overhanging, sloping'), *Rennandkelde* (1200–2) from OE *rennan* 'to run,' *Routandkeld* (13th), *Rutand(e)keld(e)* (2), *Rutendesic* (13th), *Rutandside* (1338) from OE *hrūtan* 'to roar,' *Standandestan* (13th), *Standendestayn* (13th) from OE *standan* 'to stand,' *Loutandthorn* (1244) from OE *lūtan* 'to bend, stoop.'

There are also a few names of individual interest, as *Hamlinthorne* (c. 1300) from OE *hamelian* 'distort,' *Thornlousthorn* (13th) 'thornbush without thorns' (ON *þorn-lauss*), *Hackelstayn* (13th) 'stone where flax was hackled' (ON *hekla*, OE *hæclan*), *Tunge* (c. 1300) from ON *tungu* used of a spit of land, *Pynfuleschau* (13th) probably from ME *pīnful* 'painful,' though what the sense with sceaga can be is not certain; *Fehows* (1395) from ON *féhús* 'cattle stall'; *le Spout* (1351) possibly a waterfall from ME *spūt* 'spout'; *Milemerke* (c. 1167) 'a mile mark' which is perhaps unique except for the solitary OE *mīl-gemearc* in *Beowulf*; and lastly of interest is 'a place called *Manslaughter* on Nutwith hill' (1290) which probably indicates the site of some murder.

PERSONAL NAMES IN FIELD AND OTHER MINOR NAMES

OE *Addoc (*Addocflat*, 13th), Ægelwine, Ælfwine (*Eluynhou, Elwyncherich*, 13th), Æþelw(e)ald (*Adelwaldkeld*, 12th), B(e)aldwine (*Baldineoue*, 13th), Bēda (*Bedecnol*, 13th), Beornw(e)ald (*Berewaldflat*, 12th), Cnapa (*Cnapecros, Knapetres*, 13th), Colla (*Collecrofte*, 13th, *Collesic*, 12th), Doda (*Dodecroft*, 13th), Ēadwulf (*Eadelf-, Edolfdale*, 13th), Earn (*Erneshou*, 12th), Eli (*Elesgate*, 13th), Ēsa (*Esemore*, 14th), Friðubeorht (*Frudbriscedale*, 14th), Gold(e) (*Goldesmir*, 13th), Gūðwine (*Godewynegate, Godwynhoulandes, Gudewynholme*, 13th), Gūðwulf (*Guthulvesburc*, 13th), Hēring (*Heringenese*, 13th), **Hofa (*Houekelde, Hovelunde*, 13th), *Hwassa (*Whasseho*, 13th), Lēofenath (*Lefhenadtoftes*, 13th), Lēofric (*Leverikflat*, 13th), Ōsbeorht (*Osberlyht*, 1285), Ōsw(e)ald (*Oswaldesenges*, 12th), *Pīla (*Pyleden, Pilegile, Pyleflat*, 13th), Sǣmann (*Semanthorn*, 13th), Sigemund (*Simundkelde*, 13th), Sigeric (*Siricflath, Sirikelandes*, 12th), Sigew(e)ald (*Serewaldmire*, 12th), Sigewine (*Syueneslinland*, 13th, *Siwinesriding*, 1333, *Siwinecros*, 12th), Ūhtred (*Uctredecroft*, 12th), W(e)alh (*Wallesflat*, 1260), Wīgwulf (*Wyolfesdic*, c. 1200, *Wyolmire*, 1206).

ON Álfgrímr (*Algrimhou*, 13th), Álfr (*Alfhou*, 13th), Arkil (*Arkelmire, Arkilmireflat*, 12th, *Arkilhou*, 1244, *Arkilland*, 1342), *Arnbrandr (*Arbrandwyth*, 1335), Ásgautr (*Asegothenge*, 13th), Áskell (*Askeldic*, 13th), Ásmundr (*Osemundegar*, 12th), Baggi (*Baggethwait*, 1210), Barni (ODan) (*Barnhou*, 1193–9), Bleikr (*Blaikeswath*, 12th), Brosa (*Brosehou*, 1333), Brúnólfr (*Burnolfscales*, 12th), Brúsi (*Brusegarth*, 12th), Bukkr (*Bukeshou*, 13th), Ēsi (ODan) (*Eslundes*, c. 1240, *Esebrygg*, 1389), Ēskell (ODan) (*Eskilberg*, 13th, *Eskeldic*, 1143), Forni (*Foruflath*, 13th), Fulki (OEScand) (*Fulkeholm*, 1208), Gamall (*Gamelssicke*, 13th, *Gamelriding*, 1293), Gautr (*Gauthscou*, 1204), Gísli (*Gyselecroft*, 1228), Golsteinn (*Golstaindale*, c. 1160), Grímr (*Grimescroft, Grimeshou*, 13th, *Grymesgrave*, 12th, *Grymston*, 1307), Gunnhildr (f) (*Gunildekelde*, 1243), Hámundr (*Hamundelandes*, c. 1200), Haraldr (*Haraldhou, Haraldsic*, 13th), Haukr (*Haukescou*, 12th), Hávarðr (*Hawardesdale*, 1312), Hlífólfr (*Lyolfesenge*, 1258), Hreinn (*Raineslounde*, 1338), *(H)unketill (*Unkelbek*, c. 1300), Hvelpr (*Quelpesete*, 1283), Ingimarr (*Ingemerestanes*, 13th), Íri (*Ircroft*, 13th), Jarl (*Hyarlesholm*, 1252), *Játsteinn (*Jatstaineswad*, 12th), Jókell (*Jukeleholm*, 13th), Karl (*Karleslund*, 13th), Ketill (*Ketelesgat*, 1313, *Ketelpittes*, 13th, *Katilscroft*, 12th), Kolbrandr (*Colbrandsic*, 13th), Leppi (*Lepenges*,

Lepsettynges, 13th), Múli (*Mulfosse*, 1335, *Mulecros*, 13th), Oddr (*Odescroft*, c. 1300), Ormr (*Ormesbricge*, *Hormesgrif*, 12th, *Ormescrosse*, *Ormryg*, 13th, *Ormesovenes*, 1333), Øysteinn (*Aistangarthes*, 12th), Plógmaðr (*Ploxmanflat*, 1407), Plógsveinn (*Plusweynlondes*, 1283), Rauðr (*Routhegathe*, c. 1200, *Rothtwayte*, 1407), Róaldr (*Roaldeshou*, *Roaldemyre*, 13th, *Roweldesyke*, 1407), Siggautr (*Sighedesbrigga*, c. 1300), Sindri (*Sinderthorn*, 12th), Skalli (*Scalleberg*, *Scallerig*, 13th), Skinnari (*Skynnerenges*, *Scynnerbuttes*, 1243), Sperrir (*Sperragate*, 12th), Steinn (*Stainishou*, 12th, *Staynesbrecke*, 13th), Stigandi (*Stighandebi*, 12th), Sumarr (*Somersholm*, 1282), Súni (*Sunnebeck*, 12th), *Svartgeirr (*Swargerflat*, 1303), Svarthǫfði (*Swarhovedwath*, 12th, *Swarthowflat*, H 3), Svartmundr (*Swertmundeflat*, 1407), Sveinn (*Sueinlandes*, 1193–9, *Swaynisacre*, 13th), þingólfr (*Tingolvedale*, 12th), þórketill (*Thurkilbergh*, 1241), þórr (*Thoressete*, *Thoresdale*, *Thorsbehc*, 13th), þúrr (*Thurshou*, 12th, *Thuresden*, *Tursebrig*, 13th), þyri (f) (*Tyrrehou*, 13th), þyrnir (*Thirnethorn*, 13th), Tóki (*Tokeholme*, 12th), Trani (*Traneberg*, c. 1230, *Transheued*, 1160), Ukkemaðr (*Ukkemannenge*, 1241), Úlfarr (*Hulverheved*, 1254), Úlfr (*Vlfesdale*, *Wluetueit*, 13th), Ulli (*Ulegile*, 13th), Vígmundr (*Wymundeker*, c. 1205).

OIr Cólman (*Colthmanelandes*, 13th, in Kirkdale), Dunlang (*Dunlangbrotes*, c. 1200, in Great Broughton), Finngaill (*Finegalgraft*, 13th, in Brompton on Swale), Patric (*Paterik-keld*, 13th, in Harmby).

OFr Beneit (*Beneytesberg*, 1268), Gerard (*Gerardedale*, *Gerarderiding*, 12th), Gocelin (*Gocelinenges*, 1333), Helewise (f) (*Helwysdyke*, 1407), Lambert (*Lamberttwayt*, 1329), Mansel (*Manselinges*, 1273), Norrais (*Norraysholm*, 1260), Payen (*Peyneslawe*, 13th), Petronel (f) (*Petroneldel*, 1338), Ricardus (*Richardesdaile*, 13th), Roderic (*Roderikriding*, 12th), Roger (*Rogerflat*, 13th, *Rogerpittes*, 12th), Russel (*Roselbigginges*, 1320), Walter (*le Walter Crok*, *Walteresmire*, *Walter Gille*, 13th).

Note also Isaac (*Ysaacranes*, 13th).

INDEX

OF PLACE-NAMES IN THE NORTH RIDING

The primary reference to a place is marked by the use of clarendon type.

INDEX

OF PLACE-NAMES IN COUNTIES OTHER THAN
THE NORTH RIDING

[References to place-names in Bk, Beds, Hu, Wo are not included except in a few special cases as these have been fully dealt with in the volumes already issued upon the names of those counties.]